◆ ◆ ◆ ◆

Professions and Disciplines

Functional and Conflict Perspectives

◆ ◆ ◆ ◆

Daniel W. Rossides

Bowdoin College

Prentice Hall
Upper Saddle River, New Jersey 07458

Library of Congress Cataloging-in-Publication Data

Rossides, Daniel W.
    Professions and disciplines : functional conflict perspectives/
Daniel W. Rossides.
        p.   cm.
    Includes bibliographical references and index.
    ISBN 0-13-619982-8
    1. Professions—Sociological aspects   2. Knowledge, Sociology of.
3. Social classes.   I. Title.
HT687.R67   1998
305.5′53—dc21

97-12148
CIP

Editor-in-Chief: Nancy Roberts
Associate Editor: Sharon Chambliss
Production Liaison: Fran Russello
Project Manager: Pine Tree Composition
Prepress and Manufacturing Buyer: Mary Ann Gloriande
Cover design: Kiwi Design
Marketing Manager: Chris DeJohn

This book was set in *10/11.5 Palatino* by Pine Tree Composition, Inc.,
and was printed and bound by *Courier Companies, Inc.*
The cover was printed by *Phoenix Color Corp.*

© 1998 by Prentice-Hall, Inc.
A Pearson Education Company
Upper Saddle River, NJ 07458

Printed in Canada
10 9 8 7 6 5 4 3 2

ISBN: 0-13-619982-8

Prentice-Hall International (UK) Limited,London
Prentice-Hall of Australia Pty. Limited, Sydney
Prentice-Hall Canada Inc., Toronto
Prentice-Hall Hispanoamericana, S.A., Mexico
Prentice-Hall of India Private Limited, New Delhi
Prentice-Hall of Japan, Inc., Tokyo
Pearson Education Asia Pte. Ltd., Singapore
Editora Prentice-Hall do Brasil, Ltda., Rio de Janeiro

Contents

3   *Education: Legitimating Liberal Professionalism*   **58**

4   *Academic Disciplines I*   **76**

Preface

This text has been designed for courses on the professions and on occupations and work, and as a supporting text for courses on social stratification, the sociology of knowledge, the sociology and history of science and technology, social problems, education, business, and public policy. It should also prove useful in the capstone courses in which the various disciplines and professions check their bearings, assess their progress, and compare themselves to each other.

My goals in writing this book are:

1. To stimulate thought about the professions and disciplines by providing a macro sociological analysis of them, and by looking at them alternately through functional and conflict eyes. A glance at the table of contents will show that I have included the following in the universe of professions and disciplines: the field of education, the natural sciences, literary studies, the social sciences (with a special emphasis on sociology), the applied professions, the less-established or less-powerful professions, the policy professions, and the occupations of popular and elite culture with a special emphasis on the theme of professionalism that runs through their subject matter.

2. To introduce readers to the mode of thinking called the *sociology of knowledge*. This approach seeks to understand symbols in terms of their origins and functions in sociohistorical context. In another form, this approach is known as the *social construction of reality* approach. Both approaches have played a large part in nourishing the growth in recent decades of the major creative current in science, especially in sociology, anthropology, and literary studies, which sees science as inescapably interpretive in nature.

3. To provide readers with insights and information about the professions and disciplines especially in terms of their performance of social functions and their role in the modern (especially American) system of social power. A major theme of the text explores the need for a better blend of the academic disciplines, the applied professions, and the policy sciences, all as part of harnessing them to a better performance of social functions.

The study's organizing theme is a running contrast between the functional (mainstream academic) and the conflict (radical, sociopolitical) view of the professions and disciplines. The functional view of the liberal (capitalist) disciplines and professions sees them as nonpartisan, value-free, objective pursuers of truth and appliers of knowledge. It acknowledges that the disciplines and professions have deficiencies: commercialism, bias, fraud, incompetence, monopolistic practices, jurisdictional disputes, resort to politics, and so on. To its credit, the mainstream (along with critical studies) has identified conflicts and contradictions in the professions. It now knows that professionals deviate widely from their ideals and that they contain important deficiencies. For example, the functional view no longer accepts the claim by the professions that they have a qualitatively unique knowledge base, or that they are altruistic servers of humanity. And it no longer accepts the claim that the professions are (or deserve to be) autonomous—they are beholden to powerful clients, engage in incessant turf battles, and not only subordinate their support labor, but each other. Nonetheless, the mainstream approach continues to believe that the professions are endowed with a transhistorical force, science, that their objective knowledge will gradually enter society's bloodstream, and that their method for deciding between the true and the false will one day characterize society's problem solving institutions.

The conflict view accepts the important criticisms that have emerged from the conventional view of the knowledge elites. But it goes further to argue that the professions and disciplines are essentially value-laden, political, and biased, with a highly deficient record of solving social problems. Conflict analysts argue that the liberal professions have failed to solve, or even to keep up with society's problems, because their training and operating assumptions amount to a "trained incapacity" (Veblen), especially an inability to understand the institutional-power structure that causes problems. Actually, say critics, the professions appear to be an integral part of the institutions and groups that are the cause of social problems. Far from being transhistorical, science is an emergent of history and tends to accept and serve whatever system of national power it happens to be in.

America's professions and disciplines still have a self-image and still use an ideology to promote their interests derived from the small-scale entrepreneurial economy of the nineteenth century (with many vestiges from feudalism). Knowledge elites think of themselves (not so much privately as in their public utterances) as autonomous, self-reliant, versatile, and adaptable because of their unique and superior knowledge and skills. They also claim to be serving individuals and society because their knowledge and skills are available to all, or can be, given economic growth and more funds to enlarge research and improve access by those unable to avail themselves of existing services. The academic view of the professions tends to endorse this view.

The radical view argues that the professions and disciplines are now increasingly the employees of large-scale hierarchies, their work prescribed, circumscribed, and funded by others. By and large, they are the dedicated, well-rewarded, "trusted servants" of a society (power structure) they appear not to understand. That power structure now stretches across the apexes of the various hierarchies they work for and even beyond our borders to connect with the apexes of hierarchies in other countries. The role played by America's professions in its expansion abroad, however, has not been studied and constitutes a rich field for future research.

The social construction of knowledge has come to be widely accepted in the sociology of science thanks both to academic and conflict theorists. Marxists, phenomenologists, and feminists have been especially influential in gaining acceptance of the view that science is a form of social behavior and that it depends on and is shaped by sociopolitical forces. It should be noted that creative currents in academic functionalism have also moved toward the interpretive position (for example, Jeffrey Alexander and Anthony Giddens). Analyzing the differences in the use of the interpretive method by functional and conflict analysts of the professions forms a main theme of the text.

The text also shows that our otherwise different disciplines and professions have all begun to realize that they neither generate nor apply knowledge according to the idealized traditional image. All disciplines and professions now have significant minorities that acknowledge that their particular science is inescapably reliant on metaphor, myth, narrative, stereotypes, values, informal negotiations and understandings, and so on. One of the purposes of this text is to show the diverse ways in which the disciplines and professions display this feature in common.

The social construction of reality does not mean that the principles established by physics or that structures of deviant behavior identified by sociology are false or a product of fanciful thinking. It means that knowledge is generated on a selective basis within a dominant world view that contains a hierarchy of what constitutes knowledge and what is worth knowing. In turn, that world view is constructed haphazardly and incompletely by history's power groups. Another way of saying all this is to note that science is inescapably based on assumptions from start to finish and that its principles and empirical structures are interpretations of facts, themselves collected according to assumptions.

The differences between the functional and conflict perspectives revolve around other issues besides epistemology. The conflict or sociopolitical view also argues that the academic sociology of the professions has failed to raise questions about their actual efficacy in solving social problems. In addition, when questions are raised about other issues, it is done selectively. The political activities of the professions are noted, for example, but not that the professions are *essentially* political.

The sociopolitical view also rejects the early functional view that the hierarchy of occupations and their differential rewards came from differences in the inherent complexity and intellectually demanding nature of work. One consequence of this false view, it is argued, is that the professions require excessive schooling. The radical perspective disputes the need for long years of schooling (calling the process *credentialism*) and emphasizes that most forms of work are much easier to do than we have been led to believe. Along the same lines, the academic or functional perspective has uncritically accepted the argument that the professions are meritocratic and has failed to emphasize that they are also deeply structured by racism, ethnicity, and sexism. Also not emphasized is the similarity between the way professionals exploit their support labor and the way in which it is done in the wider society. In addition, the professions and disciplines are stratified among themselves and deeply stratified internally. Indeed, the diversification of professions and disciplines is now so far advanced that the terms *doctor, lawyer, professor,* and so on are relatively meaningless. Note must also be taken that the "free" or solo professional has not only given way to professionals that live out their lives in the many bureaucracies that make up corporate capitalism, but like the rest of the labor force, they too are being squeezed and stratified by centralizing pressures.

The conventional view of the professions has also failed to identify their role in the creation of the American nation state; instead, the academic world and the professions themselves emphasize their contribution to its natural unfolding. As we see, almost all disciplines (the natural sciences, sociology, anthropology, political science, economics, history, psychology, literary studies) were shaped both in what they studied and in their conclusions about the world by the emotions of nationalism. Also missing from the mainstream's study of the professions is its neglect of the enormous amount of deviance exhibited by the professions, their similarity in this regard with America's other elites, and the skilled collusion that takes place among propertied, professional, and political elites to yield socially damaging and difficult to detect departures from both public and private norms and values.

The problem solving record of knowledge elites suggests that we must rethink our understanding of them. That same evidence suggests that improving them means more than developing a better epistemology or education. If the disciplines and professions are deficient, perhaps problematic, it may be because modern society is deficient and perhaps problematic. If we want better thinking and policies, our findings about the professions and disciplines suggest that we must redesign the groups and group networks (corporations, business associations, governing boards, research institutes and departments, voluntary groups of all kinds, including foundations and political parties, legislatures, executive branches of government, social control agencies, therapeutic organizations, advisory groups, undergraduate and graduate academic departments and professional associations) that constitute the American structure of power. If, as this study argues, a society's knowledge can never be much at odds with the power structure that generates it, then perhaps we need to stop assuming that we can improve society through what now passes for science. Perhaps we need also to think of redesigning society to yield the knowledge we need.

Daniel W. Rossides

1

Social Power, the Nature of Knowledge, and the Knowledge Professions

◆　◆　◆　◆

◆　◆　◆　◆

The starting point for an inquiry into the professions and disciplines is to ask some basic questions about the nature of knowledge and human thought: Under what conditions do knowledge and rational thought arise, do they take distinctive forms under different systems of society, what is the relation between knowledge and practice? Answering such questions is the province of the *sociology of knowledge.*

THE SOCIOLOGY OF KNOWLEDGE

Thinking about Thought

The term *knowledge* (as opposed to information, data, facts) means knowing why things or people behave as they do: the solar system, plants, the human body, a septic tank, consumers, voters, spouses, artists, scientists, theologians, groups, the human personality, society, and so on. Knowledge about causation is also a "capacity for action," as Stehr emphasizes. When, how, and why we act depends on sociopolitical conditions, as Stehr reminds us, noting that it is easier to act on natural-science knowledge than social-science knowledge.[1]

The sociological specialty, the sociology of knowledge, strives for knowledge about how knowledge itself develops. It asks, Under what social conditions can knowledge about something be generated? In studying belief, moral, and aesthetic systems, it assumes that human creations, spiritual no less than material, and whether lodged in the personality or social relations, are social and historical phenomena. The sociology of knowledge also wants to know under what conditions knowledge is put to use. What prompts the "capacity for action" to become knowledge in practice?

The goal of the sociology of knowledge, therefore, is to explain an important part of human behavior (thinking, feeling, creating symbols, evaluating).[2] In seeking answers, the sociology of knowledge can take a broad historical perspective and study, for example, the social conditions that spawned modern legal and political philosophy, Protestant-bourgeois morality, or the modern professions and disciplines. Or it can assume a microsociological form and study the emergence of norms from play groups, explain the thought of theorists by referring to their family experiences or religious background, seek to understand a natural science outcome in terms of social relations in a laboratory, or show how divorce law is constructed in part by the interaction of lawyer and client.

Analyzing the social sources of symbols is widespread and appears under various guises. The current, more fashionable term for it is the *social construction* of something, even reality itself. A great deal of our understanding of social problems, for example, has resulted from sociologists probing into socially generated definitions of crime, mental illness, mental retardation, disease, gendered occupations, and so on. Both reformers and radicals employ the constructionist perspective in an effort to show that a given phenomenon is not natural or fixed, and can therefore be reformed or replaced.

The social nature of knowledge has also been affirmed by those who refer to the various empirical sciences as *interpretive* sciences. Interpretive philosophy has influenced a wide variety of sociological (and other) studies and represents the major creative current in science over the past few decades. As we see, interpretive science argues that all human behavior, including that by professionals, is subjective (or based on cultural assumptions). It also argues that those who study human behavior also employ assumptions, assumptions that tell them what to study, what evidence is relevant, and how conclusions (interpretations) are arrived at.

The Sociology of Science

The interest in understanding science has become a flourishing subdiscipline over the past twenty-five years. The majority of studies under this heading have been about natural science, but as we see, every discipline and profession has raised questions about the nature of its knowledge. The majority of these studies of science have claimed to be nonpolitical, objective, empirical, that is, have been conducted by the same standards that the sciences being studied allege they are following.

The study of science has varied from historical studies of the rise of modern science to detailed microstudies of scientists in a laboratory. Scholars have shown affinities between such things as Protestantism, concerns about political stability, and the interests and values of the historic middle class, on the one hand, and the rise and nature of modern science, on the other. Scholars have shown how facts are constructed by the practices and technology of science (not discovered). Scholars have pointed to scientific communities, invisible colleges, and reputational (scientific) communities as ways to understand science.

The interpretive method has also played a role in the sociology of science, for example, by pointing out that scientists use hunches, stories, metaphors, myths, analogies, trial and error, and so on in their work. But a full sociopolitical (interpretive) analysis of the spectrum of sciences had yet to appear. Nonetheless, most current analysts of the sciences no longer think of them as a reflection of genius, or somehow a natural outcome of human nature freed from ignorance and superstition. Historians and sociologists have established the interrelations of capitalism and science in the dynamic world of Europe from 1100 on.

The early modern natural sciences were intimately connected with artisan traditions and problems. Early scientists, such as Galileo and Bacon, sought support from political authorities by arguing that science could help control the superstitious, unruly masses. The absolute monarchies gave natural scientists strong support because they recognized that understanding the planetary world (the main focus of early modern science) had great implications for political legitimacy.

Scholars have also gone outside the nonpolitical sociology of science to insist that understanding science requires understanding the support it receives by parties interested in the outcomes of science. The social sciences receive support from government, foundations, and reform groups and this support tends to be of a certain kind rather than neutral and nonpolitical. Chemistry, biology, and physics receive massive support by government, corporations, universities, and foundations, none given without nonscientific purposes in mind. Is there any way to discuss chemistry without referring to DuPont and Merck? Does biology have any meaning without putting it in the context of a powerful health care establishment and Medicare-Medicaid? Does physics make much sense apart from the Pentagon? And do any of the sciences make much sense without referring to the massive support they receive by the state through all phases of alleged nonpolitical, academic education?

The sociology of science has tended to rely on a conventional but now outmoded picture of the various sciences. To think of some as rigorous and factual and others as soft, diffused, and subjective is misleading. It is now widely understood that the natural and social sciences, as well as the literary-humanistic sciences are all based on value-laden assumptions derived from historically induced myths, narratives, and metaphors, crystallized through career imperatives, interpersonal negotiations, and informal understandings; in short, that all the sciences are inherently interpretive.

The sociology of science has also developed a more realistic picture of the power of science than is found among many who study or comment on it. Science is far from all-powerful and it is clear that we are not heading in the direction of becoming a scientific society as envisioned by the French Enlightenment. In addition to powerful opposition by organized religions and some secular groups, science is conducted and its knowledge is distributed selectively in keeping with the overall power structure. Indeed many findings of science are openly repudiated by both the professions and other propertied interests when these findings run counter to their core interests (for a further discussion, see "The Fiction of a Knowledge Society" later in this chapter).

The Politics of Truth

One of the major reasons that the full interpretive method has not captured the sociology of science is the difficulty of arguing that the *contents* of science are interpretive. After all, the planets do go around the sun, water does freeze at a certain temperature, germs do exist. The question of whether the findings of science are true or are interpretive figments of our imagination is a false question. The interpretive (sociopolitical) position is that the truths of science do not result from neutral acts of knowledge creation by detached observers. It also argues that the biases and false pictures that occur in science do not occur only because of human error or lack of creativity or funds. An interpretive science of science argues that the choice and funding of research and the consequences of research are deeply structured by the interests and values of power groups, including the disciplines and professions themselves.

It follows that those who practice an interpretive sociology of science also reflect interests and values. Stated simply, these are:

1. to understand how science works in order to improve its practices
2. to identify neglected areas about which knowledge is needed
3. to widen our political choices about the kinds of knowledge we need and about the purposes of science.

In analyzing the social conditions that spawn knowledge therefore (and, it should be noted, that also spawn bias, error, and ignorance), it should be remembered that the overwhelming majority of theorists in this field have assumed that knowing how knowledge emerges is compatible with the idea of truth (for example, Vico, Condorcet, Saint Simon, Auguste Comte, Karl Marx, and Emile Durkheim). Indeed, the major thrust of this perspective is that social conditions generate truth, usually over time.

The sociology of knowledge emerged from both the liberal[3] and radical traditions. Radicals and liberals both think of knowledge as a byproduct of a society committed to progress through science. Both ask a similar question: If knowledge is dependent on social conditions, what is the best way to organize those conditions to produce better knowledge? But liberals and radicals differ widely in their answers. Liberals believe that the fundamental conditions for progress in knowledge already exist: legal and political freedom, including safeguards for free speech and a free press, and education and scientific research. For radicals, a full body of knowledge, available to all, cannot occur under capitalism. The best known of the various radical perspectives is Marxism. Marxists believe that science reflects economic power—at some point, science and the entire symbolic world of capitalism ceases to be progressive (in the interests of all) and becomes ideology (the symbolic protection of an obsolete social system). Radical feminism, either alone or in tandem with Marxism, has also spawned an attack on what it considers to be a masculine (and thus biased and incomplete) body of contemporary knowledge.

The major thrust of contemporary creativity in the knowledge sciences, therefore, has generated a politics of truth. There is much misunderstanding about what is meant by the social construction of knowledge and we will navigate its waters carefully. Suffice it to say for now that only a small minority of social or humanistic scientists say truth and objectivity are not possible. Those who accuse today's creative scientific currents of being antitruth are generally those who are trying to uphold yesterday's truth (for example, creationists, politicized conservative scholars (National Association of Scholars), and natural scientists who do not understand their role as the "servants of power," who have been stung by the doubts in science-as-salvation expressed by environmentalists (and others), and who have been shaken by the breakdown of their privileged world (World War II and the

Cold War) experienced as cutbacks in federal financing and by unemployment and underemployment.

The controversies about interpretive science that will concern us are of two kinds. The first is between those who adhere to positivism (nonpolitical, objective, empirical analysis) and those who argue that a better pathway to objectivity is to employ an interpretive science (acknowledge the use of ideas, assumptions, and values in empirical science). The other controversy that will appear in the following chapters is between defenders of the ideal of truth and objectivity (both camps in the first controversy) and those who employ a radical interpretive science to argue that the irreducible diversity and unpredictability of the world and the arbitrariness of its multiple interpretive perspectives makes one truth impossible (some postmodernists). Instead of searching for trans-social, transhistorical truth, this view argues, perhaps what is needed is a democratically negotiated politics perpetually aimed at updating a working consensus on the best use of human and material resources.

The Focus of the Study

The sociology of knowledge studies all forms of human symbolic creation, whether in natural science, social science, art, literature, theology, philosophy, or popular culture. In the realm of science, sociology (along with historians and others) has devoted most of its attention to how symbols are generated in natural science.[4] Some attention has been paid to the social sources of symbol creation in other disciplines. This study focuses on all the professions and disciplines, whether in natural science, social science, literature, or the arts, whether pure or applied.

The professions have been studied rather extensively over the past seventy-five years. Scholars have sought to understand:

1. The rise of the professions
2. Their distinctive attributes
3. The relation between formal and applied knowledge
4. The social or class origins of the professions
5. The status of minorities, including women, in the professions
6. The internal differentiation and conflicts within the professions
7. The struggle by the various professions to carve out a jurisdiction (often in competition with other professions) through the elaboration of voluntary groups and ideologies, and through politics and law
8. Their relations with the state and with various kinds of clients
9. Conditions of work, in various contexts, such as solo practice, professional groups, nonprofessional groups, and small- and large-scale organizations
10. Their efforts to establish an economic base, especially through the control of entry into their ranks

11. The rewards of the various professions, especially income, and the relation of their various motivations to the health of the professions and of society

12. The distinctive nature of the professions in various national contexts

Most of the early studies of the above issues were conducted in the nonpolitical, objective style of mainstream social science (functionalism), while later studies—say in the past three decades—have been more political and critical. Many early studies investigated what the professions said about themselves or plumbed their attitudes through questionnaires or interviews. Many were case studies of particular professions and their immediate work circumstances. A trend in recent decades has been to criticize professional claims, especially by noting that they are very much interested in securing high and reliable incomes, openly engage in politics to secure their ends, do not have unique knowledge bases, and are ideological (biased in both their depictions of themselves and in their professional work).

A number of neglected areas are identified during the course of this study, and scattered studies have been brought together to give their findings greater force:

1. The professions exhibit a considerable amount of deviant behavior. Scholarship in this area has gone far beyond the conventional handwringing about the failure of the professions to curb wayward individuals (see Chapter 9).

2. Scholars have also gone beyond noting how the professions and disciplines are dependent on other elites and have begun to build a comprehensive picture of the relations among all elites. In locating the professions in the American power structure, we will point out the many similarities among them, including the way in which the professions and other elites exploit labor.

3. Scholars writing from various perspectives have noted that the professions do not apply knowledge to the problems they face in a direct manner. Some say that professionals improvise and engage in artistic interpretation, while others say that professionals create reality. These scattered studies will be pulled together and highlighted to draw out their implications for both our understanding of the professions and of society. If the professions are not objective generators and dispensers of objective knowledge, then their claim to power and its rewards must be changed. In addition, society and human behavior also cease to be objective, natural entities and processes—serious consideration must be given to the idea that society and human behavior are merely human-historical creations.

4. An interesting finding of our study points to the neglected role of nationalism in the way in which the professions defined themselves and skewed their vision of the world. What was and what is the role of the professions in helping to create and maintain the American nation state? What nationalistic values and forces shaped the professions? Is it possible to isolate notions of patriotism and national power from other considerations? As we see, natural science, sociology, anthropology, political science, economics, history, psychology, and literary studies clearly show both intended and unintended contributions to and a shaping of their subject matter to suit the needs of national development.

5. The foregoing question spills over to raise questions about the role of professions in intersocietal relations. In recent decades, the American professions have responded to the world-market economy by expanding into other countries. Currently, a number of American professional associations are lobbying to get American professional standards accepted internationally. This represents an important new dimension in the development of world-market corporate capitalism and constitutes a rich field for future research.

6. The main question that this study addresses has been neglected throughout the study of the professions. While individual professions have been critically evaluated in terms of service to individuals, groups, and categories of people, the question, How well have the professions performed their alleged social functions? has been completely ignored. Our major theme revolves around a simple question: Have the various disciplines and professions had much success in solving social problems? In an important variation on this theme, we will also ask, What role do the disciplines and professions play in either promoting or retarding the development of a responsibly organized democratic public capable of consciously managing its affairs?

In assessing the social functions of the professions, this study assumes that social problems can be solved only by a viable political system. Since the main thrust of modern professionalism has been openly antipolitical, then the mainstream professions are not likely to take the lead in expanding the questions about science and the professions that can be asked in the political arena, or in allowing a wider (democratic) scope for the activities of government. This matter takes on special urgency when analyzing American society and its professions. The United States has gone further than any other capitalist society in developing a (de facto) technocratic liberalism, and its version of professionalism, including political science and the other social sciences, may actually be working against the development of a democratic polity and society.[5] Questions must be raised, therefore, about the knowledge (both formal and applied) being generated by America's institutions and groups. Technocratic liberalism has shown that it can generate enormous amounts of knowledge (so did technocratic socialism in the former Soviet Union), but is it generating and implementing the knowledge needed to solve social problems? From all accounts, the answer appears to be no (this is an enormously difficult question and an answer in the negative is suggested at this point to balance the presumption, established largely by the professions themselves, that the answer is in the affirmative).

The key to understanding science and the professions is to see them in political terms, that is, as emerging and developing in given historical periods in response to sociopolitical conditions. Our first step in showing the political nature of science and the professions, therefore, is to illustrate briefly how they vary with type of society, and how, far from being transhistorical, they emerge, take shape, and behave in a manner consistent with historical power structures. As we see, even the idea of human reason and the belief that the world at large is rational are derivatives of a distinctive (historically abnormal) social system (see below, "Ancient Greece: The Creation of a Rational Universe by a Unique Society").

TYPE OF SOCIETY, TYPE OF KNOWLEDGE, AND TYPE OF PROFESSIONAL

Simple Societies[6]

Simple societies range from gathering-and-hunting peoples to peoples that earn their living through some combination of gathering, hunting, fishing, herding, plundering, trading, or subsistence (nonmarket) farming. For many thousands of years (at least from thirty thousand to ten thousand years ago), all humans (both women and men) lived off the natural environment as foragers: they collected food from wild plants, hunted, and fished.[7] A gathering-hunting-fishing economy produces little surplus and the members of a foraging society are relatively equal. Simple society has a simple division of labor based largely on ascriptive statuses (cultural definitions of kinship, sex, and age). The family is the basic focus of behavior and the basis of social organization.

Nonetheless, these small, often nomadic societies became highly adapted to their environment and to their problems in general. Women and men both worked hard at economic tasks though men monopolized the occupation of big-game hunter (something that led to a monopoly of military statuses in later societies and contributed to their generalized superiority to women). Those who were especially skillful at the hunt were accorded a measure of extra prestige, but it was not possible for any family to accumulate enough property to make it superior to other families over time. Though there were positions of leadership, they could not be turned into hereditary statuses and passed on to children. Gathering-hunting societies were peaceful rather than warlike. Also notable was the absence of slavery.

In simple society, no one can read or write, but there is no illiteracy. The world of "is" and the world of "ought" tend to merge. There is drought, disease, and death, but there are no social problems; that is, the culture lacks the assumption that humans, using only their own minds and efforts, can fathom the causes of undesirable occurrences and do something about them. The world view of simple society, often focused on that part of the natural environment most important to its members, constructed ad hoc with logic, imagination, true and false beliefs about the empirical world, and cemented by magic works to undercut a problem-oriented mentality and a scientific curiosity about the physical and social universe.

The two "professions" who head up and preserve the power structure of simple societies are female and male providers (gatherer-hunter) and the shaman (a religious leader who "solves" problems with magic and reassuring rituals).

Advanced Horticultural and Agrarian Societies

The momentous movement toward advanced horticultural and agrarian societies occurred when humans began to derive their food primarily from domesticated plants. The movement to farming, essentially a way to harness the power of the sun, soon led to a large number of technological developments both physical and social. The movement to advanced horticulture (a gardening, family-based form of farming coordinated by a state derived from hereditary nobles) soon led in a number of places to agrarian society (the cultivation of large plots by serf, slave, or tenant labor).

The first agrarian societies emerged out of advanced horticultural societies in the Middle East approximately 5,000 years ago. An (advanced) agrarian society is unique because it can produce food, tools, and other things, including belief and value systems, on a scale far exceeding even an advanced horticultural society. New technology, especially iron metallurgy and the plow, along with other productive techniques such as irrigation and the harnessing of animal energy, combined with such economically central sociocultural inventions as slave and serf labor, family-tenant labor, administrative structures, standing armies, forms of taxation (including forced labor), money, writing, mathematics, religion, and legal codes, resulted in a unique type and level of social existence and, of course, unique knowledge occupations.

The spurt of cultural developments, including material technology, in the relatively short time period of a few thousand years, holds important lessons for the sociologist of knowledge and for those who want to understand the professions and their place in the structure of social power. The pattern of causation is clear. The plow was a singularly important cause of increased food production—by digging deep, the plow buries weeds and releases far more nutrients than the hoe or digging stick. But a plow is really effective if made from iron and pulled by animals. This leads to new occupations beyond the familiar landlord and dependent laborer: Those who raise and tend draft animals, those who mine iron ore, and those who refine and fashion it into implements.

Successful agriculture needs a dependable supply of water and in many places this means irrigation, a prime source of new occupations and professions. Irrigation requires canal and dam builders, those who can build and operate locks, workers to maintain the vast irrigation network and supervisors to oversee the overall enterprise. The need to coordinate an irrigation system that runs beyond the jurisdiction of any locality or single landlord leads to a central government. That government needs revenues to pay for the irrigation works and that means taxes. Taxes require keeping books and thus writing becomes important and leads to still another occupation, the scribe (in those days a profession). Taxes require the use of numbers and thus arithmetic. Flooding by unpredictable rivers requires the restoration of boundaries and thus geometry emerges. Boundary disputes lead to law and law courts and more professions arise. To complete our circle of causation, the increase in food production from plow agriculture makes it possible for all these other occupations to eat while pursuing their specialized work.

The rise of complex horticultural and especially agrarian societies led to a distinct change in symbolic culture. There is a movement away from the ad hoc particularism of simple society toward universalism. One clear change is from polytheism to monotheism, something not unrelated to the emergence of a single leader (who claims to be derived from both the people and the supernatural, and sometimes to be God). The symbolic systems of complex societies, developed in response to emerging problems, were also characterized by the pervasive use of naturalistic imagery. They often had a sense of the past and of the future, but were largely present-oriented. They had a vast store of practical precepts for living as well as a line of authority to a supreme ruler. Corruption and deviance from explicitly stated norms were continuously punished and condemned. They had an image of the world in which logic, facts, magic, emotion, and value judgments were all mixed together in a noncontradictory whole.

Complex societies also exhibit a deep interest in keeping exact records about all aspects of the economy, especially crop yields and taxes, but this empirical bent did not become science as we know it. Interestingly, however, it had a similarity to contemporary data gathering: It was used to inform policymakers and to maintain the existing structure of society (for example, a careful record was kept of seasonal changes and their associations with weather changes, and priests used this information to explain good and bad crops in a supernatural context, thus effectively blocking alternative explanations and practices).

The complex feudal-authoritarian systems shaped their members in keeping with their advanced material technology. They created hereditary serfs, slaves, and tenants, and a hereditary nobility. They created new occupations and arranged them in a hierarchy of importance and a hierarchy of reward and power. The emergence of a central, or royal, bureaucracy was a momentously important historical event because it produced a social technology (professional civil servants in structured social relations) that made it possible to coordinate and control a large and diverse population. Of great importance is the increased specialization of the dominant landlord stratum, an important and indispensable development if the few are to achieve effective control of the many. The landlord class (estate) stays on the land, but it also supplies sons for the royal army and civil service (law courts, tax collectors, healers, magicians, astronomers, upper clergy). As we see, modern society does much the same with the "middle class" acting as the source of the dominant occupations in the economy, state, voluntary sector, and professions. Of supreme importance for those who want to understand the professions is the simple fact, that throughout history, professionals have been part of a wide variety of power structures and have served them without giving them much thought.

Ancient Greece: The Creation of a Rational Universe by a Unique Society

Professionalism in the West is unique because it takes place in a rationalist culture.[8] A rationalist culture believes that the lawful behavior of nature and human nature corresponds to the human brain when it is engaged in reasoning. This rational world view is true of the ancient, medieval, and modern periods and it means that the creation of a rational universe by the ancient Greeks deserves our attention. The basic question that must be answered is, If all people both before and during the time of the ancient Greeks are equal in basic capacity, why did the creation of a rational universe occur in ancient Greece?

Ancient Greece is an historical entity that developed and declined over a thousand years (roughly 1300 B.C. to 300 B.C.). Its story is first of all a result of a unique natural environment. Greece's austere natural environment promoted specialized farming, for example, olive orchards, rather than large-scale agriculture, and small rather than large centralized, self-sufficient kingdoms. The surplus of olive oil in turn spurred pottery manufacture (as containers for oil), trade in oil, and thus a simple market economy. The insufficiency of the Greek economy made it necessary for Greeks to buy and sell and eventually they became deeply implicated in market relations. The need to trade also created the unique Greek city, a center of high-density interaction among relative equals, at once a city, society, and state. By 500 B.C., the population of Athens had diversified enormously. In addition to nonworking aristocratic landowners and a substantial number of small peasants and herdsmen, the urban core had numerous small producers, shopkeepers, traders, and artisans, as well as wage-laborers. Thanks to democratic reforms, all were citizens regardless of their economic status (in the context of the Greek city-state, and unlike modern society, citizens had substantial political power). Over the years, the general insufficiency and specialization of the Greek economy generated a unique market mentality (the ability to calculate the worth of one thing in terms of another) and a unique commitment to self-government.

The small-scale Greek economy based on a tradition of small, freeholding farmers, small producers and traders, and wage laborers produced a relative equality among Greek families (especially males) and made necessary a strong emphasis on self-reliance (similar, say, to the individualism required by the settlement of the United States). The Greek stress on autonomy and equality (like the American emphasis on self-reliance) was in good part a reflection of their natural and social environment. The Greeks conceived life as a struggle, and like the ancient Jews (but in a different way), separated themselves from nature. To further self-reliance, the Greeks insisted on equal inheritance of land (among sons). But this practice eventually divided the land into parcels that were too small to support a family. One result was land concentration as the wealthy bought up bankrupt small farmers. Another was social tension because Greek society was generating a continuous supply of landless people who had expectations of autonomy and equality.

The Greeks understood the conflict between dependence on others and their tradition of self-sufficiency and it helped generate their unique political mentality. That mentality can be reduced to a simple question: how does one think about and reconcile the varied interests of quarreling equals? The existence of numerous city-states, in frequent contact, all inhabited by Greeks, but with different customs and political systems, certainly helped to stimulate thought about the nature of society. The Greeks also travelled widely outside of Greece and were aware that other kinds of societies existed besides the city-state. The need to make sense of all this was another stimulus leading to the emergence of politics as well as science, mathematics, social theory, philosophy, and the very idea that the universe is rational.

Making sense of their uniquely diverse world (a diversity which in other parts of the world had always been blanketed by mythology and authoritarianism) was greatly facilitated by the unique Greek alphabet.[9] Derived from the Phoenicians, the Greek alphabet met the three requirements of an efficient and creative writing system:

1. The visible signs must trigger the reader's memory of all the sounds that are distinctive in the language.
2. The triggering must be precise, calling forth one and only one phoneme (the smallest unit of sound) and requiring no guesswork or choices on the part of the reader.
3. The visible signs must be small in number to avoid overburdening the memory by requiring the mastery of a large list before recognition or reading can begin. The brain is biologically encoded to respond to acoustical signals, the spoken language; it has not been encoded to manage a corresponding variety of visible signs.

The Greek alphabet, says Havelock, had three important consequences:

1. There was no longer a need to rely on memory and the rhythm needed to make memory reliable. As a result considerable mental energies were released.
2. Efficient writing made it possible to record "novel statements." Under the inefficient writing systems, novelty was discouraged by the need to stay within the already cumbersome system. The "novel statements" of the West, both in natural and social science as well as the humanities, are largely due to the Greek alphabet and the ability of first Rome and then the Western European countries to develop native equivalents of the Greek writing system.

3. The Greek alphabet was also easy to learn; indeed, with it, children can learn to read almost simultaneously with learning the sounds of their oral vocabulary.

The emergence of an efficient technology of writing went beyond these three consequences. For one thing, the ease with which it could be learned complemented Greece's democratic tradition of oral discourse, unlike other writing systems which became the monopoly of a special profession in the service of oligarchy or monarchy. It facilitated interaction among the diverse social classes and categories of people. But another consequence was perhaps the most important. The ability to represent thoughts efficiently in writing meant that one could store them, revise them, sequence them, and round them out. Expressed differently, it meant that the writer could come to feel that the mind was the creator of reality, not outside forces. And not mind as shapeless consciousness, but mind as reason, as ideas in coherent sequence. It seems plausible, therefore, to conjecture, not that the Greek alphabet created Western idealism (reason as potent creator), but that it was a necessary element in that momentous invention.

The invention of reason was a response to the diversity and novelty of Greek experience. Existing side by side with religion, magic, and custom, reason eventually emerged as an autonomous force. Faced by the need to come to terms with the diversity and change spawned by a relatively complex division of labor, by foreign trade, and by warfare, the Greeks sought transcendence and certainty in the realm of abstraction. Though the Greeks preferred the logic of teleology,[10] they also invented mathematics (some will argue *discovered* mathematics).

The emergence of a universalistic culture (unifying generalizations) was prompted by the diversity, changes, and conflicts experienced by feudal-authoritarian systems. The same need to transcend the world of unpredictable experience and conflict into a realm of undisputed norms and values (truth) occurred throughout agrarian civilization. But it occurred in Greece with a unique difference—the realm of abstractions was divorced from supernaturalism and its origin was alleged to reside in something that all (male) humans had, reason.

The nature of Greek society also generated unique creations in the areas of politics and social theory, and led to new occupations and professions. By the fourth century B.C., the Greeks had invented a wide variety of knowledge fields: natural and moral philosophy, including the logic of teleology and mathematics. They had well-developed specialties in biology, medicine, physics, history, and politics. They were inventive in warfare. But they did not achieve much in the way of applied technology or in chemistry. Could it be that with plenty of slaves to tend the furnaces, they had no incentive to know more about the properties of chemicals? Could it be that with slaves and with skilled foreign workers, with a tradition in which all citizens were expected to work, and with small-scale farming and businesses, there was no motivation to develop labor-saving technology?

Interestingly, the Greeks even raised questions about their occupations and professions. Characteristically, they did so in the context of power, or rather, in relation to how a particular profession did or did not serve the common good. This occurred well before the rise of Greek democracy. The *Illiad*, written in approximately the ninth century B.C., is the story of an all-powerful human, Achilles, who can be controlled only by the gods. Here the Greeks, faced by the difficulties generated by one of their primary professions, the warrior, dealt with it in the language of mythology. As the problems of power multiplied, the Greeks were forced to deal with it in more secular, rational terms. By the fifth century B.C., Greece had generated (in addition to the typical professions of warrior and civil servant) a number of unique professions and practices: professional politicians, free-lance teachers, and autonomous academies of learning encompassing many of the basic fields of knowledge found in today's undergraduate curriculum. The controversies that raged about how society should be organized and how public policy should be generated were also controversies about elite occupations and professions: Politician (tyrant, demagogue, elected leader, and legislator), military officer, and knowledge creator (the various philosophical schools).

The burst of professional and intellectual life reflected the new diversity and discord of Greek society, but it also represented an attempt to put the world together again. The problem of diversity and discord loomed larger by the day and the Greeks devised a wide variety of secular devices in an effort to contain their leaders and overcome discord: Direct democracy, popular law courts, payment for citizen participation, ostracism and exile, rotation of office, and election by lottery. The problems they faced are still with us and we have much to say about how modern society controls (and fails to control) its powerholders and professions (and much to say about how mainstream sociological, political, and economic theorists neglect the analysis and evaluation of power).

Modern Society: Capitalism and Modern Science

The social constructionist approach to science is especially important when analyzing modern natural science because of its reputation as somehow extrasocial, extrahistorical. What follows, therefore, is a brief analysis of the development of natural science in relation to the rise and development of capitalism.

The advent of capitalism was a momentous event comparable in importance to the Agricultural Revolution. By 1500, Europe had a thriving capitalist economy anchored mostly in agriculture and commerce, but not without the stirrings of industry. Between 1500 and 1800, England and France were transformed by their respective middle classes into unique capitalist societies. From 1800 on, these countries and others underwent a process of industrialization that was to usher in today's capitalist societies and their distinctive professions and disciplines.

The first stage of capitalism (roughly 1500 to 1800) saw the advent of modern natural and social science. Basically, modern science began by abandoning the teleological worldview of the Greeks (and the medieval period), but not their rationalism or deductive epistemology. Instead of a nature composed of qualitatively different entities, all responding to fixed inner blueprints, nature became a set of abstract forces. To understand these forces, early modern science used mathematics, assuming as had the Greeks that reason was the way to get past the deceptions of experience and penetrate nature's secrets.

The climax to this stage of science came in the seventeenth century with the work of Isaac Newton. The Newtonian synthesis depicted nature as composed of material particles and abstract processes kept in orderly equilibrium by gravity, in effect, a huge machine integrating the behavior of everyday matter as well as in the furthest reaches of the solar system. Behind this grand act of reason lay centuries of experience in harnessing the energy of wind and water through machinery (the humble but indispensable origins of the Machine Age).[11]

The great breakthrough to modern science, therefore, was not only deductive (mathematical), but deeply tied to empirical experience. Indeed, a full nominalist position (ideas are names for facts) had emerged as early as the fourteenth century with William of Occam. This new empirical way of thinking reflected the need to keep a close watch on the complexities, problems, and opportunities of the burgeoning European economy. Clearly, modern science was the product of previous sociocultural systems (Greek rationalism, Greek mathematics, Christian monotheism) and the needs of the newly emerging capitalist economy and polity. In the latter respect, modern science was clearly connected to military needs and to the overseas expansion (imperialism) of Atlantic Europe.

Feminist scholars have also enlarged our understanding of the rise of modern science and capitalism. Carolyn Merchant, for example, argues that natural science, capitalism, and masculinity go together and represent a violation of the natural. For Merchant, the natural and the feminine are linked, giving us a different perspective on science, capitalism, and environmentalism.[12] For her part, Susan Bordo has used Freud to shed light on the birth of science. Bordo argues that separation from the warm, organic, "feminine" medieval world created the same anxiety that occurs when a son is separated form his mother. Descartes underwent this anxiety and solved it by making a virtue out of separation: For Descartes, the solitary, detached thinker is the agent (or method) of knowledge (or science).[13] Without rejecting Bordo's analysis, a sociology of knowledge explanation would argue that the deeply unsettling change from feudalism to capitalism had deep psychological impacts on those who had power and responsibilities for public life: Given the unusual diversity and instability of Western life, the only solution (in a rationalist culture) was to step outside life's hurley-burley and make sense of it with concepts. This epistemology became masculine because the main objects of cognition were about the things that men cared about: nature, warfare, law, the state, the economy. It also became what (male) power groups needed: not merely a cognitive way to deal with the world, but a way that freed them from responsibility from the consequences of what they did (hence the value-neutral as well as objective nature of modern science).

The eighteenth century established the Newtonian view of nature and human nature throughout Western culture. The eighteenth century also inaugurated the new stage of science, empiricism. The French Enlightenment took a revolutionary step and abandoned the Greek distrust of experience, the senses, and the world of facts. The phenomenal world, declared the *philosophes*, is orderly in and of itself and thus accessible to the thinking-sentient human being. The empirical outlook which had been gathering for centuries, received full institutionalization in the nineteenth century. The nineteenth century also inaugurated the contemporary academic disciplines and the professions. Empirical research, the growth of knowledge, and the disciplines and professions cannot be understood unless they are placed in the context of the maturing capitalist society that spawned them.[14]

Western society in the early nineteenth century was unique in a number of ways that have a bearing on the West's commitment to empiricism and the rise of the professions.[15] Above all, the advent of significant economic changes, which ran the gamut from intensified capitalist agriculture to the factory system, generated a concern for the condition of the people, especially those subject to physical deprivations. Interest in the *social question* (as historians have come to call it) was a novel occurrence in Western thought.[16] Obviously, thinkers and officials throughout history had concerned themselves with the general condition of the masses and had devised public policies to deal with it. What happened in the nineteenth century was unique because both the holders and the near-holders of power *saw their own fate* bound up with the condition of the people. Previously, those in power had simply assumed a natural and fixed hierarchic order to things and human beings. The dominant groups took the people and their suffering for granted; whatever their condition, it was ordained by nature and was normal and familiar.

By the early nineteenth century all this had changed—powerful groups could no longer take their societies for granted. In addition, the widespread changes in social life had the effect of preventing the upper classes of Europe from directly experiencing their own society—a situation that seemed to be politically dangerous to many of their members and a situation that must have been unsettling to almost all. An immediate result of this situation was a widespread desire to gain more knowledge about the social question, or condition of ordinary people: thus a vast growth of intelligence gathering by the police, government bureaus, and the emerging social sciences, and a proliferation of professions to deal directly with emerging social problems. The advent of organized empirical research in both the natural and social sciences was one of the more significant developments of this new social world.

The nineteenth century climaxed centuries of economic development to yield a capitalist economy with developed agricultural, commercial, manufacturing, and service sectors. It also saw a developed system of law, politics, and government (and especially in the United States, a far-flung system of voluntary groups and private schools). These developments produced a more specialized division of economic, political, and social labor, and it led to the rise of the modern professions. But none of this, including the rise of the professions, should be seen only in terms of the ideology that accompanied it, that is, as progress toward democracy and an ever-expanding triumph over ignorance, hunger, and exploitation. We must be especially careful not to take the claim by the professions that they are the benefactors of humanity at face value. Our history of the relation between society and its professions shows clearly that the professions serve the economically and politically powerful. The claim that the modern world is under the sway of autonomous, objective, progressive knowledge elites is highly problematic.

SOCIAL POWER, KNOWLEDGE, AND THE KNOWLEDGE PROFESSIONS

Since the ancient Greeks, Westerners have taken it for granted that:

1. Knowledge about the world can be obtained independently of time and place through the exercise of human reason (objective truth).
2. Knowledge can improve our personal and social lives.
3. There are special methods and people to provide and apply knowledge.
4. Knowledge will flow out from those who generate it to those who need to know (rulers, citizens, professionals, owners, workers, consumers).

The modern version of Western rationalism (idealism, or mind as reality and cause) is essentially continuous with the past though changes have occurred in how knowledge is obtained and in the professions who produce and apply it. As we have seen, the eighteenth century embraced the empirical method as its main avenue to truth about nature. As the French (and Scottish) Enlightenment, the eighteenth century also revolutionized the West's conception of human behavior by declaring that human nature was also subject to scientific (empirical) comprehension. The nineteenth century institutionalized the empirical method as powerful groups engaged in it and supported it. During this century, Westerners came to take it for granted that empirical science was a powerful force for good. In its various embodiments (scholarship, originality, laboratory, free press, education, learned societies, research institutes, and so on), it was soon taken for granted that science held the key to progress, and perhaps human perfectibility.

In recent decades, some have argued that the success of science and professionalism has ushered in a knowledge society and signals the end of ideology. The alleged new society has also been characterized as a *postindustrial, postmodern,* or *information* society (and in a related guise as the "end of history"[17]). In an explicit expression of the evolutionary liberal tradition in sociological theory (for example, Emile Durkheim, Charles Horton Cooley), Talcott Parsons (1902–1979) announced the reality of evolutionary progress through symbolic (mental and moral) achievement. Faith in the ability of science to produce transhistorical knowledge, and to incorporate it into the life of society continues to dominate the social and natural sciences and education. It manifests itself in the liberal (right and left) reform tradition. It appears as the explicit planning tradition. It appears throughout the liberal professions and the policy sciences, and is central to the academic study of the professions. That much of radical thought, especially Marxism, also assumes some form of rational evolution makes it even more difficult to assess critically the West's deep faith in progress through ideational activity.

The Fiction of a Knowledge Society

This study assumes that the argument for a postindustrial society is weak, and that modern capitalism has not entered into any stage that runs counter to its essence (private property as the source of economic, political, and social power). Not only is the United States not in a postindustrial world, in which it is allegedly driven by or based on theoretical scientific knowledge, but there is also no discernible trend in this direction.

The idea of a postindustrial, knowledge-based society is deeply planted and has been reinforced recently by exaggerated, fanciful claims on behalf of computer-driven integrated, interactive communication technology, the so-called information highway. Nonetheless, the idea of a knowledge-based society must be resisted, nay rejected. The most recent and perhaps the most sophisticated version of the fallacy of a postindustrial society is Harold Perkin's argument that English society, starting in 1880, left behind the class society of entrepreneurial England (just as class society left behind the aristocratic society based on land) to become a professional society.[18] Perkin argues that the professional ideal, occupation-income-and-service by a certified meritocracy, has permeated society top to almost bottom.

What makes Perkin's argument interesting and insightful is that he has anchored much of it in the success that professionals have had in turning human capital (their expertise) into income-producing property. Nonetheless, his argument is deficient, not merely because he cannot show that professionals have ceased using their power and privileges to prevent competition, or because his claim that a merit-based professionalism characterizes the basic occupational system is more than dubious. Perkin's argument is deficient because he does not recognize the co-supremacy of land, other forms of material capital, and human capital over society.

The best interpretation of the growth of white-collar occupations has occurred outside the liberal tradition. The classic analysis remains C. Wright Mills's.[19] For Mills, the new service, white-collar, or professional occupations represent a change *within* the historic middle class. Far from transcending class or industrial society, the new occupations are firmly embedded in economic, political, and social structures based on private property, managed markets, upper-level coordination, and bureaucratic administration. That significant portions of the new middle class are propertyless does not dilute their commitment (unconscious as well as conscious) to a property-oriented market society.

The belief in progress through knowledge raises two different questions:

1. Are the liberal professions supplying the knowledge needed to make the United States an adaptive society?
2. Have we entered a social stage in which knowledge animates power structures?

The answer to the first question is that they are not at present. The answer to the second is also no. But the belief that we have become or are on the verge of becoming a knowledge society remains strong, though it is not always easy to identify because it assumes various forms.[20]

Symbolic Activity and the Needs of Power

Like all symbolic activity, empirical research is related to the structure of social power. Those who accept the conventional view of the development of empirical science and of liberal political institutions as a growing emancipation from error and evil have themselves succumbed to the blandishments of power. Knowledge helps to make human beings free, but not all of them. Indeed, the knowledge that sets some people free results in the nonfreedom of others. Knowledge about how a legislature works, for example, can result in laws that free some from tax burdens while placing heavier burdens on the weak and ignorant. Empirical research can certainly contribute knowledge and help in the clarification and realization of values, but its known historic forms cannot automatically be equated with truth, morality, and the common good.

What is referred to as knowledge is also suspect because it is generated selectively according to historically induced assumptions generated by the holders of power. The use of the intelligence quotient (IQ) test is a well-known example of how assumptions enter into empirical research and how both must be related to social power. Early research into intelligence quotients was conducted under the assumption that human beings are innately unequal. As a consequence, the science of IQs became a potent instrument for creating and maintaining a capitalist division of labor—especially when educational systems adopted the IQ as the measure of native ability with the enthusiastic endorsement of the middle classes. Neglected was the counterassumption that the same facts about unequal IQs can also be interpreted as a function of social power: People are made unequal in IQ, as well as occupational skills, tastes, goals, and so on by the hierarchy of social class. This assumption gives the analyst and user of IQs a very different view of the same facts.

The connection between empirical social research and social power originated with the absolute monarchy, especially its mercantilist phase. The dynamics of internal and external power relations made it imperative that the state rationalize (bureaucratize) its operations.[21] Hand-in-hand with routine administration, the keeping of accounts, the codification of laws, and the minting and printing of money went the development of intelligence-gathering agencies: domestic and foreign spies, informers, police reports, inquiries and commissions concerning population, the state of the fishing or textile industry, surveys of public lands, and so on.

The case of England is even more instructive in understanding the power functions served by the institutionalization of empirical research. The symbolic development of England is essentially the record of acquiring, consolidating, and employing power by a dynamic middle class. In the seventeenth century, Hobbes and Locke shattered and displaced the feudal symbolic world in the name of an emergent middle class. In the eighteenth century, Adam Smith found rationality *in* capitalist society, not beyond it; Hume clipped the wings of reason, in effect saying that thought cannot be used to transcend or critically evaluate society. The nineteenth century saw the growth of a series of deductive disciplines such as economics, political science, and sociology, all within the capitalist assumptions of laissez-faire economics, utilitarianism, progress, and social Darwinism. These disciplines eventually flowered as the liberal arts—liberalism's higher education. Alongside these symbolic developments, but not linked to them until much later, grew a tradition of empirical social research, a nontheoretical grappling with the problems of an established capitalist society rapidly becoming industrialized and urbanized.

In the early nineteenth century, Britain had a well-established, though adaptable, and somewhat open set of ruling elites. There was an obvious need for intelligence, and it was assumed from the first that facts were to be used for purposes of formulating public policy. As Abrams has shown so well,[22] the basic form of research in Britain's centralized society was the massive government inquiry, and the basic roles that were encouraged were those of statistician, administrator, and reform politician. Further, Britain's dominant classes held distinctive views about society that deeply influenced the nature of empirical social research: A deeply rationalist concept of society, a focus on individuals as the basic unit of analysis, and the idea of automatic social integration and consensus through the invisible hand. Essentially, the purposes of fact gathering were to uncover the natural laws that constituted society, to expose artificial obstacles that impeded their operation, and to promote the consensual natural society through social legislation and government administration. Characteristically, researchers felt that there was no need for theory to organize their fact gathering. As Abrams points out, its characteristic units of analysis were

> the state, the individual (moral or immoral) and occasionally, the classes. What is missing is any developed concept of the social system, any extended or general analysis of structured interactions between individuals or classes,

any theory of the social basis of the state. Where there is a model of society it is typically an administrative one suffused with moral judgment . . . time and again the terms of analysis are the custodial state standing face to face with individuals in need of help, corrections, or regeneration.[23]

The relation of empirical research to sociology is instructive. Sociology grew, indeed prospered, at the end of the nineteenth century largely because many of the basic principles of early liberalism had been discredited. Of special importance in Anglo-American countries, where laissez-faire theory had taken hold, was the gradual abandonment of a belief in natural harmony and social integration through an invisible hand. Far from being even-handed and integrative, the invisible hand of the market was stroking some and punching others, subjecting society to unhealthy ups and downs, and failing to incorporate many into society. It became clear that integrative processes other than the free market had to be found or created. Everywhere in the industrial West, a late-liberal movement surfaced to spearhead a more positive and comprehensive program of social reform within the assumptions of capitalism. The development of an empirical orientation in American sociology, along with its sociocultural emphasis and its involvement in social reform, identifies it as an aspect of late liberalism. With no laissez-faire tradition to overcome, French and German sociologists (for example, Emile Durkheim and Max Weber) developed an even more pronounced sociocultural orientation and became even more involved in the political issues of the day than American sociology. In all countries alike, there was a clear recognition that empirical social research and social reform were positive forces to prevent socialism.

It is clear that the main sources of the new interest in fact gathering were government, business, and voluntary groups, and that its motives were political, economic, humanitarian, and a fear of the masses and of socialism. In a classic essay,[24] Nathan Glazer has argued that the upper classes' new interest in facts stemmed from a feeling that they were surrounded by a society they neither knew nor could know using conventional methods such as reading or personal experience. Glazer does not complete his insight, however. One of the main functions of the new interest in empirical research was to provide the dominant classes with the intelligence they needed to possess their society fully. The primary significance of the new passion for data gathering is that it helped consolidate, update, and legitimate a particular system of social control (power).

The reason that England was able to pioneer and develop the empirical arts more fully than other nations is not merely as Glazer points out, that it was the world's most advanced industrial country. All European countries were troubled by the social question during the early nineteenth century; all saw the growth of large numbers of destitute people both in the countryside and in the burgeoning industrial cities and towns. Among the major countries of Europe, however, it was only in England *that the social question was successfully separated from revolution.* Certainly the threat to civil order and to the order of society itself, represented most acutely by the Chartist movement, stimulated social research as well as political rivalry and creativity among the dominant landed and commercial-industrial classes. The defeat of Chartism, however, made England safe for liberalism, and the task of the dominant classes henceforth was to run, not to think about, their society. From then to now, the great flowering of empirical social research went hand in hand with the major achievement of British society, the successful incorporation of the working and destitute classes into a capitalist society. Empirical research supplied the intelligence for the reforms that forestalled revolution and even helped to turn socialism into reformism.

The needs of power produced a large range of overseas activities by trading companies, state-sponsored settlements, exploration expeditions, and missionary work, all of which yielded large amounts of information to aid Europe's overseas expansion. During the nineteenth century, British anthropology began largely as an arm of Britain's colonial administration, and British colonies made possible participation observation by anthropologists (field research) on a wide basis, all explicitly with a view to helping Britain administer its empire (see the anthropology section in Chapter 4).

Organized empirical research was part of the monumental formation of the centralized state that was essentially completed, though not in a uniform manner, everywhere in Europe and the United States during the nineteenth century. From the establishment of the Prussian bureaucracy under Fredrick the Great in the mid-eighteenth century to Napoleon Bonaparte's creation of the modern French civil service to the Pendleton Act of 1883 in the United States, the process of bureaucratization (rational administration) manifested itself everywhere. Britain was no exception. Britain's construction of a highly centralized state machine during the nineteenth century is perhaps a better index to the realities of social power, both there and elsewhere, than the extension of the franchise or the emergence of cabinet government.[25]

The sanctities of government and politics; the moral cloak of voluntary organizations, including churches; the iron necessities allegedly governing economic life; and the prestige of science—all served to mask the essentially partisan nature of empirical research. If one views the activities of these institutions, however, as ways of developing private solutions to public problems, then empirical research falls into place as another way in which the dominant classes solve their problems, invariably through solutions that create problems for the lower classes.

With the triumph of liberalism, starting in seventeenth-century England, philosophy and social theory no longer serviced a landed-clerical elite; symbolic culture no longer emphasized the next world and denigrated this one; and contemplation and transcendence were no longer feasible social ideals. In nineteenth-century England, organized empirical social research, in tandem with reform politics, became the main way to deal with the here-and-now. By camouflaging the here-and-now in the garb of progress through problemsolving, organized empirical research effectively preempted the future while safeguarding the present. In short, given the class uses and advantages of empirical social research, one must resist associating it with truth, morality, and the common good, even when conducted by well-intentioned professional bodies.

The Rise of the Professions: National Contexts and Variations

Though there was much talk of democratizing society by means of public education, the essential process of institutionalizing the new faith in empirical knowledge took the form of professionalism. By the late nineteenth century, a large number of groups had emerged claiming jurisdiction over special fields of knowledge: Various disciplines and professions emerged, each with its own association, subject matter, credentials, research journals, and special methods (within the overall world of empirical science). Each claimed to have knowledge about a special area of behavior and a special cluster of problems; each sought to restrict entry into its ranks through a system of credentials and licensing; and each struggled to obtain jurisdictional monopoly, high income and prestige, and autonomy from forces either to the side or below.[26] From across the spectrum of professions came similar statements and claims: We are neutral, altruistic, objective searchers for and dispensers of knowledge; we can be judged only by our fellow professionals since we possess a high and difficult to obtain knowledge base; since knowledge is power and yields virtue, our activities will be service oriented; whatever our deficiencies, we are the best guarantee of both knowledge and an improved society.

The views held by the professions about themselves, and the message they sent to the public and to the government, varied somewhat depending on time and place. The rise of the professions followed no uniform pattern, varying in terms of national socioeconomic development. Since national development shows marked differences among England, France, Germany, the Soviet Union, and the United States, differences appear in when and how the professions appeared.

The professions have been studied extensively, especially in the major countries of the West,[27] in the former Soviet Union and in some of the former socialist countries of Eastern Europe,[28] and even in a developing country,[29] but no systematic comparative study exists.[30] Actually, no complete study of the professions of any one nation exists largely because the topic is vast and definitions and approaches are unsettled.

The most important difference among national professions is the one between the United States and all other countries. Outside the United States, in both the liberal and authoritarian capitalist countries as well as in Russia and the Soviet Union, the state actively promoted the professions and employed them for public and elite purposes.[31] Clearly associated with functions deemed important to national development, the state openly established schools to conduct research and train scientists and other professionals. The state also employed professionals in large numbers, either directly or indirectly through state welfare programs. Even in England, the country that most closely resembles the United States, the professions were part and parcel of England's aristocratic traditions: elitist, public-minded, ambivalent about working for money, all in all, corporatist in outlook (the English pattern influenced English-speaking Canada and the French pattern influenced French-speaking Canada).

The professions in the United States rose without explicit state sponsorship and without a clear identification with social functions. America's professions grew up in an entrepreneurial environment, in a society with an open, decentralized economy and a state with limited responsibilities for performing social functions. Accordingly, the professions sponsored themselves: they formed associations, helped establish schools and curricula, and engaged in politics to secure legal sanctions for the standards they were creating. Accordingly, the American professions were deeply geared toward securing income from private clients and private employers, especially schools.[32]

In all this, the American professions participated in the national hypocrisy, along with business and farmers, of advocating competition while engaged in getting government subsidies and legal monopolies. The overall pattern saw powerful groups denouncing politics and government while busily using both for their own ends—the net result was to deny the masses the ability to use government for their ends. Seen in another way, the American professions, along with business and farming, were given strong support by government, but with no explicit compact that the public would receive services in return. The ideology of laissez-faire made it unnecessary that the public's exchanges with private groups be of the same order as exchanges between private parties: an exchange of equivalences.

In all these regards, the United States is unique, even when compared to other capitalist societies. Lacking a political system that could yield a sense of collective purpose, the United States is now an international anomaly: Among developed capitalist countries, it has the highest crime rates, one of the worst infant mortality rates, the highest teenage pregnancy rate, the highest divorce rate, and the worst health-care system.[33] None of this is surprising, however, given the peculiar nature of America's belief in its exceptionalism.[34] At the core of American culture is the taken-for-granted assumption that it has released human nature and placed society on the path toward reflecting the creative, though unequal, rational tendencies in human beings *qua* human beings. What is surprising is that America's knowledge elites should believe in this fantasy for so long. Perhaps the explanation is that they too benefit from the utopian image of laissez-faire, and that in any case, they are too occupied securing their place in the overall system of power to have much time to think about fundamental political and social questions.

While national context remains important for understanding the professions, the relations among nation-states have grown in importance over the past half-century. Future chapters spell out the relation between the professions and entrepreneurial America, the professions and corporate America, and the professions and America in the corporate world-market stage of capitalism. The increased concentration of the American ecnomy, its increased control of the American polity (at all levels), and its spread across the globe in search of markets, resources, and labor has had significant impacts on America's professions. The increased inequality of income in the past three decades has also stratified the professions as all groups have struggled for shares in a stagnant national pie (living standards as opposed to gross domestic product). Corporations, consumers, environmentalists, minorities, and local, state, and federal governments have all sought to change the way professions behave. For example, the heavy costs of medical care and litigation have seen strong movements to curtail the jurisdiction and autonomy of doctors and lawyers. Future chapters will outline these changes along with the negative outcomes that have appeared among teachers, professors, natural scientists, nurses, social workers, middle managers, and others.

The squeeze on the professions, or perhaps better said, the incorporation of the top levels of the professions into the top level of the political economy and the squeeze on the bottom levels of the professions has been accomplished through both private and public mechanisms. In this sense, the United States has moved more toward the European pattern, while in the meantime Europe has moved somewhat toward the American pattern. But as yet there is no clear call that the United States harness its professions to social functions. This would also require that the United States harness its economy to social functions, an idea that is too threatening to America's other and most powerful elites even to be thought, much less uttered.

SUMMARY

The text's purpose is to synthesize what is known about the professions and disciplines with a focus on the United States.

The central theme of the study analyzes how well the American professions and disciplines have performed the social functions attributed to them. It is especially interested in a variation on this theme, What is the role of the professions and disciplines in either promoting or retarding a democratic public capable of consciously managing its affairs?

The key insight into the professions and disciplines is to frame them in political terms and to assess them according to the sociology of knowledge.

The sociology of knowledge analyzes the relation between symbol creation and social conditions (or the experience of symbol creators), and is used to assess the problem solving record of knowledge elites.

The sociology of knowledge also goes by the name, *the social construction of reality*. These two concepts have helped to generate the new view of science that has appeared in both functional and radical camps, namely, that science is inescapably interpretive (sociopolitical) in nature.

The sociology of science has sought objective knowledge about science as a social process. In recent years, the interpretive method has come to the fore in the study of science, and it is now recognized that the natural and social sciences, as well as the literary-humanistic sciences use sociohistorical assumptions in their scientific work, that is, the various disciplines and professions use the interpretive method in common though only a minority in most professions and disciplines are aware that they are so doing.

The traditional questions about the professions are covered, but the focus of the study is on neglected topics such as professional deviance, the position of professionals in the overall system of power, the role of knowledge elites in creating the American nation state, and especially, whether the professions are serving positive social functions, or what amounts to the same thing, whether they are barriers to the full development of democracy.

The study's organizing perspective is that all human behavior is political, that is, a result of history and social power. It criticizes America's knowledge elites for having become part of America's pervasive system of technocratic liberalism (the reduction by capitalism of political questions to technical, means-ends issues).

Type of professional varies with type of society and this is illustrated with brief analyses of simple, horticultural-agrarian, ancient Greek, and modern societies.

The modern age of empiricism is criticized on two counts: one, the claim that it has or is ushering in a postindustrial or knowledge society is denied, and, two, far from being objective and nonpartisan, empirical research is clearly linked to and in the service of America's system of power.

A comparison of how the professions arose in modern society reveals that the American professions are unique in not having been state-sponsored (and connected to social functions in their origins). The emergence of America's professions and disciplines from America's unique entrepreneurial ethos—that is, not clearly linked to social functions because of America's foundational belief in the magic of markets—is identified as one of the reasons that America's knowledge elites have a poor and perhaps worsening record in regard to solving social problems.

The ideology of an entrepreneurial America continues to obscure the more highly concentrated and unequal America that has emerged as corporate capitalism has moved more fully into its corporate world-market stage. Present day professions and disciplines have been stratified in new ways by this movement with top levels benefiting and the rest slipping or struggling to remain in place.

NOTES

1. Nico Stehr, *Practical Knowledge* (Newbury Park, Calif.: Sage, 1992).
2. For excerpts from or discussions about almost all the major contributors to the sociology of knowledge (with the exception of feminist theorists) and for many case studies suitable for student readers, see James E. Curtis and John W. Petras, eds., *The Sociology of Knowledge: A Reader* (New York: Praeger, 1970); Gunter W. Remmling, ed., *Towards the Sociology of Knowledge: Origin and Development of a Sociological Thought Style* (London: Routledge & Kegan Paul, 1973); and Nico Stehr and Volker Meja, eds., *Society and Knowledge: Contemporary Perspectives in the Sociology of Knowledge* (New Brunswick, N.J.: Transaction Books, 1984). For a feminist sociology of knowledge that indicts sociology and its objective value-

neutral method of being biased and inherently unable to give women their due, see Dorothy E. Smith, *The Conceptual Practices of Power: A Feminist Sociology of Knowledge* (Boston: Northeastern University Press, 1990). For a similar theme in African-American feminist theory, see Patricia Hill Collins, *Black Feminist Thought: Knowledge, Consciousness, and the Politics of Empowerment* (New York: Routledge, 1991).

3. The meaning of the term *liberalism* will unfold gradually. Essentially, it refers to the acceptance of private property, private economic motives and actions, and political and legal equality as central social institutions. Thus, both Democrats and Republicans in the United States are liberals; that is, both accept the validity and superiority of capitalist/liberal society while disagreeing on how to run it. For a fuller discussion of historical European developments in liberal social thought, see *The Encyclopedia of the Social Sciences* (New York: Macmillan, 1930–35); or its successor, *The International Encyclopedia of the Social Sciences* (New York: Macmillan and Free Press, 1968); and *Encyclopedia of Sociology* (New York: Macmillan, 1992).

4. For a summary of the sociology of natural science, see Harriet Zuckerman, "The Sociology of [Natural] Science," in Neil J. Smelser, ed., *Handbook of Sociology* (Newbury Park, Calif.: Sage, 1988), pp. 511–574.

5. Technocracy refers to the antipolitical emphasis, found in both liberalism and socialism, to give over the political and social control of society to knowledge elites. For a valuable history of this perspective in the modern West and in the United States, see Frank Fischer, *Technocracy and the Politics of Expertise* (Newbury Park, Calif.: Sage, 1990), chaps. 3 and 4. The former Soviet Union openly committed itself to a society led by knowledge, especially natural science, elites (under Marxist guidelines, of course).

6. Though written from an evolutionary liberal perspective, Gerhard Lenski, Jean Lenski, and Patrick Nolan, *Human Societies: An Introduction to Macrosociology*, 7th ed., pt. 2 (New York: McGraw-Hill, 1995), provides an excellent description and analysis of preindustrial societies.

7. Anthropology and other disciplines created a male-oriented explanation of both physical evolution and social evolution into human gathering-hunting society. For the vital role played by females in both physical and social evolution (which mutually influenced each other), see Nancy Tanner, *Becoming Human: A Model of the Transition from Ape to Human and the Reconstruction of Early Human Social Life* (New York: Cambridge University Press, 1981).

8. For a history and critical analysis of social theory in the West, including a chapter on the unique social conditions that led to the invention of rationalism and social theory in ancient Greece, see Daniel W. Rossides, *Social Theory: Its Origins, History, and Contemporary Relevance* (New York: General Hall, 1998).

9. The following is based on Eric A. Havelock, *Origins of Western Literacy* (Toronto: Ontario Institute for Studies in Education, 1976).

10. Teleology understands the universe by assuming all phenomena from plants to animals to humans are driven by internal forces that, when nourished, achieve preordained ends or purposes.

11. For a Marxian analysis, which anchors Newton's theoretical synthesis in European capitalism's need to solve technical problems in water transport, industry, and war, see Boris M. Gessen, *The Social and Economic Roots of Newton's "Principia"* (New York: Howard Fertig, 1971), with a new introduction by Robert S. Cohen; originally published in 1931. For both Marxist and non-Marxist analyses showing the social roots of modern science, see Lewis Mumford, *Technics and Civilization* (New York: Harcourt, Brace, 1934); Alistair C. Crombie, *Medieval and Early Modern Science*, 2 vols. (Garden City, N.Y.: Doubleday, 1959); Samuel Lilley, *Men, Machines, and History*, rev. and enl. ed. (New York: International Pub-

lishers, 1966); and Melvin Kranzberg and Carroll W. Pursell, Jr., eds., *Technology in Western Civilization*, 2 vols. (New York: Oxford University Press, 1967).

12. Carolyn Merchant, *The Death of Nature: Women, Ecology, and the Scientific Revolution* (San Francisco: Harper & Row, 1980).

13. Susan Bordo, "The Cartesian Masculinization of Thought," *Signs* 11, no. 3 (Spring 1986): 439–456.

14. This perspective has been obscured by Thomas S. Kuhn's enormously influential *The Structure of Scientific Revolutions* (Chicago: University of Chicago Press, 1962). Kuhn's work is a useful reminder that humans, including scientists, see and behave in terms of assumptions. Kuhn argues that when natural scientists change their assumptions (paradigm), revolutionary breakthroughs occur. But Kuhn tends to call all advances in knowledge *revolutions*, thus obscuring the real revolutions—changes from one worldview, or cosmology, to another (these are very rare). Kuhn also states that he has nothing to say about the world outside of natural science (p. xii), thus supporting the view that science is a self-explanatory force, when of course it gets its impulse and direction from society, especially government and the economy.

15. For general background on the impact of the French and Industrial Revolutions on a wide variety of European countries, see Charles Breunig, *The Age of Revolution and Reaction, 1789–1850* (New York: Norton, 1977).

16. For an excellent portrait of this period and the social question, see William L. Langer, ed., *The Rise of Modern Europe* (New York: Harper & Row, 1969), vol. 14; William L. Langer, *Politics and Social Upheaval, 1832–1852*, especially chaps. 1 and 6.

17. Francis Fukuyama, *The End of History and the Last Man* (New York: Free Press, 1992).

18. Harold Perkin, *The Rise of Professional Society: England Since 1880* (New York: Routledge, 1989).

19. C. Wright Mills, *White Collar: The American Middle Classes* (New York: Oxford University Press, 1953).

20. For example, Ralf Dahrendorf, *Class and Class Conflict in Industrial Society* (Stanford, Calif.: Stanford University Press, 1959), especially chaps. 7 and 8, and Daniel Bell, *The Coming of Postindustrial Society* (New York: Basic Books, 1973). The essays in Gernot Böhme and Nico Stehr, eds., *The Knowledge Society: The Growing Impact of Scientific Knowledge on Social Relations* (Boston: D. Reidel, 1986), argue that science and knowledge are either triumphing or rearranging the relation among knowledge elites. (The essay by Richard V. Ericson and Clifford D. Shearing, "The Scientification of Police Work," is the only one to raise disturbing political questions about science, in their case, about the use of science in police work.) Charles Derber, William A. Schwartz, and Yale Magrass, *Power in the Highest Degree: Professionals and the Rise of a New Mandarin Order* (New York: Oxford University Press, 1990), provide a valuable, through shapeless, review of beliefs about the New Class (knowledge elites). It is unclear just where they stand, but their own view appears to be that professionals have power in their own right, are separate from the power of capitalists, and are engaged in a struggle with those who dispute illegitimate aspects of their power. The authors' thesis is that the professions are monopolizing knowledge and are thus preventing the full emergence of a knowledge-based society.

21. For a classic and still unsurpassed general account (well grounded empirically) of a crucial period in the formation of the modern state, the European system of states, and the profession of public administration, see Walter L. Dorn, *Competition for Empire, 1740–1763* (New York: Harper & Row, 1940), especially chaps. 1–3, and vol. 9 of Langer, *Modern Europe*.

22. Philip Abrams, *The Origins of British Sociology: 1834–1914,* pt. 1 (Chicago: University of Chicago Press, 1968).

23. Ibid., p. 48f. For further evidence of the (unintended) partisan uses of the empirical research that was established in this period and that is still with us, see M. J. Cullen, *The Statistical Movement in Early Victorian Britain: The Foundations of Empirical Research* (New York: Barnes and Noble, 1975), especially his conclusion.

24. "The Rise of Social Research in Europe," in *The Human Meaning of the Social Sciences*, ed. Daniel Lerner (New York: Meridian, 1959), chap. 2.

25. For a unique and valuable sociohistorical analysis (supplementing Dorn on the rise of public administration) of the development of Britain's centralized administration, see K. B. Smellie, *A Hundred Years of English Government* (New York: Macmillan, 1937). The rise of public administration and the use of other professions by the federal state in the United States had an aspect that looms large later in this study: Like the other capitalist societies, the United States also developed a strong central government, but unlike the other capitalist democracies, failed to give it a social mission, that is, depoliticized it, thus making its uses and benefits more available to the upper than the lower classes.

26. The nineteenth century also saw claims to autonomy by the clergy. Confronted by a secular society it could not hope to be dominant in, indeed one that was actively hostile to it, the most professional of clergy, that in command of the Roman Catholic Church, withdrew from involvement in sociopolitical issues and generated a symbolic defense of its autonomy in and power over purely spiritual and moral matters; in this regard, see Gene Burns, "The Politics of Ideology: The Papal Struggle with Liberalism," *American Journal of Sociology* 95, no. 5 (March 1990): 1123–1152.

27. For England, see Harold Perkin, *The Rise of Professional Society: England Since 1880* (New York: Routledge, 1989). For France, no general work exists, but Stephen Crawford, *Technical Workers in an Advanced Society: The Work, Careers, and Politics of French Engineers* (New York: Cambridge University Press, 1989), provides some background beyond his focus on engineers. For Germany, see Geoffrey Cocks and Konrad H. Jarausch, eds., *German Professions, 1800–1950* (New York: Oxford University Press, 1990) and Charles E. McClelland, *The German Experience of Professionalization* (New York: Cambridge University Press, 1991).

28. Anthony Jones, ed., *Professions and the State: Expertise and Autonomy in the Soviet Union and Eastern Europe* (Philadelphia: Temple University Press, 1991).

29. Peter S. Cleaves *Professions and the State: The Mexican Case* (Tucson: University of Arizona Press, 1987).

30. Comparative studies are rare in American social science, including studies of the professions. Two brief, pioneering comparative studies are Dietrich Rueschemeyer, "Contrasting Institutional Patterns of Professionalization," in his *Power and the Division of Labor* (Stanford, Calif.: Stanford University Press, 1986), pp. 118–124, and Elliott A. Krause, "Professions and the State in the Soviet Union and Eastern Europe: Theoretical Issues," especially the section, "United States, Western Europe, Eastern Europe: Comparative Issues," in Anthony Jones, ed., *Professions and the State: Expertise and Autonomy in the Soviet Union and Eastern Europe* (Philadelphia: Temple University Press, 1991), pp. 35–39. A full-scale insistance on the importance of studying the professions comparatively, with valuable material on a number of countries, including Sweden, is Michael Burrage and Rolf Torstendahl, eds., *The Formation of Professions: Knowledge, State, and Strategy* (Newbury Park, Calif.: Sage, 1990).

Eliott A. Krause has developed his comparative analytical frame by mounting full chapter analyses of the United States, Great Britain, France, Italy, and Germany; see his *Death of the Guilds: Professions, States, and the Advance of Capitalism,*

1930 to the Present (New Haven, Conn.: Yale University Press, 1996). For a discussion of this important book, see the section, "The Death of the Guilds or the Reassertion of Priorities by a Corporate World-Market Capitalism?", in Chapter 2.

31. In an interesting comparison that takes us outside the capitalist West, Graham found that American and Soviet scientists and other knowledge elites have similar concerns: scientists worry about political interference, philosophers want to protect ethics from scientists, many are concerned about the destruction of mores, and there is worry about the social and political misuse of knowledge: Loren R. Graham, "Reasons for Studying Soviet Science: The Example of Genetic Engineering," in Linda L. Lubrano and Susan Gross Solomon, eds., *The Social Context of Soviet Science* (Boulder, Col.: Westview, 1980), p. 235f.

32. For details about the way in which the American professions parlayed American mobility ideals, respect for knowledge, political power, and the cultivation of public fears and stresses into their rise and institutionalization, see "The Culture of Professionalism" in Chapter 2.

33. The United States probably also has the worst record in regard to employment and poverty (especially among children), but comparisons are difficult because cross-national indicators are compiled differently.

34. For the concept of *exceptionalism* and its embodiment in and distortion of American social science, see Dorothy Ross, *The Origins of American Social Science* (New York: Cambridge University Press, 1991).

2

American Society: Power, Knowledge, and the Professions

◆ ◆ ◆ ◆

◆ ◆ ◆ ◆

While developed societies share a common scientific worldview, this view has important variations depending on its origin and development in concrete national systems. In Chapter 1, we saw that professions vary by type of society and by historical and national variations within modern (capitalist and communist) society. The same is true of science. No understanding of the American professions is possible unless they are put in the context of America's distinctive view and practice of science.

PRAGMATISM: THE NEW SCIENCE IN THE NEW WORLD

Pragmatism: Empirical Science and the Search for Truth

The empirical phase of modern science that took hold in the nineteenth century, appeared as America's distinctive philosophy of pragmatism. Explicitly based on science and congenial to the needs of a dynamic, nontraditional society, the philosophy of pragmatism absorbed almost all of America's intellectual energy. Thanks to the favorable conditions of the New World, pragmatism emerged as a clean-cut, militant positivism that defined philosophy in terms of natural science. Unlike in Europe, the empirical phase of science in the United States was not obscured or obstructed by entrenched antiscientific philosophies. Despite rival schools, notably Hegelianism, pragmatism exercised a near monopoly in American philosophy.

The rise of pragmatism was part of a larger transformation in American intellectual culture. From the end of the nineteenth century to the 1930s, the leading figures in American social thought exhibited a remarkable uniformity in approach.[1] Pragmatism in philosophy entered directly into social theory in the person of John Dewey. As Morton White has shown, the underlying assumptions of pragmatism also pervaded the thought of Oliver Wendell Holmes (1809–1894) in law, Thorstein Veblen (1857–1929) in economics, and James Harvey Robinson (1863–1936) and Charles A. Beard (1874–1948) in history and politics. The "revolt against formalism" was an attempt to go beyond the deductive rationalism of the traditional social-science disciplines and place them on solid scientific ground. All five thinkers, said White, shared a common historicism and cultural organicism.

> By *historicism* I mean the attempt to explain facts by reference to earlier facts; by *cultural organicism* I mean the attempt to find explanations and relevant material in social sciences other than the one which is primarily under investigation. The historicist reaches back in time in order to account for certain phenomena; the cultural organicist reaches into the entire social space around him.[2]

The revolt against formalism went far beyond the rejection of deductive sociology, history, economics, political science, or jurisprudence. As Morton White points out, pragmatism faced the problem of criticizing and reevaluating the central tradition of British empiricism represented by David Hume (1711–1776), Jeremy Bentham (1748–1832), John Austin

(1790–1859), and John Stuart Mill (1806–1873). British empiricism presented a problem because it was static and nonhistorical; while it sought to base knowledge on experience, it emphasized *fixed* modes of experience. Because of this, British empiricism had become mired in the mechanistic world of Newtonian rationalism. Dewey, who was especially concerned with this question, eventually concluded that British empiricism was simply "a disguised *a priorism.*"

The goal of the pragmatic social theorists was the control of experience and the creation of desirable experience, not the passive acquisition of and adjustment to either deductive truths or fixed modes of existence. It is here that the contribution of pragmatism to professionalism is most evident. As White shows, American pragmatism was also concerned with finding truth, or more exactly, with using science to fathom the structure of fact and obtain both objective knowledge and a scientific morality. Here too, its spirit ran parallel to professionalism.

Despite flirtations with socialism and Marxism, the revolt against formalism was also a deeply conservative movement whose basic thrust was to preserve the traditional liberal structure of American society. As many commentators have noted, liberalism's core values of individualism, private property, market economy, political-legal equality, and faith in progress seeped into the marrow of American life to become a traditionalism that tolerated no competition. America's deeply ingrained liberalism is evident in the various political movements from the 1890s through the New Deal, a period characterized by Richard Hofstadter as the Age of Reform.[3] The reforms and ideas of this period attempt to realize the original definition of America as a society of free and equal individuals. Though the ideas of natural law and natural rights were gradually discarded, the individual as a self-evident category of social theory and organization remained. Instead of being rational biopsychic actors, however, individuals were increasingly thought of as emotional, highly socialized egos who needed a rational social environment to realize their true nature.

The main movements in philosophy and social science at the turn of the century, therefore, confronted America's problems head on by refining their methodology and committing themselves to social reform. Sharing the same assumptions, the social sciences became suspicious of monistic, formal theories and settled down to rethink their approach to social knowledge. By and large, they accepted the methodological implications contained in biology, constructing from them an empirical-functional orientation that was to inform the thought of almost all major social theorists. But they also continued the metaphysical dimension in modern science, seeing in the new empirical methodology a gateway to truth (known as general or systematic theory). And despite the increasingly problematic nature of the individual and the growing sociocultural flavor of the social sciences, few questioned the central liberal assumption that the individual was a significant causal entity.[4]

Stemming from the dynamic new conditions of American society, the empiricism at the heart of pragmatic philosophy brought all disciplines closer to American life. But in satisfying its craving for metaphysics, twentieth-century social science never realized that it was a product of new social conditions and that its methods and aims bore the marks of unique historical forces. As Rytina and Loomis have noted, pragmatism's attempt to derive truth from experience subjected pragmatism to social power, or the forces behind the organization and maintenance of experience.[5] In short, pragmatism never confronted the fact of social power; indeed, by stressing organic adaptation, empirical information, piecemeal reform, and education, pragmatism became the ideological agent of social power. It is of some importance, therefore, to trace the general relationship between the new phase of empirical social science and the new social (or power) structure of twentieth-century America. As Ross shows convincingly, the origins and establishment of American social science constitute a long and successful effort to link the freedom of private-property groups and science with the health and destiny of humanity (as embodied first in the American Republic), and a failure to deal with institutions, power, and the relativities of history.[6]

Pragmatism and the Emergence of Late Liberalism

The monopoly of liberalism in America is of the utmost importance for interpreting American history.[7] Save for the Southern plantation society, the United States, alone of all emerging industrial nations, had no significant social group opposed to the main ideas and values of liberalism. As such, American norms were not only congruent with the experience of Americans, but because they were so widely accepted, became thoroughly traditional. America had no continuing debate, as in seventeenth-century England and in eighteenth and nineteenth-century France, about the nature of human nature and society. Given their unanimity on fundamental questions, Americans devoted themselves to the problems of everyday life. There emerged a pattern of behavior unified by the individualistic logic that informed all institutional spheres.

As the specialized and conflicting demands of a complex economy began to affect American behavior, however, the agrarian, early capitalist version of liberalism had to be recast. The conflicts and tensions produced by hectic industrialization could neither be explained nor justified by the old faith that nature provided a cosmic guarantee of liberty, equality, justice, and harmony. Nor did the evolutionary scheme quiet the moral conscience or suit the activistic optimism of America. By the late nineteenth century, a determined critique was mounted, not only against the natural-law theory of the founders of the American Republic, but against the monistic theories of evolution as well. It had become obvious to a new breed of observers and reformers that evil—or social problems—was located not in human beings, nature, or evolution, but in the concrete, willful, and alterable policies of individuals and groups, and that these, in turn, could often be traced to outmoded institutions. Out of the pragmatic individualism of the American socioeconomic system, therefore, came a mounting critique of the intellectual and moral basis of traditional institutions and a growing feeling that America's basic institutions bred injustice and were dangerous to social survival.[8]

By the first decades of the new century, the intellectual transformation wrought by pragmatism had had far-reaching effects on American thought. The closed society, the finished morality, the fixed hierarchy of virtues, and the rationality of the individual slowly gave way to views proclaiming the open society, the developing morality, the problematic hierarchy of virtues, and the need to supplement the rationality of the individual with the rationality of social institutions. The new optimism and faith in science was based, paradoxically enough, on new insights into the passion-driven, habit-inhibited nature of individuals, who were now judged incapable of transcending the forces within or outside themselves without the aid of a humane and rational social system.

Pragmatism, therefore, represents the American response to the moral and intellectual needs of a dynamic industrial system, a system whose dynamism was confined *to perfecting existing society*. It provided the empiricism, the open-minded futurism, the moral voluntarism, and the fresh faith in mind that American capitalism needed. The inconclusiveness, diversity, and even the ambiguity of industrial life, experiences that had never before enjoyed philosophical standing, were no longer defined as departures from reason, but as features essential to a truly rational society.

The main weight of eighteenth-century liberal political and social theory was based on the assumptions and conclusions of Newtonian physics, thereby acquiring a deep ahistorical cast. The United States acquired and developed a selected version of the liberal tradition, one that emphasized the rational, self-reliant individual and the decentralized, intrinsically harmonious society whose institutions were static in their structure, but progressive in their effects. Even when this ahistorical conception of human nature and society was infused by the dynamism of evolutionary theory, the assumption that the individual was the primary datum of social science remained unchanged. Even after the evolutionary sociologies faded from the forefront of social science, the individualistic approach remained. In keeping with the American tradition of liberalism, American social science developed a naturalistic, essentially psychological, approach to human behavior; that is, it did not seriously question the ahistorical definition of human nature it had inherited.

The ahistorical bias in American culture is of the utmost importance in understanding America's professions. The United States did not develop out of a previous social system, but was founded *de novo* on two miraculously derived set of norms: Christian revelation and the natural law of secular rationalism. It emerged as a revealed society erected on religious and rational truth, a society that thought itself free of the corruptions and compromises of historical existence. It is no wonder, therefore, that social science flourished in a nation that considered itself free of the observation-distorting corruptions of history—that believed, in short, that it had achieved a perfect correspondence between human nature and social institutions.[9]

American reform movements and American social science (which were closely related) emerged out of a cultural matrix in which the idea of the potent individual had long since become the unconscious presupposition of political, social, and intellectual life. Both reformers and social scientists accepted this definition of human nature and both continued to think of society as either a natural or a created equilibrium of individuals-in-motion. Nothing illustrates better the indelible conservatism of American reform politics and social science than this twentieth-century reversion to the thoughtways and values of seventeenth- and eighteenth-century rationalism. And nothing illustrates better the central image of professionalism than the concept of the individual made especially potent by knowledge.

SCIENCE AND THE NEW SYSTEM OF POWER

The Culture of Professionalism

In a brilliant study, providing the indispensable historical background to American professionalism, Burton Bledstein has pointed to the pervasive influence of the new science on nineteenth-century American life and to the way in which it contributed and helped legitimate unequal power relations.[10] The emerging culture of nineteenth-century America was everywhere animated by the rationalizing tendencies of American capitalism. By 1870, the surge of American industrialization and its diversifying occupational system had everywhere presented opportunities for a more efficient way to conduct business and conquer or contain evil. Efficiency appeared in the mass distribution of books through subscription and rationalized marketing techniques. The important lecturing business was rationalized. Spectator sports were professionalized with the first professional baseball team appearing in 1869. Even college sports were professionalized by the development of varsity sports guided by expert staffs. During the last decades of the century, professional associations appeared in a wide variety of fields (for example, the first national professional association in law was established in 1878). A wide variety of professional schools appeared: dentistry in 1867, architecture and pharmacy in 1868, school teaching and veterinary medicine in 1879, accounting and business in 1881.

Enrollments in professional schools rose rapidly as did their length and specialization (led by medicine). By the end of the century, a huge array of associations and learned societies had appeared. Of special interest is the appearance of associations for historians (1884), economists (1885), and political scientists (1889). And in all areas there appeared a piece of paper, issued either by the state or private groups, signifying that an individual had the competence and the legal right to practice an occupation. But the connection between the academic associations and the wider political economy, including the emerging philanthropic foundations, was much deeper and far more extensive. As Silva and Slaughter argue, the emerging social sciences (between the Civil War and the 1920s) used the resources of the outer society to establish their occupational monopoly over knowledge, and in return, the social sciences (their leaders and their organizations) supported the economic and political interests of dominant groups in the wider society.[11]

The essence of the new professionalism consisted of a belief that it was possible to master nature's principles and thus acquire a mastery over the chaos of experience. Theoretical and applied knowledge (over specialized parts of worldly phenomena) would give the professional the ability to identify and control the seen and unseen factors in areas as diverse as mining, constructing bridges or skyscrapers, commercial farming, curing diseases in all parts of the body, obtaining justice, coping with poverty, establishing rational management in business and government, rationalizing politics, and even in areas such as marriage, child rearing, diet, hygiene, sex, dress, and recreation.

Armed with knowledge, the professional was a truly free, independent, autonomous individual and thus in harmony with a central theme of American culture. But, says Bledstein, the freedom of the professional had deep conservative consequences. Professional claims to competence, augmented by rituals, costumes, technology, and physical settings, resulted in the marked dependence of the professional's clients. In all of life's spheres, the public was told that it faced one evil after another: crime, strikes, political uprisings, foreign threats, diseased bodies and minds, financial losses, legal calamities, and so on. Professionals preyed on and cultivated the insecurities and fears of the public. In the wider society, industry, technology, and science were upsetting the world while at the same time offering themselves as the solution to the world's problems. In particular contexts, Allan Pinkerton in 1870 was extolling the virtues of the professional private detective in the war against the professional criminal; journalists were warning the public about the menaces in their lives and claiming that they had an objective view of them; reformers were rationalizing politics and the labor movement; and even the struggle against poverty was professionalized (a national association of social work appeared in 1874). The net result was to make ordinary persons dependent and to accept on trust that their betters knew better.

The emergence and establishment of this power relation in business, private professional practice, and the polity (politics, government, and law), then led, says Bledstein, to the emergence of professionalism as an orderly lifetime career. The role of higher education in all this was to persuade the public that those in high places were competent and trustworthy. By standardizing admissions, prescribing formal courses of study, giving examinations, and conferring degrees, higher education proclaimed that the intelligent were rising to the top and the country had a way to overcome family inheritance, political favoritism, and subjectivism.

Rounding Out Corporate Capitalism

Bledstein's insightful analysis can be augmented. The diversifying capitalist division of labor spawned a host of specialized disciplines and professions. By the closing quarter of the nineteenth century, the essentials of the American industrial system were in place and the professions and disciplines arose to do two things.

1. The applied professions emerged to grapple with the practical problems of the everyday world on a pragmatic basis: each problem was taken at face value and efforts to solve it were undertaken without relating that problem to anything much beyond itself.

2. The theoretical disciplines arose to provide the metaphysical legitimacy that all power systems seem to need. By the last quarter of the century, the American economy had been separated from any controllable or accountable connection to social functions, and economics and administration emerged as professions to tell us that economic behavior reflected a law of nature and that administering corporations was a science. The American political and legal systems were in place and political science, public administration, and jurisprudence arose to formalize them. Later, sociology emerged to proclaim the existence of a mostly-finished functional social system that needed empirically derived knowledge to lubricate its workings. And anthropology arose to separate behavior from race and fixed biopsychic structures, providing corporate capitalism with needed flexibility to shape its leaders and labor force. Anthropology also supplied a concept of culture which supplemented sociology's functionalism. Culture, claimed anthropologists, was a bounded, self-explanatory, all-purpose adaptive structure that can be understood only on its own terms (see Chapter 4 for a fuller analysis of America's academic disciplines).

The main thrust of American society, in other words, was toward a technocratic mode of addressing the world and its problems. Noble has outlined this process in terms of engineering. In an insightful analysis, he argues that capitalism appropriated scientific knowledge and technology for private ends with the help of the engineering profession and higher education. Engineering also played another role—by defining the apex of its career line as movement into managerial roles, engineers not only became capitalism's vanguard for the management of things, but for the management of people as well.[12] In a wider sense, engineering pioneered the contemporary trend toward all-purpose, abstract administrators who do not actually have to know much about the purposes of the hierarchies they are in charge of.

The emergence of rule by experts went far beyond corporate management and public administration. Efficient management was also the criterion for education and voluntary groups, including foundations and the general realm of art.[13] Though a distinct outsider tradition also emerges, the essential process was one in which most Americans, including professionals in all sectors from medicine to music, were successfully fitted into the emerging world of technocratic groups and institutions.[14]

The developing power structure of corporate America had another pattern (implicit perhaps in Bledstein): The various professions (and semiprofessions) worked in tandem to depoliticize social problems. Doctors, for example, became part of a network of medical specialties, medical associations, medical researchers, drug manufacturers, surgical and medical technologists, administrators, insurance companies, health-care financiers, city-state-federal health-care agencies, nurses, undergraduate premedical instructors, and all those in law, politics, and social science who accept the medicalization of disease, disability, mental illness, and crime—that is, accept the medicalization of socially created problems. Another example was the power network that grew around psychology. Psychology emerged to provide the human-nature underpinnings for an economic system that needed a more cerebral approach to economic and other social tasks. Its supreme achievement was the IQ examination, or rather its distorted adaptation of the intelligence test that France had developed to evaluate, not students, but its educational system. All in all, academic psychology, foundations, testing specialists, educational psychologists, school boards, teachers, and university admissions officials all foisted a highly arbitrary test on the American people, giving an enormous advantage to the upper classes in the scramble for scarce benefits (see Chapter 3 for a fuller discussion of America's educational system).

Containing Diversity and Disunity

The concern with social order and stability in early capitalist society did not end or even abate with the triumph of science and professionalism in the nineteenth century. Societies everywhere in the West relied on the agrarian idea that a stable society had to be homogeneous. The attempt to construct a homogeneous population took place on many fronts: common schools, codes of law enforced by judiciary and civil service, public morality and family-oriented holidays, and patriotism complete with myths, artifacts, national holidays, and public rituals, buildings, and monuments.

By and large, the liberal professions also relied on tradition despite their claim to have marched out of darkness into the sunlight of science. The ancient idea that a stable community had to be homogeneous prompted the removal of criminals, the mentally ill, the diseased, orphans, and other "surplus" people into special places called prisons, asylums, hospitals, and orphanages. The Christian idea that human nature is an overflowing cauldron of insatiable desires prompted professionals to see society, not as the generator of desire, but as its controller[15] (for a fuller discussion, see "Creating and Consolidating Capitalism: Professionalism and the Social Construction of Devalued People" in Chapter 9).

The Death of the Guilds or the Reassertion of Priorities by Corporate World-Market Capitalism?

Elliott Krause has called the professions (medicine, law, engineering, professors) *guilds* citing similarities to the medieval guilds of Europe between 1100 and 1450.[16] The professions as guilds reached their high point in the 1960s, he claims, and have since declined (died) under pressure from capitalism (corporations) and the state. In a valuable sociohistorical and comparative analysis—the fortunes of the above professions are followed in the United States, Great Britain, France, Italy, and Germany—Krause emphasizes the importance of the social context for understanding the professions. The death of America's guilds—to focus on the United States—has occurred, says Krause, because outside forces (capitalism and the state) have deprived them of control over themselves, their members, their workplace, and their markets. This is especially true of medicine, law, and education (engineers were never able to become a guild). Medical, bar, and educational associations have lost power, surplus labor has appeared because the state has expanded professional school enrollments, controls over professional practices have increased, and professional markets have been structured by outsiders.

Krause's analysis provides valuable comparative information about doctors, lawyers, engineers, and professors between 1930 and 1990 with some further historical background. Putting the professions into a macrocontext is also valuable. But despite flashes of sophistication (capitalism and the state are partners with the former a senior partner), Krause's use of the concept of a *guild* to understand the modern professions is not only somewhat unclear, but prevents him from seeing that the professions themselves are integral parts of capitalism. Krause depicts the modern version of guilds as having once been service oriented but now subject to profit considerations (this is a familiar criticism by those who take the ideology of the professions at face value). On the other hand, Krause is quite emphatic that the professions have always been exclusionary on the basis of race, ethnicity, and gender. The concept *guild* also prevents Krause from seeing that the modern professions are organically connected to the vital operation of capitalism in ways that differ profoundly from the connection of the medieval guilds to the society of their day. The fortunes of the modern professions have varied with the state of science, technology, and socioeconomic imperatives much as they have with farmers, manufacturers, bankers, retailers, and blue- and white-collar workers. One can draw an even tighter parallel by thinking of a doctor as human technology. As such the doctor is no different than the railroad; in a simpler age, both were dominant forms of technology but now have to compete with new and more capital–intensive forms of health care and transportation. Nonetheless, just as the railroad is still an important technology, so is the doctor.

In discussing the death of the guilds, Krause also neglects to discuss the all-important matter of income. To take doctors as an example, their income grew rapidly from the 1960s to 1995. He also fails to focus on the immediate social context that doctors must now practice in—the sprawling health-care establishment of hospitals, drug and medical-supply companies, pharmacies, laboratories, nursing homes, health insurers, medical schools, research institutes, charities, and local and federal agencies. The share of GDP that went to health care in the United States rose to about 13 percent in the 1990s, approximately twice as much as in other capitalist societies. By not focusing on the health-care establishment as an important and growing sector of the American capitalism, Krause fails to see the medical profession as an integral part of a profit-oriented constellation of health-care businesses, including all those that refer to themselves as non-profit. The rapid expansion of the health-care industry from the 1960s on, fueled by the blank check given to it by both public and private forms of health insurance, meant opportunities for large profits by all health-care providers (except subordinate labor). The cost of the overall system became a heavy burden on American business, especially corporations that had foreign competitors, and a concerted effort began as early as the 1970s by business to reduce its health-care costs. To understand the changing fortunes of doctors, therefore, one must see the full sociopolitical context, namely, one set of capitalist interests curbing their costs in another sector of capitalism, and the dominant form of capitalism (highly organized bureaucratic structures) asserting itself in the lucrative health-care field still characterized by small scale, inefficient practices and groups. Given America's laissez-faire tradition, the curb on and the rationalization of the health-care industry could not take the course of establishing national health insurance as in other capitalist countries. The way out was to fragment the world of insured into individual systems run for companies by powerful cost-conscious HMO insurers, and for the government to institute rate controls over doctor and hospital fees. The way out was to develop huge for-profit hospital chains and for-profit health insurers. By the mid-90s overall increases in doctors' income and health-care costs as a percent of GDP had both been arrested (though both remain high and are much higher than in other capitalist countries). What has resulted is not the death of the physicians' guild, but the restoration of priorities by a corporate world-market capitalism: large is better than small, capital is more important than labor.

Krause is better at recognizing how lawyers are tied tightly to the corporate world even when they are dealing with legislators and government. In regard to professors, he cites government and business policies that have cut back overall support for higher education and have divided and pitted the various academic disciplines against each other. But in regard to law and education, there is no focus on the legal or educational establishment (as opposed to lawyers and professors) as adjuncts (junior partners) of the capitalist political economy. While Krause notes that doctors, lawyers, and professors are highly stratified and that their lower levels are distinctly struggling, he fails to note that capitalism has treated the professions in the same way that it treats its entire labor force.

Krause's focus on the professions as guilds makes it appear that if we are to have better professions we must return to an earlier era, this despite his many statements citing monopolistic practices and bias against miniorities during those times. He also fails to note the class nature of the professions, then and now, and says nothing about their dismal record of providing services and solving social problems. While it is important to note that the simpler age of the professions is over, it is also important not to take their ideology at face value. The professions have always taken their identity from capitalism, and studying their changing fortunes must be done in terms of the changes from entrepreneurial to corporate capitalism and from the latter to corporate world-market capitalism.

Krause does provide a valuable section on the impact of the European Economic Community on Europe's professions (pp. 273–279), but he does not identify the ECC as itself a response to world-market corporate capitalism, nor does he see the latter as the context for understanding the fortunes of the professions (and citizens) of both the developed and developing world.

That any separation of the professions from corporations and the state is misleading can be seen in another way. The professions, corporations, and the state are all deeply oligarchic and profoundly prone toward monopolistic control of their respective spheres of action. All hide behind the alleged operative principles of equal opportunity, meritocracy, and progress through research, science, technology, individual competition, and public service. Krause is insightful when he points out the similarity between a dynamic capitalism that destroyed the medieval guilds in order to establish an economy based on freely exchangeable goods, services, and labor and what has occurred over the past few decades. What he has failed to note is that capitalism and its professions have never been characterized by their common ideology. Stated perhaps too simply, the political economy of the United States requires that health costs be curbed because they threaten the profitability of the rest of the economy. Along the same lines, the costs of litigation must be curbed and thus the concerted attacks on liability and poverty lawyers. One can also see the system-wide nature of the updating of American capitalism by noting the efforts to curb costs in higher education and other costs of government that are not directly related to the welfare of business. A final way to understand the changing fortunes of the capitalist professions as a reassertion of capitalist priorities is to see this many-sided process as the triumph of those who profit from material capital over those who merely profit from human capital.

INTELLECTUALS: A PROFESSION IN DECLINE?

From the ancient Greeks to the nineteenth century, the intellectual (known by different names, of course) was a leading professional. During this period, intellectuals were those who dealt with a seamless world of causation. They were at once both metaphysical and practical, at home in both natural and social science. They could focus on literature, politics, or theology. Their expertise lay in their familiarity with both perennial and current issues and the ideas required to deal with them. Some of them defended the status quo and some attacked it. Some generated knowledge and others codified it. Despite their substantive differences, intellectuals were those who were at home in the world of ideas and who sought to persuade other educated people that their ideas were important to humans and society.

Intellectuals are here distinguished from scholars, professors, specialists, empirical researchers, non-partisan social and natural scientists, and so on. The latter rarely focus their scholarship on trying to figure out what kind of society they belong to; intellectuals, on the other hand, tend to be consciously for or against the world they live in. They are also different from the Knowledge Class, the New Class, technocrats, or the intelligentsia, and all other such designations (these terms merely refer to educated people or to experts). Intellectuals claim the gift of prophecy. As astronomer-priests forecasting the weather (so vital to crops in agrarian society) to social philosophers forecasting prosperity, depression, or war, intellectuals are those who predict about matters important to powerful publics.

The decline of the intellectual "profession" occurred from roughly 1850 to 1950. The decline occurred because of the onrush of science and its specialization, which is also the story of the development of higher education. Of course, the rise of science and the narrow, artificial disciplines of academe reflected the surge into industrialism and the end of the simpler ages of agrarianism and commercial capitalism. Today, forecasts and predictions are cast in more tightly circumscribed terms by academic and professional specialists: meteorologists, economists, military experts, demographers.

Early professional social scientists such as Sumner, Ward, and Veblen were also intellectuals who involved themselves in the larger issues of the day. Early historians were prone toward writing for the general public. But by the 1920s, the various disciplines had settled into the empirical investigation of smaller issues, including a concern for depoliticized social problems. Henceforth the trend was clear: America's cerebral energies were being splintered into specialties, the members of which wrote, not for the general public, but for each other.

American intellectual culture thrived from the 1930s to the 1960s, helped by the puzzling shocks of depression, fascism, communism, and Cold War.[17] Some segments of this intellectual ferment became disenchanted with the radicalism of the 1930s and became more centrist, even conservative, in regard to domestic and foreign policy.[18] After the 1950s, the world of intellectuals developed into its present pattern: a neoconservative or right-liberal wing, a left-liberal wing, and a radical left-wing composed of Marxists, radical feminists, radical environmentalists, radical ethnic and racial theorists, and politically charged academics who have developed American Studies programs or who espouse a political interpretation of literature (the deconstructionist perspective). If one defines an intellectual in this way (as someone who is eager to change something in the sociopolitical world), then intellectuals are alive and well. No longer free-lance writers living in Bohemia, they now work for research institutes, journals, magazines, policy institutes, reform groups, and so on. They even exist on college and university campuses.

The decline of intellectuals, however, can be argued on two fronts. One, they are now so scattered and diverse that their influence on the life of society may be much smaller than it once was. Small numbers of intellectuals writing (or creating) for a small and powerful set of elites, concentrated in Paris, say, or New York, may once have been influential. Today, American intellectuals are scattered in many cities, appear in many public journals from *Dissent* to *Commentary*; in many scholarly journals such as *Public Inter-*

est, Telos, and *Signs;* and in many newspapers such as the *Wall Street Journal* and the *New York Times.* Framed differently, there seem to be many small publics, focused around racial, ethnic, sexual, and environmental groups, and the like, rather than a large one capable of being swayed by broad intellectual arguments.

The decline of intellectuals may also be seen in the fact that many educated people, both as college graduates and as college faculty, consider themselves to be nonpolitical. There may no longer be a public for intellectuals to write (or create) for. Nothing better signifies the demise, or rather domestication, of the critical intellect than the fact that millions of students are busy acquiring abstract, nonpolitical knowledge under the direction of professional specialists in artificial, life-removed subject matter.[19] Russell Jacoby has deplored the decline of intellectuals (evidenced, he claims, by the absence of young intellectuals and the continued prominence of intellectuals from earlier decades) and attributes the decline to the explosive growth of higher education after World War II.[20]

A third argument, implicit in the others, is that the political economy of advanced capitalism, aided by communication technology, is transforming knowledge into private property and gradually absorbing public spaces and relations (including politics) with commercial artifacts and messages. The dangers that modern society poses to the critical intellect and to vital publics has been voiced again and again, for example, by the Frankfurt School, Herbert Marcuse, C. Wright Mills, and Jürgen Habermas. We come across the work of the most prolific and accessible contemporary scholar to voice alarm at socioeconomic and technological trends in capitalism that threaten the intellect and politically vital publics, Herbert I. Schiller, in Chapter 8.

THE SOCIOLOGY OF THE PROFESSIONS

The study of the professions is fairly recent, but interest in them goes back to the very origins of modern social science. Actually, the academic (mainstream) study of the professions is continuous with the technocratic tradition found in Condorcet and Saint Simon and with the acceptance of the emerging capitalist division of labor by liberal sociologists such as Spencer, Durkheim, Sumner, Ward, and Cooley. In short, the study of the professions is itself part of the positive evaluation of science that dominates the West.

This positive outlook on knowledge is also characteristic of analysts in the sociology of knowledge tradition, most of whom assumed that the social source of knowledge was compatible with the idea of truth and progress. In American sociology, argues Fuhrman, the main formative figures, for example, Sumner, Ward, Giddings, Small, Ross, and Cooley, all stressed the social nature of knowledge and its utility to society. These theorists were all squarely in the liberal tradition and their thought was conservative. They saw society as a plurality of causal agents, as something which moved slowly and whose outcomes, including knowledge, were progressive.[21]

Fuhrman refers to the main sociological tradition in early American sociology as "social-technological" as opposed to a more political view of knowledge which he calls "critical-emancipatory." The former corresponds largely to what is here called the *academic* perspective while the latter is close to what is here called the *sociopolitical* perspective.

The Academic (Functional) View of the Professions

The study of the professions by mainstream academics has resulted in a considerable body of knowledge.[22] Early analysts had assumed that the professions had unique attributes and that they emerged in a distinct sequence. By the 1970s, research had revealed that professional claims to a unique knowledge base, autonomy, altruism, service, and self-monitoring were not true. In all cases, one found degrees of truth rather than absolutes. Also, analysts could find no discernible stages that marked the emergence of the professions—on the contrary, the professions displayed great historical and national variations. In addition, some academic analysts argued that the professions have been losing power to clients, other elites, or the state (deprofessionalization), while some claim that they are being proletarianized.

In recent decades, theorists have looked at the professions (to use Ritzer's and Walczak's word) in terms of "power." The professions openly seek to exclude others, work politically to get the state to give them monopolies, and engage in incessant turf battles. "Power" theorists have noticed that the professions grew concurrently with a corporate economy and the expanding rational-legal state.

"Power" theorists, however, still lack a theory of modern society. Implicit in the work of academic "power" analysts and of Ritzer's and Walczak's account of their work is the assumption that power in modern society is fluid, competitive, dynamic, and guided by science and liberal social and political norms. In short, "power" theorists accept the idea that modern society is what it says it is, a pluralistic system based on open, fair, competitive, meritocratic processes.

The academic perspective on the professions is similar to the way in which mainstream social science has seen modern society. Until recently, most social scientists took it for granted that progress was a law of history and that the West was simply leading humanity out of its dark past. More concretely, sociologists, perhaps the majority in the United States, saw the basic trend of the past six hundred years as a growth in the adaptive capacity of society. Mainstream sociologists (and social scientists) argued that modern society (by which they usually meant the capitalist democracies of the West) has or represents:

1. Increased social differentiation toward functional specialization (a shift from diffused ascriptive statuses to specific, achievement statuses)

2. The emergence of abstract, disposable facilities (money, technology, rational law, abstract labor force, abstract electorate, abstract nature)—in short, a rational market economy, polity, and society
3. The emergence of a hierarchy of statuses known and accepted by most in which norm-role obligations are arranged in a structure of priority, thus providing predictability, stability, and direction
4. A growth of knowledge (provided by natural and social science)
5. The application and transmission of knowledge through the professions and education to yield higher living standards and social adaptation
6. The rise of rational organizations (bureaucracies) to ensure efficiency in the economy, professions, voluntary sector, and government

In recent years, sociologists have become less sure about where the overall trend of modern development is leading. Despite a revival of the evolutionary perspective, sociology (along with the other social sciences) is no longer so sure that economic and technological growth is automatically good for society. And it is not as optimistic as it once was about the ability of the professions, electorates, or markets to direct society and solve its problems. Accordingly, there is now a fairly wide difference of opinion about modernization in general. The liberal (capitalist) faith in the adaptive capacity of economic and political markets, aided and directed by professionalism, has been severely qualified. Beyond liberalism, radicals argue that modern society has long been bankrupt and is sustained only by imperialism and the victimization of many of its members.

In recent studies by two prominent mainstream analysts, the new more realistic picture of how the professions deviate from the above ideals has been accepted.[23] Their studies contain valuable information about professionalism and some of the professions. But even when they acknowledge that they are focusing only on selected questions, they create the impression that objectivity about partial aspects of their subject is possible. Even as they stress careful empirical analysis, their endless qualifications and denials that global statements are possible (all is contingency, no trends or developments exist), in effect, wed empirical analysis to the status quo. Even as they stress the political-legal supports received by the professions, their analyses depoliticize the politics of professionalism. In short, Freidson and Abbott do not generate knowledge as a prompter of action (to use Stehr's term, they are not generating knowledge as capacity for action).

In summary, the academic or functional view of the professions sees them as the outcome of the growth of knowledge and explains their proliferation since the nineteenth century as a response to social need and the imperatives of science. From this perspective, the professions result from objective, transhistorical, meritocratic processes. Functional analysts of the professions are themselves professionals and therefore speak the language of facts, function, and progress through scientific knowledge. Talcott Parsons, who helped enormously to establish the functional view of the professions in sociology during the 1950s and 1960s, saw them as the spearhead of the developing democratization of modern society. Just as the early capitalists had superseded feudal aristocrats, argued Parsons, the professions are leading the way past property and toward meritocracy. The emerging professions represent a marriage of objective knowledge and its applications.[24]

The early functional perspective on the professions bore a deep kinship with the innocent optimism of early sociology. Pioneer sociologists such as Condorcet and Saint Simon down through Lester Ward and Charles Horton Cooley equated modern society with the growth of knowledge through science. Parsons's functional view of the professions saw them as an integral part of the modernization process in which sacred-agrarian-ascriptive society gives way to a secular-industrial-achievement society based on the institutionalization of knowledge.

The current academic outlook on the professions, represented by theorists such as Freidson and Abbott, depicts the professions as part of the political process. Gone is the assumption that professions have risen above the vulgar pursuit of power and dispense their various services altruistically in a nonpartisan manner. Instead, a new empirical realism has emerged about them. Large, conclusive abstractions about the professions, we are told, are not possible and there is no indication that research will eventually lead to a final understanding of them. There are endless qualifications that must be made to all statements about them. There is this nuance and that to be pursued. All is contingency, fluidity, and realignment. Nowhere does the new empirical realism embed the professions in any macrosocial structure (Freidson does give a valuable, nonpolitical analysis of the many ways in which professionals are related to the state: licensing, accreditation, certification; as expert witnesses; in labor law; in the formulation and implementation of legislation; and in setting state-enforced standards in a wide variety of areas). Nowhere are questions raised about the actual efficacy of the professions as among individuals, social classes, or society-at-large. Throughout, the impression is given of a rather messy, but distinct upward thrust of knowledge through professionalization with an ensuing social betterment. Throughout there are conflicts, which in the lexicon of liberalism means competition to ensure the triumph of the most worthy.

When all is said, there is not much difference between the old and the new functionalism. The new functional perspective still assumes that modern society is institutionalizing knowledge via professionalism (compare the concepts of *postindustrial society, high-information society, managerial revolution*) and that the professions emerge from and represent a meritocratic-based, pluralistic system of power.[25] The only difference is that the process of making society more rational is now messier and less linear than the old functionalism.

The Sociopolitical (Radical Conflict) View of the Professions

The radical conflict perspective rejects the assumption that the professions are objective creators and carriers of objective knowledge.[26] This assumption, combined with the assumption that modern society is on a progressive-evolutionary trajectory, has failed to note that the professions have a poor record of problemsolving. The conflict perspective has come to the fore because it best accounts for strategic facts, especially the fact of widespread professional failure in solving social problems.

Today, we know that both science and the professions are social phenomena and reflect the society in which they occur. In the capitalist world, the professions are best understood as forms of publicly sanctioned private property.[27] Seen from this perspective, the liberal professions, which for the sake of argument can include upper-level corporate managers and high civil, military, and elected officials (most of whom have received professional educations), belong to the upper classes of capitalist society. The professions enjoy high income, the highest prestige, and great power in liberal (and socialist) society. Their historic achievements and their creative conflicts should not obscure the fact that they are the main beneficiaries of their own competence (and incompetence).

The occupational prestige studies of the past fifty years have consistently shown that the American public accords the professions and disciplines top ratings. The high income of many professionals is well-known. But as Bok has shown, the reward structure of the United States bears little relation to labor-market theories. Not only is there no competitive labor market for talent in the United States, but, says Bok, American private-sector executives, doctors, and lawyers, not only make far more than ordinary workers compared to other nations, but these three occupations are also deeply stratified (beyond any measure of merit) with a few at the top making far more than their colleagues, again in comparison to other nations.[28] In broader context, these three occupations are part of a general pattern forming the dual labor market: managerial and professional workers, unionized workers, and workers in oligarchic industries or extremely large organizations are not subject to labor market competition as posited by mainstream economists.[29]

The radical conflict perspective focuses on the mutual support that the professions give each other as they operate at or near the apex of the state (civil and military), corporations, hospitals, research institutes, law firms, universities, laboratories, and so on. The interchangeability of professionals is further evidence of a power structure whose main priority is its own survival. Lawyers and physicists, for example, can serve any cause, organizational structure, or country. Administrators can administrate anything. Retired military officers can be usefully employed at the apex of corporations, schools, or law enforcement agencies.

The sociopolitical perspective also defines the process of knowledge creation as an arbitrary social process. The academic and applied professions, as seen by the sociopolitical perspective, define their subject matter in narrow, artificial terms assuming that other factors are constant or inconsequential. Essentially, each divorces a slice of phenomena or a problem from the sociohistorical context that gave it birth. Each assumes consensus about the world outside its domain. Each assumes no need for priorities in knowledge—each can exist if it allows the others to exist and this implies no invidious distinctions among them. Thus, for example, natural scientists pursue what they feel are the frontiers of knowledge across a broad front unaware that priorities are being set for them by corporations, governments, the military, churches, and so on.

Though the impression is created that all knowledge is useful and that seekers of knowledge are advancing on all fronts, the fact of the matter is that the enterprise of knowledge generation is biased, haphazard, and leaves many areas uncovered. Actually, the structured nature of the ignorance and ineffectiveness of the entire spectrum of disciplines and professions leads straight to the deepest level of concern about them: Are they organized to provide social adaptation and social self-determination? The answer is no. In keeping with the overall capitalist outlook on society, American elites deny the need for anyone, any group, or any process to be in charge of society.

Far from being detached respondents to evil, argue radical critics, the liberal professions provide biased definitions and explanations of problems, thereby setting up arbitrary parameters to how society responds to problems. Not only are their explanations and approaches faulty, but by actively exaggerating the complexity and dangers of problems, they help create the anxious, passive clients they need for their services. Born in the heyday of early industrialism, when society was in the throes of deep conflict, when massive social changes were upsetting social routines, the professions were an ideal way to create the impression that an abstract science (personified in the academic and applied professions) could handle the multiple new evils of industrialism, ideal because professionals were derived from and in the service of the property groups that were causing the problems.

Professionals, say critics, must stop thinking of themselves as value-free pursuers of knowledge and as value-free practitioners. The liberal professions share this value-free perspective with the overall liberal belief in a value-free market economy and objective electoral markets leading to non-partisan government. The false belief by owners, managers, lawyers, mathematicians, accountants, engineers, biologists, doctors, soldiers, physicists, politicians, philosophers, domestic and foreign policy experts, journalists, educators, economists, psychologists, and social scientists that they are nonpartisan goes a long way in explaining their formalism, failure, and irresponsibility.

Professional thought and action not only have value consequences, but many of the consequences are negative. Critics argue that the professions must acknowledge that they are making value judgments and that much of their work is "political" in nature. But to acknowledge the value implications of their work would threaten elite authority for who is able to claim expertise and objectivity about values. To acknowledge the importance of values would subject elites to the judgment of laypeople.

Regardless of how they are seen, the salient fact about the liberal professions is their universal lack of effectiveness in dealing with social problems (as opposed to their greater success in dealing with the problems of some individuals and groups, and in compiling formal, academic, socially sterile knowledge). The liberal professions are also characterized by basic procedures that are suspect (for example, peer review), by significant num-

bers of incapacitated practitioners,[30] and by significant numbers of criminals (see Chapter 9, "The Professions and Deviance," for a fuller discussion).

The accepted definition of what constitutes a professional is still a matter of considerable dispute.[31] The radical conflict or sociopolitical perspective argues that a profession is an occupation that has succeeded in keeping
its numbers low in relation to need, or has devised other ways to guarantee
itself high material benefits regardless of performance (primarily through
state financing or state-granted monopolies). In short, the defining characteristic of contemporary professionals is that they provide support services,
including ideological cover, for their respective societies (capitalist and socialist, fascist, liberal democratic, or authoritarian) and are rewarded by
being exempt from the shortcomings of these various societies. In the
United States, it is especially clear that professionals profit from a market
society without being subject to all its workings. When ordinary labor is in
surplus, unemployment occurs, but a surplus of surgeons consistently leads
to huge numbers of unnecessary surgeries at high and rising prices. How efficient and how fair is it that the public finances research in technology,
drugs, and agriculture, but receives no return either in royalties or lower
consumer prices when the research becomes profitable? Why is it that the
state finances much of the education of professionals and grants them a
legal monopoly to practice, but is not permitted to set standards in regard to
credentials or performance?

The radical view given so far is a composite of liberal and Marxist perspectives. In recent decades, new forms of radicalism have arisen from phenomenology, linguistic-literary studies, feminism, and African-American
thought. An important source of this new radicalism is the thought of
Michel Foucault who has profoundly influenced social theory, literary criticism, feminism, critical legal studies, and specialists in sociology and psychology.[32] Foucault argues that knowledge comes from *discourse* and that
there is no method, scientific or otherwise, that yields truth. Discourse is
whatever it is possible to say under given historical power structures. The
knowledge claims of modern natural and social science and its applied professions are arbitrary, argues Foucault, but appear objective because they
have power behind them and can thus enforce consensus.

Foucault's analysis of the history of social-control agencies (prisons,
asylums, schools, hospitals) has obvious implications for the professions
and disciplines. To Foucault, modern control systems are arbitrary and do
not deserve to be given metaphysical or so-called objective status. Traditional epistemology's claim to objective truth is really a disguised interpretive philosophy (we must use arbitrary assumptions in our empirical sciences). Further, the power/knowledge that an arbitrary science establishes
gets imposed on people and this is what has happened in the fields of deviance (mental illness, crime), punishment, and sexuality. The social-control
agencies of modern society and their professions are based on arbitrary notions of normality. They, along with the social sciences and humanities, are
forms of power, and interpretive science gives us a way to resist domination

by other people's alleged truths. Indeed, social-control structures violate the need of human beings to express their own forms of knowledge. Accordingly, Foucault invites resistance to the knowledge claims of power groups and their so-called rational or scientific control systems. As we see, Foucault has appealed to a wide variety of dissident groups.

Relying on a variety of perspectives, feminism has generated a rich body of criticism of the professions and disciplines. In Chapter 1, we pointed to the way in which Nancy Tanner helped correct the male-oriented picture of human and social evolution in anthropology. Dorothy E. Smith and African-American feminist theorists have rejected the objective, value-neutral, impersonal methodology of sociology as inherently biased against women.[33] Catherine A. MacKinnon has indicted the entire legal system as a masculine bias against women.[34] Sandra Harding has pointed to masculine bias in the natural sciences.[35] And feminist and nonfeminist writers have mounted a deep criticism of the literature profession for slanting the curriculum against women, African Americans, and all other minorities.[36]

Our survey of radical thought has not exhausted the indictments that have been made of the professions (for example, we have not discussed the criticism of the law and lawyers by the Critical Legal Studies movement and the deep criticisms that have been leveled at liberal journalism).[37] But enough has been said to make it clear that regardless of whether they focus on social or natural science, or on the classics in literature and philosophy, radicals reject the assumption underlying objective empiricism, namely that a fixed and finished neutral observer can find the truth about a fixed and finished reality. Instead, radicals stress the historicity of both thinking and facts. They stress the need to develop new forms of thought in keeping with the movement of history. They stress the inevitable political-value nature of science.[38]

Perhaps radical conflict thought can be summed up as an attempt to blend analysis and policy, the factual and the ideal, and scholarship and politics. Liberals, on the other hand, feel obligated to don another hat when they advocate reform or pass judgment on what they find. Radical thinkers assume that theory must be about the concrete experiences of people, especially the dominated, in concrete historical societies, and that it must have policy relevance for presentday society (as opposed to mainstream liberalism, which seeks transhistorical knowledge about no society in particular).

SUMMARY

Though modern societies share a common scientific world view, they have developed distinctive national variations of it.

Pragmatism is America's distinctive version of empirical science. At first a philosophy oriented toward the control of experience and the creation of desirable experience, pragmatism became a philosophy of adjustment bent on perfecting existing society. In this sense, it became synonymous with liberalism and professionalism, one aspect of the overall liberal monopoly.

The culture of professionalism that emerged in the nineteenth century reflected the rationalizing tendencies of capitalism.

The essence of professionalism was the belief that the principles governing the physical and social worlds could be discovered and that this knowledge would make possible the solution to every imaginable problem.

Embodying this worldview, a host of special professions arose each with a career pattern (framed largely in terms of acquiring academic education), associations, journals, rituals, costumes, physical settings, and so on. Each carved out a sphere of competence, claimed exclusive jurisdiction because of its possession of a unique knowledge base, and worked to achieve a legal monopoly over a cluster of problems. Each also worked hard to create a demand for its services by publicizing the evils that surrounded the public.

The largely self-sponsored upward mobility and success at institutionalization by the American professions were part of the growing concern of the emerging industrial system with the problem of order and the need to develop new social-control agents.

The culture of capitalism shifted away from entrepreneurial capitalism in the late nineteenth century (early liberalism) toward a corporate capitalism (late liberalism). The professions were an integral part of this shift providing the practices and ideologies that legitimated the shift from a small-property economy to a concentrated political economy.

The deep specialization of Western science in the nineteenth century signaled the decline of intellectuals, symbol creators who have a society-wide influence.

The sociology of the professions has two branches: the academic and the sociopolitical. The academic analysis of the professions has undermined all the claims of the professions (unique knowledge base, autonomy, service, altruism, self-monitoring). Nonetheless, mainstream academics continue to view professionals as part of the fundamental process of modernization, the steady progress toward a knowledge-based society.

The sociopolitical view of the professions sees them as power groups that receive more income, prestige, and power than their knowledge and ability warrant. The professions are anchored in artificial subject matter and their efforts, especially efforts to solve social problems are far from successful. They do not utilize available knowledge, are biased in their definition of problems, and create dependency among their clients. The professions must come to realize that science is value-laden and that solutions to problems must involve all those affected, that is, can come about only through a democratized polity.

Significant changes in the professions have occurred over the past few decades but laments about their commercialization or death are misplaced. Changes in the professions have been largely to weld them tightly to a more fully profit-oriented world-market corporate capitalism.

The sociopolitical indictment of the professions stems largely from liberal and Marxist sources. It also includes the work of Foucault who denies the possibility of objectivity and regards the professions as arbitrary control structures. The professions have also come under attack by both white and black feminists who see a pattern of masculine bias running through all of them.

The overall criticism of science and the professions, generated by both the academic and sociopolitical camps, emerges from a common recognition that science and the professions are sociopolitical and historical in nature. If their deep deficiencies in performing personal, group, and social functions are acknowledged and connected to the type of society of which they are a part, then curbing these deficiencies requires not only redesigning science and the professions, but changing the political economy that they serve.

NOTES

1. The following account draws heavily on Morton White, *Social Thought in America: The Revolt against Formalism* (Boston: Beacon Press, 1957).
2. Morton White, *Social Thought in America*, p. 12.
3. *The Age of Reform* (New York: Knopf, 1955). A supplement to White's analysis, this book is expressly concerned with the middlebrow figures that helped to spark America's three great reform movements: Populism, Progressivism, and New Dealism. Though Hofstadter distinguishes between the moralistic and absolutist character of Populism and Progressivism and the more realistic and opportunistic character of the New Deal, it should be noted that no serious challenge to the core beliefs and values of liberalism emerged from any of these movements.
4. In their survey of American sociology, *The Development of Modern Sociology* (New York: Random House, 1954), Roscoe and Gisela Hinkle emphasized the pervasive American consensus on "voluntaristic nominalism," the "assumption that the structure of all social groups is the consequence of the aggregate of its separate, component individuals and that social phenomena ultimately derive from the motivations of these knowing, feeling, and willing individuals" (preface, p. v). Major strands of mainstream sociological theory and most theory texts have continued this tradition of confusing the individual with individualism.
5. Joan Huber Rytina and Charles P. Loomis, "Marxist Dialectic and Pragmatism: Power as Knowledge," *American Sociological Review* 35 (April 1970): 308–319.
6. Dorothy Ross, *The Origins of American Social Science* (New York: Cambridge University Press, 1991), uses the concept of *American exceptionalism* to show the metaphysical basis of American social science (economics, history, political science, sociology) from the founding of the Republic down through 1929 and the triumph of scientism (instrumental positivism in sociology, neoclassical economics in economics, and their eventual offshoots, rational-choice and public-choice theory).
7. For a pioneering contribution to the understanding of American history as a liberal monopoly, see Louis Hartz, *The Liberal Tradition in America* (New York: Harcourt Brace, 1955). For a sophisticated Marxian analysis with the same theme, see Herbert Marcuse, *One-Dimensional Man* (Boston: Beacon Press, 1964).

Chapter 9 explicitly discusses whether cultural monopoly (or cultural *hegemony*, to use Antonio Gramsci's term) has increased in recent decades.

8. For an early depiction of the correspondence between pragmatism in philosophy and social science and middle-class experience from the Civil War to World War II, see Thelma Herman, "Pragmatism: A Study in Middle Class Ideology," *Social Forces* 22 (May 1944): 404–410.

9. For a valuable analysis of political science along these lines, see Bernard Crick, *The American Science of Politics: Its Origins and Conditions* (Berkeley: University of California Press, 1959).

10. Burton J. Bledstein, *The Culture of Professionalism: The Middle Class and the Development of Higher Education in America* (New York: Norton, 1976).

11. Edward T. Silva and Sheila A. Slaughter, *Serving Power: The Making of the Academic Social Science Expert* (Westport, Conn.: Greenwood Press, 1984).

12. David F. Noble, *America by Design: Science, Technology, and the Rise of Corporate Capitalism* (New York: Knopf, 1977).

13. This is one of the themes of Paul J. DiMaggio, ed., *Nonprofit Enterprise in the Arts: Studies in Mission and Constraint* (New York: Oxford University Press, 1986).

14. Edward Arian, *Bach, Beethoven, and Bureaucracy: The Case of the Philadelphia Orchestra* (Tuscaloosa: University of Alabama Press, 1971) shows how the old rich exercised strict control over the finances and type of music played by professional classical musicians. For a followup to Arian's theme, see Stephen R. Couch, "The Orchestra as Factory: Interrelationships of Occupational Change, Social Structure, and Musical Style," in Arnold W. Foster and Judith R. Blau, eds., *Art and Society: Readings in the Sociology of the Arts* (Albany: State University of New York Press, 1989), chap. 16.

15. For an interesting discussion that argues that anthropology's central concept of culture (allegedly a coherent body of norms and values that supplies boundaries and positive controls) was a vague and illogical answer to the Christian doctrine of original sin (human nature as boundless desire), see Christopher Herbert, *Culture and Anomie: Ethnographic Imagination in the Nineteenth Century* (Chicago: University of Chicago Press, 1991).

16. Elliot A. Krause, *Death of the Guilds: Professions, States, and the Advance of Capitalism, 1930 to the Present* (New Haven, Conn.: Yale University Press, 1996).

17. Terry A. Cooney, *The Rise of the New York Intellectuals: "Partisan Review" and Its Circle* (Madison, Wisc.: University of Wisconsin Press, 1986), and Alan M. Wald, *The New York Intellectuals: The Rise and Decline of the anti-Stalinist Left from the 1930s to the 1980s* (Chapel Hill: University of North Carolina Press, 1987).

18. Richard H. Pells, *The Liberal Mind in a Conservative Age: American Intellectuals in the 1940s and 1950s* (New York: Harper & Row, 1985).

19. For a fuller discussion of the American educational system, see Chapter 3.

20. Russell Jacoby, *The Last Intellectuals: American Culture in the Age of Academe* (New York: Basic Books, 1987).

21. Ellsworth R. Fuhrman, *The Sociology of Knowledge in America, 1883–1915* (Charlottesville: University Press of Virginia, 1980).

22. The following relies heavily on George Ritzer and David Walczak, *Working: Conflict and Change*, 3rd ed. (Englewood Cliffs, N.J.: Prentice Hall, 1986), chap. 4.

23. Eliot Freidson, *Professional Powers: A Study of the Institutionalization of Formal Knowledge* (Chicago: University of Chicago Press, 1986), and Andrew Abbott, *The System of Professions: An Essay on the Division of Expert Labor* (Chicago: University of Chicago Press, 1988).

24. Talcott Parsons, "The Professions," in David H. Sills, ed., *International Encyclopedia of the Social Sciences* (New York: Free Press, 1968), vol. 12. Parsons is here an early advocate of what later came to be known as the concept of *postindustrial*

society (for a fuller discussion of this concept, see "The Fiction of a Knowledge Society" in Chapter 1.

25. Freidson, perhaps the leading academic (mainstream) analyst of the professions, has explicitly endorsed the present system of professionalism by stating it as an ideal worth fighting for politically; see Eliot Freidson, "Professionalism as a Model and Ideology," in Robert L. Nelson et al., eds., *Lawyers' Ideals/Lawyers' Practices: Transformations in the American Legal Profession* (Ithaca, N.Y.: Cornell University Press, 1992), chap. 6. Interestingly, Freidson's endorsement is not based on an evaluation of all the criticisms of the liberal professions, but because the present system is abstractly better than the other two possibilities, the free-market approach on the right and the approach on the left and the right that stresses order, efficiency, and comprehensive services. The present monopoly by experts is better than monopoly by capital or the state, he concludes. Why the professions cannot be thought of ideally as being embedded in a genuinely pluralistic power structure in which a democratic public holds them accountable for the performance of functions is not clear.

26. The radical conflict view presented here is a composite of ideas from numerous sources. It should be clear that the analysts discussed under the term *academic* have contributed many ideas useful to a more political, critical outlook here called *sociopolitical*, for example, George Ritzer and David Walczak, *Working: Conflict and Change*, 3rd ed. (Englewood Cliffs, N.J.: 1986), pp. 79–85, and George Ritzer, "Professionalism, Bureaucratization, and Rationalization," *Social Forces* 53 (1975): 627–634. Some important ingredients in the radical view of the professions may be found in T. J. Johnson, *Professions and Power* (London: Macmillan, 1972); T. J. Johnson, "The Professions in the Class Structure," in Richard Scase, ed., *Industrial Society: Class, Cleavage, and Control* (New York: St. Martin's Press, 1977), chap. 4; and Magali Sarfatti Larson, *The Rise of Professionalism* (Berkeley: University of California Press, 1977). Sources for recent radical outlooks on the professions will be given shortly. Fuller discussions of individual disciplines and professions are found in later chapters.

27. Carolyn J. Touhy, "Private Government, Property, and Professionalism," *Canadian Journal of Political Science* 9 (December 1976): 668–681.

28. Derek Bok, *The Cost of Talent: How Executives and Professionals Are Paid and How It Affects America* (New York: Free Press, 1993). It should be noted that while Bok's analysis has radical implications, he himself is a liberal. He accepts the myth that America is a meritocracy, or rather that it, including education, is generating talent despite the fact that income does not emerge from competitive forces. His analysis has little on the essentially class nature of education and little on whether executives and professionals are effective—his only concern is that American talent is poorly distributed in favor of an overpaid private sector and that professors, teachers, and federal civil servants are not paid enough.

29. For a recent study confirming dual labor market theory with a full bibliography of the relevant literature, see Arthur Sakamoto and Meicher D. Chen, "Inequality and Attainment in a Dual Labor Market," *American Sociological Review* 56 (June 1991): 295–308.

30. Compiling data about a wide variety of professions and semiprofessions, as well as executives, set in the context of a competitive capitalism that "values only material gain, wealth, and power," Phillips has shown that America's most valued occupations suffer from a wide variety of mental and physical health problems: E. Lakin Phillips, *Stress, Health, and Psychological Problems in the Major Professions* (Lanham, Md.: University Press of America, 1982). There has been no followup to Phillips's global analysis, though individual professions have done or have commissioned research on themselves in order to identify the impaired and to institute preventive measures.

31. Freidson's definition of a professional is someone who has higher education credentials. Freidson's reliance on the criterion of academic credentials is no accident. Much of the study of the professions (which claim to be value-neutral possessors of skills and knowledge) has been done by value-neutral academics who are themselves part of the professional world.
32. Michel Foucault, *Madness and Civilization: A History of Insanity in the Age of Reason*, tr. Richard Howard (New York: Vintage, 1965); The Order of Things: An Archaeology of the Human Sciences (New York: Vintage, 1966); *The Archaeology of Knowledge and the Discourse on Language* (New York: Harper Colophon, 1969); *The Birth of the Clinic: An Archaeology of Medical Perception* (New York: Vintage, 1975); *Discipline and Punishment: The Birth of the Prison*, tr. Alan Sheridan (New York: Vintage, 1979); *The History of Sexuality: An Introduction*, vol. 1 (New York: Vintage, 1980); *The Uses of Pleasure: The History of Sexuality*, vol. 2 (New York: Pantheon, 1985).
33. Dorothy E. Smith, *The Conceptual Practices of Power: A Feminist Sociology of Knowledge* (Boston: Northeastern University Press, 1990), and Patricia Hill Collins, *Black Feminist Thought: Knowledge, Consciousness, and the Politics of Empowerment* (New York: Routledge, 1991).
34. Catherine A. MacKinnon, *Toward a Feminist Theory of the State* (Cambridge, Mass.: Harvard University Press, 1989).
35. Sandra Harding, *Whose Science? Whose Knowledge? Thinking from Women's Lives* (Ithaca, N.Y.: Cornell University Press, 1991).
36. For an example of a feminist critique of literature and purported classics, derived from Foucault, see Chris Weedon, *Feminist Practice and Poststructural Theory* (New York: Oxford University Press, 1987). For a fuller discussion of gender bias in the literature professions and curriculum, see "Literary Studies" in Chapter 5 of this volume.
37. For a discussion of these criticisms, see Chapters 6 and 7.
38. It should be noted that there are disputes among radicals, especially between Marxists, who affirm the objectivity of knowledge and the main goals of Western rationalism, and some postmodern thinkers, who enunciate a relativism running counter to Western rationalism.

3

Education: Legitimating Liberal Professionalism

◆ ◆ ◆ ◆

◆ ◆ ◆ ◆

The starting point for an in-depth understanding of America's unique version of liberal professionalism is America's distinctive educational system. As we see, American education has been assigned many functions, none of which has been performed well, and most not at all. The failure of education, however, is not a failure to incorporate the lower classes and minorities into the academic world as most think. Its failure is the mistaken decision to establish the academic world in the first place and call it education.

AMERICA'S FAITH IN EDUCATION

Thomas Jefferson wanted a society that allowed human nature's best to emerge and rise to the top as leaders. In Jefferson's time this idea was revolutionary just as a similar idea in Plato's *Republic* had been revolutionary. Both Jefferson and Plato thought of a society led by high-ability individuals recruited from all class levels. And both stressed the importance of education in developing a natural elite and thus a well-ordered society. Jefferson was as proud of his part in establishing the University of Virginia as he was of writing the Declaration of Independence.

Jefferson's faith in education as a way to reveal those qualified to occupy positions in the division of labor was combined later with a faith in free markets and free elections to become America's social philosophy of "nonegalitarian classlessness." For Americans, it became axiomatic that there should be no arbitrariness in the relation between social rewards and personal worth. Since the founding of their new Jerusalem, Americans have believed that it is they who at long last had found the way to realize nature's hierarchy of talent and put unequal rewards on a just and natural basis. For Americans, the key to overcoming the artificial barriers of social condition (and eventually even race, religion, ethnicity, and gender), and to revealing the true universe (and hierarchy) of individuals is equal opportunity and competition in the spheres of economics, politics, and education.

In this trinity of free markets, education holds a special place in American hearts. It is alleged to have great power to improve people and solve problems; nothing is more characteristic of an American faced with a problem than to attribute it to a lack of education. The power of education is thought to be enormous, largely because Americans attribute great power to ideas and knowledge. This faith in ideational causation (actually a faith in the power of truth over ignorance and evil), along with the difficulty of running a regionally, racially, economically, and ethnically diverse society, has led the United States to assign a heavy burden of functions to education. Given their belief in biopsychological causation, Americans find it easy to equate the absence of formal barriers to education and the existence of free public schools with equality of opportunity.[1] For an American, an opportunity is something one seizes or makes use of; inequality in any field is simply the record of those who did not have it in them to profit from opportunities available to all.

During the 1960s, two distinct strands of sociological research on education appeared. One adopted a functional position more or less in line with the mainstream American tradition derived from Thomas Jefferson. The other strand was a many-sided conflict perspective (liberal, Marxist, African-American, feminist) that focused on class, race, and gender, and the power of the social structure to explain success in school and after.

The Functional Position

The early research on father-to-son mobility reflected the broad acceptance in sociology of the basic tenets of American liberalism (capitalism). From its beginnings until the 1960s and 1970s, American sociology envisioned the United States as an open society based on and progressively realizing universalistic principles. Universalism meant that science and achievement statuses were displacing nonscientific beliefs and statuses centered on ascription. Society was gradually developing objective criteria for evaluating people and positions. In time, all particularistic evaluations based on family, religion, race, and sex would be displaced by achievement criteria. Science, efficiency, rationality, and achievement would eventually triumph over any religious, philosophical, or humanistically derived beliefs and values that could not be empirically verified.

From Cooley to Parsons, and from Sumner to Davis-Moore, American sociologists had an image of society as a functional division of labor headed by natural elites as determined by competition, science, and achievement criteria. The United States was an open society, and whatever barriers to achievement remained were being dismantled. The occupational system already embodied the principle of merit as established in open-market competition. The occupational hierarchy was essentially a functional differentiation based on a growing consensus of what each occupation was worth. Already the rational division of labor had produced a large and growing middle-level sector in the American population. The causes of progress were technology, education, urbanization, industrialization, and the growth of specialization and formal organizations. In this overall process of modernization, education had a special importance because one could actually observe the meritocratic process in action and understand how individuals were attaining their status in society.

This is the context in which early mobility studies were conducted.[2] Now known as the *status attainment* perspective, early mobility studies assumed that American society had already become a meritocracy (the theorists rejected the local community studies that had discovered deep nonmeritocratic class structures, claiming that they were not representative of the nation at large). Taking the United States at face value, status-attainment theorists focused on individual characteristics, essentially asking: Who has the basic American values and how did they get them?

The pioneering and extremely influential study in this regard was by Blau and Duncan, who found that class background influences the mobility-achievement process with middle-class and above parents providing an impetus to occupational success. But, argued Blau and Duncan, the individual's personal characteristics also count and this is reflected in education.[3] Their analysis of this process was extended by other analysts found a relation between class and success, but did not evaluate this relation critically. They found personal characteristics and small-group experiences (related to class) that led to educational and occupational success, but again they did not disapprove. They found school systems that fostered success by those who came from the better classes, but again status attainment theorists did not interpret their findings, in effect endorsing them.[4]

The reason that status-attainment scholars did not raise questions about what they found is that they assumed that the middle class (and above) represented the valid march of history, or rather, the forces of science, rationality, and individual achievement. Thus, it is right and proper that the middle class (and above) should produce sons who have the personal attributes that lead to success, and that educational institutions should embody the universalistic values that were progressively enveloping all of society. The role of the objective, value-neutral researcher is simply to lay bare this objective, historical process.

The net result of status-attainment theory did more than merely endorse the idea that the upper classes, the individual, and education were central to achievement and the idea of meritocracy. It also endorsed the idea that American society was essentially meritocratic and progressive.

The Conflict Position

Conflict sociologists who analyze education differ profoundly from not only the status-attainment theorists (who themselves have begun to modify their position), but from the basic beliefs of most educators, public officials, national leaders, and the lay public. Sociologists in the conflict tradition have reinterpreted past findings, and by using new assumptions, have come up with a radically different view of education.

In fashioning their perspective, conflict sociologists built on the main tradition in stratification analysis. Earlier research going back to the Lynds's *Middletown* study of 1927 and Hollinghead's *Elmtown* study in the 1940s had established the class basis of education. Conflict sociologists were also inspired by an insight in the Coleman Report (1966), namely, that education appears to have little independent power in its own right (this report will be discussed shortly). Running counter to basic American beliefs, conflict sociologists argue that education is merely a way to transmit class position from one generation to the next and to hide the fact that the basic power over occupation and income lies in the economy itself.

The starting point for understanding education, therefore, is the little known fact that education has little power in its own right; causation flows from society to education, not the other way around. All who have studied education agree that the class-derived personality of the incoming student explains almost all educational behavior (not teachers, curricula, facilities, or school budgets). Those who succeed, as well those who are average or failures in school, are largely a result, not of the school, but of the families and thus the social classes from which they come.

The process by which families perpetuate themselves at given class levels can be better understood if we remember that parents' class position is a heavy determinant of children's performance in school. Parents at the upper levels of the class system provide their children with the motives and skills that ensure academic success. In turn, success in school means high income and occupation, and thus high class position, a process that is then repeated in the next generation. At lower class levels, parents provide their children with lower levels of academically relevant interests and skills, and fewer opportunities for personal enrichment, all of which is reflected in a lower level of school performance. In turn, poorer school performance leads to poorer jobs and lower income. Since job markets are increasingly controlled by educational credentials, here again class achievement is tightly circumscribed by class ascription. Of the many functions of American education, the legitimation of this process of inheritance is surely one of the least understood by American policymakers.

From the 1970s on, the main creative currents in stratification research have come out of the conflict tradition. In regard to mobility, conflict theorists criticized the status-attainment model as narrow and biased, narrow because of its focus on occupation, and biased because of its focus on personal characteristics. Status-attainment analysis, argued critics, was directly in line with mainstream liberalism and functionalism.[5] As such, the status-attainment model overlooked essential processes in the overall process of mobility. Occupation is too broad a term; hence, one must include important distinctions such as occupational power and complexity of skills. And fundamental structural forces in the economy and society are central to mobility. Property relations are crucial in maintaining continuity among generations in the upper class and controlling the admission of new members. Property relations as economic concentration, and in static versus dynamic sectors in the economy, are also central to mobility.[6] The actions of professional associations and trade unions in controlling labor flows, the actions of government, the behavior of foreign countries, and so on—all are important to how well each generation fares. All in all, the conflict perspective has made *structural* (or socially induced) mobility (or lack of) central to how sociologists think of mobility and stratification.

The conflict tradition has produced a vastly different picture of education than the one found in mainstream American thinking and in status-attainment research. Far from being a progressive force reflecting progressive middle-class values, the school is basically a class phenomenon, ensuring the success of the established classes and the failure of the lower classes. Research has conclusively established the power of social class no matter what type of behavior is investigated: expenditure per pupil, attendance, educational aspirations, IQ and achievement tests, years completed, grades, diplomas, and degrees. The upper classes even benefit more from remedial courses. Of great importance was the finding that class determines who goes to college and to what type of college. By and large, attendance and completion of four-year colleges is a monopoly of the upper classes.

On the surface, of course, the class nature of education can be reconciled with traditional views by stressing the need to expand, even equalize, educational opportunities for the lower classes. Indeed, this has been the main thrust in education throughout American history. But the real problem with education has not yet been stated. As we see below, the impotence of academic education is complete—research has revealed that *success* in America's schools and universities is not only class-determined, but that it *does not lead to and cannot be associated with positive performances either in the economy or in politics.*

Higher Education: The Capstone of Class Education

Through much of its history (approximately from 1500 to 1850), the nascent class society of the West required little formal training or education in the socialization process. By mid-nineteenth century, the social need for literacy generated a system of mass public education, and at the end of the nineteenth century the free high school was on its way toward becoming a standard feature of American education. Between 1900 and 1940, enrollment in America's high schools rose from about 5 percent to over 90 percent of the relevant age group. But in the post-1945 period the terminal high-school systems were asked to expand their college preparatory programs as the United States inaugurated a system of mass higher education. In 1940, only 15 percent of eighteen- to twenty-one-year olds were enrolled in institutions of higher education; by 1970 this figure exceeded 50 percent. Since the 1960s, both graduate training and professional training have increasingly become the gateway to upper-level occupations.

American institutions of higher education developed in a decentralized fashion during the nineteenth century. As a result, a vast variety of "special-interest" colleges emerged: Colleges for each of the many Protestant denominations; for Roman Catholics and for Jews; for men or women only; for whites or blacks; for farmers, engineers, or teachers; for inhabitants of a given town, city, or state; for adolescents or adults; and for the rich and not-so-rich.[7] While the composition of the governing boards of institutions of higher education was necessarily affected by this diversity, analysts agree that, by and large, such boards exhibit a common trend: A decline in the power of clergy and a corresponding rise in the power of businesspeople and professionals. Though there are variations among institutions, it is clear that farmers, manual workers, lower white-collar workers, ethnic and racial minorities, intellectuals, scientists, labor union officials, and artists (as well as women and young adults) are not represented on governing boards in proportion to their numbers or importance.[8]

Barrow provides a valuable Marxist analysis of higher education as an adjunct to corporate capitalism.[9] Assuming a collaboration between business and state to favor capital accumulation, Barrow sees the restructuring of American higher education between 1894 and 1928 as the incorporation of education into the political economy. Thus, education was increasingly viewed as a business, as amenable to efficiency measures, and as something that represents an investment that has to pay off.

The basic trend outlined by Barrow seems to have accelerated. Today, most major research universities and their faculties are in financial partnership with private corporations. The research facilities of higher education are subsidized by public money (with no provision for sharing gains with the public). And while this arrangement is alleged to help make America economically competitive, a large amount of the sale of American research knowledge goes to foreign corporations.[10]

It is of considerable interest that higher education can no longer claim to be an interconnected, multilevel meritocracy. It is what it has probably always been, a fragmented set of unrelated, noncompetitive clusters. High-quality, high-prestige institutions, both private and public, continue to emphasize elitist goals (pure research, liberal arts, preservation of the cultural heritage, an intellectual atmosphere of free inquiry). Such goals also further faculty members' professional careers and assign a low priority to teaching, especially at the undergraduate level. Lower-quality, lower-prestige institutions, usually public, appear to have given up trying to compete with front-ranking universities and have come to be characterized by different goals: vocational programs, applied research, teaching, service to the immediate community, and equality of opportunity.[11]

It should surprise no one to learn that higher education is deeply implicated in our class system.[12] But it is important to insist on viewing higher education as a class phenomenon and to resist the notion that colleges are attended exclusively by an elite of personal merit, and that such extraneous factors as class, race, ethnicity, religion, and gender, though perhaps influential at the lower levels of schooling, have somehow been overcome or neutralized by the time students enter college. The student bodies of our colleges and universities not only do not include all the available academic talent, but are also havens of class privilege.

Class influence over entry to higher education takes a number of forms. First, local school districts are often homogeneous by income and are thus class-based. This means a vast difference in the amount of money spent on education from one district to another. But more important, it means that students entering school are already programmed either for success, mediocrity, or failure. This process is institutionalized by the high school tracking system in which students are assigned to programs by IQ or previous academic achievement, that is, essentially by class and gender.[13]

All this leads to differential access to higher education with large numbers of youngsters with academic ability dropping out of high school or not going on. And tracking continues in higher education because class again determines what quality of four-year school one attends and whether or not one attends a junior college. In addition, class is also related to type of programs selected once in college. The conclusion reached by Bowles and Gintis for the U.S. and Bourdieu and Passeron for France, that education in capitalist society is a process of social reproduction, is difficult to avoid.[14]

Small and Different Worlds: The Academic Profession

The term *academic profession* has no referent; it is an abstraction left over from the early years of higher education when a small, homogeneous collection of colleges provided a tiny number of people with the then available amount of knowledge. Burton Clark has painted a disturbing picture of present day higher education in which little unity can be found. There is mongrelization (my term) among types of school ranging from medical to hair styling schools, from research universities to community colleges. There is mongrelization of subject matter ("it is virtually impossible", says Clark, "to name a subject that someone, somewhere, will not teach"). And subjects have splintered into subspecialities and beyond into topics, most with their own association and even journals. There is hierarchy and separation among the various departments within a school and all are separate from "the pieties of curricular integration."

The teaching faculty of higher education has lost economic ground over the past decades (in addition, enormous disparity in income and teaching loads exist among the various schools and among disciplines). And while some instructors enjoy great autonomy, some have been put back under the control of trustees, and many are under the sway of clients (the student-driven bottom third to bottom half of institutions). Perhaps nothing is more telling than the fact that fully over forty percent of instructors in higher education are temporary and lack income, benefits, security, or career prospects. The academic profession is really (in Clark's words) one of small and different worlds.[15] This exploitation of professional labor is matched by the exploitation of other educational labor (secretaries, clerical help, graduate and laboratory assistants), a pattern of exploitation that has its counterpart in all professions.

EDUCATION'S FAILURE TO PERFORM SOCIAL FUNCTIONS

Education is alleged to perform four distinct functions: (1) transmit the culture, (2) promote social solidarity, (3) provide for personal development and selection by merit, and (4) generate knowledge and update society. That it has failed and failed badly on all counts comes as no surprise. What is surprising is the continuing belief that education can and should perform these functions! To understand why (academic) education cannot perform any positive function, let us frame our beliefs about its role in society into two general purposes: one, to prepare (sift, train, and sort) the young for an ever-more demanding occupational hierarchy, and two, to prepare them for citizenship. As education was assigned ever-more explicit economic and social functions, Americans came to think of it as a natural or objective process for sorting out and training the talent manifested in each generation so that these functions could be served. This belief is now so universally accepted that it is almost impossible to raise questions about it. Of course, Americans have been openly critical of their educational institutions. They have spent and will no doubt continue to spend enormous amounts of time and energy debating their performance. What the empirical record suggests, however, is that America's fundamental premises about education are wrong; that is, a sizable amount of evidence indicates *that formal education bears no positive relation to economic behavior or to citizenship.* If anything, education is associated with negative economic and political consequences. The implications for the professions are enormous.

The Myth of Education as the Generator of Human Capital

Ivar Berg indicted education as a "great training robbery" as far back as 1970.[16] Summarizing the considerable evidence on the relation between formal education and work performance and satisfaction, as well as a study of his own, Berg found no relation between formal education and work productivity, low absenteeism, low turnover, work satisfaction, or promotion. If anything, he found an inverse relation between amount of formal education and occupational performance. While the studies reported by Berg varied with regard to the type and reliability of their data, the impression gained from reviewing data on blue-collar, white-collar, and engineer-scientist workers is that formal education plays one simple role: It determines where one enters the occupational system. What is crucial, in other words, is that employers *believe* that formal education makes better workers and therefore use it as a criterion for hiring. *But once hired, workers with more and less formal education exhibit no significant difference in work performance.* The only apparent difference is in income, because workers with more formal education enter the labor force at higher levels and change jobs more often.

Berg also found no relation between formal education and success in the military or the civil service. This was borne out in the early 1980s, in one highly demanding occupation (air controller). When President Reagan fired striking air controllers, the Federal Aviation Administration was forced to train new controllers quickly. Significantly, no difference in performance was found between high school and college graduates. To cite another example, the demand that teachers have undergraduate and even graduate degrees is associated with high turnover and departure from the profession. Thus Berg and others suggest that formal education is mostly a means of assigning credentials that control the supply of labor, and thus access to jobs and income. Given the close relationship between class and the acquisition of educational credentials, the American system of education is thus, as much as anything else, a way of transmitting class position from one generation to the next.

The association of formal education with positive economic outcomes has been exploded by Randall Collins's sophisticated and intensive analysis of this overall question. Reviewing the literature and the data on the increased schooling required for employment in the United States, Collins found that education is better understood as a status-conferring process by means of which dominant groups seek to control occupations by imposing irrelevant cultural requirements than as a reflection of the greater skills needed on the job due to technological change.[17]

School achievement does lead to higher occupations and income. But one need only look at the large difference in income between those with one to three years of college and those with four years to realize that employers honor credentials, not knowledge. In addition, those who do well in school cannot be shown to become better workers and citizens because of their schooling. Researchers have been unable to find a positive relation between grades or test scores, and success in later life.[18]

Our graduate and professional schools are no exception to the general ineffectiveness (lack of payoff for the general public) of American education. American graduate schools turn out professors who are untrained in education and teaching. Medical schools have faculties oriented mostly toward research and curricula that are overlong, technocratic introductions to a specialized medicine which neglects the patient as a whole person and is indifferent to health. Law schools teach students to memorize legal materials while neglecting almost all the things that real-life lawyers do (interviewing clients, negotiating, performing in a court of law). Business schools teach their MBAs to manipulate symbols and analyze financial statements while failing to stress that the world of business means negotiation, personnel evaluation, product development, labor relations, marketing, sales, and so on. And none of these graduate and professional programs has valid admission standards, and none has any evidence that graduates perform better for having attended its program.[19] What they all have in common is that they sharpen the minds of our professional elites by making them narrow; they do not sharpen them by discussing the important issues of the day: How do we generate full employment, how do we provide justice and health care for all, and how do we educate to attain these goals?

The absence of a positive relation between success in school and positive results for society is most easily understood by the fact that employers are not much interested in abstract cognitive achievement. When asked what kind of people they prefer, the world of business answers: individuals who hunger for work, can always give it all they have, can see a job through, and who have self-confidence, a zest for life, and a sense of direction in life. The business world's list of desired qualities does not even mention cognitive ability. That is probably why grades in school do not correlate with occupational success after school. The same is true of professional education—no study has ever validated a connection between grades in medical school, law school, business school, and so on with later professional success.

The idea that schools create human capital is understandable in a capitalist society and it is not surprising that it is supported in academe by mainstream economists. Economists are able to continue this myth because economics is largely a deductive science out of touch with the more empiri-

cal disciplines (more evidence of educational failure). Mainstream economists make a number of assumptions, long since contradicted by empirical
research, that prevent them from questioning the relevance of higher education to economic growth.[20] They mistakenly equate the higher earnings of
college graduates as proof that they are contributing to economic growth.
They assume that the correlation of growth in education and economic
growth is causal. But Randall Collins has shown that America's system of
mass education came *after* the breakthrough into sustained economic
growth. Also, the explosive growth of higher education from the 1950s on in
the U.S. correlates with a *slowdown* in productivity.[21]

The Myth that Education Promotes Citizenship

The failure of education to provide positive economic outcomes also
applies to the world of citizenship. In the nineteenth century, Americans believed that education in a common school would provide moral and intellectual cement to bind the nation together. Children would acquire a shared
outlook and spirit by growing up together under adult supervision. The
idea of a common curriculum in a common school was inspired by, or at
least congruent with, the social experience of most Americans in the early
nineteenth century. Most Americans had Protestantism, Newtonian cosmology, farming, and small-town life in common, which no doubt made it natural for them to think in terms of a common school. Later, the common
school was also seen as a corrective to the increased diversity brought about
by urbanization and immigration. Even when the school was diversified at
the high school level, the faith persisted that educational homogenization
was gradually taking place and that ever higher levels of education (years
of schooling) were good for society.

Almost a century and a half after the advent of mass public education,
Americans are probably no more united by common values and beliefs acquired through education than they were before public education. The public also displays ignorance about a large range of public matters as well as a
lack of interest in politics.[22] Why Americans persist in thinking of education
as a mechanism for promoting social integration through homogeneity cannot be explained with precision. Whatever its source, however, the ideology
of homogeneity in education (equality of opportunity, objective-national
norms, universalistic professional standards, national accreditation, national programs) helps to conceal an unfair contest for social position. In
fact, beneath the rhetoric of homogeneity and universalism, American society has created wide diversification. It has diversified its high school system
so much that even students who attend the same school receive different
educations; it has created a highly diversified hierarchy of colleges, universities, and junior colleges; it has diversified its entire elementary and high
school systems by class as a result of residential segregation and the tradition of the neighborhood school; and it has taken class diversification one
step further to create severe racial isolation in all parts of the nation, creating more racial segregation in schools than existed in the 1960s. But educa-

tional diversification, disguised by the rhetoric of equality and competition, serves important latent functions. The truth of the matter is that the American educational nonsystem does create social stability, but in a manner extremely incongruous with normative ideology: The class-based educational system, in which youngsters start out and largely remain in separate tracks, protects those with power and legitimates the failure of those without power.

The lack of positive outcomes for higher education can also be seen in the fact that the United States has long had a surplus of college graduates. Unlike other capitalist societies, the United States uses college graduates in a large number of supervisory positions with no increase in productivity. The real purpose of these supervisory positions is to act as a buffer between the upper class and the working-lower classes and to disguise the unwarranted rewards of the upper classes (American executives, for example, have far higher incomes relative to their workers than executives in any other capitalist society).[23] Recently college graduates have noticeably begun to take over jobs that high school graduates have held[24] (earlier research established that one-third of college graduates reported that they were in jobs that did not require a college degree).

Education does not have positive outcomes because knowledge as such cannot be related to behavior in any one-to-one relation. People who *know* that AIDS is not easily transmitted continue to discriminate against AIDS victims. Individuals who *know* that condoms reduce the risk of acquiring AIDS nonetheless do not use them. Teenagers who take sex education courses do not avoid pregnancy any more than teenagers who do not take such courses. Doctors who take courses in nutrition do not incorporate knowledge about nutrition into their practices. Students who take language courses do not know more about foreign countries than students who do not take such courses. And so on. Actually, schools do not stress knowledge that can be used. Schools stress abstract skills presumably applicable to social policy or personal problem areas. But everything we know about learning tells us that humans behave in this way (know how to apply knowledge) only if they are trained to do so! In addition, the skills in abstraction that graduates have must be utilized in well-defined settings: for example, corporations, hospitals, law firms, schools, foundations, and civil service bureaucracies. Perhaps the easiest way to see and remember the failure of academic education is that businesses are training as many employees at all levels as there are students in all four-year colleges and graduate programs combined at a cost equal to all expenditures for the same schools.[25]

A recent massive (800-page) compilation of all available research on the impact of higher education on students confirms the above themes. The authors report that we do not have much research on the specific impact of higher education on students and that research in this area is declining. Second, what can be established points to an only modest impact of higher education on students. Though it is not possible to disentangle the characteristics of students, the aging process, and outside influences from the effects of education (because of how research has been designed), college seniors tend to have an array of cognitive skills that presumably they acquired in college. Changes in attitudes and values in the realms of politics and sex roles (presumably in the direction of enlightenment) are modest and may be declining. There is no evidence supporting higher education's claim that it enhances economic productivity (what evidence exists is negative), though there is evidence that a college degree leads to occupational advancement and yields a small amount of job satisfaction (largely, remember, because employers falsely believe that education enhances productivity and place college graduates in the better jobs). Pascarella and Terenzini also confirm that there is no evidence to support the belief that selective, prestigious colleges have a greater impact on students than less selective schools.[26]

The fact that higher education seems to promote cognitive skills does not mean that improving such skills should continue to be the main thrust of reform efforts. Quite the contrary, abstract cognitive skills have no direct payoff in better workers or citizens. And the same applies to higher education's success in promoting "better" attitudes about politics and gender: Better attitudes about politics and gender are not the same thing as better behavior. College graduates pursue their own interests just as others do, deviating quite widely in their behavior from their own attitudes and from American ideals in general.

Why does a failed education endure? Or rather, how does it serve the interests of America's power groups? For one thing, it helps sustain the myth that the upper classes derive from meritocratic processes based on equal competition. Its prolonged and irrelevant system of credentials curbs labor flows into the good jobs, ensuring power groups control over the income, prestige, and power of upper-level occupations. A prolonged and irrelevant education also ensures the success of the children of the upper classes, thereby solving the problem of how to transmit class advantages to offspring without seeming to violate the achievement ethic.

All this suggests that academic education is not a separate institutional compartment. But its value to the outer society goes beyond its class-based system of selection for occupations and its ideological claim that it is serving the common good by producing better workers and homogeneous, knowledgeable citizens. In the late eighteenth century, Cambridge University pioneered the use of examinations to evaluate how well *individuals* had absorbed its learning. Here began the process whereby individuals were graded by alleged objective abstractions (letter grades, numerical scores) to see how much of an alleged objective curriculum they had grasped. Here began the process in modern society, in other words, whereby concrete power processes impose themselves on concrete individuals. The practice of systematic training in reading and writing, and grading through examinations, or disciplining students and ultimately society, was intensified at West Point between 1817 and the 1830s for elite students (and adopted for the masses starting in Massachusetts in the 1850s). West Point graduates spread the use of management by numerical monitoring to manufacturing processes and corporate administration.[27] Eventually, of course, the use of alleged objective criteria and data spread to all aspects of American life to give America's governing classes and professions the false belief that they had found a way to administer and direct their society (the analysis of the claim to objectivity by American's professions is the main theme of this study. For the pervasive use of mathematics to buttress that claim, see "Mathematics" in Chapter 5, "Administrators and Executives" in Chapter 6, "Accountants" in Chapter 7, all of Chapter 10, and "Knowledge and Policy as Expressions of Power" in Chapter 11).

Understanding the impotence of academic education goes a long way in understanding the performance shortfalls of both the separate academic disciplines and our various professions. Ironically, as each profession and discipline confronts its shortfalls, it tends to reassert its dedication to the education that is the problem in the first place! The participation of the disciplines and professions in this failed system is thus sincere and not deliberate ideology. Beyond their understanding lie the latent functions of education for the knowledge elites. One, education's emphasis on mastering abstract symbols helps perpetuate the myth that society is under the guidance of knowledge elites. And two, education serves as a scapegoat: By blaming it for social problems and assigning it the responsibility for performing social functions that it clearly cannot perform, our elites deflect attention from the fact that they are the cause of problems and that they bear the responsibility for solving them.

Professionals and the Ritual of Research

The call for research is a favorite among professionals. The faith in research is understandable. Through it much knowledge has been generated and many wondrous products have appeared. But our understanding of the role of research in education and modern society has been limited, at least until recently. Lately, a fuller and different picture of research has appeared. Those who specialize in the analysis of the relation between thought and society have begun to realize that there may be no such thing as objective or pure research. What passes for objective research appears to be a search for what elites want knowledge about. Objective knowledge, in turn, is what elites agree on. Seen in this way, America's research is largely into things that business, government, especially the military, and the professions want knowledge about.

Research is an ineffective ritual because its findings are either not used or used selectively to further the interests of power groups. Research does not only not solve social problems, but it is an honored way to postpone tackling them. As we see later, neither basic nor applied research is directed toward revamping the institutions and groups that are causing social problems in the first place. Research is done largely to enhance the technical skills of elites or to enhance social-control structures (for example, law enforcement, educational psychology, to make a class-biased school system work better, or provide welfare programs for the economically distressed). Higher education is an integral part of the world of research and in this respect serves important power functions, not the least of which is to legitimate social power by its pretense of providing objective knowledge for a functionally differentiated set of progressive institutions and professions.

Education, Educational Reform, and Ideology

Organized as a college or university, the academic profession is sanctioned by the state as either a private or autonomous public "corporation" with the right to decide on the qualifications for entry into the other prized professions. Ideology aside, it is clear that American education serves the needs of America's power groups (see the section, "The Culture of Professionalism" in Chapter 2 for Bledstein's argument that higher education in America emerged as largely a middle-class phenomenon which yields a social order without democracy and deflects attention from the social sources of problems). To protect and further their interests, power groups (including educators) have created the myth that success in school is related to performance outside of school (to the benefit of both individuals and society). One outcome of this myth is that it permits power groups to postpone tackling social problems by referring solutions to schools and the young.

For over a hundred years America's elites have asked education to produce better citizens, promote equality, curb delinquency, poverty and unemployment, provide skilled labor, and upgrade productivity; it has failed and must fail on all counts for the simple reason that what happens in classrooms bears little relation to what happens outside.[28] It is difficult not to believe that the latent function of education is to legitimate an illegitimate academic profession, and, in the process, to serve a similar function for its component disciplines and the professions derived from them. Beyond that it is also clear that education's main latent function is to provide the means that enables the upper classes to turn their property (land, factories, office buildings, profits, income, etc.) into other property forms (the cognitive and personality skills of their children, the ability of their children to acquire academic credentials), a social process which not only contributes to the hereditary transmission of property, but which forms a vital link in disguising a political economy centered on the interchangeability of material and human capital.

The implications of all of the above for the education of professionals can be stated simply. Ability is probably far more widespread than is now believed by our professions and other leaders. Those who educate professionals should gear what they do to creating personalities that are trained to apply knowledge and to solve problems in the real world (the major way to solve problems is by redesigning social institutions and creating adaptive, knowledgeable citizens, workers, and consumers). The overall image that should guide education is that competent professionals and ordinary citizens can be turned out much more readily and sooner than anyone suspects and that only the overall reduction of unnecessary inequality deserves the name *democratic reform*.

SUMMARY

American education is thought to serve a number of valuable social functions. This belief has become part of the mores and cannot easily be questioned. Research on education has established that it is a class phenomenon through and through. Research reveals that education is a hugely diverse nonsystem and that this includes higher education and the academic disciplines. Not only is each academic discipline fragmented beyond coherence, but the various disciplines, despite some interdisciplinary work, are also sitting at separate tables.

More ominously, research has also established that academic and professional education exhibits no positive relation to the performance of social functions, either by elites or ordinary citizens.

The right kind of education requires abandoning abstract learning and the ritual of research. Education must be connected directly to the performance of economic, political, family, and personal roles.

The latent functions served by education are to hide the failure of American institutions, groups, and elites, and to provide an undeserved legitimacy for itself, its various disciplines and professions, and the liberal social system.

NOTES

1. Equality of opportunity as an equal chance at the starting gate should not be confused with equal access to education of some sort or with proposals to provide different or more effective educational opportunities for diverse social classes.
2. For much of the above context, see J. David Knottnerus, "Status Attainment Research and Its Image of Society," *American Sociological Review* 52 (February 1987): 113–21.
3. Peter M. Blau and Otis D. Duncan, *The American Occupational Structure* (New York: Wiley, 1967).
4. David Featherman and Robert M. Hauser, *Opportunity and Change* (New York: Academic Press, 1978), and William H. Sewell and Robert M. Hauser, eds., *Schooling and Achievement in American Society* (New York: Academic Press, 1976).
5. Patrick M. Horan, "Is Status Attainment Research Atheoretical?" *American Sociological Review* 43 (August 1978): 534–41.
6. E. M. Beck, Patrick M. Horan, and Charles M. Tolbert II, "Stratification in a Dual Economy," *American Sociological Review* 43 (October 1978): 704–720.
7. Christopher Jencks and David Reisman, *The Academic Revolution* (Garden City, N.Y.: Doubleday, 1968).
8. For a pioneering study of, and still our most comprehensive body of empirical data on, the composition and attitudes of governing boards, see Morton A. Rauh, *The Trusteeship of Colleges and Universities* (New York: McGraw-Hill, 1969).
9. Clyde W. Barrow, *Universities and the Capitalist State: Corporate Liberalism and the Reconstruction of American Higher Education, 1894–1928* (Madison: University of Wisconsin Press, 1990).

10. For background on the absorption of natural science by industry (and the military), see David Dickson, *The New Politics of Science* (New York: Pantheon, 1984), and Sheila Slaughter, *The Higher Learning and High Technology: Dynamics of Education Policy Formation* (Albany: State University of New York Press, 1990). For a summary of developments (in the long-term transformation of higher education into an adjunct of corporate capitalism), see Russell Jacoby, "The Greening of the University: From Ivory Tower to Industrial Park," *Dissent* 38 (Spring 1991): 286–92.

11. Burton R. Clark, *The Academic Life: Small Worlds, Different Worlds* (Princeton, N.J.: Carnegie Foundation for the Advancement of Teaching, 1987).

12. The ability of the upper classes to get their children through college much more successfully than the lower classes has a long history of documentation by social stratification research. For the latest analysis, based on census and other data, tracing the relations between family income and college enrollment and graduation from 1970 to 1988—which clearly indicates "substantial stratification by income", especially in four-year colleges—see Charles F. Manski, "Income and Higher Education," *Focus* 14, no. 3 (Winter 1992–93): 14–19.

13. James E. Rosenbaum, "The Structure of Opportunity in School," *Social Forces* 57 (September 1978): 236–56; "Track Misperceptions and Frustrated College Plans: An Analysis of the Effects of Tracks and Track Perceptions in the National Longitudinal Survey," *Sociology of Education* 53 (April 1980): 74–88; Jane Gaskell, "Course Enrollment in High School: The Perspective of Working-Class Females," *Sociology of Education* 58 (January 1985): 48–59.

14. Samuel Bowles and Herbert Gintis, *Schooling in Capitalist America* (New York: Basic Books, 1977) and Pierre Bourdieu and Jean-Claude Passeron, *Reproduction in Education, Society, and Culture*, trans. Richard Nice (Newbury Park, Calif.: Sage, 1977).

15. Burton R. Clark, *The Academic Life: Small Worlds, Different Worlds* (Princeton, N.J.: Carnegie Foundation for the Advancement of Teaching, 1987). Clark's careful, comprehensive, and elegantly written analysis stays inside higher education, assuming it to be a knowledge-driven, self-contained entity that is generating its own deficiencies. One feels the absence of any discussion of the socioeconomic basis of education as well as the failure to note that higher education is not performing the functions attributed to it. A comparative analysis, Philip G. Altbach, ed., *Comparative Perspectives on the Academic Profession* (New York: Praeger, 1977), also stresses the diversity and drift of the academic profession across developed and developing countries as it comes under pressure from the outside to do more and more for business, government, and clients, both old and new (to the middle and upper classes have been added the working class and those who have hitherto been excluded from the benefits of higher education because of race, ethnicity, sex, age, or disability). A useful discussion of the academic disciplines as each having its own "culture" (different views of method, goal of research, national versus international focus, education, and so on) is provided by Henry Bauer under the heading "The Antithesis," *Social Epistemology* 4, no. 2 (1990): 215–227.

16. Ivar Berg, assisted by Sherry Gorelick, *Education and Jobs: The Great Training Robbery* (New York: Praeger, 1970).

17. Randall Collins, *The Credential Society* (New York: Academic Press, 1979). For a pioneering study that discovered that high-quality colleges have relatively little impact on the future occupations of their students, since the type of student they recruit more adequately explains future success, see Duane F. Alwin, "College Effects on Educational and Occupational Attainment," *American Sociological Review* 39 (April 1974): 210–223.

18. Michael R. Olneck and James Crouse, "The IQ Meritocracy Reconsidered: Cognitive Skill and Adult Success in the United States," *American Journal of Education* 88 (November 1979): 1–31; Michael Useem and S. M. Miller, "The Upper Class in Higher Education," *Social Policy* 7 (January–February, 1977): 28–31.

19. For the lack of positive results from professional programs for doctors, lawyers, and business executives, see Andrew Hacker, "The Shame of Professional Schools," *Harper's* 263 (October 1981): 22–28. For a full analysis that comes to the same conclusion, see Robert Klitgaard, *Choosing Elites* (New York: Basic Books, 1985).

20. For example, William E. Becker and Darrell R. Lewis, eds., *Higher Education and Economic Growth* (Boston: Kluwer, 1993).

21. In later chapters we also see that equal educational achievements by racial, ethnic, and gender minorities do not lead to equal results in economic status.

22. Norval D. Glenn, "The Distribution of Political Knowledge in the United States," in Dan D. Vimmo and Charles M. Bonjean, eds., *Political Attitudes and Public Opinion* (New York: Longman, 1972). Astonishingly there has been no followup of Glenn's pioneering study, with one recent exception; for survey evidence of a decline of interest and knowledge about politics among young adults, see *New York Times*, June 28, 1990, p. 1. For the failure of high-school history texts even to take on the function of preparing students for democratic citizenship, see the section "History" in Chapter 4.

23. Eric Olin Wright and Bill Martin, "The Transformation of the American Class Structure, 1960–1980," *American Journal of Sociology* 93 (July 1987): 1–29. Wright and Martin also argue that owners and managers receive more income than is warranted even holding education, occupational status, age, and job tenure constant.

24. *New York Times*, June 18, 1990, p. 1.

25. Nell P. Eurich, *Corporate Classrooms* (Princeton: Carnegie Foundation for the Advancement of Teaching, 1985). The cost to business (ultimately to taxpayers and consumers) is much higher if employee wages and benefits are included. The education by governments of their employees would raise the figures for both costs and the number of students still more.

26. Ernest T. Pascarella and Patrick T. Terenzini, *How College Affects Students: Findings and Insights from Twenty Years of Research* (San Francisco: Jossey-Bass, 1991).

27. For fascinating details of the origin of the examination and its spread through West Point to the American economy, all seen as origins of accountancy, see Keith Hoskin and Richard Macve, "Writing, Examining, Disciplining: The Genesis of Accounting's Modern Power," in A. G. Hopwood and Peter Miller, eds., *Accounting as Social and Institutional Practice* (New York: Cambridge University Press, 1994), chap. 3.

28. For a valuable historical overview and analysis, see Richard DeLone's report for the Carnegie Council on Children, *Small Futures: Children, Inequality, and the Limits of Liberal Reform* (New York: Harcourt Brace Jovanovich, 1979).

4
Academic Disciplines I

◆ ◆ ◆ ◆

◆ ◆ ◆ ◆

The far-reaching indictment of education that has emerged over the past seventy-five years of research has been matched by similar indictments of individual academic disciplines. These disciplines are professions in their own right, of course, and form the foundations from which the various applied and policy professions are derived (see Chapters 6–8, 10). In analyzing the various professions in this and later chapters, we continue earlier themes: Are the professions autonomous, objective, and nonpolitical? Are they adaptive and do they generate the knowledge needed to solve social problems? Do the professions monitor themselves and curb wayward members? Is there a trend toward a Knowledge (Postindustrial) society in which knowledge is supplanting property, political power, and social class to become the axial principle of society?

The academic disciplines and applied professionals give the appearance of being autonomous and it is best to put that appearance in a more realistic context at the outset. The concept *autonomy* means to be self-propelled and self-correcting. It is an important value to Americans (and also goes by the names of freedom, liberty, and individualism). America's professions have used the basic principle of freedom to establish their unique autonomy from collectively enforced responsibilities for the collective good. By autonomy, elites mean the right to be let alone to pursue their interests, to not have outsiders telling them what to do. Their autonomy, and that of Americans in general, adds up to the collective good because of America's fetishistic belief in the magic of markets: the social good for American elites is guaranteed by economic, political, and educational markets sustained by fiduciary and professional norms.

Beneath this ideology is a far different reality. If by markets, one means equal competition on the basis of full information, then markets are nowhere to be found. If by professionalism, one means the nonpolitical pursuit and application of knowledge, this too is absent from American life. If by autonomy, one means the ability of individual professionals to find satisfaction in their work, then here too reality and ideology diverge. If by professional, one means a group of individuals united by a common ethic, practicing under common conditions, and linked to social functions, then here again one will be disappointed.

The reality is that the academic disciplines and applied professionals are highly subjective (they create reality as they translate formal knowledge into applied knowledge or as they negotiate reality with nature, each other, clients, patients, students, and so on). As we see in this and following chapters, every discipline from the social to the natural sciences as well as literary studies is questioning its epistemological base. All are discovering that the alleged objectivity and value neutrality of empirical fact-gathering is a fiction; all scientists use myths, metaphors, stories, hunches, and socially derived assumptions in their work. Until that is acknowledged, the fiction of Olympian detachment will continue to favor economic and state interests and run counter to the interests of ordinary people, especially the poor, racial-ethnic minorities, and women.

The various professions and disciplines are also highly political, internally differentiated and stratified, embedded in bureaucratic settings, and subject to outside monitoring by other bodies, including governments. Professionals share a common economic interest (how to ensure secure income against the vagaries of markets without being subject to outside evaluation by those who want to link income to performance). Not only does the overall separation of the professions and other elites from accountability for the performance of social functions lead predictably to large amounts of incompetence and crime by our upper classes, but, more ominously, to a society without direction.

Our survey of the academic disciplines will not pursue all these themes with equal emphasis. It can be taken for granted that access to these disciplines is class-based, that the practice of them is in bureaucratic settings, that there are internal and jurisdictional disputes among them, that their membership is highly stratified and differentiated, and that, like all elites and professions, they rest on exploited labor, only partly explained by racism and sexism. Our major focus is on the scientific shortfalls of the academic disciplines and their failure to develop socially useful knowledge.

SOCIOLOGY

Sociology as the Ideology of Corporate Capitalism

Sociology was creative during the emergence and establishment of capitalism, especially in France and Germany which experienced the shock of modernization (social-system change) in traumatic terms. Its creative period (1750–1914) was one in which inquiry became social theory (what variables help explain the structure and movement of total societies?). During the twentieth century, however, sociology went the way of the other social sciences and became a profession. Taking the nature of society for granted (especially in the United States), it began to study it empirically in a value-free way. By the 1960s, it had become an integral part of capitalism, no longer able to analyze and evaluate it from the outside.

Twentieth-century sociological theory up to the 1960s saw the establishment of a deeply skewed world view disguised as science. From Cooley and Thomas down through Herbert Blumer and Talcott Parsons, sociological theory was essentially a way to legitimate corporate capitalism. It did this in two ways:

1. It established the social-action paradigm as the dominant mode of thought for sociologists. The social-action paradigm is admirably suited to the needs of corporate capitalism. Individuals, according to social-action theorists, live in a world of scarcity requiring incessant choices. With these simple words, sociology accepted the biopsychological view of behavior,

put the explanation of good and evil on individuals, and effectively by-passed the institutional-power explanation of human behavior.

2. The Chicago School (1920s and 1930s) had a lasting negative influence on sociology. Its main contribution to corporate capitalism was to sever social problems from their cause (the political economy) and to create the impression that they emerged from individuals and local circumstances, all subject to reform.

The social-action orientation not only focused on the choices of individuals, but had a pronounced bias in favor of ideational and normative causation (symbolic interactionism, functionalism).

Sociology as Evolutionary Liberalism: Talcott Parsons

The thought of Talcott Parsons, America's leading sociological theorist from the 1930s to the 1970s, illustrates all of the above. By and large, Parsonian thought deflected attention from the meaning of the Great Depression and helped support American liberalism during the Cold War by developing a naive functionalism which took all the fictions of American liberalism at face value: Ascription has declined and will continue to decline; equality of opportunity is distinctive and real; law is the central control and adaptive mechanism of modern society; bureaucracy is important, but the trend is toward associationalism; society is deeply pluralistic; the old laissez-faire capitalism of the nineteenth century is dead; property has given way to occupation; and occupations are filled by merit as determined by education.

Education held a special significance for Parsons. It is the third revolution of modern times, with the French Revolution in politics and the Industrial Revolution in economics composing the first two. Education and the professions go together to ensure a society based on achievement. The professions, argued Parsons, are replacing the power of property just as the early capitalists replaced feudal aristocrats. As a marriage of objective knowledge and application, the professions are the spearhead of the developing democratization of society.

On all of the above counts, Parsons was wrong. By Parsons's time, and during his lifetime (1902–1979), a burgeoning empirical tradition had unearthed an America that was widely divergent from its beliefs about itself (beliefs that Parsons never questioned). The Lynds, for example, had uncovered in *Middletown* (1927 and again in 1936) an America that should have inhibited Parsons from assuming a correspondence between American ideals and behaviors. A vital tradition of social stratification theory (Weber, Cooley, Veblen) and especially stratification research, starting with the seminal works of W. Lloyd Warner, John Dollard, James West, St. Clair Drake and Horace R. Cayton, August B. Hollingshead, and Floyd Hunter, had splashed itself all over mainstream sociology in the 1940s and early 50s to question the alleged meritocratic basis of American social stratification. In 1951, C. Wright Mills's *White Collar* raised serious questions about the bureaucratization and concentration of the American economy. Michael Harrington's *The Other America* (1962) and Rachel Carson's *Silent Spring* (1962) raised still further questions about American society (Why after more than a century of industrialization does so much poverty exist? Is industrialization ruinous to nature?). All of the above (and more) were books that were current and well known during Parsons's creative years. In addition, Parsons, who ignored Marx when he canvassed ideas for his social theory, did not pick up on the Marxian-influenced theory of imperialism, now known as dependency theory, that emerged in the 1950s starting with Paul A. Baran and which blossomed in the 1960s and 1970s thanks to such thinkers as Andre Gunder Frank and Immanuel Wallerstein.

Parsons's reluctance to cite the overall polity as an integrative mechanism is also significant. American elites have consistently denied a positive role for the state, even though they use it extensively. Essentially, the negative view of the polity from Madison and Jefferson through Sumner, followed by indifference to it by Cooley, Thomas, and Parsons, allowed American elites to use the state for their interests while denying its use to the masses. Parsons does emphasize the integrative function of law, but this is part of his misplaced faith in the nonpolitical professions and the nonpartisan state.

Sociology as Disguised Evolutionary Liberalism: Anthony Giddens

The early optimism and certainties of the immediate post-World War II period no longer characterize creative liberals. In an effort to update sociological theory, the British sociologist Anthony Giddens has abandoned the explicit evolutionary-progressive premise behind American sociological theory. His own theory about society and how to reconstruct sociology is called *structuration*. Society, he argues, is not an external entity imposing itself on individual actors, as an assortment of structuralists have claimed, but an interplay between the actor as a socialized being and other actors. In this interplay, "knowledgeable actors" engage in a give and take. By give and take, Giddens means interpreting each other's behavior and learning from each other (Giddens's terms for this foundational process are "double hermeneutics" and "reflexive monitoring").[1]

For Giddens, the concept of *structure* is not an objective thing but consists of "rules [norms] and resources [economic]"—more or less similar to Parsons' concept of "abstract disposable facilities." *Social system* refers to concrete interaction regularities (institutions). Together, structure and social system both *constrain* and *enable* individual actors. The concept of power, he argues, should be incorporated into this scheme by thinking of rules and resources as a *transformative capacity*, that is, as abstract forces that allow change to take place. One must be careful, Giddens warns, to avoid the dichotomy or dualism of individual versus society or subjective versus objective. Instead, he argues, and this is the linchpin of his theory, there is a "duality of structure," actors and rules and resources are one and the same thing, opposite sides of the same coin.

Fundamental to Giddens's thought is the concept of knowledgeable agent, the individual actor as rational cause. Individuals have a *practical consciousness* exhibited in a huge inventory of both simple and complex social skills. These skills, acquired from society, harden into *routines*, which simultaneously ward off the unconscious and its anxieties (yielding "ontological security") and produce the overall social system. Individuals are capable, when pressed, of explaining why they behave as they do ("discursive consciousness"). The double hermeneutic also applies to knowledge elites—much of the knowledge generated by the professions and disciplines is about what lay people already know. Any new knowledge is absorbed by lay people as they come into contact with knowledge elites. All in all, the knowledgeable activities of actors, both lay and professional, reproduce society as well as change it in the light of new knowledge. Human actors are learners and society is thus a learning machine.

Though generalizations about society, like the ones he has just made, are possible, society itself cannot be defined, says Giddens, and he warns against using the allegedly autonomous nation state as a bounded and definable entity. Modern society is now global and societies interpenetrate. Society is not definable because it is also becoming something else as actors learn and because it is also filled with unanticipated consequences. Social behavior, remember, is highly structured and reproduced at the micro level by the enormously skillful interaction displayed by ordinary individuals, and by a process of creativity represented by the interaction of knowledge elites, especially those in social science. The latter, remember, is itself in a double hermeneutic relation with its subject matter. It gets to know what actors already know and adds knowledge that eventually becomes part of society. Social science is not lagging behind natural science because it is not standing detached from its field of study in search of laws. It *is* its field of study and has had considerable success in generating what it is that actors are behaving according to.

Giddens advocates adopting this approach as the way to think of policy as well as sociological method and theory. One does not develop knowledge first and then intervene. Just as actors monitor their own interactions and negotiate their meanings, thereby improving themselves, just so reformers should immerse themselves in the world they are studying, thereby gaining a better position to bring insights from other areas into whatever context they are in.

The methods of natural science and social science are now understood, says Giddens, to be postempirical, by which he means postpositivist. The subject matter of each is different (the natural world is not subjective and cannot act back to initiatives by natural scientists), but both natural and social scientists use, whether they know it or not, an interpretive method. Sociological theory in the nineteenth and early twentieth century mistakenly coalesced, argues Giddens, around the core concept of industrial, modern, scientific society in contrast to agrarian or sacred, feudal society. By imitating the false empirical method of the natural sciences, says Giddens, socio-logical theory hardened into the "orthodox consensus" of "functionalism and naturalism" in the 1960s led by Talcott Parsons. Giddens feels that he has escaped the dead end of functionalism and naturalism by blending its good parts with phenomenology or interpretive sociology, and by redefin-ing the nature of modernity.

Though Giddens carefully mentions everything important about soci-ety and theory in his commentaries, his own theory is curiously selective. He argues that power is a pervasive part of society, but it does not figure much in his own theory. Actually, there is a conspicuous absence of hierarchical power and social class in his theory, and little emphasis on groups as actors, though on occasion he mentions that the state and social movements are important (he has almost no reference to corporations and other complex organizations and certainly overlooks them as the central actors in current capitalism). Gid-dens also states that social life is a process of negotiating, but there is little em-phasis on this idea in his own theory—the idea remains a liberal one, meaning negotiation among equals leading to contracts, with no acknowledgment that the differentials of power in modern society make negotiation decidedly one-sided (owners–workers, men–women, and so on).

Giddens's most explicit statement about modern society, not buried in his commentaries on other theories, in his small essay *The Consequences of Modernity* (Stanford University Press, 1990). In it, he develops a theory that he claims is different from those of Marx, Durkheim, and Weber (who were too deeply embedded in false comparisons of modern and premodern), as well as different from the postmodern outlook of Jean-Francois Lyotard (the latter sees "a shift away from attempts to ground epistemology and from faith in humanly engineered progress"). Rather, Giddens claims, we are witnessing a period in which "the consequences of modernity are becoming more radicalized and universalized than before."

The modern period, or society in the West from the seventeenth cen-tury on, is marked by discontinuities, by rapid and comprehensive change, and by distinctive institutions. The dimensions of modern society and its achievements, dangers, and discontinuities must be seen as a series of processes:

1. The separation of time and space from any locality or type of experi-ence and the use of these abstractions to order life
2. The disembedding of social systems, or the lifting of social relations out of particular contexts, and restructuring them in terms of abstract time and space
3. The reflexive ordering and reordering of social relations by the contin-uous generation of knowledge

Knowledge elites are engaged in a "double hermeneutics," the observer in-terpreting the observed, the latter interpreting the former, and both incorpo-rating each other's observations. Thus, "sociological knowledge spirals in and out of the universe of social life, reconstructing both itself and that uni-verse as an integral part of that process."

Modernity, concludes Giddens, is not Weber's "iron cage" of instrumental reason or Marx's oppressive property system, but rather a "juggernaut—a runaway engine" whose speed and direction cannot be known or controlled. The juggernaut of modernity (modern society) has many good and many bad features, all in complex interaction with each other.

But underneath Giddens's argument is an unabashed liberal focus on the adaptability of existing society through knowledge (though he hedges continuously) and a faith in the hidden logic of unintended outcomes (the liberal market mentality). By saying everything, by giving all sides of every issue, Giddens creates the impression of Olympian objectivity. What he has done, though, is to endorse capitalism by openly identifying its warts, but saying it also has the most good features possible: integration, self-identity, growth, openness, and so on. Nowhere in his discussion of modern institutions does he refer to the concentrated economy, the primacy of the corporation as a social actor, the plutocratic polity, the poor, substantial and chronic unemployment and underemployment, minorities (including pronounced gender inequality and inequity), the state as a supporter of a capitalist way of life, or imperialism. Giddens argues that a focus on the nation-state as society is a mistake, but the net result is not to show the outward thrust of the main engine in the modern world, the political economy of the Western nations and its five centuries of imperialism. The result is to hide that engine in abstract talk of global processes.

Perhaps the most important thing about contemporary capitalist societies is that its leaders in practical life, public life, and in the world of knowledge seem incapable of running their domains with any degree of certainty or equity. There seems no awareness in Giddens that contemporary societies, while continuing to produce economic growth, have been unable to turn that growth into growing standards of living, or to curb what appear to be mounting pathologies, including deeply alienated electorates. One reason could be that much of liberal social science is a grappling with ideas, not the structure of social power.

Despite many references to how the abstract processes he is identifying reach out to bring individuals to life (the enabling process), what his selective abstracting has done is to remove the impact of society on the aggregate of individuals, thus giving their fate over to existing power groups. In other words, Giddens is guilty of committing modernism, the use of selective ideas to create a fictitious, depoliticized, nondemocratic world based on noninterpretive, objective analysis. In short, there is more than a hint of functionalism and evolutionism in Giddens's thought. Deep down he has provided a late-liberal appreciation of the social nature of behavior and of the uses of the state in the emergence and maintenance of capitalism, something much needed in mainstream American theory. But he has also cut that world off from scrutiny by:

1. Emphasizing that there is no continuity with the past
2. Stressing that there is no better future
3. Saying nothing about creating a better future through political action

Instead we are a "juggernaut" beyond control lurching into an unknown future. Giddens seems unaware that his depiction of society as a juggernaut contradicts the heart of his earlier theory—society as a duality of structure in which human interaction constrained and enabled by an abstract culture continually reproduces itself and adapts through new knowledge. In the final outcome, Giddens's theory is a defense of corporate world-market capitalism against early liberalism, socialism, and postmodernism alike.

Overcoming the Spectrum of Bias

The formalism of mainstream sociological theory was accompanied by a large variety of biased research and theorizing in special areas. Here we are not talking of error or bias on the part of particular individuals, but of pronounced tendencies shaping the basic character of sociological specialties. To its credit, sociology has itself raised serious questions about its perspective in regard to small group analysis,[2] family research,[3] racial assimilation,[4] social stratification,[5] gender,[6] and social problems and deviance.[7] The enormous complexity of sociology makes it difficult to say how well it has fared in overcoming the above deficiencies. There is little doubt, however, that the mainstream still thinks of itself as a science and still defines science as a nonpolitical, value-free, objective empiricism. There is also little doubt that important currents from both liberal and radical sources have begun to see sociology as an interpretive science.

Sociology's Deficient Introductory Text

The introductory textbook is perhaps the best indicator of a discipline's strengths and weaknesses. The introductory text in sociology has generated a long series of complaints:

1. Introductory texts are ad hoc in their discussion and presentation of concepts and subject matter.

2. While they stress the social sources of behavior, texts fail to discuss society as a system of power (power is treated as simply a topic instead of as a pervasive feature of all social relations).[8]

3. Introductory texts discuss conflict sociology, but fail to distinguish between capitalist and socialist modes of conflict thought.[9] Texts tend to be critical, but in a narrow, disguised manner. Almost all texts begin by undermining the validity of common experience (by pointing out that many popular beliefs are not true). But texts rarely challenge the beliefs that validate the power of elites and the professions. Here texts expound a conflict sociology, but only to set up the authority of liberal elites, including itself, as over against the vulgar and obsolescing beliefs of ordinary people and lesser elites. Incredibly, almost all introductory texts have little or nothing on the professions, and what they have, takes them at face value.

4. Introductory texts lose sight of American society by universalizing purely American phenomena. By assuming that American society is the terminal of historical development they fail to raise questions about the basic nature of the United States. Genuine historical and comparative analysis renders *all* behavior problematic, including society itself. This requires comparative research, which is largely absent in the United States (and elsewhere for that matter).[10]

5. Given item 4, it is not surprising that introductory texts in sociology (at least until the last few years) have neglected intersocietal relations. Given item 4, introductory texts are complacent about modernization in the West and in the developing world. Most introductory texts have ignored the most important development in sociology (and social science) over the past few decades, world-system analysis. Modern society can no longer be thought of as a naturally progressive process and its problems simply the problems of adjustment. And single societies can no longer be thought of as ultimate units of study (even one as large and as relatively self-sufficient as the United States). The interaction and interpenetration of societies are thus vital to understanding given societies, or elements therein, but this cannot be learned from the introductory text in sociology.

6. Introductory sociology texts tend not to provide full coverage of economic and political institutions perhaps in deference to their older, fellow disciplines, economics and political science. The economy and polity, however, are the central institutions of American society, and a sociology that slights them while concentrating on other institutions is doomed to irrelevance. Too often introductory texts stimulate awareness about personal life, exotic variations on households, religious cults, and sexual deviance, but fail to give individuals what they need most, information and ideas about the institutions that have the most influence on their lives, the economy and the political-legal system. What this means is that American sociology is largely residual—its subject matter consists of the scraps left over by economics and political science. Ironically, sociologists have no need to apologize when it comes to economic or political analysis—sociology has contributed as much to our understanding of the capitalist economy and polity as any other discipline.

7. Introductory texts have been apolitical for most of their history reflecting sociology's search for professional status. In recent years texts have begun to introduce policy issues, but on an ad hoc basis. To a large extent, texts both old and new tend to be reformist and thus tend to accept American society. By and large, the United States is seen as a society with problems (solvable problems), never as a problem society in need of major restructuring.

8. Perhaps the most important criticism of introductory texts is that they do not give students the best available picture of American society. Sociology takes it on faith that the other disciplines are doing their job and that enlightenment will somehow emerge from the overall educational process.

But of course the other disciplines are also defective and all share (have a stake) in the multiple myths of education. In many ways, sociology's absorption by American society can be told in terms of its reliance on education to supply it with goals, careers, and clients.

The bland introductory text also reflects sociology's need to reach its audience through textbook companies publishing for national markets. It reflects the need to secure employment at schools where deviation from a bland liberalism is quickly noted and punished. Sociology shares much with the other liberal professions. It developed unobjectionable generalizations by becoming ahistorical and abstract. Its focus on the concrete rarely questioned the host society or its power groups. And it institutionalized a wide range of biases within an ethnocentric professionalism. Not much appears to have changed since C. Wright Mills's indictment that sociologists were ad hoc, theoryless, case-oriented, and biopsychological, that they were eager to have deviants conform to an unproblematic normative order, biased in favor of rural, small-town life, all in all, formalistic believers in a vague, readymade, multicausal social world that was organically evolving toward an ever more harmonious blending of parts and which had no discernible levers of power.[11]

In a recent analysis, Aggar has argued that the introductory text reflects a market-driven consensus about scientific method (texts invariably argue that the objective empirical method is the same in sociology as in the natural sciences), about theory (all theory can be divided into functionalism, symbolic interactionism, and conflict theories), and contains biased pictures of Marxism and feminism. Aggar argues that his study of the three main sociology journals also reveals a narrow atheoretical empiricism.[12] And most recently, a study of forty introductory sociology texts published between 1950 and 1989 revealed that they had biased and inadequate discussions of gay males and almost no discussion of gay females.[13]

Racial, Ethnic, and Gender Minorities in Sociology

The ascent to professionalism by liberalism in the nineteenth century meant an arid specialization: economics and political science took the economy and polity respectively for their domains leaving sociology with important residues such as the family, urbanization, deviance, social stratification, and minorities. Sociology's record in these areas is notable. Despite its liberal bias, it did enormously important work early in its life in regard to minorities, especially African Americans. Lately, its work has expanded to include ethnic and gender minorities.

Sociology has one of the best records of any of the disciplines in regard to generating and accepting minorities, especially women, into its ranks. Women have made considerable progress in obtaining doctorates in sociology and now make up 25 percent of sociology faculty.[14] This increase was partly due to softness in the academic labor market in the 1970s and progress in sociology for women may have reached a plateau. And like in the rest of higher education, women sociologists have not obtained a proportionate share of upper rank and authority positions. In sociology, we also encounter another pattern in the professions—even when women make impressive entry gains, they tend to go (are shunted?) into less prestigious, less rewarded specialties. In sociology women specialize in family, medical, population, aging, and gender studies.

Creative Currents

The main outside forces that are challenging mainstream sociology are Marxists (a small but creative group that has done much to influence social stratification, urban sociology, imperialist-development theory, and feminism), phenomenologists (most of whom are liberals and do not do much real challenging), radical feminists (here again there is a singular lack of real influence largely because sociology early developed a liberal feminism), and gay theorists (progress here will be slow given the recent analysis of the way in which introductory sociology texts bias the analysis of homosexuality).

Finally, sociology has creative currents emanating from specialized studies of neglected topics. But this only serves to highlight the fact that the formalism of the main stream hides the fact (as is true of the entire range of disciplines and professions) that there is no such thing as sociology, only a thousand specialities and subspecialities.

ANTHROPOLOGY

The two disciplines that have generated the strongest radical perspectives are literary studies (see Chapter 5) and anthropology. Since World War II, anthropology has not only generated a strong radical perspective, but may also be unique in having had radicalism pervade its main stream. The feminist critique of the older anthropology has already been cited. Of special note is the wideranging critique of the foundations of cultural anthropology, its claim to be an objective, empirical (field research) science, by a wide range of thinkers.

The general indictment of anthropology is that during its early and maturing professional stages, it explored and reported on the outer world, not objectively as it claimed, but in terms of the sociopolitical concerns that anthropologists acquired as members of their home countries. The use of Western ideas, values, and concerns, which varied depending on changing social conditions at home, yielded deeply biased pictures of the non-Western world. This has been richly documented by Kuklick's history of the most developed national anthropology, Great Britain's.[15]

Anthropology as the Ideology of the British Upper Classes

British anthropology was explicitly connected to the political concerns of the British upper classes from the early nineteenth century on. It engaged in all the traditional questions of liberal social theory: What is legitimate political authority, how does change occur, what are the rights and duties of individuals? It offered itself as a way to make reform at home and the management of colonies easier. And the general thrust of its scholarship varied with Britain's fortunes. As Britain prospered in the early to mid-nineteenth century, anthropology saw progress as a universal law and primitive peoples as part of it. By World War I, British optimism had withered with the decline of its economic fortunes. As political turmoil at home increased and the British masses increased their demands, British anthropology separated the idea of economic growth and the good life. The non-Western world was now seen as a way to conceive a good life without a growing material base. During the 1920s and 1930s British functionalist anthropology crystallized, thanks especially to A. R. Radcliffe-Brown (1881–1955) and Bronislaw Malinowski (1884–1942). Anthropological functionalism constructed a concept of culture as a fundamental process of social control and stability through custom (mores). Functionalism redefined individuals to make them part of a functioning whole, and since faith in progress had been abandoned, it abandoned history. Kuklick suggests that since World War II, anthropology's major new contribution to knowledge has been its awareness of its own biased history.[16]

Anthropology as Interpretive Quest

Awareness of its biased history and of the high barriers that prevent the establishment of an objective, empirical science is now a characteristic unique to anthropology in the social sciences (matched in America's symbolic culture only by literary studies). Alone of the social sciences, anthropology has acknowledged its failure and has accepted the need for new beginnings.[17] But even within the new beginnings, foundational questions have appeared. The major thrust of anthropology has now centered on understanding culture as a symbolic system. Pioneered by Clifford Geertz, symbolic anthropology is now an interpretive quest for establishing the deep meaning ("or webs of significance") of cultural systems. Keesing, applying Marxian ideas with phenomenology, has questioned this approach on three grounds.[18] One, knowledge and meaning in a culture are created and controlled by those with power. Two, knowledge and meaning form ideologies masking economic power and other privileges. And three, the difficulties of reading a culture as text have not been fully acknowledged. Cultural symbols allow for different readings and there is still a tendency to impose Western meanings on them. It is added confirmation that anthropology is unique among the social sciences that all eight commentators on Keesing's essay, by and large, agreed with him.

Nonetheless, anthropology has maintained its faith in science by searching for the greatest amount of truth possible. To this end it has adopted three new approaches: new fieldwork practices to minimize bias by the ethnographer, a focus on overlooked aspects of culture such as poems and fiction, and attempts to reduce bias against women and other minorities.[19]

ECONOMICS

The Ascent to Formalism

Early economics (1750–1850) was a worldly social philosophy anxious to understand the real world of human society. By mid-nineteenth century, it had begun its ascent to irrelevant formalism: It became a science and a profession. Despite some variety of perspective and even some occasional heresy, economics settled into an arid formalism. In keeping with the main thrust of Western rationalism, it forsook history and social analysis to search for the truth about a narrow, artificial subject matter—in its case, something called an economy. The economy is real, said economists, and can be understood as a natural system either in or in search of equilibrium. Basing itself largely on deductive rationalism, economics declared that mathematics was the key to understanding how the economy worked. From the 1930s to the 1960s, economics became the most prestigious profession in the social sciences. With the advent of Keynesianism, many believed that it had at last based itself squarely on the fundamental principles underlying economic behavior. But in the 1970s, disillusionment set in as economists confronted stagflation (low growth and high inflation), which their principles said could not happen, and as they realized that they were unable to predict the up and down movements of the economy even in gross terms.

Criticism of economics has centered on its strong penchant for theory, deduction, rationalistic rigor, and mathematics, and its failure to grapple directly with the actual world of economic behavior. Leontief argues that 50 percent of the articles in the *American Economic Review* have no data, and many that have "cooked data".[20] Simon argues that no bad theory in economics goes unrewarded and that he knows of no other science that purportedly is about the real world where statements are made regularly that are contrary to fact.[21] And in a witty technical analysis by an accomplished mathematician-economist, comparing the mathematical approach in economics (allegedly experimental and objective because based on random data) and nonexperimental inference based on experience, Leamer argues that both are the same. Both are based on assumptions, neither are based on data (facts are never given, but are defined phenomena), and neither is objective inference. In Leamer's words, *whim* and *fragility* are fundamental dimensions of science and fundamental dangers: Whimsically-chosen assumptions underlie analysis and lead to conclusions that are fragile because they collapse when assumptions are altered.[22] Davis and Hersh, quoting Kenneth Galbraith, also argue that requiring competence in mathematics for economists, in addition to atrophying judgment and intuition, serves as a way to control labor flows.[23]

Economics at the micro level can be useful (corporations have begun to use economists to assess concrete markets and no longer find them useful as macrolevel analysts). Macroeconomics, however, has had no success at predicting or analyzing the economy as a whole. The reasons are numerous:

1. The economy is changing and becoming more complex.

2. The economy as a whole does not exist apart from the economic behavior of government departments, professions, hospitals, churches, universities, the world market, foreign governments, and so on.

3. Unable to understand the above, economists cannot understand that there are other values in the world besides efficiency. Not knowing this is why they are not good at understanding efficiency itself. Thus economic actors strive for security, work satisfaction; political actors want to reallocate resources to achieve justice; and so on.

4. The basic assumption in economics of an interest-maximizing individual or group is faulty. Not only do actors not behave in narrow efficiency terms, but actors have long memories and behave in terms of their overall experience with the economy. Thus each generation has different memory banks and different ways of interpreting the world.

5. The image in economics of a fluid system of prices and actors in search of equilibrium, thus ensuring efficiency, is also faulty. The concept of equilibrium, however inappropriate, has been borrowed from the natural sciences to form the basic interpretative paradigm of economics (and as we see, in disguised form it also undergirds the other liberal social sciences). The concept of balance is also central to how agrarian elites look at the world.

6. The basic indices that economists use are based on arbitrary and debatable assumptions (for example, unemployment, inflation), tend to turn socially created facts (for example, unemployment) into natural facts, are obsolete (the basic Index of Economic Indicators is anchored in manufacturing, and has changed little since it was first developed in 1937 despite the fact that over two-thirds of our economy is now geared to services), or fail to account for large amounts of economic data (for example, the underground and informal economy).

Economics also suffers because of its theory of modernization—see "The Academic (Functional) View of the Professions" in Chapter 2). And it has also developed a false picture of the international economy to match the false one it has of the domestic economy. International economics emerged during the post–World War II period as an extension of laissez-faire domestic economics. Liberal economists simply looked at the world economy in the same way that they looked on the domestic economy: Economic drives and interests are given; economic behavior is a natural process that can and must be severed from non-rational politics and national customs; trade and investment must be free (private); and nations must pursue what they are best suited for in a grand global division of labor. If all this takes place, argue liberal economists, a mutually beneficial world economy will emerge and with it prosperity, stability, and peace. Socialism and communism, they argue, are wrongful limits on natural domestic and international economies, which, ultimately are part of a one-world economy.[24]

Economics and Public Policy: Keynesianism as Technocratic Formalism

Economists stress the scientific nature of their work and decry artificial interference with the natural economy they say they have uncovered (or are still uncovering). As such, they feel free to advise governments and politicians and to educate the young. The high point of economics as public policy is Keynesianism whose main attraction is that it holds out the promise of a nonpolitical, nondivisive way to provide a technical fix to whatever ails the economy. But even though Keynesianism is a nonstructural approach to the economy and thus bound to fail, Republicans and Democrats each remain committed to their separate versions of it.

Keynes argued that the economy is not governed by an inherent process of equilibrium. The economy contains no principles that will produce full employment (the full use of material and human resources). Economic groups, especially business firms, but also labor unions, professions, and other private groups want control, not competition. Thus the economy as a whole lacks the flexibility (markets) that ensures adaptation to new conditions. Over time, there is disequilibrium. Savings do not all go into productive investment; demand can falter and snowball into recession, and even depression, as business cuts back production. Thus, argued Keynes, the government has a continuous and legitimate role in directing the economy.

Though never clear on what the government's role is, Keynes suggested that government could keep the economy growing in a balanced manner (full employment with price stability) in three ways: by acting as a consumer (for example, government spending for housing or public works), by cutting taxes to give private consumers or producers more money to spend (even if it means a public deficit), and by adjusting interest rates (the price that consumers and producers pay for credit) either to stimulate or to slow down consumption and investment.

The two dominant American political parties have both adopted Keynesianism, but they interpret it differently. The Democratic party emphasizes government spending and giving tax cuts to individual consumers to stimulate the economy (demand-side economics), while the Republican party rejects government spending and emphasizes giving tax cuts to business to stimulate economic growth (supply-side economics). But the U.S. experience with a *mixed economy* (a private economy dependent in important ways on government activity) is not overly positive. Democratic administrations have had some success in stimulating the economy by enhancing consumer demand but have been unable to control inflation. The Republican administration of 1980 inaugurated an approach emphasizing tax cuts for producers. After more than a decade of experience with supply-side economics, almost all analysts agreed that tax cuts for business and well-to-do individuals did not succeed in producing more capital investment or in improving productivity.[25]

Gordon argues that mainstream economics is diverse and more than willing to acknowledge that it has no principles or indubitable truths about how the economy works. But in their public utterances, American economists hew to a narrow party line—here, they say, are the principles that must guide public policy. In knee-jerk unison, they refer to the absolute need to reduce government deficits, government spending, government regulations, and taxes on capital and income. Even mainstream economic research has questioned these alleged principles. Like a Greek chorus, public-policy economists chant free trade, liberate the market, and reduce the power of trade unions. Again, even mainstream research cannot substantiate such conclusions.

Gordon's reason for the narrow and stunted public policy discussions in the United States (Continental European economists differ significantly from American economists on all economic issues) is that our think tanks and policy institutes, the media, and politicians and their staffs promulgate these mainstream formalisms. In addition, introductory economics textbooks enunciate them as laws, graduate training and graduate school textbooks are far removed from the actual economy, the labor market for economists is tightly controlled and standardized by fifteen or so graduate schools, and economists have yet to acknowledge the role of metaphor, appeals to authority, and other nonscientific assumptions underlying their science.[26]

Economics, the Poor, and Minorities

Adam Smith's *The Wealth of Nations* understandably focused on how wealth is created. Unfortunately, economics has continued this focus long after it became obvious that society and its economy was also a potent generator of poverty. Though a few economists have done some serious work on poverty, the field has failed utterly to include poverty as an organic feature of capitalism and thus a topic central to its life. Unable to analyze the economy in a sociohistorical context, economics has failed to acknowledge the indispensable role of surplus, cheap labor in the creation of wealth. And it has been unable to acknowledge the indispensible functions that the poor perform for capitalism.[27] Today, it is unable to see that the global market economy has disconnected large numbers of Americans from meaningful work and has systematically lowered the standard of living of most other Americans. Largely, a captive of professional pretensions and benefits, and enjoying strong confirmation of its empty theories from both major political parties, economics continues to stress the fetish of economic growth. Unfortunately, the indicator used for measuring growth, the Gross Domestic Product, is a useless tangle of contradictions and distractions (for a fuller discussion of this and other indicators, see "Reconstructing Our Basic Indicators" in Chapter 11).

Uninterested in poverty, it is understandable that economics has shown virtually no interest in racial and ethnic minorities or in women. Its lack of interest in minorities also stems from the fact that minorities, including women, are in short supply as members of economics departments. Given its focus on abstract economic growth, nonexistent rational man, and magical meritocratic processes, economics is utterly unable to understand that capitalism both undermines and creates minorities and that it exhibits a greater trend toward the latter than the former.

African Americans, for example, were deeply deprived of the personality and family traits needed to function in American society by slavery and segregation. Their condition improved between 1875 and 1950 because of their movement into the lower reaches of the northern industrial economy (and wartime labor shortages). But their position stagnated and for many deteriorated after 1950 thanks to the movement of capital outside the northern economy to cheap labor areas in the United States and abroad, and to increased educational requirements that only the established middle classes could meet.

The neglect of women by economics is comprehensive, from showing no interest in housework as work, arbitrary disparity in pay for similar work, a gender gap in income and authority for the same education and experience, and for continuing to hang on to its assumption that economic behavior is impersonal, rational, and self-interested and should be studied in the same way, an assumption that is masculine bias as well as scientifically faulty.[28]

Deep down, economics confuses its artificial ideal world with reality, a simple but fatal confusion of "ought" and "is." Like elites in general, it resists new ways of thinking, having become a knee-jerk formalism. In Kuttner's words, there is no free market in ideas in economics. Like all the academic disciplines, economics has floundered on the false distinction between a theoretical and an applied science. Like them, it will improve its validity and usefulness only if it enters public policy (read social policy) with both feet.

Critics charge that economics has achieved theoretical rigor by ignoring many important variables (technology, politics, government, law, religion, education, crime, international events). Theoretical vigor (empty generalizations) is also achieved by ignoring the history of economic institutions and comparative economic systems. One searches in vain in mainstream economics for serious discussions of poverty, ethnic and racial minorities, and women (has feminism affected economics at all?). Is there any understanding in American economics that government regulations are not only inescapable but a positive force for efficiency (as well as inefficiency)? Do economists understand that much of how we allocate resources depends on tax and other legislation? Are they aware that other capitalist societies define the basic categories of economic analysis (for example, capital, savings, labor) differently?[29]

The formalism of American economics and its inability to provide useful predictions and policies has led to some soul searching among economists. On the whole, however, the profession has been highly resistant to change. Tightly organized, and with a secure base in academe, the profession listens to and rewards only the faithful. Until economists are simply those who have decided to focus their historical, political, and sociological knowledge on economic behavior, economics will continue to impoverish the mind and society. By becoming a technical, deductive, value-free discipline, economics is unable to talk about its own subject matter.[30]

POLITICAL SCIENCE

The Sociology of a Nonpolitical Discipline

At a 1990 roundtable discussion of the nature of contemporary political science, sponsored by the American Political Science Association, political scientists agreed that their discipline is characterized by fragmentation and descensus.[31] All agreed that the field lacks a defining core and that the need for unity is urgent. Various proposals were made to bridge the differences among political scientists: reliance on political theory, more critical self-awareness, more commonsense discussion of politics, and so on.

The roundtable also revealed that political scientists cannot talk about themselves in political terms anymore than they can talk about the United States in political terms. Almost all political scientists are liberals, whether they espouse behavioralism, rational-choice theory, eclectic analysis, or natural law philosophy. No one at the roundtable discussion mentioned that political science reflects society and that it is in disarray because society is in disarray. Aside from socialist, and perhaps some Thomistic and self-conscious anti-modern theorists, mainstream political science is an expression of and an unwitting defense of capitalist democracy, American-style. O'Brien, for example, shows the pull of time and place in American political science. In the period after World War II, while their country was prosperous and exercised world leadership, American political scientists optimistically promoted democracy at home and abroad. As troubles developed at home during the sixties and as American power went into relative decline in the seventies, American political scientists began to stress elitism, stability, and value consensus.[32]

Lowi has criticized political science for moving away from "judgmental and evaluative thinking." Starting in the nineteenth century with the call for a science of administration (which presumed the "American system was permanent," paralleled by the association of political science with reform (which also presumes the system is sound), political science eventually succumbed completely to public-policy analysis and economics (ways to shut off debate with impressions of certainty). For Lowi, political science has become what it studies, an adjunct of the state, in effect, a nationalized discipline supplying legitimacy to an unexamined society.[33]

Sustaining Formalism

Like the other social sciences, political science also became a profession and a special discipline in the nineteenth century, and it too suffers from irrelevance and formalism.[34] The emptiness of political science is not as apparent as the emptiness of economics because it has not succumbed as fully to the quantitative, value-free perspective. Political science departments still teach the history of political theory and while they may pretend that the past is but prologue to the present, students cannot escape learning at least some history and gaining some awareness of the sociology of knowledge (or how symbols tend to reflect social conditions unbeknownst to the symbol makers). And formalism is curbed because political science is forced to go outside the presuppositions of the field to study interest groups, campaign financing, the mass media, and so on.

The view of modernization in political science is as deficient as it is in the other social sciences—see "The Academic (Functional) View of the Professions" in Chapter 2. Almond has written the summary statement for a recent collection of mainstream essays on Third World political development. His essay congratulates mainstream modernization theory in political science, affirms the empirical, value-neutral approach, and dismisses dependency theory altogether.[35] Lucien Pye's presidential address (1991) to the American Political Science Association said that the collapse of state socialism has vindicated modernization theory. Other political scientists, seeking to explain the changes in the USSR and Eastern Europe, also rely on the core assumptions of political science (politics can be explained without recourse to history, economics, and sociology). The net result is to create the false impression that representative government in the same thing as democracy and that something called a market society actually exists, or can be established.

The main thrust of mainstream political theory seems to have gone in the direction of rational-choice theory, or political actors can be understood in the same way as economic actors, as rational choosers,[36] and in the direction of philosophy.[37] In a masterful summary of the relations among political theory, political science, and politics in American history, Gunnell has shown how political theory, anchored in academia, created a fictitious concept of a "great political theory tradition", while ignoring the central tradition in Western social theory of trying to relate theory and practice—in short, American political theory is not about politics. Along the way, political science, via its invention, political theory, sought to provide an ideological basis for American liberalism as well as a rationale for the U.S. as a world power, something especially apparent during the 1930s and 1940s. As for the rest of political science, it adopted an objective, nonpolitical approach to political behavior based on a different myth, that it was modeling itself on natural science.[38]

Political Science and Minorities

Political science pays considerable attention to racial and ethnic minorities and to women, but only as political actors in a nonproblematic political and social system. Thus there are studies of voting by these various minorities and analyses of constitutional questions revolving around representation and about matters of special interest to minorities. But there is no awareness of the failure of American society to integrate its minorities, including women, and more importantly, of its apparent inherent inability to do so. As with economics, political science has yet to ask itself: Can the United States really function without a large and steady supply of victims?

Political science lacks a large enough contingent of African, Hispanic, and Asian Americans and of women of all races among its ranks to be influenced along the above lines. Political science seems to have been almost as completely unaffected by feminism as economics though some valuable work by women on women in the history of political theory and in the modern state has emerged.[39] Marxist political scientists are the main opposition to mainstream political science, but they appear to be small in number and to work outside the main stream. As with all marginal groups in all spheres of knowledge production and transmission, from left to right and including feminists, Marxist political scientists have their own journals, associations, caucuses, and centers of influence.

The professionalization of political science has pulled it deep into liberal society. By adopting an apolitical perspective, it ceased being about politics. By becoming ahistorical and quantitative, it lost sight of the changing impact on politics of the economy, religion, and other social variables. As is true of the other liberal disciplines, its narrow, value-free focus means that it can analyze only means in a taken-for-granted world of ends. Unlike the great political economists of the past, it cannot address its own subject matter, what polity best serves what set of human values?[40] Domestic political science hides the United States, while comparative political science hides the rest of the world.

HISTORY

History as Mainstream Social Science

History was once social and moral analysis framed as a story. It became a profession in the late nineteenth century and has gone the way of the other academic disciplines. It is now a fragmented collection of subspecialties, each of which speaks only to itself and whatever batch of students it happens to have. And it too is filled with the same arguments that occur in other disciplines: quantitative versus qualitative methods, value-neutrality versus the use of value judgments, objective versus interpretive analysis.

American history has been enriched by critics, mostly Marxists and feminists, who have pointed out the many biases of mainstream historians. Marxist historians have provided new perspectives on slavery, work, the Progressive movement, the New Deal, and foreign policy. Feminist scholars have also revised our basic perception of the past. As noted earlier, anthropology (a form of history) has had to change its view of biological evolution as well as social evolution to give females their due, thanks to feminist scholars. And, as also noted earlier, feminist scholars have changed our view of the history of social theory and of natural science.

History and the Politics of National Identity

Mainstream history's biggest failure is the high school history text. Critics argue that American high school history textbooks are highly deficient and biased, *leaving out what appear to be the main variables and happenings in our history* (it is important to note that which is left out is whatever is disagreeable or controversial).[41] To make history agreeable is also to make it dull which requires considerable effort. It also requires framing facts in one way and leaving out facts. A recent analysis of the five leading high-school history texts also finds them to be seriously deficient, amounting to fluff and failing in all respects in imparting the knowledge and values needed by a democratic citizenry.[42]

One reason why high school history texts are false, beset by the further sin of dullness, is well known: Publishers must gain adoptions from state and local school boards and the latter tell them what is permissible and non-permissible in America's classrooms. Here as elsewhere, the professional is profiting from a market society without being subject to its workings. Understanding the political pressures that have dumbed down our high school history texts might lead one to assume that the authors knew more than they wrote. In one of our rare looks at college history texts, analysts report that these texts fail by a wide margin to provide a balanced discussion of science and technology.[43] Science and technology in college history texts are depicted as natural, inexorable forces that lead to positive social consequences. There is no mention of the use and misuse of science to justify racism and sexism. The politics of science and technology for national defense, in war, for research, for nuclear development, and so on are absent. The role of science and technology in fostering economic concentration, polluting the environment, and creating an excessively costly, depersonalized health-care system are also overlooked.

The 1994 report of a national commission to establish new (up-to-date) standards in the teaching of high school history raised considerable opposition from conservatives who objected to the report's critical tone and its failure to celebrate America as a democracy along with its heroes.[44] Two things are important about the controversy: one, the refusal of historians to acknowledge the inescapable role of interpretation in science, and two, their failure to recognize that history is as much as anything, a political struggle to control how a nation's identity is defined. Failure to recognize these two things can be substantiated by simply noting that historians were surprised that the report led to serious controversy.

History as the Analysis of the Possible

History emerges from consciousness of change. It leads to curiosity as to where institutions come from and what causes they are subject to. History is about the real world of past, present, and future. History is always in tension with static absolutes, with the myths of a given culture. But history is also a collaboration with myth, sometimes wittingly, sometimes not. American historical thought, for example, has undergone stages in keeping with America's central myths. Except for a brief period, roughly 1890 to 1940, it has been mostly a handmaiden of Christian and liberal myths. Even when it emerged from myth in the first half of this century it did not go much beyond American liberalism.[45]

Novick discusses the profession of history in terms of the standard of objectivity. This standard was upheld until 1914, challenged between the two World Wars, and reasserted during the Cold War. Today, says Novick, the field is characterized by widespread uncertainty and division, and the ideal of objectivity has become problematic.[46] Ironically, division and uncertainty have tended to polarize and foster an ahistorical argument about truth. Instead of providing a picture of the past to help us cope with the present and create a future, history either philosophizes (we can or cannot understand the totality of history), or aspires to become a science. In either case, history is dominated by an ahistorical standard of truth. Here it joins the other social sciences in affirming the status quo (the myths by which we see and do not see). Here it loses control of history to those who are more interested in myth than useful knowledge. Here all lose control of the past to those who make it serve the present (for example, by writing the history of World War II to glorify America, or rewriting the history of the Vietnam war to protect America from blame). At its best, American history has never been on a par with European history. At its worst, it has helped America "wander out of history."

Susman quotes Van Wyck Brooks approvingly to say that historians should be looking for a "usable past." That is certainly a first step. This is not a call to invent the past, but to relate the past to present problems. It is not a call for subjectivism against objectivism, but an honest interpretive analysis that sheds light on a current policy problem.[47]

On a still broader level, history is the way in which we can reflect on what we are and what we can be. Genuine history is not an American (or German, Japanese, or other nationality) looking at the past using current American eyes. History is the making of various worlds by humans and its study offers the possibility of a wholesale restructuring of life. The key originator of an important aspect of this view of history was Giambattista Vico (1668–1744), who argued that the facts that historians deal with (unlike natural science) are not data (givens), but human creations.

The philosopher who more than anyone developed this point of view was R. G. Collingwood (1889–1943). Collingwood's objective was to establish the field of history as something different from philosophy and from science (positivism).[48] The main tendency in Greek thought, said Collingwood, was based on an anti-historical metaphysics. The idea of history, however, was clearly developed in the work of Herodotus, the first to use the word *history* to imply an inquiry into what human beings *qua* human beings had done. Though Collingwood ranks Herodotus and Socrates as the two innovating geniuses of the fifth century B.C., he points out that

Herodotus had no successors (with the possible exception of Thucydides), whereas Socrates had many.

The failure of Herodotus to attract followers, said Collingwood, is crucially important for understanding the history of the idea of history. The Greeks became sensitive to history for the simple reason that they had experienced the violent fluctuations of social change. They came to feel that the world of flux could never be an object of cognition. No knowledge gained through the sensory perception of the inconstant world was reliable; only that based on the stationary could properly be called knowledge. Thus, the uncertainty of temporal existence prompted the Greeks to search behind events for an unchanging substance. Thus history itself engendered the mode of thought that outlawed the historical as knowledge.

But, says Collingwood, the actual history of philosophy shows it to be a reflection on social change, a qualitative shift from one mode of experience, for example, agrarian to early capitalism, stimulating deep reflection on and changed conceptions of the nature of mind. Thus philosophy, and by implication social science and history, is essentially a reflection on the possibilities presented by human experience. That American history is a search for universals only in the American experience means that American citizens and policymakers have been cut off from the full possibilities of human life by yet another of the social sciences.

SUMMARY

A summary of the academic disciplines appears at the end of Chapter 5.

NOTES

1. Anthony Giddens, *The Constitution of Society: Outline of a Theory of Structuration* (Berkeley: University of California Press, 1984).
2. Lewis A. Coser, "The Functions of Small-Group Research," *Social Problems* (1955): 1–6; "Presidential Address: Two Methods in Search of a Substance," *American Sociological Review* 40 (December 1975): 691–700.
3. Veronica Stolte Heiskanan, "The Myth of the Middle-Class Family in American Sociology," *American Sociologist* 6 (February 1971): 14–18.
4. L. Paul Metzger, "American Sociology and Black Assimilation: Conflicting Perspectives," *American Journal of Sociology* 76 (January 1971): 627–647.
5. Wayne J. Villemez, "Explaining Inequality: A Survey of Perspectives Represented in Introductory Sociology Textbooks," *Contemporary Sociology* 9 (January 1980): 35–39. For earlier criticisms of bias in American stratification analysis, see John Pease, William H. Form, and Joan Huber Rytina, "Ideological Currents in American Stratification Literature," *American Sociologist* 5 (May 1970): 127–137, and Lewis A. Coser, "Presidential Address: Two Methods in Search of a Substance, "*American Sociological Review* 40 (December 1975): 691–700. Also see the discussion of status attainment theory in Chapter 3.
6. For an outline of types of sexist bias in research, see "Sexist Biases in Sociological Research: Problems and Issues," report of the Committee on the Status of Women in Sociology, American Sociological Association, *Footnotes* 8, no. 1 (Jan-

uary 1980): 8–9, Sharlene J. Hesse, Ina B. Burnstein, and Geri E. Atkins, "Sex Roles Bias in Public Opinion Questionnaires," *Social Policy* 10, no. 3 (November/December, 1979): 51–56, and Rosalie H. Wax, "Gender and Age in Fieldwork and Fieldwork Education: No Good Thing Is Done by Any Man Alone," *Social Problems* 26, no. 5 (June 1979): 509–522. For a more general analysis, see Judith Stacy and Barrie Thorne, "The Missing Feminist Revolution in Sociology," *Social Problems* 32, no. 4 (April 1985): 301–316.

7. C. Wright Mills, "The Professional Ideology of Social Pathologists," *American Journal of Sociology* 49 (September 1943): 165–180 (Mills notes that prominent sociologists also exerted these biases in the textbooks they wrote); R. E. Hilbert and Charles E. Wright, "Representations of Merton's Theory of Anomie," *American Sociologist* 14 (August 1979): 150–156; and Alexander Liazos, "The Poverty of the Sociology of Deviance: Nuts, Sluts, and Preverts [sic]," *Social Problems* 20 (Summer 1972): 103–120.

8. Warren R. Papp's examination of fifty introductory texts, published between 1977 and 1980, reveals a consensus on Weber's macrolevel definition of power with emphasis on legitimated forms of power; see his article "The Concept of Power: Treatment in Fifty Introductory Sociology Textbooks," *Teaching Sociology* 9 (October 1981): 57–68. Papp criticizes the absence of microlevel discussions of power as poor teaching. This absence, plus the small and highly formal discussion of macrolevel power in introductory texts, is also poor sociology.

9. Robert E. Wood, "Conflict Theory as Pedagogy: A Critique from the Left," *Teaching Sociology* 10 (July 1983): 463–485.

10. For an indictment of sociology's lack of interest in comparative research, see Paul Hollander, "Comparative Sociology in the United States and Why There Is So Little of It," in Scott G. McNall and Gary N. Howe, eds., *Current Perspectives in Social Theory*, vol. 2 (Greenwich, Conn: JAI Press, 1981), pp. 21–29. For an indictment of American social science as parochial, see Frederick H. Gareau, "The United States as a Center of Social Science," *Social Science Quarterly* 65 (September 1984): 840–847. In an article following Garneau's, Norval Glenn argues that American sectarianism also stems from narrow specialization within social science and within each of the social sciences; ibid., 848–853. For the continued lack of comparative and historical materials in the introductory text, see Stephen K. Sanderson, "The Provincialism of Introductory Sociology," *Teaching Sociology* 12, no. 4 (July 1985): 394–410. The lack of an international context in the entire undergraduate sociology curriculum was found by a task force, formed by the ASA Committee on International Sociology; see *Footnotes*, February 1993, p. 8.

11. C. Wright Mills, "The Professional Ideology of Social Pathologists," *American Journal of Sociology* 49 (September 1943): 165–180.

12. Ben Aggar, "Do Books Write Authors? A Study of Disciplinary Hegemony," *Teaching Sociology* 17 (July 1989): 365–369.

13. Sarah Rengel Phillips, "The Hegemony of Heterosexuality: A Study of Introductory Texts," *Teaching Sociology* 19 (October 1991): 454–463.

14. Patricia A. Roos and Katherine W. Jones, "Shifting Gender Boundaries: Women's Inroads into Academic Sociology," in Jerry A. Jacobs, ed., *Gender Inequality at Work* (Thousand Oaks, Calif: Sage, 1995), chap. 11.

15. Henrika Kuklick, *The Savage Within: The Social History of British Anthropology, 1885–1945* (New York: Cambridge University Press, 1991).

16. For valuable essays providing concrete details about the use of Western ideas (for example, Western legal concepts such as rights, duties, and property), as well as an emphasis on how Westerners, including anthropologists, created the tribal identities they claimed existed, and changed their ways of formulating their depiction of colonies to suit economic interests and to create the illusion that the gap between colony and home country was narrowing, see George W. Stocking, Jr., ed., *Colonial Situations: Essays on the Contextualization of Ethnographic Knowledge*

(Madison: University of Wisconsin Press, 1991). For an indictment of anthropology, not only for inventing the idea of a primitive society but for hanging onto the empty ideal for so long (since it served the interests of liberals, Marxists, imperialists, and nationalists), see Adam Kuper, *The Invention of Primitive Society: Transformations of an Illusion* (New York: Routledge Press, 1988).

17. See for example, Clifford Geertz, *Works and Lives: The Anthropologist as Author* (Stanford, Calif.: Stanford University Press, 1988), and George W. Stocking, Jr., *The Ethnographer's Magic and Other Essays in the History of Anthropology* (Madison: University of Wisconsin Press, 1992), especially chap. 8.

18. Roger M. Keesing, "Anthropology as Interpretive Quest," *Current Anthropology* 28 (April 1987): 161–176.

19. For a valuable analysis that links positivist ethnography in anthropology from the 1920s to the 1960s to the parallel rise of ethnographic studies of American subcultures in sociology, and links both to postmodernist critiques, see Andrea Fontana, "Ethnographic Trends in the Postmodern Era," in D. R. Dickens and Andrea Fontana, eds., *Postmodernism and Social Inquiry* (New York: Guilford Press, 1994), chap. 9.

20. Wassily Leontief, "Interview: Why Economics Needs Input-Output Analysis," *Challenge* (March–April, 1985): 27–35.

21. Herbert A. Simon, "Interview: The Failure of Arm Chair Economics," *Challenge* (November–December, 1986): 18–25.

22. Edward E. Leamer, "Let's Take the Con Out of Econometrics," *American Economic Review* 73 (March 1983): 31–43.

23. Philip J. Davis and Reuben Hersh, *Descartes' Dream: The World According to Mathematics* (San Diego: Harcourt Brace Jovanovich, 1986), p. 101.

24. For a well-written and balanced presentation and defense of the liberal position, see Franklin R. Root, *International Trade and Investment*, 7th ed. (Cincinnati: South-West Publishing Co., 1994). (This is also the major textbook on international economics used in American business schools.)

25. The harm done by economics in public policy also takes the form of cost-benefit analysis (see the section on cost-benefit analysis in Chapter 11).

26. David M. Gordon, "'Twixt the Cup and the Lip: Mainstream Economics and the Formation of Economic Policy," *Social Research* 61, no. 1 (Spring 1994): 1–33. Gordon's reference to the monopoly power of a small number of graduate schools over the labor market in economics is a good example of the absence of supply and demand markets in labor in general and the professions in particular. Derek Bok, *The Cost of Talent: How Executives and Professionals Are Paid and How It Affects America* (New York: Free Press, 1993), argues persuasively that there is no competitive labor market for talent and that U.S. institutional biases promote overcompensation for the private professions.

27. Herbert J. Gans, "The Positive Functions of Poverty," *American Journal of Sociology* 78 (September 1972): 175–189; widely reprinted.

28. For a general discussion of the discipline along the latter lines, see Julie A. Nelson, *Feminism, Objectivity, and Economics* (New York: Routledge, 1996). For concrete examples of racial, ethnic, and gender bias in the various professions, see later in the chapter and the text.

29. For a valuable critique of mainstream economics that revolves around the arbitrary nature of many of its main assumptions, see Fred Block, *Postindustrial Possibilities: A Critique of Economic Discourse* (Berkeley: University of California Press, 1990).

30. For much of the above, see Melville J. Ulmer, "Economics in Decline," *Commentary* 78 (November 1984): 42–46; Robert Kuttner, "The Poverty of Economics," *Atlantic Monthly* 255 (February 1985): 74–84; and Lester Thurow, *Dangerous Currents: The State of Economics* (New York: Random House, 1983).

31. *PS: Political Science & Politics* 23 (March 1990): 34–43.

32. For an analysis of American political science from this perspective, see Donal Cruise O'Brien, "Modernization, Order, and the Erosion of the Democratic Ideal," in David Lehmann, ed., *Development Theory* (Totawa, N.J.: Frank Case, 1979). For a similar critique of British anthropology as a follower of Britain's national fortunes, see the section on Anthropology.

33. Theodore J. Lowi, "The State in Political Science: How We Became What We Study," *American Political Science Review* 86, no. 1 (March 1992): 1–7. The use of the social sciences by the state was done explicitly in Europe, but since World War II, Europe has followed the American model (namely, either the open or the indirect use of empirical knowledge to manage a technocratic state).

34. Stefan Collini, Donald Winch, and John Burrow, *That Noble Science of Politics: A Study in Nineteenth-Century Intellectual History* (London: Cambridge University Press, 1983).

35. Gabriel A. Almond, "The Development of Political Development [Sic]" in Myron Weiner and Samuel P. Huntington, eds., *Understanding Political Development* (Boston: Little, Brown, 1987), pp. 437–478.

36. See, for example, James M. Buchanan and Gordon Tullock, *The Calculus of Consent* (Ann Arbor: University of Michigan Press, 1962). Important attempts to understand political phenomena from this perspective have also been made by Anthony Downs, *An Economic Theory of Democracy* (New York: Harper Row, 1957) and Mancur Olson, *The Logic of Collective Action: Public Goods and the Theory of Groups* (Cambridge, Mass.: Harvard University Press, 1965).

37. See, for example, John Rawls, *A Theory of Justice* (Cambridge, Mass.: Harvard University Press, 1971), and Robert Nozick, *Anarchy, State, and Utopia* (New York: Basic Books, 1974).

38. John G. Gunnell, *Between Philosophy and Politics: The Alienation of Political Theory* (Amherst: University of Massachussetts Press, 1986), and a followup history, *The Descent of Political Theory: The Genealogy of an American Vocation* (Chicago: University of Chicago Press, 1993). A similar development, based on a fictitious tradition of classic literature as a support for America as a world power, occurred in the humanities: see "Literary Studies" in Chapter 5.

39. See, for example, Arlene W. Saxonhouse, *Women in the History of Political Thought: Ancient Greece to Machiavelli* (New York: Praeger, 1985), and Catherine A. MacKinnon, *Toward a Feminist Theory of the State* (Cambridge, Mass.: Harvard University Press, 1989).

40. Arguing from a conservative perspective (there is a human nature; life is tragic; humans have to be helped to be better; society is a great conversation about values, God, and how to live), David M. Ricci, *The Tragedy of Political Science: Politics, Scholarship, and Democracy* (New Haven, Conn.: Yale University Press, 1984), makes similar charges, though he does not identify political science's downfall with capitalism. Political science, he argues, is now a narrow professional group, its product emerges from the way university departments are organized, and it cannot address the basic value issues that have always marked the field.

41. Jean Anyon, "Ideology and United States History Textbooks," *Harvard Educational Review* 49 (August 1979): 361–386; Frances Fitzgerald, *America Revised: History Textbooks in America* (Boston: Little Brown, 1979).

42. Paul Gagnon, "Why Study History," *Atlantic Monthly* 263 (November 1988): 43–66.

43. J. L. Heilbron and Daniel J. Kevles, "By Failing to Discuss the 'Civics' of Science and Technology, History Textbooks Distort the Past and Endanger the Future," *Chronicle of Higher Education* 35 (February 15, 1989), p. A48.

44. For background, see Karen J. Winkler, "Who Owns History," *Chronicle of Higher Education*, 61 (January 20, 1995): 10ff.

45. Warren I. Susman, *Culture as History* (New York: Pantheon, 1973), chap. 1.
46. Peter Novick, *That Noble Dream: The "Objectivity Question" and the American Historical Profession* (New York: Cambridge University Press, 1988).
47. For a valuable example, Richard E. Neustadt and Ernest R. May, *Thinking in Time: The Uses of History for Decision-Makers* (New York: Free Press, 1986).
48. R. G. Collingwood, *The Idea of History* (New York: Oxford University Press, 1956); first published in 1946.

5
Academic Disciplines II

◆　◆　◆　◆

◆　◆　◆　◆

THE NATURAL SCIENCES

Attacks on science and knowledge elites are common in Western history. The Bible equates knowledge with the fall of humankind. In the modern period, traditionalists disputed claims by science that it could establish truth and virtue, and warned that science and technology had negative consequences. But until recently, attacks on science were largely from the outside by theologians, romantic artists, disgruntled workers—criticism of science *from within science* was rare. In recent decades, however, the sociology of science has raised doubts even about that holy of holies, basic scientific research in the natural sciences.

The Academic Sociology of Natural Science

The old faith in science can be seen in the sociology of Robert K. Merton. Merton's explanation of how science works was directly in line with the French Enlightenment and the main current of liberalism. Scientists, argued Merton, are animated by four shared norms:

1. Universalism: Science is above race and nationality.
2. Communalism: Scientific knowledge belongs to everybody and should not become private property.
3. Disinterestedness: Scientists should not let self-interest interfere with or bias their work.
4. Organized skepticism: Scientists should systematically search for truth, they should never accept theories on faith, and they should be skeptical until the facts show otherwise.[1]

The triumph of this view of science created the impression that a full-bodied, reality-based knowledge-generating process, with distinct and identifiable properties, had emerged and that deviations from it came from the outside or were vestiges of the past. The history of natural science, however, tells a different story.

The Conflict Sociology of Natural Science

Sociologists in the conflict tradition have shown that the norms allegedly governing the behavior of scientists are consistently violated.[2] Natural science's claim that it is apolitical and based on universal norms and values has been challenged and rejected. Natural scientists have been found to be secretive, political, ambitious, and prestige-conscious. Serious doubts have been raised about the peer review process governing grants and publications.[3] A recent, pioneering national survey of faculty and graduate students in chemistry, civil engineering, microbiology, and sociology found that various forms of misconduct (plagiarism, the use of fraudulent data, misuse of facilities for personal gain) were far from rare.[4] Suspicions have also grown about the traditional belief that pure or basic research precedes and is necessary to the development of technology.[5] We have also now begun to realize that knowledge-makers are employees who work for governments, foundations, or profit making businesses and that their work is used for a variety of purposes only partly understood by the scientist employees. We now know that knowledge is private property in a number of different senses and that its alleged generation for the public good is highly suspect. In short, scientific ideals form an ideological smokescreen which shields science from evaluation, helps it raise money, furthers careers, and helps some groups and harms other groups.

Natural science's deviation from ideal norms is far more than the deviance of individuals or the result of special circumstances. An entire discipline may overlook an anomaly (an observed fact that cannot be explained by existing theory) for decades, even centuries.[6] There are doubtless correctable deficiencies in natural science, but its embeddedness in history and society, especially the central power structure of given ages, comprises its core identity. It is now more fully understood that natural science represents social behavior and that being a scientist affords one no special protection against the biases and values of one's society or era. Despite their brilliance at science, the ancient Greeks failed to develop an empirical science, or to use science for the creation of technological devices because (for one thing) they had slaves. The English spearheaded the rise of empirical science largely to serve the needs of industry, warfare, and imperial expansion. German scientists served both the Kaiser and Adolph Hitler. In short, natural scientists are integral members of national communities and willingly use their knowledge to further national ambitions of varying kinds, including war, conquest, and genocide.

An important latent function in the relation between natural science and government was revealed in a recent study by Chandra Mukerji.[7] In an insightful study of marine biologists, Mukerji argues that natural scientists do not really understand the essential process of government funding. What really takes place, says Mukerji, is that scientists get money to do autonomous research (which they justify politically with clichés about serving the economy and national defense), and in exchange, the government gets the cultural authority of science for its policies. The best way to see this, says Mukerji, is to realize that the government often does not care about results: Its main purpose is to develop an *elite reserve labor force* that is on hand to use as experts, either singly or as aggregates, during emergencies. Government purposes are achieved by funding basic research through the National Science Foundation and the National Institutes of Health in order to determine what constitutes *quality* in natural science and by using large sums of *soft* (uncertain, scarce) money to create a dependent force of scientists across a wide spectrum of specialized fields.

It is also worth noting that scientific discoveries do not always occur because goal-oriented professionals are following institutionalized scientific procedures. Though one needs a motivated and skilled person, it must be noted that a significant number of important scientific and technological discoveries have been made by accident.[8]

○ Science as a Legitimating Facade

The use of natural science by government (which means, of course, by the governing elites that dominate the political process) to justify both specific politics and uphold the social order as such deserves an extra word. Robert Wuthnow has pointed to the way in which the emergence of distinct nation states during the fifteenth and sixteenth centuries helped the rise of modern science. The absolute monarchies of that era gave science extensive support, not for the practical benefits it might bring, but to acquire legitimacy by associating their regimes and the emerging nation state with higher learning and the cosmic forces that learning had uncovered (climaxed by the politically useful Newtonian world scheme of balance).[9] In an age of religion and political conflict, science also served as a way in which the state could claim that it was in tune with the natural normative order that transcended historical diversity and uncertainty.

By the end of the sixteenth century, natural scientists were communicating easily across Europe and belonged to many scientific academies besides those in their native country. Scientists also found it easy to move from one country to another as nation states vied for the legitimacy that they provided. The association of science with the state had many consequences for the nature of science. Above all, science could now claim to be nonpolitical and autonomous, public-spirited, and in pursuit of knowledge for its own sake.

The relation between the state and science has continued into the present. Today, the priorities of not only natural science but all science, including scientific education, are deeply influenced by the state. Of course, science today is used more openly for the practical benefits it might bring. But, the state still obtains legitimacy from science, and it still gains it for its nonscientific policies. Natural scientists throughout the federal government help justify debatable policies in regard to health care, agriculture, energy, land use, and so on. A parallel can be found in economics, which pretends to be science, but in reality provides a legitimating facade for biased policies throughout the federal system, most especially through the Council of Economic Advisors, the Federal Reserve Board, the Department of the Treasury and Commerce, and the Department of Energy.[10] One thing has changed, however—the easy pretense that government policies are scientific appears to have ended.

Plant Science in the Service of Power

A comprehensive sociohistorical analysis of plant science[11] raises serious reservations about the alleged neutrality of science. From 1492 on, Western imperial powers took plants from their colonies to study at botanical gardens at home. This was part of a vast transfer of plants from one colony to another and from colony to home country in order to spur export agriculture and to secure a food supply at home. The rapid development of plant science after 1900 made it possible to pursue another strategy for profit. Selling seeds was not profitable as long as farmers could reproduce their own seed (perennials). And it was not possible to develop a market for seeds as long as government agricultural research stations were distributing their knowledge and finished products free.

The development of hybrid corn yielded the opening wedge of a private-profit business in seeds. In the 1920s and 1930s, seed breeders worked for and final achieved legislation that gave legal protection to private property in plant knowledge. This opened the way for pressure on government to curtail its practice of distributing knowledge free, and to discontinue research on perennials, on how plants resist disease through their own germplasm (rather than through the addition of bacteria, a patentable process), and on plants suitable for small agricultural regions with special conditions.

The genetic revolution of recent years has spurred the privatization of plant knowledge and its protection by the state. This process has ominous implications. Human-made plants tend to replace plants that evolve naturally, thus reducing the stock from which we can learn how plants survive and adapt to changing conditions. Synthetic plants require fertilizer, pesticides, and irrigation; not surprisingly, there is a deep tie among seed breeders and oil and chemical companies. And plant science, along with other technology, has led to economic concentration in seed breeding and supply as well as in agriculture. Along with other factors, plant scientists are part of a private-profit economy that has spurred food production, but has also had serious adverse effects on developing societies, American farmers, and the natural environment.

The New Politics of Science

The vast enlargement of the natural sciences since World War II has been associated with military victory, national prestige, national defense, better health, and economic competitiveness. Though some doubts were raised about natural science during the late '60s and early '70s, and research support faltered, a huge new surge of support for science emerged in 1975. And as Dickson points out, the Reagan administration in the early 1980s accelerated the long-term process linking government funding of research (direct subsidies and tax expenditures) to private advantage (via industry and universities), a process that is turning knowledge into private property and rendering science policy largely immune from democratic control.[12]

The corporate world has also taken the initiative in this area, for one thing, by clearly linking American economic competitiveness and business profits to the need to improve human capital. From elementary school to university, business leaders have stressed abstract academic skills, especially those in natural science. Alongside the theme of human capital, there is also the theme of high technology as the key to the future. These initiatives by business have been supported by federal government funding for technological research with the results turned over free to private business. Higher education and especially its natural science faculties, have eagerly sold their facilities and brains to become part of an evolving industrial-government-education complex.[13] Here again, there is little doubt that education and its professions are an integral part of the capitalist economy.

In recent years, the politics of science has come into its own. Fear, based on actual and potential harm from such things as pesticides, drugs, nuclear energy, and computers has made people and elites much more aware of the political nature of science. The questions keep rising no matter how high the tangible benefits. Even the mighty achievements of American agricultural science have given it no protection against serious criticism. Critics point to a deep bias in agricultural research in favor of fertilizers, pesticides, and machinery, a failure to do research into the harm caused by these technologies, and a neglect of other ways to accomplish the same ends. And politically aware critics have pointed to the links among agricultural research by government and universities, government agencies, university governing boards, chemical and petroleum companies, farm implement manufacturers, credit interests, giant food chains and distributors, and industrial farms (agribusiness). After a half century of damage to soil and water through pesticides and fertilizers (and to the small-farm sector of the agricultural economy), the National Academy of Science announced in 1990 that pesticides and fertilizers are not necessary to a productive agriculture!

Natural Science and Racial, Ethnic, and Gender Minorities

Census and Bureau of Labor Statistics categories for classifying occupations are not reliable—indeed, their use has contaminated American stratification and mobility studies for their entire history. Our data for minorities in the sciences and engineering have been compiled by the National Science Foundation using these and other sources. A study focused on doctorate holders (see Table 5–1) does give some useful precision to the data presented. Though gains have been registered over the past two decades, minorities, especially African Americans, Native Americans, and Hispanics have not made any significant gains let alone breakthroughs. The major explanation is lack of class resources. Asian Americans seem to be doing better than African or Hispanic Americans, but one should not assume that Asian Americans (a diverse group of old and recent immigrants) have found an answer to minority problems. White women are doing the best of all minorities because of their considerable class resources, but they still suffer from what appears to be significant gender discrimination.

Sonnert has conducted an empirical analysis (from a functional-academic perspective explicitly distinguished from the sociopolitical perspective) of the careers of men and women with similar postdoctoral fellowships.[14] What he found is that in biology (which has large numbers of women) a gender gap was not significant. In the physical sciences, mathematics, and engineering, a significant gender gap exists in academic rank and tenure. It should be noted that achievement after the fellowship was taken fully into account.

TABLE 5–1 Female and Minority Proportions of Doctoral Science and Engineering Workforce, by Degree Field: 1991

PROPORTION OF SCIENCE
& ENGINEERING WORKFORCE

	Female	Black	Asian	Native American	Hispanic
			Percent		
Total science and engineering	18.8	2.1	9.8	0.2	1.8
Sciences	21.7	2.2	7.3	0.2	1.8
Physical sciences	8.9	1.1	11.3	0.1	1.7
Mathematics	10.2	1.1	10.7	0.1	2.2
Computer sciences	11.8	0.5	20.3	0.1	1.7
Environmental sciences	9.6	0.2	5.3	0.2	1.0
Life sciences	24.0	1.9	7.8	0.2	1.6
Psychology	38.1	3.1	1.6	0.2	2.0
Social sciences	23.9	4.2	5.6	0.2	2.1
Engineering	3.4	1.2	23.1	0.2	1.9
Aeronautical/astronautical	2.0	1.4	19.3	*	1.5
Chemical	3.7	0.8	24.4	*	1.2
Civil	3.6	2.4	23.0	0.2	2.0
Electrical/electronic	2.5	1.3	23.3	0.1	1.9
Materials	6.0	0.9	25.2	0.2	3.0
Mechanical	2.1	1.4	26.7	0.1	2.0
Nuclear	2.8	0.3	18.8	*	2.8
Systems design	13.4	5.8	15.8	*	4.3
Other engineering	3.2	0.3	20.9	0.4	1.5

NOTE: * = no cases reported.

SOURCE: National Science Board, *Science & Engineering Indicators—1993*, (Washington, D.C.: U.S. Government Printing Office, 1993), p. 81.

The Social Construction of Natural Science

The sociology of the natural sciences has suffered from a preoccupation with whether natural scientists, working in the academic, nonpolitical tradition, are capable of making sound empirical statements about how nature works. The answer to this question is yes. Those who dwell on this issue are guilty of being academic.[15] The real issues about natural science (and mathematics) are the social and political purposes to which they are put. For example, there is little doubt that chemistry can make true statements about the ingredients that make up fertilizers and pesticides. But like the social sciences, chemistry (and the natural sciences) is a selective (biased) process that obtains knowledge about the things that the powerful want knowledge about; it is merely one participant in an overall process that leaves us systematically ignorant (because it asks some questions and does not raise questions that the powerful do not have interest in, or often, would rather not know the answers to). Thus, no testing on the possible harmful side effects of pesticides and fertilizers was done until the harm began to appear. And no research was done comparing natural with artificial agriculture up to the time that the National Academy of Sciences issued a report saying that pesticides and fertilizers are not really needed. As we saw earlier, college history texts offer no guidance on natural science and technology. And neither do the rest of the knowledge elites as each allows the others to pursue their careers unencumbered by embarrassing or career-thwarting questions about their activities.

The endorsement of natural science's ability to make valid empirical statements does not mean an endorsement of how scientists think they are producing knowledge. The reason that empirical science as currently practiced in natural science is suspect is that scientists are not aware that the entire enterprise of science (as well as philosophy, literature, art, and so on) is founded on assumptions, and that choices about what to study and not study are political. Phenomenologists and feminists (who are sometimes the same) have done much in recent years to bring the arbitrariness of science and our biased picture of it into relief. Phenomenologists have stressed the way in which natural scientists are embedded in a sociopolitical tradition and that they are not detached observers using transhistorical methods to establish objective reality.[16] Some analysts focus on microlevel interaction in the laboratory,[17] while others stress a full set of sociocultural variables such as funding, previous knowledge, the educational process, career interests, multiple goals, and arbitrary assumptions.[18] For their part, feminists tend to reject (liberal) objective empirical science because it is impersonal and presupposes an outside observer studying a finished reality. Since that outside observer is male, the facts that are seen and the goals of knowledge tend to be those that are consistent with male values and thus incomplete and biased.[19]

The social construction of natural science means that the purposes and consequences of science are its most important features. This means further that purposes and consequences are rightly subject to discussion and negotiation by a democratic public. Understanding and acting on this knowledge is also important to reducing the power of technocratic elites and thus allowing a democratic public to emerge.

MATHEMATICS

Mathematics and Western Rationalism

Mathematics has played an important role in Western science. The use of mathematics to garner knowledge is apparent in ancient Greece, becomes prominent in the seventeenth century, and becomes prevalent in both natural and social science from the nineteenth century on.[20] The success of mathematics in the modern era seemed to confirm the Greek assumption that human reason has a structure that corresponds to the outer world. When Newton and Lebnitz (and others) invented calculus to provide a logic for the developing science of physical motion, it was thought that they had discovered it.

The development of probability mathematics has special importance for modern natural and social science. Its construction over three centuries was seen as part of a developing rational world. The core idea of probability, namely that chance occurrences are lawful and that uncertainty can be calculated precisely, is older than the nineteenth century. Major beginnings in probability mathematics were made during the seventeenth century by Pascal and Fermat and numerous advances occurred in the eighteenth century; but it was only in the nineteenth century that both the logic of probability and its application came into their own. A rich future for probability mathematics was predicted in a major treatise by Pierre Laplace (1749–1827), an individual conscious of his place in the historical development of the subject and of his role as a synthesizer.

Throughout the nineteenth century probability mathematics was applied to one field after another, reaping a rich harvest of knowledge. Perhaps more than anyone else, it was Darwin who stimulated interest in the scientific potential of the logic of possibilities. His discovery of the lawfulness of random mutations in biological evolution was a dramatic confirmation that one of the most complex portions of the empirical realm was rational.[21] The statistical nature of phenomena appeared across a wide variety of fields. Mendel (1822–1884) and Galton (1822–1911) made important applications of statistical laws to biological and psychological phenomena; Maxwell (1831–1879) and Boltzmann (1844–1906) formulated the behavior of gas molecules in statistical terms; and such later scientists as Max Planck (1858–1947) and Werner Heisenberg (1901–1976) established that the atom was statistical in nature.

During the nineteenth century the logic of probability was also applied successfully to the study of social phenomena. Its record in this regard is not unimpressive, even in comparison with natural science. The origins of statistical reasoning about social phenomena are traditionally dated from the work of two seventeenth-century Englishmen, John Graunt (1620–1674) and William Petty (1623–1687), the founders of "political arithmetic." But the credit for first conducting empirical research on human behavior (suicide, crime) using probability mathematics goes to Quetelet (1796–1874). For a sociology of how advances in probability theory reflected social interests after Quetelet, see the section "The Social Construction of Mathematics: Numbers and Social Power," below.

While the development of probability produced no crisis for mathematics in general, this was not true of nineteenth-century developments in geometry. To understand this crisis, one must appreciate the reverence with which geometry had been held from the Greeks on. Because geometry seemed to possess unity and permanence amidst an irrational world of diversity and change, Greek philosophy thought of it as the core of mathematics and the bastion of human rationality. Of special importance in the Greek view of geometry was the fact that in the development of mathematics from Pythagoras to Euclid, mathematical reasoning was defined, not only as being internally logical, but as resting on axioms that were consonant with the external world. It is not surprising, therefore, that mathematics was given ontological status and that thinkers believed that the human mind (as it expresses itself in mathematics) and the world of nature at large were not only orderly, but identically orderly. All that changed during the nineteenth century, even as science was enjoying its heyday.

The Relativity of Mathematics and Its Reduction to Method

Overshadowed by Aristotelian logic until the late Middle Ages, mathematics emerged during the early period of modern science to spark an incredible expansion of knowledge. Indeed, so striking was the success of the mathematical method in uncovering nature's laws that each day seemed to bring added confirmation that nature was constructed along mathematical lines. But even during the height of its success, the definition of mathematics as a unitary system of symbols was being challenged. Out of the work of Lobatchevsky, Bolyai, Gauss, and Riemann came a number of non-Euclidean geometries, all of which rested on axioms that contradicted those of Euclid. This development eventually afforded new insights into nature, the most important of which was Einstein's theory of relativity. Of great significance to modern intellectual life was the fact that out of non-Euclidean geometry came a sense of the *relativity* of mathematics itself. The axioms of Euclid were no longer considered axiomatic except in a logical sense; that is, they were not indubitable truths about physical nature lodged in the human mind, but only subjective estimates about the structure of nature. Far from being ontological in nature, mathematical axioms, to use words made famous by Henri Poincare, were "conventions, disguised definitions," mental forms that, far from constituting the foundations of being, were simply "advantageous" assumptions. Mathematical reasoning, in other words, was not a feature of the human mind that corresponded to the features of nature, but, like the rest of human ideas, a product of experience. The nature of mathematics, in short, was to be found, not only in philosophical or logical analysis, but in history, or again to quote Poincare, in "ancestral experience."

Significantly, mathematics was exalted as well as humbled by these developments. By freeing itself from its dubious links with nature—that is, by emptying itself of content and remaining true to its primary function, the development of abstractions—mathematics was able to construct a larger series of logical structures and provide a continuous flow of new and hitherto unsuspected insights into nature. Mathematics, in short, had become a *method*, a fate that the nineteenth century had in store for mind in general.[22]

The Social Construction of Mathematics: Numbers and Social Power

The nineteenth century crisis in mathematics identifies a current inside science that ran counter to the idea of an objective reason able to make contact with an objective reality. Since then, it has also led to a better understanding of the social roots and history of mathematics (now thought of as a cluster of ununitable logics derived from experience to cope with experience). We now know that Babylonia and Egypt developed a practical mathematics clearly connected to trade and to boundary restoration after flooding. But the use of mathematics to observe and predict the movement of the stars holds special interest. The ability to connect the behavior of stars with seasonal changes, weather, and flooding was economically valuable (one knows when to prepare for planting and flooding for example). But this knowledge had even greater value to those who owned it once it became a claim that priests had access to the supernatural. The effect of this claim was to turn technical knowledge into an emotional, diffused support for unaccountable social power (for aristocracy and monarch as well as priests).

The connections between social power and the use of numerical symbols is clear from then to the present day. Also clear is the development of mathematics in keeping with sociohistorical development, especially the problems faced by governing classes. Large, complex society needs to count its population, for example, to determine how many are of military age, who is to pay taxes, and how much. In contemporary America, a diverse cluster of censuses provide data for many different government programs, for private business use, and for apportioning representation to Congress itself.[23]

The historical development of probability mathematics after Quetelet's pioneering research reveals a relationship of great interest to the student of the professions. Analyzing the advances in statistical theory made by Francis Galton, Karl Pearson, and R. A. Fisher between 1865 and 1930 in Great Britain, MacKenzie argues that all three men were eugenicists and that this interest not only prompted their mathematical creativity but that it also represented the social interests of the British professional middle class. Eugenics is a belief that behavior is a function of heredity and supports the idea that social inequality results from inequality in human nature, a belief of obvious value to professionals. By and large, the process uncovered by MacKenzie connects with the widespread use of social Darwinist ideas, IQ testing, and biopsychological explanations in the Anglo-American world from that time to the present. MacKenzie concludes his analysis by arguing that mathematics is not a finished, timeless world of Platonic ideas waiting to be discovered but that both it and science are socially constructed (though not necessarily invalid because of it) in keeping with historical experience and social interests.[24]

The various meanings of objectivity and the social and political importance of mathematics have been insightfully analyzed by Theodore Porter.[25] Mathematics is a valuable communication device because parties to an interchange can understand each other (or presume that they can). It is a way in which a larger social entity can transcend local realities, as well as a way to replace trust from intimate personal knowledge with trust in abstract objective numbers.

The use of objective data is also used to protect government and its various agencies from political pressure. Cost-benefit analysis, for example, helped the U.S. Corps of Engineers in its struggles with other agencies and political opponents. Today success is not as easy because all groups employ mathematical arguments to support rival positions. Porter also points out that the same protection against others is sought by the various disciplines which use quantitative data to establish disciplinary boundaries. Weak disciplines make a fetish of methodology while established disciplines tend to be quite casual about how they conduct their business. Camic and Xie bear this out in regard to disciplines and also argue that the use of statistical analysis in the United States was a result of rivalry among academic institutions.[26] The pioneering adoption of statistical analysis by Columbia University in psychology, anthropology, sociology, and economics did not occur because theorists were "more astute about the future of statistical analysis." It occurred because Columbia University was engaged in fierce competition for resources and rank in American higher education and because there was intense struggle by the various disciplines to establish themselves. New disciplines faced the "newcomer's dilemma": how does one display conformity to accepted scientific norms while differentiating oneself from others? Statistical analysis solved this problem both for the university and for the separate disciplines. Incidentally, the use of statistical analysis by Cattell in psychology, Boas in anthropology, Giddings in sociology, and Moore in economics, precedes its use in American natural science.

We also know, argues Porter (and so does MacKenzie), that so-called objective data and findings represent a consensus within a professional community. Objectivity as knowledge beyond transitory interests, emotions, values, and politics (from Plato to Comte and on to liberal technocracy, scientism, positivism) has been replaced by the idea that objectivity is whatever disciplines, professions, and powerful groups agree on in their respective spheres at any given time.

In the past, objectivity as metaphysics (or as the law and will of God) created the moral idea of objectivity as impartiality, fairness, and justice in a hierarchic society. Under liberalism, the concept of objectivity as derived from mathematical, empirical science served to depoliticize the exercise of power. Under both systems of universal truth, the concept of objectivity was antidemocratic in that it upheld the authority of upper-level groups to define reality. Both modern and postmodern thinkers have declared an end to traditional concepts of objectivity. We now understand that all symbolic systems, including mathematics and mathematically based knowledge, are based on sociohistorically determined assumptions. We know that even carefully done and accurate mathematically expressed systems and indicators do not facilitate communication, achieve consensus, or generate trust (for the pervasive power uses of numbers, see such items as IQ, grading, accountants, cost-benefit analysis, and social indicators in the Index).

Mathematics as Ideology and Gatekeeper for the Professions

The realization that mathematics lacks unity and that it is not a template for either nature or human nature has been slow in penetrating the various professions. It has not been fully realized, in other words, that quantitative and qualitative reasoning are not different ways of thinking. In short, the various professions have yet to accept that mathematics is a means, not a structure that must be obeyed because it must have its counterpart in phenomena. Mathematics as an end in itself continues in mathematics departments, but even here it is a formal or academic subject and seems to be shunned by students who prefer to learn their mathematics from departments of applied science.

The requirement that students in economics, business, or any other social or humanistic discipline be adept at mathematics is really a way in which the professions control labor flows into those professions. Not only are some white males, ethnic and racial minorities, and women being prevented from entering these disciplines, but the subject matter of these areas is being falsified by the excessive emphasis on mathematics.

The use of mathematics as a part of the effort to develop an objective science of this or that is ideological to the extent that it creates the impression that the present way of looking at nature and society is the only way. The use of mathematics to make human behavior appear like nature (fixed structures) has been a major fallacy in social science since Quetelet. The use of mathematics to create the impression that our array of social indicators (for example, unemployment rate, GDP, capital investment, crime rate) gives a true picture of society is extremely harmful. The use of mathematics in cost-benefit analysis is particularly harmful, a flagrant example of the ideological maintenance of the status quo through the professional misuse of reason (for a fuller discussion of cost-benefit analysis, see Chapter 11).

Mathematics and Minorities

Racial, ethnic, and gender minorities have not entered the discipline of mathematics in numbers proportionate to their size. Though ideologies have appeared claiming that the reason has to do with innate characteristics, the obvious explanation is social class. Readers should also recall that even when women mathematicians display equal achievement to men in winning prestigious postdoctoral fellowships and equal achievement thereafter, they experience a gender gap in academic rank and tenure.

PSYCHOLOGY

Psychology's Special Affinity with Anglo-Protestant Liberalism

The rise of capitalism promoted individualism and the ideology that individualistic behavior reflected forces in the individual as a biopsychic being. At first the interest in the individual (say from John Locke through Thomas Jefferson) was blended with interests and values in economics, politics, and the like. The contemporary psychological approach to behavior stems from the nineteenth century when psychology became a professionalized science. Since that time professionalized psychology has been associated with the spread of liberal society and most clearly with the center of the "individualist view of society, the Anglo-Protestant core countries" (United States, Canada, United Kingdom, Australia, New Zealand).[27]

Psychology's focus on the individual has had an important negative result since the individual as such has little to do with behavior. Clearly, the human biology and psychology are needed for human behavior, but are not its sources. The ahistorical, asocial, apolitical nature of psychology also appears in Freudianism (and the thousand and one schools of psychotherapy), or the idea that we do not need to know the history of humanity, only the history of individuals.

Psychology's focus on the individual leads to the same "blame the victim" approach found in other disciplines. Caplan and Nelson report that in a study of sixty-nine articles on African Americans in professional psychology journals, the overwhelming emphasis was on their personal deficiencies.[28] Psychology achieves a measure of relevance when it becomes a social psychology and focuses on personality. But even here it rarely gets beyond the small group, innate motives, or artificial experiments.

The establishment of scientific psychology in the nineteenth century consisted largely of using scientifically colored words to continue the old psychology from Locke through Bentham, or the imaginary liberal social world made up of self-propelled, rational individuals.[29] Psychology, or the belief that human nature is understandable as a cause in its own right, received enormous support, not merely from the general current of Anglo-American liberalism (the individual as reality), but from universities, foundations, industry, the military, and public schools. By and large, both academic psychology and applied psychology framed themselves to suit the ideological and practical needs of the American power structure.[30]

Centering Psychology in Social Structure

Academic psychology established itself by supporting the popular view that Americans were the vanguard of an emerging human nature. It further ingratiated itself by assuming that middle class individuals were the first to poke their heads out of history. It established itself in higher education in various ways, one of which was to use college students as a research base (it is common in psychology to require students to participate as research subjects as part of course requirements). It became popular because both teachers and students (like the rest of us) enjoy talking about themselves. Psychologists David O. Sears and Robyn M. Dawes have criticized their colleagues for biasing their research by over-reliance on college students as subjects. It is a mistake, says Sears, to equate the college student (a loner good at paper-and-pencil tests) with the human race. It is not necessarily true, says Dawes, that college students (controlled and competitive) are an expression of human nature, and it is not necessarily a good idea to use them as a model for judging others.[31]

Academic psychology is unique among the academic disciplines in being a minority in its own field: The large majority of psychologists are practitioners or professionals who deal with patients and clients (see Chapter 7). Academic psychology has its various schools and its methodological conflicts. The scientific or research-oriented branch of psychology tends not to go anywhere until it introduces sociocultural factors. It is difficult not to believe that academic psychology should be relegated to a natural science subspecialty, say, neurochemistry, and psychology as such, be classified as an applied profession.

The career of psychologist Jerome Bruner illustrates the problem that academic psychology faces. In an illustrious career, Bruner has pointed out that we perceive, intend, and otherwise behave in terms of sociocultural factors, and that the role of the psyche as a set of variables is to all intents and purposes negligible. Bruner does stress that individuals actively participate in their world somehow leaving a role for the psyche. Had Bruner clearly stated that the ability and skills with which individuals both act and react are culturally derived, he would have reached a position well known to common sense and social science since the time of the ancient Greeks. What is noteworthy about Bruner's career is that he has been considered a deviant by mainstream psychology.

The career of Kenneth J. Gergen also illustrates creative deviance in psychology. Even more than Bruner, Gergen has gone beyond the objective empiricism of his field to embrace a postmodern vision of psychology.[32] Whereas the modern period stressed reason, impersonality, and observation, the postmodern self, he argues, is marked by multiplicity, change, and ambiguity. Individuals must now look beyond themselves to find reality—ours is to be a constructed world, says Gergen, not because we have discovered reality, but because we have negotiated with others and reached a decision about what its structure should be.

Gergen is aware that he is taking psychology in the direction taken by postmodernism in literature, phenomenology, anthropology, and feminism. His explanation of why the modern world is being superseded tends to focus rather simplistically on communication technology (this has made possible the multiple messages that have "saturated the self"). In his most recent book, Gergen has clearly shoved psychology into sociology: the personality or self emerges from interaction with others. Just as the self is constructed by social relationships, so must the psychologist openly embrace a constructionist stance.[33]

LITERARY STUDIES

Literature: How the Powerful (and Powerless) Think and Feel about the World

Literature has played an important role in the life of the West from the ancient Greeks to the present. Throughout Western history literary works were prime ways for the upper classes, whether ascendant or ascending, to record their experiences and politicize their concerns among themselves.[34] Since literature was about the upper or ascending classes, it was also used by the upper classes as their primary resource in educating their young through the nineteenth century.

Literary works in the past had an authority similar to that of science in the modern period. Even after the advent of modern science, literature continued to press its authority by distinguishing itself from science: As opposed to the arrid, impersonal world of natural and social science, claimed exponents, literature represented the full spectrum of human experience (its values, joys, sufferings, struggles, triumphs, and so on). In the twentieth century, the defenders of literature added another dimension when they aspired to become a profession.

The Professionalization of Literary Studies, or Finding One's Place in the Structure of Power by Marginalizing Minorities

Lauter argues that the idea of a literary canon (a select list of the most important writers of literature) emerged in the 1920s and virtually eliminated works by black and female authors, and literature about the working class.[35] By the 1950s, the college undergraduate read "only" works of white males devoted, by and large, to the values and interests of the middle and upper classes. It is interesting that female writers had a considerable following before this period and that females were active in teaching college literature and as an organized public of readers. All this changed as professionalization generated a male monopoly over literature after the 1920s.

The professionalization of literature emerged through the Modern Language Association (reorganized in the 1920s giving power to white males who attended conventions) in conjunction with the vast expansion of higher education: thus the standardized curriculum by specialists. In addition to yielding power and prestige to the few, the urge to construct a canon was also motivated by the belief that the United States had become a world power and needed a great literature. The emphasis on national power and politics made the world of female writers (love, marriage, domesticity) seem unimportant. Also important in excluding female writers was the practice of periodizing literature: the "Puritan Mind," "Romanticism," "Realism," and so on. This is similar to writing history in terms of palace revolts, revolutions, and wars. Here again there was a tendency to rule out the focus in female writers on life's continuities, enduring cycles, and everyday life. Lauter concludes that because of these trends, all representing white upper-class male power, in conjunction with the economics of publishing for national markets, an arbitrary literary canon became deeply institutionalized.[36]

The attempt to break out of the straitjacket of the "canon" is best discussed in terms of American Culture Studies, which began in the 1930s as a reaction to an imputed inferiority of American art and literature. By the 1960s, especially because of continental European influences, the American Culture Studies movement began to focus on the place of minorities in American literary studies. Today it represents an active, politicized struggle by some academics to change the picture of the world found in the classics (especially Western literature, including some of the classics in the social sciences). There are many separate emphases within this movement centered on questions of truth, social class, race, ethnicity, gender, and sexuality.

The critique of the humanities as nonclassic, that is, as lacking validity, or a claim to be truth, has relied heavily on phenomenology, especially as found in Derrida and Foucault. Jacques Derrida is a radical *interpretive* thinker (or phenomenologist in the tradition of radical hermeneutics). Max Weber, a pioneer in the development of interpretive sociology, combined traditional epistemology (positive science) with *verstehen*, or understanding. In Derrida, these are radical opposites; indeed traditional science and philosophy, or the search for the one objective truth, is dead because impossible. In its place is knowledge through the exercise of subjective processes. Rather than repress subjectivity, we release it because it is all there is (objective science is simply disguised subjectivity). Subjectivity both creates knowledge and confronts previously created knowledge to create more. Since we all bring different things to whatever is out there, we create diverse forms of knowledge when we confront the world. Thus, there is not one truth, but "plural truths."

Derrida's focus is on texts, which represent attempts to represent the one reality. But texts cannot do this because they rely on unverifiable metaphors, on words that have multiple meanings, and ultimately on language, especially syntax, which renders meanings intelligible only in context. The inability of philosophy to establish truth also means that there can be no progress in knowledge.[37]

Foucault, also a radical phenomenologist, argues that Derrida leaves us with no way to fight power. Analyzing texts is not all there is; we must also be practical and do things, or have policies. There may be plural truths, but some have power behind them and some do not. What Foucault does is to show that traditional epistemology's claim to objective truth is really a disguised interpretive philosophy (we must use arbitrary assumptions in our empirical sciences). Further, the power/knowledge that an arbitrary science establishes gets imposed on people and this is what has happened in the fields of deviance (mental illness, crime), punishment, and sexuality. Thus, concludes Foucault, the social-control agencies of modern society (animated by the applied professions that we discuss in Chapters 6 and 7) are based on arbitrary notions of normality. Literature, as well as the social sciences are forms of power, and (implies Foucault) interpretive science gives us a way to resist domination by other people's truths.

Understandably, the American Culture Studies movement and feminists have relied more on Foucault than Derrida to challenge the idea that higher education's classics (literary works that were declared enduring depictions of reality and embodied in the curriculum between the 1920s and the 1950s) are representative of human experience and creativity. In politicizing the canon of literary classics, critics have also pointed out that literature by or about the working class, and black, female, Hispanic, and gay writers (not to mention other minorities) have all been deeply under represented, which also means that the experience of these minorities is rendered unimportant, even nonexistent.[38]

The Marxist Defense of Rationalism and Objectivity

Writing from a Marxist standpoint, Jameson argues that the philosophy of interpretation has gone too far and represents an empty relativism, in effect, an attempt to institute symbolic reality for material reality. The attempt to substitute symbols for reality, he argues, is found throughout modern literature and modern philosophy. These disciplines all exhibit a general movement against balanced "interpretation" or "commentary" and toward "metacommentary," by which Jameson means formalism.

"All great twentieth century schools of literature and philosophy—whether those of pragmatism or phenomenology, existentialism, logical positivism, or structuralism—share a renunciation of *content*, find their fulfillment in formalism, in the refusal of all presuppositions about substance and human nature, and in the substitution of method for metaphysical system."[39]

There is truth, says Jameson, to much in the debunking of literature and philosophy, but that is no reason to give up on the need to interpret (even those who deny its need in their search for transhistorical processes do it largely by smuggling in content, or rather, interpreted content). Literature (and symbolmaking) must be reanchored in history as Marx intended. Both elite and popular culture interpreters must promote awareness about the historical predicaments that people find themselves in. Jameson defends George Lukacs as a pioneer in this regard. Despite deficiencies, Lukacs kept the essential Marxian goal alive: How does one connect symbols and history and thus promote a critical consciousness about history's shortfalls and opportunities?

Jameson provides two examples of what a Marxist interpretation of literature consists of. When a novel provides a complete and fully satisfying plot (Jameson's example is Fielding's *Tom Jones*), one should not thereby assume that one is dealing with a literary form that can be understood in the abstract. A full and satisfying plot convinces us that its elements cohere and display the properties of logic. But, argues Jameson, the plot that works does so in relation to a particular moment in history, to the possibilities in a given stage of social development. In the same way, plots that do not work (say the melodrama of the mid-nineteenth century) indicate the loss of social coherence. More significant in the breakdown of social reality is the psychological novel in which actors analyze *themselves* because the atomization of society prevents them from having social experiences that would warrant analysis and narration. Thus, an alleged unity of personality is substituted for the unity of social action, and its alleged completeness now replaces the full and satisfying plot as real.

Jameson's other example of the need to turn formal categories of analysis into historically grounded interpretation is his critique of Susan Sontag's thesis about science fiction. Sontag's thesis is that the science-fiction movie expresses our anxieties about existence and the prospect of universal annihilation. Jameson argues Sontag's analysis remains on the surface and takes science fiction on its own terms, in its disguise so to speak (thus it and Sontag act as censors). Does not science fiction, asks Jameson, also celebrate the scientist as a fantasy figure doing free, satisfying work, work not bound by rigid schedules, work as a primary relation between master and apprentice, work as a personal activity with a clearly perceived end, work that gives power, work as intellectual, and thus (falsely) believed to be easy—in short, nonalienated work that harkens back to an earlier stage of capitalism and perhaps our memory of medieval guilds? And perhaps science fiction provides a way of reliving our togetherness in war, a disaster now serving as a substitute emergency that allows us to draw on our memory banks of a vanished coherent world. One need only substitute the word professional for scientist to gain insight into not merely science fiction but the entire range of popular culture.[40]

SUMMARY

The main academic disciplines in American higher education were analyzed in terms of their self-definitions in Chapters 4 and 5. The questions asked about them were: Are they autonomous and nonpolitical? Do they monitor themselves and remain up-to-date? Are they contributing to a knowledge society? Are their members recruited through a meritocratic process, either free of or freeing itself from class bias, racism, ethnic bias, and sexism? Above all, are they turning out objective knowledge and knowledgeable graduates that have positive consequences for society?

The mainstream of the academic disciplines was found wanting in regard to all of the above questions. Based on criticism and research found in both the academic and sociopolitical perspectives, it is difficult to substantiate the claim that the United States is being guided by nonpolitical, value-free, objective, empirical disciplines in the natural and social sciences, or that the humanities have a nonarbitrary body of classics representing the truth about the human condition.

The mainstreams of the academic disciplines do not only not know themselves, but they appear seriously out of touch with social reality. Two different positions can be taken about the criticisms of the academic disciplines that have emerged from liberal and radical analysts. One is that objectivity is still a feasible goal, but science and literary studies must henceforth include an interpretive, sociohistorical dimension (to yield a truth that will uphold either capitalist or socialist perspectives while at the same time satisfying minorities). The second perspective is that a full understanding and commitment to interpretive science denies the possibility of truth and yields only a politics of negotiated, transient truths.

NOTES

1. Robert K. Merton, "Science and Democratic Social Order," *Social Theory and Social Structure*, enl. ed. (New York: Free Press, 1968), chap. 18; originally written in 1942.
2. For studies in the conflict tradition in the natural sciences, see Michael Mulkay, *The Social Process of Innovation* (New York: Macmillan, 1972); Ian I. Mitroff, "Norms and Counter-Norms in a Select Group of Apollo Moon Scientists," *American Sociological Review* 39 (August 1974): 579–595; and D. O. Edge and Michael Mulkay, *Astronomy Transformed* (New York: John Wiley, 1976); Michael Mulkay, "Sociology of Science in the West," in Michael Mulkay and Vogin Milic, *The Sociology of Science in East and West* (Beverly Hills, Calif.: Sage, 1980); Rita Arditti, Pat Brennan, and Steve Cavrak, eds., *Science and Liberation* (Boston: South End Press, 1980); Stanley Aronowitz, *Science as Power: Discourse and Ideology in Modern Society* (Minneapolis: University of Minnesota Press, 1988); Steven L. Goldman, ed., *Science, Technology, and Progress* (Bethlehem, Penn.: Lehigh University Press, 1989); and Evelyn Fox Keller and Helen E. Longino, eds., *Feminism and Science* (New York: Oxford University Press, 1996).
3. For widespread "cronyism, elitism, and conflicts induced by self-interested competition" in the peer review process (p. 165) and a conclusion that it "seldom operates according to strictly meritocratic criteria" (p. 125), see Daryl E. Chubin and Edward J. Hackett, *Peerless Science: Peer Review and U.S. Science Policy* (Albany: State University of New York Press, 1990).
4. Judith P. Swazey, Melissa S. Anderson, and Karen Seashore Louis, "Ethical Problems in Academic Research," *American Scientist* 81 (November–December, 1993): 542–551.
5. For a discussion of this latter point, which concludes that we should suspend judgment about this question, see E. Layton, "Conditions of Technological Development," in Ina Speigel-Rosing and Derik de Solla Price, eds., *Science, Technology, and Society* (Beverly Hills, Calif.: Sage, 1977), pp. 206–207.
6. For important examples from physics, biology, and geology, see Alan Lightman and Owen Gingerich, "When Do Anomalies Begin?" *Science* 255 (February 7, 1991): 690–695.
7. Chandra Mukerji, *A Fragile Power: Scientists and the State* (Princeton, N.J.: Princeton University Press, 1989).
8. Royston M. Roberts, *Serendipity: Accidental Discoveries in Science* (New York: John Wiley and Sons, 1989).
9. Robert Wuthnow, "The Emergence of Modern Science and World System Theory," *Theory and Society* 8 (1979): 215–243.
10. For a pattern at the Department of Energy similar to the one found by Mukerji among marine biologists (the government is not interested in results but in bor-

rowing the authority of social science), see "The Cases of Energy Researchers and BART Engineers" in Chapter 11.

11. Jack Ralph Kloppenburg, Jr., *First the Seed: The Political Economy of Plant Biotechnology, 1492–2000* (New York: Cambridge University Press, 1988).

12. David Dickson, *The New Politics of Science* (New York: Pantheon, 1984).

13. For the story of how higher education and its professions have blended with the business world in the field of biotechnology, see Martin Kenney, *Biotechnology: The University-Industrial Complex* (New Haven: Yale University Press, 1986). For further evidence of the eagerness of higher education for corporate support, see Sheila Slaughter, *The Higher Learning and High Technology: Dynamics of Higher Education Policy Formation* (Albany: State University of New York Press, 1990).

14. Gerhard Sonnert with the assistance of Gerald Holton, *Gender Differences in Science Careers* (New Brunswick, N.J.: Rutgers University Press, 1995).

15. For example, Harriet A. Zuckerman, "The Sociology of [Natural] Science," in Neil J. Smelser, ed., *Handbook of Sociology* (Newbury Park, Calif.: Sage, 1988), pp. 511–574.

16. Anthony Giddens's elaboration of the interpretive tradition in sociology explicitly includes natural science as relying on subjectively derived assumptions; see his *New Rules of Sociological Method: A Positive Critique of Interpretive Philosophies* (New York: Basic Books, 1976).

17. Bruno Latour and Steve Woolgar, *Laboratory Life: The Social Construction of Scientific Facts* (Beverly Hills, Calif.: Sage, 1979).

18. Tom Jagtenberg, *The Social Construction of Science* (London: D. Reidel, 1983).

19. The identification of mainstream empirical natural and social science with masculine bias is a pervasive theme in radical feminism across many disciplines. Perhaps the leading commentator and publicizer of creative work in feminist epistemology is Sandra Harding; see Sandra Harding, *The Science Question in Feminism* (Ithaca, N.Y.: Cornell University Press, 1986); Sandra Harding and Jean F. O'Barr, eds., *Sex and Scientific Inquiry* (Chicago: University of Chicago Press, 1987); Sandra Harding, ed., *Feminism and Methodology: Social Science Issues* (Bloomington: Indiana University Press, 1987); and Sandra Harding, *Whose Science? Whose Knowledge? Thinking from Women's Lives* (Ithaca, N.Y.: Cornell University Press, 1991).

20. Morris Kline, *Mathematics in Western Culture* (New York: Oxford University Press, 1953).

21. Even here one must use the sociology of knowledge to understand the theory of evolution. It required centuries of coping with social change, and seeing benefits from it, that made it possible for Westerners to think positively about change and thus about evolution.

22. The changed view of mathematics is analyzed by Morris Kline, who decries its movement toward pure abstraction and away from nature and applications; see his *Mathematics: The Loss of Certainty* (New York: Oxford University Press, 1980).

23. For valuable if noncritical essays along these lines, see William Alonso and Paul Starr, eds., *The Politics of Numbers* (New York: Russell Sage, 1987).

24. Donald A. MacKenzie, *Statistics in Britain, 1865–1930: The Social Construction of Scientific Knowledge* (Edinburgh: University of Edinburgh Press, 1981).

25. Theodore M. Porter, *Trust in Numbers: The Pursuit of Objectivity in Science and Public Life* (Princeton, N.J.: Princeton University Press, 1995).

26. Charles Camic and Yu Xie, "The Statistical Turn in American Social Science: Columbia University, 1890 to 1915," *American Sociological Review* 59 (October, 1994): 773–805.

27. David John Frank, John W. Meyer, and David Miyahara, "The Individualist Polity and the Prevalence of Professionalized Psychology: A Cross-National Study," *American Sociological Review* 60 (June 1995): 360–377.

28. Nathan Caplan and Stephen D. Nelson, "On Being Useful," in Irving Louis Horowitz, ed., *The Use and Abuse of Social Science*, 2nd ed. (New Brunswick, N.J.: Transaction, 1975).
29. For an analysis, see David E. Leary, "Communication, Persuasion, and the Establishment of Academic Disciplines: The Case of American Psychology," in Richard Harvey Brown, ed., *Writing the Social Text: Poetics and Politics in Social Science Discourse* (New York: Aldine De Gruyter, 1992), chap. 6.
30. For a more detailed picture of how an ineffective psychology was nonetheless useful to the American power structure, see the section on psychotherapists and applied psychology in Chapter 5.
31. *Chronicle of Higher Education,* June 26, 1991, p. A5.
32. Kenneth J. Gergen, *The Saturated Self: Dilemmas of Identity in Contemporary Life* (New York: Basic Books, 1991).
33. Kenneth J. Gergen, *Realities and Relationships: Soundings in Social Construction* (Cambridge, Mass.: Harvard University Press, 1994).
34. It also provided an outlet for oppressed peoples (for example, the Irish and the African Americans).
35. Paul Lauter, "Race and Gender in the Shaping of the American Literary Canon: A Case Study from the Twenties," *Feminist Studies* 9 (Fall 1983): 435–463.
36. Lauter purposely omits the treatment of literature about the working class and says little about black literature. Nonetheless, while extra factors may be needed to explain their exclusion, Lauter says his analysis pertains to all literature excluded from the canon.
37. Jacque Derrida, *Of Grammatology*, tr. Gayatri C. Spivak (Baltimore: Johns Hopkins Press, 1976); *Writing and Difference*, tr. and intro. Alan Bass (Chicago: University of Chicago Press, 1978); *Positions*, tr. and annt. Alan Bass (Chicago: University of Chicago Press, 1981); and *Margins of Philosophy*, tr. Alan Bass (Chicago: University of Chicago Press, 1982).
38. For an example of a feminist critique of literature and the purported classics, derived from Foucault, see Chris Weedon, *Feminist Practice and Poststructural Theory* (New York: Oxford University Press, 1987).
39. Frederic Jameson, "Metacommetary," *The Ideologies of Theory: Essays 1971–1986, Vol. I: Situations of Theory* (Minneapolis: University of Minnesota Press, 1988), p. 3. Our discussion of Jameson's thought relies on this seminal essay. His other writings are collected in *The Ideologies of Theory: Essays 1971–1986*, vol. 2, *The Syntax of History* (Minneapolis: University of Minnesota Press, 1988). The most accessible of Jameson's work is *Marxism and Form: Twentieth Century Dialectical Theories of Literature* (Princeton, N.J.: University of Princeton Press, 1971).
40. The study of popular culture (folklore, film, television, popular music) has revealed a powerful theme extolling professionalism (see Chapter 8 for a fuller discussion).

6

The Applied Professions

◆ ◆ ◆ ◆

◆ ◆ ◆ ◆

PUTTING KNOWLEDGE INTO PRACTICE

This study distinguishes between two ways of putting knowledge into practice, the applied professions (treated in Chapters 6 and 7) and the policy professions (treated in Chapter 10). The theme of these chapters reduces to a single question: Is the knowledge generated by mainstream professionalism being institutionalized, that is, yielding positive and growing benefits for individuals, groups, and society?

THE APPLIED PROFESSIONS

The applied professions are derived from the academic professions and bring knowledge to bear on a variety of problems. The success of the applied professions is well publicized (by the professions themselves and the mass media), bringing fame and fortune both to the professions and to some of their outstanding members. The failures of the applied professions are usually transformed into the failure of individual practitioners and criticism of both the professions and wrongdoers is routinely done behind closed doors.

To understand the applied professions, one must be wary of liberal ideology, especially its depolicizing doctrine of progress (today's disappointments will be dissipated by tomorrow's achievements). Not only must the applied professions be seen as part of a system of power, but the disparity between their claims and their performance must not be obscured by the fog of futurism. In short, the professions must be analyzed sociopolitically as well as academically.

The following categorization and analysis of applied professionals is organized in terms of how they are popularly perceived. Our analysis will show that popular evaluations hide a deeper reality: all professions are deeply fragmented, largely ineffective in performing social functions, and are lodged in the upper levels of the American class system. In short, the applied professions are not derived from a society-wide competitive, meritocratic process, neglect the needs of the lower classes, especially the poor and minorities, and judged by their own norms and values are an integral part of an illegitimate system of power.

PHYSICIANS

The Academic Approach to Medicine

Medicine has been the most studied of the professions. The early academic study of medicine stressed its success at curing diseases and overcoming disabilities through objective, empirical, value-neutral science and technology. The later academic study of medicine took a more realistic view: analysts noticed that medicine did not always live up to its ideals, that it did not have a unique knowledge base, and that it was active in protecting its income and privileges. The academic view was augmented powerfully by analysts employing the sociopolitical perspective.

A Monopoly for Profit, Not for Health

Medicine has a legal monopoly over the treatment of disease and disability, a monopoly that emphasizes value-free knowledge, technology, research, and until recently has been able to stress solo practice for private income. Of enormous importance for understanding both the successes and deficiencies of medicine is its success in separating a mechanistic, biologically based body of knowledge from the rest of the human body (personality), as well as from society (the source of the personality and of many illnesses and disabilities), and establishing it as an autonomous, monopolistic approach to bodily malfunctions.[1]

The monopoly of medicine has led to a long history of blocking alternative ways of dealing with disease and disability, especially other forms of health care and proven ways of using emotional supports to facilitate recovery (incidentally, Americans are flocking to both useful and harmful alternatives to traditional medicine[2]). Medicine has also developed an implicit or *de facto* monopoly on how we approach health (preventive medicine means individuals voluntarily getting checkups or changing unhealthy life styles, not public-health measures). The prestige of medicine has also led to a medicalization of many forms of behavioral problems, most notably crime and mental illness. The latter has more or less blocked approaches that see a need to reorganize a sick society if we are to curb crime and mental illness.[3]

The U.S. population has enjoyed rising levels of health and life expectancy since the end of the nineteenth century. But our life expectancy is lower than many European countries and Japan, our death rate from heart disease is far higher than the nearest country, our immunization of children rate (50 percent) is the lowest in the industrial world, and many countries have a better infant mortality rate than we do. Medicine in the United States is characterized by excessive specialization and by technological fetishism, all within an ethic that stresses an objective, value-free, scientific approach to curing and restoring patients.

American medicine is also characterized by a deep commitment to research. This commitment is associated with medical education and helps to socialize each generation of doctors to carry on in the technocratic tradition. Medicine's research orientation gives prestige to those who are hunting down cures for exotic diseases. It helps to explain why doctors do not look on patients as whole persons and have failed to recognize that patients have an emotional and social life that has an important bearing on health and successful treatment. Another consequence of the research orientation is the neglect of ordinary diseases and diseases that do not fall in any specialty (for example, the long neglect of alcoholism). A great deal of medical practice is routine and becoming a doctor could become standardized (and thus take less time and cost less). But professions fear standardization (not without some good reason, of course) and their excessive emphasis on research helps keep alive the myth that they have a unique knowledge base. The strong research tradition in medicine, for example, has generated cures but it has also created the false belief that doctors are the only ones that can battle the mysterious world of disease.

Health care in the United States is a thoroughgoing private profitmaking business. In this, the United States stands alone among all industrial countries. America's radical commitment to for-profit, but nonmarket medicine has had predictable consequences: oligarchy, much higher costs for the same or often less results than other countries, unnecessary and incompetent treatment, and a relative neglect of ordinary Americans, especially the health needs of minorities (including women) and the poor. Research has shown that anywhere from one to 2.5 million unnecessary operations are performed each year, causing over 10,000 deaths. The misuse and overuse of (overpriced[4]) drugs by doctors causes over 30,000 deaths per year and the hospitalization of hundreds of thousands.

The United States probably has the best medical technology in the world and some of its doctors are the world's best. But excessive specialization, duplicate technology, surplus hospital space,[5] the poor distribution of doctors, hospitals that lack salaried doctors, and so on make for bad and overly expensive medicine. Until recently, doctors' demand for autonomy was matched by a demand for autonomy (in the name of market efficiency) by medical supply corporations, drug companies, medical technology manufacturers, health insurers, medical research and charity organizations, and nonprofit and for-profit hospitals. All enjoyed large profits (including foundations and charities) under monopoly conditions. But the cost of medical care affected the profits of American businesses, both directly in the case of their employees and indirectly through taxes to pay for Medicare and Medicaid. Starting in the 1980s and accelerating in the 1990s, actions by corporations, state and federal governments, and private health insurers began the trend toward a highly concentrated, leaner, for-profit health-care industry. As a result, new and extensive controls over how doctors practice have come into place. The overall system is still producing monopolistic profits but its share of GDP and the share going to doctors have begun to shrink along with shrinking professional satisfaction.

Medicine as an Interpretive Science

Doctors exhibit a wide variety of subjectivity in their professional activities not much different in extent from all other professionals. Far from being objective, value-free applicators of knowledge, they make diagnoses and prescribe according to false class and gender stereotypes. Proven remedies, for example, for asthma and ulcers, are not used. Useless or suspect remedies, such as heart by-pass surgery and mastectomies, continued to be used long after they have been proven to be ineffective or unnecessary. Medical practices are supported by outside forces. Doctors' bias toward technology, including drugs, and away from preventive medicine and alternative approaches to health care, for example, is supported by our method of financing health care. Doctors are paid only if they perform concrete acts of medical intervention.[6] Doctors are not paid if they chat with patients to put them at ease, or if they use their authority to get patients to change their life styles or follow treatment. Considerable evidence has also appeared that many patients would recover if let alone rather than have a wide variety of medical procedures administered to them. And approximately ten percent, or 50,000 doctors, are incapacitated but still seeing patients (another 2 percent or 10,000 doctors are impostors).

The interpretive nature of medicine emerged in a national study of health-care practices.[7] Striking differences in medical treatments and costs were found in areas of medical uncertainty: breast cancer, prostate cancer, heart trouble, and back pain (for example, in some parts of the country, up to 33 times more radical mastectomies were performed, rather than breast-saving lumpectomies). Researchers isolated medical interpretation (the behavior of doctors) by controlling for age, type and amount of insurance, cost, and results (those who paid more or received more medical care were not healthier). Doctors tend to adopt the approach of their schools and region and change if they go elsewhere to practice. Higher costs and more services were found where supply was greatest—instead of competition lowering costs, supply was driving demand in violation of alleged economic law. Or stated differently, uninformed patients, unsupported by outside bodies, simply accepted the subjective judgment of their doctors as objective.

The interpretive nature of medical practice also leads to medically sound decisions. Data that point to different treatment for male and female patients do not necessarily mean that sexist discrimination is at work. Women, for example, receive far fewer heart surgeries than men, which suggests neglect. What is at work, however, is legitimate medical discrimination—women develop heart trouble at a much later age than men when they are also suffering from other problems and surgery is much riskier. Here we see added confirmation that a professional (doctors) must exercise interpretive judgment and that professionals who are analyzing the behavior of others (the researcher) must do likewise.[8]

Far from being based on science and objectivity, the medical world, like all other professions, is an interpretive science thoroughly embedded in the moral and political values of the American upper classes. It, along with all the disciplines and professions, must be placed in the context of social power, and evaluated as to values served and values denied.

America's Health-Care System as an International Anomaly

The U.S. health-care system is markedly different from all other societies, capitalist or socialist.[9] Health care in the United States began as and has remained a private-profit system providing different health care to the various classes and costing an average of twice as much as in any other developed capitalist society for health results that at best are the same. The United States spends huge amounts of money on its health-care system, but since there is no effective counterweight to the providers of health-care services and products, prices, incomes, and profits are largely set by the providers. All in all, the medical establishment has succeeded in obtaining public financing without public supervision, direction, or control (recent pressures to curb medical costs may change all this though the result may be to simply move profits from one sector of the health establishment to another). And to make matters worse, there is no direct positive relation between money spent on curative medicine and better health.[10] All other developed countries have national health insurance (private medicine financed by comprehensive public insurance), or socialized medicine (public medicine providing free medical care), and costs are contained and standards maintained because the government acts as a monitor and negotiator on behalf of the public.[11] Some rough equivalents of these systems exist at the local level in the United States[12] but, on the whole, the American system (actually nonsystem) is an international freak, costing (to repeat) an average of twice as much as any other developed society for the *same health results.*

Medicine, Class, and Minorities

Many studies over the past decades have shown a relation between social class, on the one hand, and health and life expectancy on the other. Studies agree that the lower classes suffer more from all diseases (and have much higher rates of infant mortality). Whether judged by income, occupation, or education (or a mixture of these), the lower classes live significantly fewer years than the upper classes (some narrowing of life expectancy rates has taken place). The lower classes are also more likely to be uninsured (out of a total of approximately 42 million uninsured in 1995) and the uninsured do not utilize ostensibly free health services.[13] By and large, the lower classes have poorer health and life expectancy because of their class status (the lack of medical services aggravates their problems). They are more subject to work-related diseases, disabilities, and deaths. Their lives are more stressful, including the health-debilitating stress of unemployment. They know less about how to maintain health and suffer both from deprivation (hunger affects millions) and from the wrong foods and other style of life habits.[14] And as Dutton points out, the health-care delivery system is oriented toward middle and upper income levels, and barriers to using health-care facilities are an important part of the low use of health services by the poor.[15]

Wornie Reed's comprehensive analysis of African-American health and health care dramatizes the enormously adverse health consequences of low socioeconomic status.[16] African Americans suffer higher rates of all serious diseases. In consequence, blacks live shorter lives, black males about seven years fewer than white males and black females five years fewer than white females. After paying into the Social Security system since 1936, black males reached an average life expectancy of sixty-five only a few times during the 1980s and have barely been able to stay at sixty-five since. Since the retirement age will rise gradually over the coming years and health care for the poor is likely to decline after 1996, the average black male may never qualify for a Social Security pension.

Infant mortality rates and birth complications are shamefully high in the United States and especially prevalent among low-income, unmarried teenagers, and thus more prevalent among black Americans. Successful federal programs, such as Maternal and Child Health (MCH) and Maternal and Infant Care (MIC), have been either reduced and turned over to the states or are not available to all because of inadequate funding and outreach. These will both become less adequate if the health-care "reforms" proposed by the Republican Congress of 1995–96 ever become law.

Lead poisoning is an enormously important health hazard and derives from lead paint in old buildings and old industrial sites (and of course from gasoline before lead was removed). These sites are found disproportionately where blacks live and it explains why lead poisoning rates for blacks are much higher than those for whites. The impact of lead on the body impairs cognitive functioning and causes a wide variety of serious diseases. Cleaning such sites has low priority for public officials. Smoking, alcohol, and homicide are further scourges among African Americans.

Health care for African Americans is uniformly inferior, largely a case of money, less insurance, less useful insurance, few health services and personnel serving African-American areas, and a severe shortage of African-American health-care professionals and auxiliary personnel. While shortages of personnel exist for all American racial and ethnic minorities, the shortages are especially acute for African Americans. These shortages will be aggravated if the 1996 proposals by the medical establishment to cut back on medical school enrollments are enacted.[17]

Well-to-do women probably receive the best medical care possible. But the large majority of women are subject to the negative consequences of class and sexism. Working- and lower-class women, like their male counterparts, do not receive the same medical care received by the middle class and above. But in addition to deprivation by class, broad segments of the female population, including women above the working classes, are treated differently by the medical profession (but readers should remember that data require interpretation and different treatment is often medically sound). The different, often damaging treatment of female patients is no doubt a result of the pervasive sexism of American society. But it is also due to the fact that women are excluded from the upper reaches of the health-care professions.[18]

Changes in the Medical Establishment

Research into the power structure inside the medical world has revealed a shift away from physician autonomy toward power sharing, power confusion, and personal resentment by doctors of oversight by outsiders and of excessive paperwork. Recent polls indicate that 40 percent of doctors would not enter medicine if they had it to do over, and recent trends indicate that many doctors are retiring much earlier than is customary, or moving into medical work that does not require contact with patients.[19]

An early shift in power occurred when doctors had to use hospital facilities and share power with hospital administrators. But recent years have produced a more important change—to curtail burdensome health-care costs, governments, employers, and insurance companies have imposed controls on how medicine is practiced. Large, powerful, for-profit health-care maintenance organizations (HMOs) have appeared which insure patients and deliver them to doctors and hospitals provided certain norms are adhered to. Doctors are paid a set sum for each patient, expensive tests and procedures are discouraged, and complaints have arisen because doctors are asked not to give patient information about alternative treatments. The trend toward HMOs has even prompted a movement on the part of doctors to organize with hospitals to form their own health insurance organizations, something that requires legislation to exempt them from anti-trust laws.

The movement toward competitive managed health-care markets has also forced many hospitals to merge and has greatly increased the size of for-profit hospital chains. All of this has also squeezed the nonprofit Blue Cross insurance systems across the country and many have applied to become for-profit companies (a struggle has ensued between them and state governments because they are being asked to pay back to the public a portion of their assets that have accrued because of their tax-exempt status).

The impact of structural changes in health care has caused a significant shift among medical students toward primary care (favored by HMOs). It has also caused a decline in work satisfaction among doctors and a small but growing number have joined labor unions. In 1995, average physician income dropped for the first time. The above shift in power can also be called a diversification of medical policy making, or forcing doctors to share decision making with insurance companies and governments. Whether this diversification generated in the name of efficiency and profit can produce better health care is highly problematic. The unusually high percent of GDP that goes to the health-care establishment in the United States may stabilize or even decline slightly, but will continue to cost far more than in other capitalist societies for the foreseeable future. What we may be seeing, in other words, is merely a redistribution of excessive profits among the various health-care sectors.

Bypassing the Medical Establishment

The problem with medicine goes deeper than the fact that the public pays and overpays for most of the education, equipment, and income of doctors and other members of the medical establishment. It goes beyond excessive specialization, overeducation, uncontrolled costs, fraud, maldistribution of medical staff and facilities, and the failure to root out imposters and incapacitated doctors.[20] It goes beyond the neglect of the poor and minorities, including women. It goes beyond the failure to nourish and extend student idealism by medical school.[21] And it goes beyond the highly structured class, racial, ethnic, and gendered nature of the medical profession. The deeper problem is that both good and bad health come from social institutions, especially the economy (good food, clean air and water, safe workplaces, and secure employment). Medicine (and the medical establishment, including such auxiliaries as Blue Cross-Blue Shield and single-disease associations such as the American Cancer Society) is largely a way (unintended) to protect the American economy from being reorganized to promote health.

Disease and disability are largely caused by how a society lives, essentially by its economy and other institutions.[22] By medicalizing disease and disability, medicine (and its support groups such as drug companies, medical supply corporations, hospitals, insurance companies, higher education, the American Cancer Society and other single-disease or disability groups), has depoliticized the issue of good and bad health. By and large, our resources are devoted to coping with the results of a bad social environment rather than with promoting good health. And our pronounced commitment to private solutions to a public problem (the social generation of disease and disability) is undoubtedly related to the backwardness of American practices in a number of areas (the glaring deficiencies that have appeared in recent years in our public disease-detection systems, lax enforcement of occupational safety, inadequate measures of public hygiene and treatment among the lower classes, and the failure to immunize half of our children).

Reforms, derived from proven experience, are easy to list: comprehensive national health insurance, better practices (such as hospitals staffed by salaried doctors), national licensing, review boards with significant representation by nondoctors, a reduction in the social distance among doctors, other health practitioners, and patients, accepting and routinizing the growing use of nurse practitioners as primary-care doctors,[23] and a medical education devoted to supplying the number and type of health practitioners that society needs. The latter holds exceptional promise: training can be shortened, stress can be placed on treating the whole person (both as a physical and emotional being), the special needs of the various classes, ethnic groups, and each sex can be emphasized, and the number of specialists can be strictly limited by need.[24] Planning our labor needs in medicine would be good practice for planning them in all spheres of the economy and society.

The approach to medicine outlined above downgrades medical elitism while producing more of the values improperly attributed to it. But the biggest advances in health lie in *bypassing the medical establishment altogether*. American culture mistakenly associates health with medicine and good medicine with private medicine. Not only do these false associations produce adverse health values, but other values are violated, values such as efficiency, productivity, and equality. The health of the American people has improved largely because of better food, water, and sanitation. Future advances in health can come about only if further advances are made in the conditions of health, which now include the need for safe workplaces, secure economic status, healthier life styles, and a safe environment.

Health should be a fundamental human right and its promotion built into the social structure. A healthy population is also a more productive one. Resources not needed for treating cancer and malformed babies can be devoted to helping businesses construct safe, nonpolluting workplaces, communities to clean up waste dumps, and farmers to break their dependence on fertilizers and pesticides. Note, that to improve health is also to improve the economy and vice versa—to improve the economy will yield the side benefit of better health.

LAWYERS

The Academic Picture of Lawyers and Law

Lawyers ideally think of themselves in ways similar to other professions and to the academic disciplines as well: objective, value neutral, empirical, nonpolitical. And like them, they blend their self-identity with their subject matter, in this case, with the law.

Lawyers think of law as an objective, apolitical, autonomous code of norms marked by consensus, implemented by experts, and serving the common good. Along with other elites, lawyers believe that law reflects the considered judgment of the community and is thus binding on it. Law, they believe, contributes to social stability and helps society adjust. Despite faults, law embodies society's highest moral values and seeks goals that most agree on. The U.S. Constitution provides boundaries, stability, and the values that make America work. Law as a set of procedures guarantees everyone and every group a fair hearing. The adversarial tradition embodies the best values of competitive capitalism ensuring justice through the victory of the most able and deserving. True, there are many conflicting opinions about law and the judicial process, but this is because law is in the thick of things busily solving problems and helping individuals, groups, and society adapt to new conditions. The law may lag behind society, but that is not necessarily bad since it forces people to think before they act.

The Conflict Picture of Lawyers and Law

The law may integrate and stabilize society, argue liberal and radical critics, but it also preserves the bad with the good. Law is best seen as an instrument for legitimating and supporting existing power groups be they priesthoods, landed aristocracies, business people, professionals, or dictatorships. While it may sometimes express the common interest, law usually expresses the interest of the strong and neglects, even overrides, the interests of the weak.

The law may rest on a considerable consensus, but it is also marked by conflict and contradiction. Americans break the law in large numbers and engage in litigation far more than other people, argue critics, precisely because the law does not rest on consensus. Legislatures enact ambiguous and contradictory laws, not because legislators cannot write or think clearly, but because legislatures themselves do not rest on consensus. Americans engage in litigation because they are a diverse people who no longer have norms in common governing their lives. All this leads to poor law enforcement. Laws expressing only a majority consensus often lack enforcement teeth (for example, fair employment and fair housing laws). Though there is broad consensus on the need for law and order, the most important forms of criminal behavior cannot be controlled because they are committed by powerful business and professional groups, often in conjunction with public officials. (See Chapter 9 for a fuller discussion of professional deviance.)

Liberal and Radical Critiques

Two forms of criticism of mainstream law have appeared, liberal and radical. The legal realism school that emerged early in the twentieth century saw deficiencies in the law, but remained liberal in that it presupposed that reforms were possible. An example of liberal realism is the summary of deficiencies in the American legal system by Derek C. Bok.[25] Bok charges that American law (for example, labor law, antitrust law, work-place safety regulations) cannot be related to the public interest (to verifiable results in each specific area). Legal scholars do little research into the legal system as such. The legal field, like medicine, is succumbing to bigness. The United States, says Bok, has far more lawyers than any other industrialized society, which not only channels huge numbers of able people away from fields in which they are needed, but once in place these lawyers (like surplus surgeons) create work whether needed or not. The legal system caters to the rich and powerful and neglects the interests of the middle, working, and lower classes. America's law schools have done little to counter all this—legal education, or learning how to think like a lawyer, means memorizing unique cases and knowing how to find variations in detail. Teaching students to think like lawyers, argues Bok, "has helped to produce a legal system that is among the most expensive and least efficient in the world." Ironically, concludes Bok, "the blunt inexcusable fact is that this nation, which prides itself on its efficiency and justice, has developed a legal system that is the most expensive in the world, yet cannot manage to protect the rights of most of its citizens."

Liberal realism has also exposed the way in which the world outside the law helps to create the meaning of law. Rather than being an objective body of rules, the law emerges from the interaction of lawyer and client. When the client is a powerful corporation, lawyers tend to bow to their clients. But even when clients are not powerful, lawyers (and the law) are much influenced by them. In their study of a nonrepresentative sample of divorce lawyers and their clients (marked by an absence of prominent lawyers and clients from the upper classes), Sarat and Felstiner show how the meaning of the law emerges from social interaction rather than from the application of knowledge by a professional. The power of the professional is fragile, they argue, because clients undergoing divorce insist on talking about their entire life circumstances thus making it impossible for lawyers to stick to technical legal analysis. Here we see the social construction of legal meaning as the outcome of differing assumptions about law and justice. The intense and often chaotic interaction in law offices and the social construction of meaning is not a question of weak or incompetent lawyers—the entire process and product emerges from the very definition of a lawyer—rather than being merely a skilled interpreter of an objective body of law, the lawyer must also act on behalf of a client, and this means that the law must be interpreted to suit the client's nonprofessional interests and values.[26]

Sarat and Felstiner have sought to put their study in the context of an emerging tradition of interpretive legal scholarship by referring to both liberal and radical analyses. But interpretive, or sociopolitical, legal analysis is far more advanced than they allow, and their study, at bottom, is about one small part of a relatively secondary world of law, the divorce problems of ordinary people using available legal help. A far different, more foundational, picture of the social construction of law, has emerged from the Critical Legal Studies movement (which has Marxist, phenomenological, and feminist components). From a radical perspective, for example, members of this movement would argue that Bok's analysis, however insightful, assumes that law can be reformed without reforming the basic capitalist system. And they would argue that Sarat and Felstiner are really analyzing the disorderly personal relations generated by late corporate capitalism. Their analysis illustrates in yet another area, how professionals have to cope with and patch up victims of a non-functional social world.

The basic assumption guiding the Critical Legal Studies movement is that the law, from the U.S. Constitution through statutes, cases, lawyers, judges, and law schools, is constructed by legislatures, who are themselves constructed by a political process largely controlled by those with money, knowledge, and organizational skills. While feminists have made important contributions to defining the law as an arbitrary, unjust construction (for example, Catherine A. MacKinnon's analysis of the masculine bias that permeates the law, illustrated with penetrating case studies of sexuality, rape, abortion, and pornography laws[27]), the major thrust of radical legal scholarship has focused on the class nature of law. Our example is drawn from the work of M. J. Horwitz.[28]

Horwitz has argued that American law was drastically altered during the formative years of the republic, primarily through judicial interpretations, to favor some property owners over others. The eighteenth century tended to regard law as stemming from community customs derived from natural law. Property was defined as the absolute right to enjoy something and to be able to prevent others from interfering with that enjoyment. From 1780 to 1860, argues Horwitz, the legal conception of property was drastically altered to mean that one had the right to develop and use property regardless of injury to others.

Not surprisingly, argues Horwitz, the changed meaning of property was accompanied by a change in the meaning of a contract. In the eighteenth century, a contract had to be fair and could be set aside if it was not. By mid nineteenth century, a contract was enforceable even if its provisions were patently unfair. The law was simply reflecting a fact of economic life: Strong commercial and industrial interests were using their competitive advantages to exploit smaller businesses, consumers, and workers, and they legalized their exploitation by putting it in the form of a contract. They also protected their economic power by getting the courts to reduce their responsibility for damages (in keeping with the new dictum that the central meaning of property was the right to develop it), and juries gradually had their power to make judgments and award damages on the basis of fairness curtailed. Once all this had been accomplished, legal philosophers sanctified the results by arguing that law is neutral, objective, and apolitical, that is, they created the formal discipline of jurisprudence.

Law, Property, Class, and Income

The legal profession has enjoyed enormous growth in numbers, prestige, power, and money rewards since the nineteenth century.[29] It accomplished this by restricting entry into its ranks by erecting both necessary and unnecessary qualifications, by excluding women and minorities, and by promoting demand for its services while setting fee schedules (price fixing). Some theorists argue that all this was functional for society because it improved quality, promoted justice, and helped integrate a dynamic and diverse population. Others argue that the legal profession acted as a typical occupation: While talking of community ideals and service, it actively promoted its own interests through restrictive practices, state licensing, and state financing (legal expenses are tax deductible, tax-supported lawyers for the poor). Still others argue that the legal profession is the arm of business interests, helping to promote a capitalist way of life (both the good and bad in it), and that the law firm is itself a capitalist enterprise actively extracting surplus value from lower-level employees, including junior partners and beginning lawyers.

The legal profession has a poor record of initiating law reform, having opposed or lagged behind almost all minor and major reforms of the American legal system. Internally, it is deeply divided into elite and non-elite lawyers living and working in very different class worlds. Divided into different bar associations by class, it is further divided by race, sex, religion, and ethnicity. The diversification and conflicts of American society have progressed to a point where the lawyers needed to litigate these conflicts have become so diversified that one can no longer talk of a legal profession.[30] Understandably, only minimal standards for the field can be established by the American Bar Association.

The power of wealth (owners of both large and small businesses) to generate more income for themselves and their managers than is warranted by education, occupational status, age, or job tenure has been shown by Wright and Perrone.[31] The power of wealth to generate income is also a characteristic of the professions. Here we are dealing with two forms of wealth: human capital and capital as ownership of material productive property. Given the unusual autonomy of the American professions, some of them make unusual incomes in relation to professions in other capitalist societies (doctors are a prime example). In addition, doctors, lawyers, and professors can turn their practices into lucrative businesses by setting up laboratories, law firms, and commercial ventures to exploit research findings (no matter that human capital and research are largely financed by tax money).

In a rare analysis of a particular profession (lawyers in Toronto, Canada) John Hagen identifies two stratifying relations—core sector, large firms (representing large businesses) versus peripheral firms (representing individuals and small businesses) and male versus female lawyers. Lawyers in core firms earn more than lawyers in peripheral firms, with the owners of large firms making substantially more than their lawyer employees. Thus law is deeply stratified reflecting the stratification of the larger capitalist economy.[32]

The growth of the large law firm and the decline of solo and small-firm practice reflects not so much the abstract demands of efficiency and service, but the needs of corporate capitalism. These needs are two-fold: one, the dominant corporations need specialized legal services to help them adapt to a fast-changing world, and two, the overall system of capitalism needs the elite law firms to provide the coordination and to spearhead the reforms that are necessary among the business community, government, politics, and private bodies.[33] These needs have resulted in the transformation of the elite levels of the profession into a business—the large law firm is indistinguishable from the rest of the corporate world (which helps explain, of course, why the interpenetration among them is so complete). Like medicine, not only has it become (largely?) a business, but again like medicine, its leading edge is being played out in bureaucratic forms.[34]

Law and Racial, Ethnic, and Gender Minorities

Jewish, Irish, Italian, and other ethnic groups from European or Canadian backgrounds have done well in law (though few recent studies exist). African Americans have not done well in law and have segregated practices.[35] Very little is known about Hispanics and Asian Americans in law (or in most of the professions for that matter).

Women have entered law schools in impressive numbers, but they find it difficult to reach the heights of prestigious law firms (become partners[36]), the upper echelons of Washington, or join law school faculties.[37] Here, as in the world of business, and under current practices, women professionals have found it difficult to combine motherhood and successful careers.

Earlier we reported John Hagen's study of the legal profession to illustrate the power that property has over income. Hagen's study was actually focused on gender inequality and revealed a gender gap of 25 percent in income after controlling all other relevant variables.[38] Studying the same group five years later, together with a survey of entrants to law in Ontario between 1975 and 1990, Hagan and Kay also provide a wealth of details about the lives of male and female lawyers (work satisfaction, changing jobs, leaving the profession, the burden of children and housework faced by women, and so on).[39] Contrasting the human capital (or rational-choice) approach with the gender stratification approach, Hagan and Kay find that both approaches have something to offer, though they highlight gender discrimination. While the authors are aware that the thrust of corporate capitalism has led to concentration and centralization in the ownership of law firms, and that owners (partners) make the bulk of their income from the labor of their overworked employee lawyers, their extended suggestions for changing gender discrimination say nothing about the need to change the power of property to exploit labor (which would continue even if women became partners at a rate equal to men and made the same income).

A recent American Bar Association report notes that despite the fact that American women have increased their numbers to half of law school enrollments and to 27 percent of all lawyers, they still lag badly in pay, promotions, partnerships, and professorships at law schools.[40]

Reforming the Legal Establishment

Law schools have been criticized for not training lawyers to be lawyers. Thus, they neglect all the things that most lawyers need: knowledge about court procedures, how to interview clients, how to negotiate, how to deal with a large variety of social strata. Legal education (represented by one elite law school) has been criticized for shaping students toward the ideology of corporate capitalism and away from idealistic concerns.[41] Another study reports that student interest in public interest law (law that affects the poor, civil rights, environmental, and consumer law) and public interest careers (providing legal representation for those who would do without if they had to rely on their own resources) dropped dramatically from the first to the third year of law school as students experienced the deep bias toward corporate law in the legal profession.[42] This tendency reflects, of course, the major development in the field, the steady growth of the legal profession as a business and as an adjunct to corporate capitalism. A national survey also reveals that women students achieve poorer grades (on blindly graded final examinations) and do less well in achieving academic honors than men students, holding grade point admission averages and Law School Admission Test scores constant. Analysts remained puzzled as to why this is so—one plausible guess is that a male faculty and a competitive atmosphere favor male students.[43] No questions were raised as to whether single minded competition (the adversarial tradition) makes better lawyers or yields more justice.

A study of nonlawyer judges (59 percent of whom had no education beyond high school) found no significant difference between them and lawyer judges.[44] These findings while limited to one state (forty-three states use nonlawyer judges) are tantalizing in their suggestion that here as elsewhere there is overcredentialing in how we fill our occupations. This finding augments the new realism about law and lawyers that sees them as part of an overall system of power composed of both legitimate and illegitimate elements. The new realism rejects the image of law as the cutting edge of reform—legal rights are often empty formalities and legal reform (for example, civil rights) modernizes power relations rather than changes them. The new realism rejects the image of society that sees it as an arena of free behavior bounded by a framework of impartial, commonly accepted legal rules and procedures. Like the other professions, lawyers cannot understand their subject matter, the law, nor will they, until they understand history, the impact on law of economic and other interest groups, and the use of law by power groups to legitimate their illegitimate interests.

Lawyers and bar associations (and legislators) have sensed that things are amiss. The problems addressed and the reforms proposed, however, only highlight how little they understand the law and the legal system. For example, they have successfully supported the Legal Services Corporation (a federally subsidized way to provide legal services for the lower classes) against the efforts of the Reagan–Bush administrations of 1980–92 to abolish it, only to see the program crippled illegally by said administrations (further crippled by the Republican Congress of 1994–96). The main opposition by the Republican party to the Legal Services Corporation is that its lawyers have fought to enforce laws already on the books on behalf of workers, consumers, and the poor. This is a good example of the upper classes using and misusing their political power and the law to maintain their power over the lower classes.

The legal profession and judiciary have also tackled the problems of the high cost and justice-denying delays in public trials by encouraging and mandating negotiated convictions, mediation, and private trials before rented (retired) judges. In some mediation cases, the record shows better compliance with agreements than in similar cases where conclusions are reached in and imposed by courts. But the entire trend toward out-of-court settlement may also be part of a wider trend in education and public services toward privatization (mediation firms are lucrative businesses) and more class justice (the wealthy and the powerful can pick and choose whatever dispute resolution process suits them. It may also constitute an erosion of America's ability to enunciate and maintain through public adjudication the fundamental values underlying law that Americans have in common.[45]

Lawyers and bar associations (and legislators) have focused on another problem, which they have misdefined, providing another example of how American elites, by focusing on a social problem directly and without a theory of power to guide them, cannot see or solve said problem. The relation of law and the legal system to the capitalist system of society has been framed (misdefined) by the legal profession as a clash between professionalism and commercialism.[46] Stating the issue in this way presupposes that professionalism (the objective, nonpartisan, fiduciary dispensation of skill and knowledge), because desirable in a conflict-ridden society, is thus achievable.

The relation between law and capitalism has also been misdefined in an otherwise insightful analysis of why lawyer employees work an excessive and inefficient number of hours (despite a preference for less work even if it means less pay).[47] Using a sociological approach (the power over behavior of groups) to understand why alleged market principles are violated by the two large law firms studied, three economists point to the fact that the partners who share in the profits of the firm use hours worked as an indicator of who will be a hardworking income-producing future partner. The authors also say that a more efficient labor policy is not possible unless all firms are compelled to honor employee preferences since stand alone firms would be flooded with applicants and be at a competitive disadvantage. Also welcome is the sociological insight that the performance of individuals can have a large impact on group productivity in a large variety of settings, the authors specifically suggesting that their findings about why lawyers are trapped in a rat race are also applicable to software engineers, research teams, and corporate executives. The authors offer two other insights derived from their analysis. One, law firm practices make it difficult for women to qualify for partnership (given their work burdens outside of paid work and the fact that lawyers tend to marry other hard working professionals), and two, partners selected in the current manner, are also those selected for leadership posts in the profession, something that may prevent the profession from adjusting organizational life to cope with the new demographic composition of the American population.

The authors' insights about the legal professions could conceivably have led to another larger insight. Had they put their insights into a macro-sociological setting, they could have identified an institutional system in which the owners of law firms join the owners of other forms of capital in a common need to derive profit from employees. This system forces many into a competitive process (society as a rat race) with many negative features, not the least of which is economic concentration and its corollary, political domination.

Society, Power, and Law

The idea of law as a way to transcend the biases of self-interest (class, ethnicity, race, gender, geography, and so on) has a long history (Plato, Aristotle, Roman law, Jeremy Bentham, Emile Durkheim, and, of course, American constitutional law and mainstream jurisprudence). In the light of Montesquieu's relativism about all social norms, including law, the Marxist and Durkheimian identification of type of law with type of society, or Miller's identification of type of justice with type of society,[48] and the rather full comparative study of lawyers and the law that is now available,[49] one needs to ask, Is a transhistorical professionalism possible under capitalism any more than other historical societies? No matter how much a competitive, market society needs to generate a sense of fairness in its process of producing winners and losers, can it be done through a professionalism that exhibits a massive embeddedness in the very institutions and class hierarchy that it presumably should transcend? As Miller's essay suggests, the idea of fairness (or equal rights, or individual merit), emerged early in the modern period when a small-scaled capitalist economy began to replace unequal feudal relations (lord-serf) with market exchanges of (presumed) equivalent value between individuals. The ideals of law may have been approximated to some extent or reasonably been assumed to be achievable up to the nineteenth century. But these ideals are highly problematic in an era of high economic concentration, highly unequal social classes, and a pronounced plutocratic polity. The real question about law and lawyers is the same one that must be asked of all the professions and disciplines: How can society achieve legitimacy and effectively solve problems when its professions and the norms and values they implement are part and parcel of the problems they are allegedly solving?[50]

ADMINISTRATORS AND EXECUTIVES

The science (and incipient profession) of management emerged in the United States in the 1830s and 1840s in keeping with the practical problems of manufacturing (Springfield Armory) and transportation by railroad. Building on the new system of education that graded *individuals* (using a hierarchy expressed by letters and numbers) on reading and writing through examinations (a system begun at Cambridge University in the late eighteenth century but perfected with a vengeance by West Point Military Academy between 1817 and the 1830s), the Springfield Armory and America's new railroads began the practice of keeping precise accounts (West Point graduates were prominent leaders in these enterprises). This practice helped in increasing productivity and in coordinating far-flung, multi-unit enterprises like a railroad. And it was the first time that accounts were kept so that managing for the future and aiming for specific goals, including profit, was attempted. In the context of economic expansion in the early decades of industrialization, bureaucratization was a large aid in generating efficiency an productivity.[51] But with mature industrialization, the American version of bureaucratization has developed many practices that thwart efficiency, productivity, and accountability.

Ideal versus Real Bureaucracies

One of capitalism's most important inventions is bureaucracy (which it brought to fruition during the nineteenth century). A bureaucracy (also known as a complex organization) is a group organized to ensure efficiency and responsibility. Described in ideal terms, a bureaucracy is an administrative structure in which a hierarchy of statuses, separated from other statuses, is given specified duties and rights. The statuses are occupied by employees selected by stated qualifications. Employees are expected to establish a career, that is, make a long-term commitment to the enterprise. The equipment and facilities that employees use to perform their duties belong to the group.

Actual bureaucracies deviate from this ideal. Behavior within corporations, schools, foundations, hospitals, law firms, the military, and government agencies varies somewhat from the enterprise's official blueprint. While different theories of complex organizations abound, the key idea for making sense of them is power.[52] Bureaucracies belong to or are controlled by somebody, and represent, not so much efficiency and responsibility as the power of property. Both private and public bureaucracies create an image of nonpartisan public service, but in the final analysis they represent the heart of *corporate* capitalism.

A long scholarly tradition, from Frederic Taylor in the early part of the century to present day public administration, business administration, and organizational theory, has sought to perfect the science of management.[53] These efforts, however, have helped to cloak the deep trend toward economic and political centralization and concentration. This trend has also been hidden by analysts who argue that corporate capitalism has undergone a managerial revolution (well-educated managers have replaced property as the organizing principle of capitalism). Of course managers are also property owners and share fundamental class interests with owners in any case. The trend toward a concentrated political economy is further obscured when it is called the End of Ideology, a Knowledge Society, a High-Information Society, a Postindustrial Society, the rise of Professional Society, or the End of History (see "The Fiction of a Knowledge Society" in Chapter 1). Narrow, technical studies of organizations in a taken-for-granted world also obscure the trend toward and the reality of concentrated power.

The basic managerial style in the United States stresses individual responsibility within a hierarchical structure. Orders come from on high, responsibility is from the bottom up. Within this ethic, the manager is free to hire and fire (subject to labor and civil rights law and to labor union contracts). The corporation is the stronghold of the managerial ethic, but it is also the model for managerial styles in government, the military, religion, education, health care, and voluntary groups.

Hierarchy and specialization have their uses, but also create problems. We now know that an efficient bureaucracy does not necessarily mean centralization and steep hierarchy. Workers must feel free to exercise skills and assume responsibilities. Cooperation among workers and worker participation in management yield better and more work. Excessive centralization, hierarchy, and specialization breed insecure workers, clog communication lines, and result in employees who "feather their nest" and carve out turfs.

In recent years, the managerial style of American corporations has been seen as a barrier to corporate innovation, productivity, efficiency, and long-term investment. The American executive is an individual careerist who moves a great deal among different companies, putting down few roots and developing only temporary loyalties, a practice that contrasts sharply with Japanese custom. The American executive is subject to pressures to produce profits every quarter and thus cannot take the long view or argue for investments that will take years to pay off. Again this runs counter to Japanese practice. Centralized control around one dimension leads to inefficiency, and the hierarchical structure promotes social distance between adjacent levels and chasms between managers and workers. As a result, it is difficult to harness the experience and skills of those directly involved in creating products or providing services.[54]

Corporations strive to make their operations seem fair and just as well as efficient. Today the personnel director serves as the corporate conscience in this regard, in effect linking organizational behavior to broad concerns about social and individual justice in the outside world. Organizations have many features not directly linked to efficiency or work. But such things as company newsletters, titles, company bowling teams, and retirement parties are vital to fostering loyalty and commitment. And the pretense that ranks, income, and benefits can be determined through scientific assessment helps to give the organization legitimacy in the eyes of its members. Nevertheless, and despite the claims of "scientific management" and "scientific personnel work," the process of recruiting, testing, interviewing, hiring, and training new members of an organization is largely a legitimizing facade, not science.[55]

The American Science (Ideology) of Management

The science of management, like the social sciences, is not so much science as *American* science. Generated in a culture based on universalistic secular principles and supported by a gigantic continental market, American symbolic culture stressed quantitative studies when it did research and universal principles when it reached conclusions. Flushed with victory in World War II, and able to take the functioning of society for granted, management science did the same thing as the social sciences—it concentrated on developing abstract, universalistic principles. This meant American phenomena were deemed somehow natural. The result in management science was to validate American practices that had little to do with America's economic success. The economic boom of the 1950s and 1960s, when management science came into its own as a profession, was largely due to the pent up demand created by the Great Depression and World War II. It was also due to the fact that the other capitalist societies were either exhausted or in ruins, that is, America's postwar economic success was an artifact of monopoly.

American management science did little comparative work and failed to see that American practices were culture-bound. Decades after many American companies have become global corporations and the American economy faces serious competition from abroad, American management science has still not engaged in comparative research to uncover other managerial styles and understand the cultures that spawn them.[56] This no doubt is part of the explanation for the poor showing by American employees abroad: between 16 to 40 percent return home early (each premature return costing $100,000) and approximately 30 to 50 percent who stay in their overseas assignments are considered ineffective or marginally effective by their firms.[57]

The deficiencies of management science are connected to deficiencies in business education.[58] In turn, business education is hampered by its reliance on mainstream economics.[59] Professionalized managers administer policies made by governing boards (or by policymaking committees, agencies, councils, etc. depending on the type of activity). By and large, policymaking bodies have homogeneous memberships, often despite laws requiring diversification. For example, no progress has been made by the U.S. State Department in obeying the Foreign Service Act of 1980 which requires that America's diplomatic corps be representative of the American people. Corporate boards, university trustees, hospital boards, and presidential advisers[60] are still composed of like-minded individuals. The chances are high that up to ninety percent of the governing boards of American universities have had no training in education. Probably no one on the board or staff of a hospital understands where health comes from. And women, blue-collar workers, blacks, Hispanics, the handicapped, and gays are underrepresented on policy-making bodies throughout American society. Managers, therefore, are subject to policy groups of like-minded individuals who fail to generate the ideas needed for good decisions. And leaders in general are subject to a narrow pipeline of information guarded by a narrow circle of like-minded advisers. All in all, homogeneous policy bodies, mechanically organized, one-dimensional bureaucracies, an obsolete managerial style,[61] and connections among power groups across the apexes of society,[62] all go together to make up a major reason for America's economic, social, and political shortfalls.

Despite the trend toward all-purpose administrators, the field of administration is split up into business, public, hospital, welfare, recreational, and voluntary (nonprofit) administration. Of these, public administration is solidly established with a large association and a journal. Nonetheless, all forms of administration fail to measure up to what we know about complex organizations. A simple question about American bureaucracies (collectively, corporate capitalism) yields an important insight: Why does the United States use so many college graduates in its private and public administrative structures, including the military, in comparison with other developed capitalist societies? The only reason is that unnecessary educational requirements and unnecessary layers of personnel, act as a buffer and camouflage to enable the top people to reap rewards far above those available to their counterparts in other developed capitalist countries.[63] It is a telling fact about the large corporations that make up the heart of the American economy that their executives pay themselves and that there is no relation between income and the size and performance of their enterprises whether judged against other corporations or similar bureaucracies in public utilities, government, or the military, either in the United States or in other developed capitalist societies.[64]

Management and Racial, Ethnic, and Gender Minorities

The African American is not a property-owning middle class—black households that have middle-level incomes receive them largely through double earners and from public employment and public service programs, leaving them vulnerable to cutbacks (as has happened from the Reagan administration of 1980 on through the Clinton administration from 1992 on). In addition, many blacks who hold "managerial" positions tend to be in public relations and affirmative action positions even when they have professional qualifications in other fields.[65] Given the recessions of 1979–83 and 1989–92 and the continuing pressure of having to compete with all types of labor in the developing world, African Americans are even in danger of losing the gains they made between 1875 and 1950.

Data for Hispanic, Asian, and Native Americans are framed in terms of the Census Bureau's broad category of Managerial, Technical, and Professional. The data clearly show that these minorities have not entered this category in proportions to their numbers, but exact studies of particular professions are lacking.

The American occupational system is deeply segregated by sex. Though less true today than thirty years ago, almost all occupations are either female or male dominated. Income differences have also persisted with women earning about 65 to 75 percent of men's despite having the same education[66] and the same occupation.[67] In addition, many *comparable* occupations show large disparities in earnings.

Some narrowing of the gender gap occurred from the 1970s to 1980s, but the reasons are no cause for optimism. A large part of the relative advance of women was due to setbacks suffered by males during the deindustrialization of the American economy. Another part was due to polarization among women as a small group advanced into the better paying occupations, while most women, especially black women, fell behind. The business world's accelerating thrust to lower labor costs by using temporary and part-time workers, or going abroad, will continue to hurt all workers, but lower-level women more than men and probably black women the most. In addition to a steepening hierarchy of income among all workers, including a cleavage between most workers and an upper level of well-protected knowledge workers, there appears to be a strong trend toward increased occupational segregation by gender and race.[68]

While much of the structure of sex segregation was publicized by feminist scholars during the 1970s, it is only in the past few years that research has isolated the relevant variables in this area and has been able to tackle concrete questions. In particular, recent research has been able to refute many of the erroneous reasons advanced as to why women fare less well than men in the workplace.[69] The major reasons alleged to explain gender inequality are: biology, lack of motivation, desire to have families, failure to invest in education, and lack of experience. All these assertions have been refuted. Women value success in business just as much as men and they have actually invested more time in education than men. They are also discriminated against even when they are suitably experienced. By carefully controlling for factors that women share with men, recent studies have shown that disparities in income and authority are due to gender bias.

In recent decades women have made considerable relative increases vis à vis men in college enrollment, graduate and professional education, and in entering management and professional occupations. Women's gains are impressive if one uses census categories—for example, they posted 30 and 40 percent increases in jobs classified as managerial, executive, and administrative in 1980 and 1990 respectively. But as Barbara Reskin and Catherine Ross show, women are concentrated near the bottom of organizational hierarchies, supervise workers of their own sex, and have lower earnings and lower authority despite the fact that their education and experience is similar to men.[70]

ENGINEERS

The Academic View of Engineering

A pioneering national survey of engineering graduates in industry and government yielded valuable information about their social background, education, occupational and value commitments, and career decisions and experience.[71] One finding, that engineers do not have shared professional values, is partly because there are so many different kinds: civil, chemical, electrical, mechanical, industrial, metallurgical-mining-petroleum, and aeronautical. The lack of community, which Perrucci and Gerstl considered unusual, along with the fact that engineers were mostly employees, is now a characteristic of professions in general. The authors also noted that the distinct class nature of recruitment into engineering made them similar to other professions (a finding that they interpreted, along with all their findings, under the assumption that the United States was on the move toward a meritocracy based on science). They also noted the apolitical and narrow education received by engineers and wondered if their lack of a fuller humanistic-social science education was a bad thing.

Perrucci and Gerstl provide a good example of mainstream (functionalist) sociology taking the social world at face value. The U.S. is a society on the move, developing and recruiting the most talented into its elite occupations. The professions perform valuable functions for society. "Law, medicine, and the clergy played an important integrative role in society by institutionalizing a relationship of trust between strangers in crisis situations." But these professions deal with the problems of individuals and their concern with society is only in the aggregate sense. Engineering, however, like the technical-scientific professions in general, is moving more and more toward solving problems through technological means. What the movement into system-analysis and system-building in regard to cities, pollution control, transportation, education, and crime control holds only the future will tell. The new technology raises serious questions about its use: Totalitarian control through centralized data banks, criteria for judging effectiveness, and autonomy of decision-making, thus making external control impossible. The integrative functions of professionals, continue the authors, require a service ethic that will create trust and cohesion between them and clients.

In any case, say Perrucci and Gerstl, the professions are aiding social integration and adaptation by being part of a stratification system based on "universalistic performance criteria that make rewards available to all who qualify in terms of ability." The emerging meritocratic system provides social and political stability and new integrative bonds among those who share the new image of a fluid mobility system based on ability.

The Conflict View of Engineering

The sociology of the professions, as well as sociology, has moved beyond this age of innocence. But the deep affinity of early functionalist sociology with technocratic liberalism became transparent when it studied an openly technocratic profession, engineering. Nonetheless, Perrucci and Gerstl raised issues and pointed to problems that have since been resolved by research. We now also know a great deal about national variations in engineering.[72]

Whalley's study of British engineers helps resolve many of the questions raised about engineers (and can be generalized to other professions). Are they autonomous because of their knowledge? Do they have separate career lines within an organization? Are they being deskilled (either deprofessionalized or proletarianized)? Walley answers all these questions with the concept *trusted worker*. Property owners find it necessary to the efficient operation of a profitable enterprise to create trusted workers out of engineers, that is, expert help who combine their expertise with managerial roles and fuse it into the productive process.

As for the claim that engineers are part of an evolving scientific society based on objective knowledge, we now know this to be mostly wishful thinking that closes the large and stubborn gap between the is and the ought worlds of liberalism. As noted earlier, citing Noble, engineers, along with higher education, helped create the technocratic mode of administration characteristic of American corporations. This made American corporations excessively hierarchic, impersonal, and rigid. This way of solving the problem of assembling and employing capital and organizing a labor force became the model for the administration of government departments, schools, hospitals, foundations, museums, and so on, as well as the disciplines that study administration and organizations. Engineers, in other words, contributed to the formation of a technocratic America. The engineering mode of problem solving is also consistent with the ineffectual way in which Americans and policy professionals think about social problems. We are now aware that the technological orientation of medicine, psychotherapy, law enforcement, education, pollution control, agriculture, sports, national defense, communication, and transportation[73] has had at best mixed results with most analysts tending toward a negative balance sheet.

Engineering and Racial, Ethnic, and Gender Minorities

Engineering has probably the largest percentage of white males among the major professions. Racial, ethnic, and female minorities have low representation in engineering as in all the natural sciences, including mathematics (see Table 5–1). An analysis of women in engineering based on a random sample of engineering graduates (1976–85) reports that the increase of women with bachelor degrees in engineering, after rising significantly, seems to have leveled off at 15 percent of the total.[74] The authors report that engineering has a strong male-oriented culture, but that this varies by type of workplace. Women do much better when the workplace has a weak emphasis on male values, something that occurs in areas with new engineering applications. They also cite liberal and socialist feminist arguments about another barrier that women face—the wider society. Liberals tend to stress gender role socialization that impedes interest in engineering and burdens women with family responsibilities. Socialist feminists refer to the same process as power relations at home, school, and work.

McIlvee and Robinson use a conflict-structural approach to provide valuable insights into women in engineering, especially through a focus on the culture of the workplace. Their one oversight is surprising given their reference to the middle class origins of engineers, especially true of women, and their acquaintance with socialist feminism. Their suggestions for improving the participation of women in engineering call for activism, affirmative action, changes in workplace power relations, and better public services. Nowhere do they recognize that helping women merely means a redistribution of resources restricted artificially and without functional justification by a private-property economy (of which the professions are an integral part). A full structural approach would recognize that unless the economy is directed to increase the number of good jobs, then what is good for some will be bad for others in our zero-sum society.

SUMMARY

The Western tradition sees knowledge as something that has practical applications. Thus the modern world of abstract knowledge producers is matched by a large range of applied professions.

The applied professions all exhibit serious deficiencies. Briefly, these are as follows.

Physicians: Our most powerful and by far best-rewarded profession does not have a unique knowledge base, restricts entry with excessive educational requirements, practitioners rely on routine, often outmoded remedies, are often biased and mistaken, are part of a highly political medical establishment, and are erroneously associated with better health and life expectancy (the latter come from better food, water, hygiene, economic security, and so on). By and large, the medical profession and establishment are unwitting protectors of an unhealthy social environment. Unlike other capitalist societies which have national health insurance (or socialized medicine as in the case of Great Britain), the non-market, unregulated, medicine-for-profit American system costs twice as much as other countries for results that at best are the same.

Lawyers: Lawyers are deeply stratified by social class, race, ethnicity, and gender, and by the class of their clients. These forces, in addition to the emergence of an almost numberless increase in specialized fields and sub-fields of legal practice has rendered the term *lawyer* almost meaningless.

The law has been criticized as being the expression of power—far from having an objective legal system (the rule of law), the United States has a class-based legal system in which the legal rights of the majority are nonexistent. Lawyers are also overeducated and display various forms of incompetence. The American Bar Association has lagged behind on almost all issues of law reform.

Administrators and Executives: The myth of scientific objective management has eroded as more and more evidence has appeared that managers and America's defective administrative structures are a main cause of economic shortfalls.

Engineers: Engineers epitomize technocracy and have been rewarded by having careers in management where they helped create the mechanistic, inflexible, and wasteful American version of bureaucratic administration. They have been superseded by managers trained in finance and law (these managers have also been miseducated for business).

Racial and ethnic minorities have made some gains in the professions, but are far from being represented in proportion to numbers. The reasons are largely because racial and ethnic minorities lack class resources: steady, well-rewarded employment and personalities that come from stable family and community life.

White women from the middle and upper classes have made gains into the professions, but they tend to be segregated within them and have not been able to translate their commitment, education, or experience into income and authority comparable to that of similarly qualified males.

NOTES

1. For some fascinating essays along these general lines, see Margaret Lock and Deborah R. Gordon, eds., *Biomedicine Examined* (New York: Kluwer, 1988).
2. Gina Kolata, "On the Fringes of Health Care, Untested Therapies Thrive" and "In Quests Outside the Mainstream, Medical Projects Rewrite the Rules," *New York Times*, June 17–18, 1996, p. 1.
3. For a highly critical analysis of the American Medical Association as a "political entity that claims to be tending to the public's health, while in reality looking after doctors' interests," see Howard Wolinsky and Tom Brune, *The Serpent and the Staff: The Unhealthy Politics of the American Medical Association* (New York: G.P. Putnam's Sons, 1994).
4. Drugs sold in Canada by American drug companies cost far less than the same drugs in the United States: *New York Times*, October 22, 1992, p. D1.
5. The U.S. specialization rate is more than twice as high as most European countries, over 40 percent of U.S. hospital beds are empty at any given time, and we

have far greater quantities of expensive technology, such as CAT scan machines, than comparable industrial countries: *New York Times*, March 1, 1993, p. A15.

6. For a comparison of the higher use of estrogen by American fee-for-service doctors as opposed to its use by British salaried doctors, see "Professionals versus Professionals: Public Policy as Negotiated Reality among the Powerful," in Chapter 11.

7. As reported by Gina Kolata, *New York Times*, January 30, 1996, p. c3. The study by Dr. John E. Wennberg et al., *The Dartmouth Atlas of Health Care* (1996), is distributed by the American Hospital Association (Washington, D.C.).

8. For a fuller analysis of the reasons why male and female health-care data are often legitimately different, see Andrew G. Kadar, "The Sex-Bias Myth in Medicine," *Atlantic Monthly* 274, no. 2 (August 1994): 66–70.

9. For a valuable set of case studies of a large variety of societies, essentially showing that the medical profession, while powerful everywhere, has undergone ups and downs depending on national-historical variations in its relation to state and capital forces, see Frederic W. Hafferty and John B. McKinlay, eds., *The Changing Medical Profession: An International Perspective* (New York: Oxford University Press, 1993). For an analysis of medicine (and other professions) in the United States, Great Britain, France, Italy, and Germany, see Elliot A. Krause, *Death of the Guilds: Professions, States, and the Advance of Capitalism, 1930 to the Present* (New Haven, Conn.: Yale University Press, 1996)—discussed as "The Death of the Guilds or the Reassertion of Priorities by Corporate World-Market Capitalism?" in Chapter 2. For the abnormal rise and nature of the professions in general in the United States, see "The Rise of the Professions: National Contexts and Variations" in Chapter 1.

10. Thomas McKeown, *The Modern Rise of Population* (London: Edward Arnold, 1976); John Powles, "On the Limitations of Modern Medicine," in David Mechanic, ed., *Readings in Medical Sociology* (New York: Free Press, 1980). For a summary of research in this area, see John B. McKinlay and Sonja M. McKinlay, "Medical Measures and the Decline of Mortality" (1977), in Peter Conrad and Rochelle Kern, eds., *The Sociology of Health and Illness*, 4th ed. (New York: St. Martin's Press, 1994), selection 1.

11. For an analysis of Canada's health-care system, which provides health services and outcomes equal to the United States at considerably less cost, and which refutes empirically all objections raised by those who advocate private, market-oriented medicine, see Theodore R. Marmor and Jerry L. Mashaw, "Canada's Heath Insurance and Ours: The Real Lessons, The Big Choice," in Peter Conrad and Rochelle Kern, eds., *The Sociology of Health and Illness: Critical Perspectives*, 4th ed. (New York: St. Martin's Press, 1994), selection 41.

12. For example, Rochester, N.Y., has much lower health costs because Blue Cross/Blue Shield is the lone insurer and, backed by business—especially Kodak—negotiates fees and prices with health providers.

13. For a summary of the literature and a discussion, see S. Leonard Syme and Lisa F. Berkman, "Social Class, Susceptibility, and Sickness," and Karen Davis and Diane Rowland, "Uninsured and Underserved: Inequalities in Health Care in the United States," both in Peter Conrad and Rochelle Kern, eds., *The Sociology of Health and Illness: Critical Perspectives*, 3rd ed. (New York: St. Martin's Press, 1990), selections 2 and 22. The former is also in the 4th ed. of this work, selection 2.

14. The uninsured also receive negligent, medically inflicted injuries at more than twice the rate of insured patients regardless of race, gender, income, or type of hospital: *New York Times*, November 4, 1992, p. C16.

15. Diana B. Dutton, "Explaining the Low Use of Health Services by the Poor: Costs, Attitudes, or Delivery Systems?" *American Sociological Review* 43 (June 1978): 348–368.

16. Wornie L. Reed with William Darity, Sr., and Norma L. Roberson, *Health and Medical Care of African Americans* (Westport, Conn.: Auburn House, 1993).

17. *New York Times*, January 24, 1996, p. 17A.

18. For some pioneering analyses, see Susan Schiefelbein, "The Female Patient: Heeded? Hustled? Healed?," *Saturday Review* 7 (March 29, 1980): 12–16, and Marian Sandmaier, "Alcoholic Invisible: The Ordeal of the Female Alcoholic," *Social Policy* 10 (January–February, 1980): 25–30.

19. *New York Times*, March 9, 1993, p. 1.

20. The trend across the country to increase the number of nondoctors on medical review boards has resulted in more decisions going against doctors. A national licensing system is still needed to prevent doctors barred in one state from practicing elsewhere and to weed out imposters.

21. Howard Becker and Blanche Geer, "The Fate of Idealism in Medical School," *American Sociological Review* 23 (February 1958): 50–56.

22. Frederic D. Wolinsky, *The Sociology of Health*, 2nd. ed. (Belmont, Calif.: Wadsworth, 1988), pp. 7–25.

23. *New York Times*, November 22, 1993, p. 1.

24. Double credit should go to Harvard Medical School: one, because it has revamped its medical education along some of these lines, and two, because significant departure from routine is rare among front-runners. See Daniel C. Tosteson, "New Pathways in General Medical Education," *New England Journal of Medicine* 322 (January 25, 1990): 234–238.

25. Derek C. Bok, "A Flawed System," *Harvard Magazine* (May–June 1983): 38ff. Bok, former president of Harvard University, is also a former dean of Harvard Law School.

26. Austin Sarat and William L. F. Felstiner, *Divorce Lawyers and Their Clients: Power and Meaning in the Legal Process* (New York: Oxford University Press, 1995).

27. Catherine A. MacKinnon, *Toward a Feminist Theory of the State* (Cambridge, Mass.: Harvard University Press, 1989).

28. *The Transformation of American Law, 1780–1860* (Cambridge, Mass.: Harvard University Press, 1977).

29. The following is based on the comprehensive and insightful analysis by Richard L. Abel, *American Lawyer* (New York: Oxford University Press, 1989).

30. Richard L. Abel, "The Transformation of the American Legal Profession," *Law and Society Review*, 20, no. 1 (1986): 7–17.

31. Erik Olin Wright and Luca Perrone, "Marxist Class Categories and Income Inequality," *American Sociological Review* 42 (February 1977): 32–55.

32. John Hagen, "The Gender Stratification of Income Inequality Among Lawyers," *Social Forces* 68 (March 1990): 835–855.

33. In addition to Abel, see John P. Heinz and Edward O. Laumann, *Chicago Lawyers: The Social Structure of the Bar* (New York: Russell Sage Foundation and American Bar Foundation 1982), and Robert L. Nelson, *Partners With Power: The Social Transformation of the Large Law Firm* (Berkeley: University of California Press, 1988).

34. For an interesting analysis of what it is like to practice in a large, medium, and small firm as well as a public agency and a corporate law department, see Michael J. Kelly, *Lives of Lawyers: Journeys in the Organizations of Practice* (Ann Arbor: University of Michigan Press, 1994).

35. Richard L. Abel, *American Lawyer* (New York: Oxford University Press, 1989). In addition to Abel, a number of studies provide valuable background on racial and ethnic minorities: Erwin O. Smigel, *The Wall Street Lawyer: Professional Organization Man?* (New York: Free Press, 1964); John P. Heinz and Edward O. Lauman, *Chicago Lawyers: The Social Structure of the Bar* (New York: Russell Sage Foundation and American Bar Association, 1982); and Geraldine R. Segal, *Blacks*

in the Law: Philadelphia and the Nation (Philadelphia: University of Pennsylvania Press, 1983).

36. The U.S. Supreme Court has ruled unanimously that partnership firms are not exempt from the civil rights laws.

37. For an old but still relevant study, see Cynthia Fuchs Epstein, *Women in Law* (New York: Basic Books, 1981).

38. John Hagen, "The Gender Stratification of Income Inequality Among Lawyers," *Social Forces* 68 (March 1990): 835–855. Income disparities exist regardless of the size of firm.

39. John Hagan and Fiona Kay, *Gender in Practice: A Study of Lawyers' Lives* (New York: Oxford University Press, 1995).

40. Nina Bernstein, *New York Times*, January 8, 1996, p. 9.

41. Robert Granfield, "Legal Education as Corporate Ideology: Student Adjustment to the Law School Experience," *Sociological Forum* 1, no. 3 (1986): 514–523.

42. Robert V. Stover, ed. and intro. Howard S. Erlanger, *Making It and Breaking It: The Fate of Public Interest Commitment During Law School* (Urbana: University of Illinois Press, 1989).

43. *New York Times*, February 10, 1995, p. A25. The article has details about male and female achievement at the University of Pennsylvania Law School.

44. Doris Marie Provine, *Judging Credentials: Nonlawyer Judges and the Politics of Professionalism* (Chicago: University of Chicago, 1986).

45. For a discussion, see Doris Marie Provine, "Justice à la Carte: On the Privatization of Dispute Resolution," and Bryant Garth, "Public and Private Justice: Issues in Ideology, Professional Interest, Information, and Private Governance," both in Susan S. Silbey and Austin Sarat, eds., *Studies in Law, Politics, and Society* (Greenwich, Conn.: JAI Press, 1992), vol. 12 (Part B), part IV.

46. For background on the American Bar Association's concern with this issue, the commission it sponsored to study it, and a collection of essays forming a first step in the ABA's Program on Professionalism, see Robert L. Nelson, David M. Trubek, and Rayman L. Solomon, eds., *Lawyers' Ideals/Lawyers' Practices* (Ithaca, N.Y.: Cornell University Press, 1992).

47. Renée M. Landers, James B. Rebitzer, and Lowell J. Taylor, "Rat Race Redux: Adverse Selection in the Determination of Work Hours in Law Firms," *American Economic Review* 86 (June 1996): 329–348.

48. David Miller, "Social Justice in Sociological Perspective," *Social Justice* (New York: Oxford University Press, 1976), chap. 8.

49. For a wide variety of case studies of law and lawyers in the developed countries (though not Eastern Europe or the former Soviet Union) and in selected developing countries, as well as comparative theories about them, see Richard L. Abel and Philip S. C. Lewis, eds., *Lawyers in Society*, 3 vols. (Berkeley, Calif.: University of California Press, 1988–89). For the former Soviet Union, see Louise I. Shelley, *Lawyers in Soviet Work Life* (New Brunswick, N.J.: Rutgers University Press, 1984), and Eugene Huskey, *Russian Lawyers and the Soviet State: The Origins and Development of the Soviet Bar, 1917–1939* (Princeton, N.J.: Princeton University Press, 1986). For coverage of a variety of developing countries, and for theoretical perspectives, tuned to the special world of development, see C. J. Dias et al., eds., *Lawyers in the Third World: Comparative and Developmental Perspectives* (Uppsala, Sweden: Scandinavian Institute for African Studies; New York: International Center for Law and Development, 1981).

50. The relative powerlessness of law and the courts when they are opposed by powerful groups is discussed in Chapter 11.

51. For background and bibliography on the above as part of understanding the origins of accountancy, see Keith Hoskin and Richard Macve, "Writing, Examining, Disciplining: The Genesis of Accounting's Modern Power," in A. G. Hop-

wood and Peter Miller, eds., *Accounting as Social and Institutional Practice* (New York: Cambridge University Press, 1994), chap. 3.

52. Charles Perrow, *Complex Organizations: A Critical Essay*, 3rd ed. (New York: Random House, 1986).

53. For a critical history claiming that Taylorism is ideology, not science, and cannot bridge the gap between management and labor, see Stephen P. Waring, *Taylorism Transformed: Scientific Management Since 1945* (Chapel Hill: University of North Carolina Press, 1991).

54. For a summary of the many studies showing that the American managerial style generates bad work and bad morale, see Alan Farnham, "The Trust Gap," *Fortune* 120, no. 14 (December 14, 1989): 56–78.

55. Harrison M. Trice, James Belasco, and Joseph A. Alutto, "The Role of Ceremonials in Organizational Behavior," *Industrial and Labor Relations Review* 23 (October 1969): 40–51.

56. For a valuable analysis showing the American roots of American management science and the need for comparative analysis to develop a genuine universal science of administration, see Nakiye Avdan Boyacigiller and Nancy J. Adler, "The Parochial Dinosaur: Organization Science in a Global Context," *Academy of Management Review* 16, no. 2 (April 1991): 262–290.

57. J. Stuart Black, Mark Mendenhall, and Gary Oddou, "Toward a Comprehensive Model of International Adjustment: An Integration of Multiple Theoretical Perspectives," *Academy of Management Review* 16, no. 2 (April 1991): 291.

58. For an indictment of business education as excessively specialized and out-of-touch with business realities, including the new global economy, see Lyman W. Porter and Lawrence E. McKibbin, *Management Education and Development: Drift or Thrust into the 21st Century?* (New York: McGraw-Hill, 1988). For an interesting radical feminist criticism of this report as merely reasserting the patriarchical values and practices characteristic of business, see Marta B. Calas and Linda Smircich, "Thrusting Toward More of the Same with the Porter-McKibbin Report," *Academy of Management Review* 15, no. 4 (October 1990): 698–705. See also "Education's Failure to Perform Social Functions" in Chapter 3, especially the discussion of the MBA.

59. For a wide-ranging critique of the negative results from business education's alliance with mainstream economics, see Milton Leontiades, *Myth Management: An Examination of Corporate Diversification as Fact and Theory* (Oxford, England: Basil Blackwell, 1989).

60. In his study of the political leanings of White House staffs, John H. Kersel reports that the key advisers to President Reagan were extremely homogeneous, essentially Reagan clones, as reported in the *New York Times* (August 27, 1983), p. G7. William Domhoff, "Where do Government Experts Come From?" In G. W. Domhoff and T. R. Dye, eds., *Power Elites and Organizations* (Beverly Hills, Calif.: Sage, 1987), chap. 10, shows that the President's Council of Economic Advisers is drawn from the corporate elite and a narrow spectrum of elite foundations, think tanks, research institutes, and private policy organizations.

61. For a discussion of the powerful impact of the engineering profession on management during the formative period of corporate capitalism, see David F. Noble, *America by Design: Science, Technology, and the Rise of Corporate Capitalism* (New York: Knopf, 1977). For an earlier discussion of how the natural sciences are adjuncts to the capitalist political economy, see "The Natural Sciences" in Chapter 5, and "Science and the New System of Power" in Chapter 2.

62. Michael Useem, *The Inner Circle* (New York: Oxford University Press, 1984).

63. Articles criticizing excessive executive pay have appeared frequently in *Fortune*. CBS News reported (May 20, 1991) that chief executive officers in the

United States are paid 85 times as much as average workers, whereas the ratio in Germany is 23 to 1 and in Japan 17 to 1.

64. Erik Olin Wright and Luca Perrone, "Marxist Class Categories and Income Inequality," *American Sociological Review* 42 (February 1977): 32–55.

65. Sharon M. Collins, "The Marginalization of Black Executives," *Social Problems* 36 (October 1989): 317–331.

66. U.S. Bureau of the Census, "Money Income of Households, Families, and Persons in the United States: 1992," *Current Population Reports*, P60-184 (Washington, D.C.: U.S. Government Printing Office, 1993), Figure 2.

67. U.S. Bureau of the Census, *Statistical Abstract of the United States 1995* (Washington, D.C.: U.S. Government Printing Office, 1995), Table 677.

68. Annette Bernhardt, Martina Morris, and Mark S. Handcock, "Women's Gains or Men's Losses? A Closer Look at the Shrinking Gender Gap in Earnings," *American Journal of Sociology* 101, no. 2 (September 1995): 302–328.

69. For two readers that reflect this new research, see Ann Helton Stromberg and Shirley Harkess, eds., 2nd ed., *Women Working* (Mountain View, Calif.: Mayfield, 1988), and Jerry A. Jacobs, ed., *Gender Inequality at Work* (Thousand Oaks, Calif.: Sage, 1995).

70. Barbara F. Reskin and Catherine E. Ross, "Jobs, Authority, and Earnings Among Managers: The Continuing Significance of Sex," in Jerry A. Jacobs, ed., *Gender Inequality at Work*, chap. 5.

71. Robert Perrucci and Joel E. Gerstl, *Profession Without Community: Engineers in American Society* (New York: Random House, 1969).

72. For Great Britain, see Peter Whalley, *The Social Production of Technical Work: The Case of British Engineers* (Albany: State University of New York Press, 1986). For France, see Stephen Crawford, *Technical Workers in an Advanced Society: The Work, Careers, and Politics of French Engineers* (New York: Cambridge University Press, 1989). For Germany, see Charles E. McClelland, *The German Experience of Professionalization: Modern Learned Professions and Their Organizations from the Early Nineteenth Century to the Hitler Era* (New York: Cambridge University Press, 1991). For the former Soviet Union, see Edward Gloeckner, "Soviet Engineers as a Professional Group," in Anthony Jones, ed., *Professions and the State: Expertise and Autonomy in the Soviet Union and Eastern Europe* (Philadelphia: Temple University Press, 1991), chap. 4. For Mexico, see Peter S. Cleaves, *Professions and the State: The Mexican Case* (Tucson: University of Arizona Press, 1987).

73. For a case study of engineers awash in a large-scale project, BART (Bay Area Rapid Transit) system, which was a poorly conceived, one-time dodge to circumvent popular control, see "The Cooption of Professionals: The Cases of Energy Researchers and BART Engineers" in Chapter 11.

74. Judith S. McIlwee and J. Gregg Robinson, *Women in Engineering: Gender, Power, and Workplace Culture* (Albany: State University of New York Press, 1992).

7

The Less-Established or Less-Powerful Applied Professions

♦ ♦ ♦ ♦

♦ ♦ ♦ ♦

A large group of applied professions has sought to achieve collective upward mobility by developing a professional ideology and adopting professional practices, for example, publishing journals, creating associations, and requiring long years of schooling. Many have failed to establish themselves as professions, but even those that succeed somewhat must practice in settings or for clients that render them less powerful and less rewarded than other professions.

It is clear that all professions, and the institutions in which they are embedded, are in service to a particular kind of society, corporate, world-market capitalism, a society that in the past fifty years has become to use Giddens's term, an accelerating juggernaut. Throughout our analysis, we have pointed out that a greater understanding of the professions often requires going beyond the self-definitions that the professions have of themselves. Thus the medical profession also makes sense as a way to disguise the damage done to human health by the assorted hazards of corporate capitalism. Lawyers function to legitimate the power of property and its new forms, and to smooth away the unnecessary damages done by businesses, other interest groups, and governments. The function of executives and engineers is to construct the organizations (human capital) and the machines and buildings (material capital) that make up the heart and guts of corporate capitalism.

The professions and semiprofessions analyzed in this chapter also serve corporate capitalism in ways that are not fully intended or understood. Teachers, social workers, computer specialists, applied psychologists and sociologists, and detectives are agents of social control. Journalists transform foundational events and issues requiring collective action into apolitical, unconnectible episodes. And as we now see, psychotherapists (along with help from applied psychologists and others), strive to restore and reincorporate into an unproblematic society the identities shattered by the juggernaut of corporate capitalism.

PSYCHOTHERAPISTS: PSYCHIATRISTS, CLINICAL PSYCHOLOGISTS, AND OTHERS

The Lack of Consensus

Mental illness is extremely diverse and there is no accepted explanation of the causes of many of its various manifestations. Psychotherapists themselves are extremely diverse and have not achieved even a working consensus on how the field should be defined or which therapies are effective. Psychiatrists have medical degrees and can prescribe drugs and admit patients to hospitals. Some practice psychoanalysis (derived from Freud) which is a lengthy exploration of childhood experiences to explain present problems. Clinical psychologists and social workers have professional degrees and are eligible for insurance payments for treating mentally ill patients. Along with marriage-family counselors and clergy (and friends and relatives), psychologists and social workers rely on various kinds of "talk" therapy.

Psychiatry has declined in recent decades (numbering about thirty-six thousand in 1990) and there are now more clinical psychologists and marriage-family counselors (forty-two thousand and forty thousand respectively) than psychiatrists, while clinical social workers now number eighty thousand.[1]

A large number of experimental studies are under way to test the validity of various approaches to mental health. But hanging over the head of the psychotherapy profession(s) is the knowledge that nontherapists have had as much success as trained therapists and that the various therapies used by practitioners have all had equal rates of (modest) success against all disorders. One important implication in all this is that what patients lack and need is someone to talk to in order to restore the morale taken from them by the general social environment. Also hanging over the head of the psychotherapy professions is the well-known fact that practitioners pay little attention to research findings.[2]

The Failure to Perform

As the above suggests, the basic flaw in the mental-health profession may be its anchorage in medicine and psychology. Psychiatry (which requires a medical degree, or rather, which is a medical specialty) has not been overly successful in curing people. Over time, mental health has been increasingly associated with psychology, but here too no great success can be reported. Mental-health specialists have no tests or diagnostic devices that identify mental illnesses and they have had only limited success with their various therapies (confinement, drugs, surgery, shock treatments, one-on-one and small-group interaction).

In a classic study, Rosenhan showed that normal individuals were not identified as normal by mental-health experts when they pretended to have a psychological problem. These individuals were admitted to a wide variety of psychiatric hospitals where they behaved normally. Their normal behavior was noted in hospital files, but hospital authorities never suspected that the patients were normal. Interestingly, the real patients found it easy to identify them as normal. Later, these findings were presented to the staff of a research and teaching hospital to conduct another experiment—the staff was asked to be on the outlook for pseudo patients. Though no pseudo patients appeared, 43 out of 193 applicants for psychiatric treatment were judged to be pseudo patients by at least one staff member, and 19 were judged to be pseudo patients by a psychiatrist and at least one other staff member.[3]

In another study, clinicians were asked to identify normals, neurotics, and psychotics among those who had taken a wide variety of basic tests. Not only did they do no better than chance, but they were inconsistent when asked to repeat the diagnosis a few weeks later. In addition, experi-

enced clinicians could not distinguish between homosexual and heterosex-
ual men, or find any difference in their level of adjustment, again on the
basis of standard tests.[4]

The Pressure to Medicalize Mental Illness

The evolution of the bible of the profession, the *Diagnostic and Statistical Manual of Mental Disorders* (DSM), is an attempt by psychiatry to
achieve consensus by anchoring the field in biomedicine (and, of course, to
exclude rivals). The 3rd edition that appeared in 1980 and in revised form
in 1987 claimed that it represented an accumulation of research findings
and that the field had made great strides in improving diagnostic reliability. But as Kirk and Kutchins argue, *DSM-III* offered only description, had
no new causal findings, and its claims of improved diagnostic reliability
were based on faulty, unreliable, poorly reported, and poorly interpreted
research. Through an analysis of how the manual was constructed, Kirk
and Kutchins conclude that behind the elaborate network of committees
and research groups that allegedly compiled the manual's material according to strict scientific standards was a small, self-selected group that
made arbitrary selections and decisions. Central to the entire enterprise
was an attempt to define the problem of diagnostic reliability in technical
terms and thus make it appear that mental illness was an objective medical
specialty.[5]

The manual is in wide use, but is used differently by different
practitioners. A fourth edition (1994) made the same claims as the sponsors of DSM-III, but critics, including Kirk, argue that it is no different
from previous editions—indeed, it includes all the disorders listed in
the third edition.[6] Perhaps the most negative fact about the field of
psychotherapy is that the first edition of the manual in 1952 listed 106
disorders (up from 59 listed by the American Psychiatric Association
in 1917), the second had 182, the third had 262 in 1980, and 292 in its
revised 1987 form. In addition to protecting their turf by using the
rhetoric of science, the psychiatric profession is also mindful that unless it
lists specific disorders it cannot hope to have its practices covered by
health insurance.

Bypassing the Psychotherapy Profession

Moving away from psychiatry proper, one sees a different picture.
To their credit, the psychotherapy professions appear to be coming to terms
with the reality of mental illness, or rather, their failure to understand
it. Many have begun to recognize that emotional problems are normal, that is,
most of those who are troubled are normal individuals facing normal problems encountered by attempting to live up to American norms. By distinguishing between the small number who are seriously ill (either because of
chemical deficiencies or severe traumas) and the vast majority who can be

helped with an eclectic mix of brief treatments, the psychotherapy professions are moving toward social psychology and sociology. Until they complete this move, they will continue to misdefine the causes of problems and rely on false stereotyping, including the present tendency (shared with medical doctors) to have different images and explanations of mental health for men and women.

The most promising perspective on mental health is to anchor policies in a social-class context. Research indicates that the lower classes suffer more from it and get poorer and less effective treatment. Ultimately, of course, the treatment for mental health must come from public policies that curb the unnecessary stresses and deprivations that are endemic to the American class system. The overall problem with the psychotherapy profession is the failure to understand that mental health comes from living in a healthy social environment, one that provides a congruent, stable world of meaning and material sustenance. By looking for its source in the private individual and trying to cure it through private professionals, mental-health specialists are inadvertent protectors of a liberal social system that warps and destroys many of its members.[7]

APPLIED PSYCHOLOGY

Serving Power: Testing

Applied psychology began in World War I when psychologists used testing to help the military evaluate individuals and place them in the niches for which they were allegedly best suited by nature. During the 1920s, applied psychology expanded and began to advise corporations, schools, universities, and governments on how to evaluate individuals and fit them in, especially through the use of testing. They also began to advise parents on how to raise children and to advise individuals on how to solve personal problems. All in all, they became "architects of adjustment" who simply took society for granted, ignored workers, women, and minorities, and using Darwinian ideas, thought of the human psyche as something that should adjust to its environment.[8]

Applied psychology hitched its wagon to testing in the early decades of the twentieth century and has resisted the knowledge that tests (IQ, SAT, LSAT, MCAT, GRE, and so on) are class based and might have some value if used in that light. But the idea that tests reveal the basic natural hierarchy of talented individuals is too useful to their clients (the upper classes, schools, corporations, governments) for psychologists to listen to criticism. Not only do tests not predict how individuals behave outside of schools, but their predictive power about success or failure in school is weak. A recent study, for example, revealed that the GRE has almost no value in predicting success in America's graduate programs.[9]

Serving Power: Counseling

The problems with applied psychology can also be gleaned from the following case studies. A study of how a group of male and female psychologists, school psychologists, and male and female public school teachers ranked 53 stressful experiences for teenagers (for example, the death or divorce of a parent, a car accident, moving to a new town or school, dropping out of school, required to attend summer school) compared to how teenagers (aged fourteen to seventeen) ranked the identical list showed a wide disparity in how each group ranked the items. Not only does this cast doubt on professional competence, but the psychologist who reported the results of the study referred to the professionals as "adults" who were misinterpreting the experiences of the "young."[10]

In another study, young children and a group of adults (made up of child experts, teachers, and college students) rated twenty items in terms of stressfulness (for example, a new baby brother or sister, being caught stealing, having an operation, being sent to the principal's office). The adults tended to agree strongly, but their ratings were markedly different from those of the children. That is to say, the child experts were no different from teachers and both experts and teachers were no different from college students, and all were wrong.[11] Erroneous stereotyping is rampant among elites and professionals and perhaps worst in the field of psychotherapy (for a fuller discussion of professional bias within the context of deviance, see Chapter 9).

A third study comparing school psychologists in an urban, bureaucratic setting with psychologists in a suburban, less bureaucratic setting found that the former stressed objectivity and testing and saw themselves as serving educators, while the latter focused on students and sought whatever information might be helpful in serving them.[12] The author stresses the influence of organizational setting and argues that suburban schools are part of a "moral community" that invite psychologists to tackle the various value and other conflicts in their work. The urban school psychologists, dealing largely with minority students, used allegedly objective tests to counsel students, in effect, enacting the latent consequence of all tests (including the influential academic tests that students are subjected to), social control in the name of the existing class system.

Counseling has its roots in American psychology and has been especially remiss in addressing the special needs of minorities. This failure has its first cause in the lack of minority representation in both the American Psychological Association and the American Counseling Association. Continued failure to redirect these organizations eventually led to a protest movement within counseling and then to a separate group (the Association for Multicultural Counseling and Development) and journal. This movement is significant not merely because minorities are projected to form one-third of the American population in 2000, but because its focus on all forms of sociocultural phenomena, including social class, could pull all of psychology in the same direction. The multicultural movement in psychological counseling has climaxed its efforts with a valuable handbook.[13] Unfortunately, the movement has not been able to escape the scientism that mars mainstream psychology.

JOURNALISTS

The Social Construction of News

Like professionals in medicine, law, and the natural and social sciences, journalists define themselves by the ideals of objectivity, empirical accuracy, and nonpartisanship. But here, and even before it occurred in the other professions and disciplines, a new realism has surfaced. In his classic analysis of the day-to-day routine of journalists on a small-city newspaper, framed in terms of the "reality construction perspective," Fishman shows how deeply constrained newsreporters were by the logic of a profit-oriented, bureaucratically run newspaper. With the organization spelling out the where, what, when, who, and why of news reporting, with private and governmental groups and individuals supplying the majority of their facts and interpretations, and with their corresponding American way of looking at things, journalists *create* a highly selective body of news. News is really a way of not knowing, a highly ideological way to create reality.[14]

Journalism depoliticizes by alleging that it is objective. We now know that objectivity is a fiction invented by elites to protect themselves against each other. We know that journalism has neither the time nor the money to cover the news fully or carefully (and still remain profitable). We know that journalists lack the expertise and experience needed to get beneath the surface of substantive issues. We know that journalists become dependent on their sources, most of whom are powerful groups and individuals. We know that journalists work in bureaucratic settings in a highly concentrated business.

We are also aware that the news is a socially created reality that supports the status quo and (this may be especially true of television news) creates dependency and undermines reflexivity (the ability to see oneself as an active participant in the formation and control of social reality[15]). TV news does not encourage viewers to explain and understand social and personal problems in terms of the larger socioeconomic world. And it does not present alternative public or private policies for viewers to choose from. Instead, it presents viewers with a taken-for-granted world, a fixed "objective" world in which people are acted upon. In this world, action takes place in terms of unquestioned cultural a priori about the family, government, capital, labor unions, the legitimacy of experts, and other countries.[16] The basic causes in the world are different types of individuals, fixed impersonal institutions, and sinister or unstable foreigners. In this sense, TV news is part of the overall symbolic world that constitutes the basic outlook of all the theoretical and applied sciences and all the professions. As part of the larger culture, TV news does not control by imposing itself on viewers—perhaps more important is its ability to connect with the already fashioned personality of its viewers and to involve them in a mythical world common to both.[17]

Newscasts pretend to have an authoritative picture of what is going on in the world. They consist of fragmented bits of information in vivid word and picture. They appear omniscient because of their technical ability to conquer space and time. But all this undermines understanding and promotes passivity. Broadcast journalism rarely encourages action by its audience or works to empower it by locating personal troubles in public and private institutions. And it rarely provides historical background so that the audience can learn from the past and locate itself in an ongoing process of social creation.

Journalists as Ethnocentric Servants of Power

Analysts have shown that the news media are distinctly ethnocentric and provide a false picture of the world-at-large, especially the developing world.[18] The two American international news agencies (Britain and France have one each and the former USSR had one) routinely support United States and Western interests in their news reporting. Elliott and Golding have found that the British news media have created a typical image of developing nations (they imply that the same is true of news media in all capitalist countries):

1. Developing countries are depicted only in terms of political, military, or economic crisis.
2. Direct British interests are highlighted in any news from a developing country.
3. Events are invariably framed in an East–West Cold War perspective.
4. The structure of the developing country is simplified—countries are seen in terms of their national leader and conflicts are reduced to tribal or religious disputes. National, regional, and racial stereotypes are also widespread.
5. Foreign news stories are framed within a narrow range of story cycles that limit the possibilities open to the developing country.

Western news media assume that it is normal for a developing country to strive to meet Western standards. Because of their reliance on Western news agencies and journalism training, developing countries devote more attention to the developed world than to other developing countries, and as is done in the West, they focus mostly on political leaders, defining political action as that done by elites and equating official diplomacy with the substance of international politics and conflict.[19]

Journalism and the Politics of Corporate Capitalism

As we saw with medicine and law, both broadcast and print journalists work for large profit-seeking organizations. Brint argues that journalism and other professions have suffered a loss of autonomy as markets have stripped away some of the protection that they once had against such forces.[20] Brint's analysis is framed in terms of his overall thesis, that the once nonpolitical, nonprofit professions, motivated by a service-scholarship ethic, have become experts for hire, experts who are oriented toward markets and income. Brint's thesis is a common one that surfaces continuously in the individual professions and is based on the dubious assumption that the professions were once separate from and above the capitalist economy.

It is closer to historical reality to see the professions as essentially capitalist actors who invented ideals of service, objectivity, and so on to enhance their market capabilities. What Brint and others are observing is change within an unchanging capitalist world. Thus change has led, in journalism as elsewhere, to corporate world-market capitalism. News organizations are not merely dependent on advertisers—they are big businesses in their own right whether in newscasting, newsprint, or as parts of giant, and increasingly, global, multimedia corporations. In any case, there is little doubt that the news media exhibit a strong trend toward monopoly.[21]

Organizational dependence is not the only constraint on journalists. They are also extremely dependent on their sources, who often are people in power, that is, those who make news. Given this overall context, it is not surprising that journalism often falsifies by accepting the facts as presented by politicians and representatives of interest groups. It collaborates with political figures and police departments at budget time to create false crime waves.[22] It falsifies by omitting facts—for example, in reporting on elections in El Salvador in 1984, it hailed the large turnout as a victory for moderation forgetting to note that voting in El Salvador is compulsory. Journalism falsifies by discussing a limited range of reform proposals as the only choice open to Americans. Journalism falsifies by faithfully reporting what government officials have to say. And journalists who report on science consistently portray it as humanity's best hope and fail to raise critical issues about it.

In an important empirical study of the impact of TV newscasts on public opinion, Iyengar found that the *episodic* framing of the bulk of newscasting (the depiction of particular acts by individuals, particular events, individual perpetrators or victims) as opposed to *thematic* format (putting the episodes in an explanatory context) reduced the public's ability to attribute acts and events to societal factors and to the actions of elected officials.[23] Hundreds of acts of terrorism, for example, were reported during the 1980s, but virtually no reports on their socioeconomic or political antecedents. In addition to terrorism, crime and poverty were reported episodically, racial inequality featured both episodic and thematic reports, and unemployment was primarily thematic. With the exception of unemployment, the public was sensitive to the format employed. The influence of the format used by TV news is resisted by other variables (for example, party affiliation and political ideology, but not level of education). Nonetheless, depending on the format it uses, TV news has the power to raise or lower the public's ability to hold political officials accountable. Iyengar's conclusion is that it lowers the public's ability to hold elected officials and social factors responsible for social problems, not least because it prevents the public from seeing the interconnections among "episodes," for example, unemployment and crime.

Another careful study, this time of the personality of elite journalists (in the context of the national media), reports that elite journalists are fairly homogeneous in origin (upper-middle class, Eastern urban, nonchurchgoing) and in personality (they are politically liberal and alienated from traditional norms and institutions, to the left on social issues such as abortion, gay rights, and affirmative action, and would like to strip power from traditional holders and empower black leaders, consumer groups, intellectuals, and the media).[24] All this leads them to give the news a left-liberal slant as judged by long-term coverage of nuclear safety, busing, and energy issues. The slant given to these questions (which occurs on all issues, say the authors) can be seen in two ways: American executives consistently see all issues differently than journalists (on tests), and the journalists veer toward the left in comparison with experts on nuclear safety, busing, and energy.

The authors tend to conclude that journalists cannot be objective (that is, they do not make the mistake of criticizing them for not being objective). But their study creates the impression that executives have sounder judgment than journalists, and assume that the experts are objective. Instead of realizing that executives and experts are no different than journalists (one or another form of liberal bias), the authors' purpose seems to be to discredit journalists, not so much for displaying bias, but for being biased on the liberal left. Somehow journalists are biased because personality tests reveal that they are anti-authority and their need for power is stronger than their need for achievement. The authors would have also been wise to be suspicious of experts in testing.[25]

Public confidence in newspaper and television news has dropped significantly in the past decade or so (part of a general loss of confidence by the American people in their institutions and professions). In a paper to the American Political Science Association's annual meeting, Kathleen Hall Jamieson argues that journalism's standing had suffered because it focuses on the maneuvering of public participants and their attacks on one another and fails to report on the substantive content of policy proposals.[26] Jay Rosen has also pointed to the tendency by journalists to focus on the strategy of public actors and to connect public life to the wider American value of winning. And by claiming to be objective, journalism tags all others as subjective. All in all, concludes Rosen, the desire to be objective is really a desire "to be free of the results of what you do."[27] His judgment about journalism is applicable to all the professions and disciplines.

Journalism, perhaps especially TV news, is politically biased despite, or perhaps because of, its strenuous effort to be objective and nonpartisan. To achieve objectivity, it searches out and affirms the broadest area of agreement. By focusing on social consensus, it neglects conflict, special points of view, and the possibilities for change. The world it creates is seen as unchanging and unchangeable. Investigative journalism (for example, *60 Minutes*) focuses on rotten apples and ignores the barrel (the institutions of capitalism). In-depth coverage of issues (the news documentary) has all but disappeared from television: the prime-time public is not interested, it represents a loss of profit, and it only causes controversy. The demise of the Fairness Doctrine (the requirement that different positions on issues be given) means that the discussion of public issues is wholly subject to the power of money. And journalism, again especially television news, has become an integral part of the new politics, the ability of candidates to create a false world through a careful management of symbols: privately produced film that is presented as news, and staged news events and photo opportunities at which little of substantive value is said.[28] The emergence of public or civic journalism in the elections of 1994 and especially in 1996, spearheaded by grants from the Pew Foundation, is an encouraging sign. Here news organizations determine what issues the public is interested in, stress them in their election coverage, and prod the candidates and parties to discuss them.

The press clearly is an integral part of internal American power relations[29] transmitting national news from the standpoint of the upper-middle class and from a distinctively American value standpoint.[30] By and large, the press depoliticizes social problems even as it promotes a corporate liberalism at the national level and an entrepreneurial liberalism at the local and regional level.

Journalism and Racial, Ethnic, and Gender Minorities

An analysis of how the Los Angeles riot of 1992 was reported by the *Los Angeles Times*, the *Chicago Tribune*, the *Atlanta Constitution*, and the *New York Times* exemplifies the problem faced by African Americans (and all other racial-ethnic minorities) when it comes to news reporting. By focusing on the event, and because there is so little positive, offsetting coverage of African Americans, the reports tended to blame blacks for the riot—that is, there was very little causal explanation of why riots take place.[31]

African Americans have a long history of publishing their own newspapers and other vehicles of information, but such efforts cannot overcome the biased image created by the white press since white America does not read the black press. The biases of the white newsworld will not be overcome until more African Americans hold decision-making positions in newspapers and newscasting organizations.[32]

Women are prominent in reporting the news on television, but they are not very well represented in decision-making positions in journalism. White women in the upper classes tend to have considerable class resources and thus have a certain measure of political power. What this means is that issues important to them get aired in American politics and journalism.

ACCOUNTANTS

American accountants have many of the attributes of a profession (long years of schooling, journals, associations). But, on the whole, they suffer from prestige problems, being ranked by the American people lower than dental hygienists and elementary school teachers, and even the more established levels in accountancy are in distinct service to powerful clients.

Accounting is still widely regarded as a technical science providing objective-neutral knowledge about the economic health of individuals, firms, hospitals, schools, governments, and so on. Along with those who compile our social indicators (Gross Domestic Product, unemployment rate, income data, and so on), accountants are the bookkeepers of our civilization, the ones we rely on to see how things are going. Technically, accountants audit the books to see if an enterprise has given a true accounting of itself. Owners, legislators, citizens, consumers, and so on want to know if an enterprise is generating enough revenues to cover costs and turn a profit, if taxes are staying ahead of spending or reducing deficits, and of trends in these areas. But creative scholarship has caught up with accounting just as it has with the other professions and disciplines.

The most advanced scholarship on accounting is British[33] and the reasons are easy to understand. Great Britain has a long history as a developing capitalist society in which both the deficiencies and the virtues of its various classes are transparent. British scholars, therefore, have been able to see accounting as a developing science, that is, as a science with a history of serving the different needs of a developing capitalist society. By seeing accounting as a social activity, British scholars could see any number of things that cast doubt on it as objective and neutral. By assigning numbers to the behavior of humans, accounting changes how we think of behavior, in effect, creating reality. The use of numbers also provides the created reality with metaphysical standing (objective truth) and connects it to a host of other values, for example, choice and efficiency. And by inventing new ways to calculate the meaning of cost, profit, investment, assets, depreciation, and so, accounting provides society with an adaptive capability.

The new view of accounting now studies it in terms of national context, as a part of an organization's decision making system, as a way to cope with other organizations and interests, and in relation to other institutional sectors. From the accumulating research, fundamental connections between the economy and state were identified. It was also established that managers do not make rational decisions with or without accounting, but operate in a world of multiple ambiguities (the fiction that accounting leads to rational decisions perpetuates the fiction that life is under rational human control and direction). Nonetheless, financial officers have come to dominate the management of enterprises. The scholars in this collection suggest strongly that accounting has no essence and cannot be considered objective and neutral. Instead, accounting is part of our myth structure, an interpretive science that performs ceremonial functions and is used by owners to marginalize and closely monitor labor. But the conclusion drawn from all this is not what one would expect (that accounting be defined in sociopolitical terms). Miller's introduction-and-summary concludes by stressing that the creativity of accounting in the past promises an even more creative future, thus presenting great opportunities for creative research. In short, accounting is somehow taken out of history and its role in the exercise of social power and turned into an autonomous academic discipline.

The material revealed by British scholarship can be interpreted differently. As we saw earlier, the use of numbers to create what is real and unreal, desirable and undesirable, has become a pervasive social practice providing social-control and adaptive functions for corporate capitalism. We are now in a social world in which mathematics is used (with the help of the computer) to give a number to every aspect of behavior and every unit of society from the individual to complex organizations, including international organizations. In short, behavior and groups are being closely monitored to see if the values and beliefs of the upper classes are being adhered to. Accounting is merely another aspect of the use of numerical symbols to exercise and legitimate social power (which, by definition, should be problematic in a national political culture). Indeed, the use of arbitrary ways to assign numbers to the behavior demanded by power groups has the consequence of making that behavior the meaning of rational (for a fuller discussion, see "Mathematics" in Chapter 5).

Like all the professions and disciplines, accountants rely on assumptions, in their case, accounting rules. In accounting, as elsewhere, there are no bedrock axioms that correspond to reality—only data collected and assembled according to assumptions. Readers should recall that the assumptions used by economists, political scientists, and so on to define their basic concepts are far from settled, or the most advantageous. Concepts such as *capital, profit, work, productivity, debt, deficit, inflation, tax, spending,* and so on are all problematic. Many are used, however, as if they were objective depictions of reality (perhaps less so today than in the recent past). In any case, the bottom line about accounting and all the knowledge professions is that there is no bottom line.

Current efforts to improve private and public accounting standards are important, though they stem largely from pressures by disaffected property and professional groups, not from a healthy desire to politicize how we run our affairs. This is to say that improvements in accounting standards are still being portrayed as part of a developing science. Nonetheless, improvements are valuable both for private and public decision making. To give two examples of needed improvements: banks are required to keep capital reserves, but there are no standard measures for computing them; defining the ownership of private pensions is lacking in both accounting practices and in public law.

Better accounts are important and the accounting profession, working through a private body (the Financial Accounting Foundation which selects members of the Financial Accounting Standards Board), whose functions have been delegated to it by the Securities and Exchange Commission, continuously strives to improve the definitions used to compile the accounts of corporations. For example, it is currently trying to get businesses to state their assets in current market values. But too much faith should not be put in this process. It has been established, for example, that accounting is not information on which decision making is conducted. Instead, the information in a company statement provides "ritual assurance. An account or statement symbolizes competence, displays authority, inspires confidence, affirms the legitimacy of decisions made, and establishes the validity of [alleged] ongoing intelligent choice."[34]

Despite improvements, therefore, accounting (like all social indicators and all academic knowledge) is not knowledge as a prompter of democratic choice and action. The success of the SEC in broadening the public-interest representation on the Financial Accounting Standards Board in 1996, will no doubt lead to better definitions, but that does not mean that a rational-choice economy and society is on the way. Higher standards or better definitions are no substitute for an open discussion of what standards a responsibly organized public should adopt in order to manage society's fortunes.

The most important changes needed in accounting rules are in the public sector. Though every single public indicator contains arbitrary and debatable assumptions at its base, one important example, actually, the most important, will suffice for now (for needed reforms in our social indicators, see Chapter 11). The federal budget, the core subject of most political discussion, does not contain the elementary distinction between capital and overhead spending. No business, hospital, law firm, foundation, or household could function effectively without this distinction and yet the United States is attempting to do so. In a real sense, it is not the United States that has decided not to use this all-important distinction—it is the powerful private groups, the same ones who employ that distinction to manage their private affairs, who insist that it not be used for managing the public's affairs. The reason is obvious—not to count large sums of public spending as capital (or social investment) allows politically conservative groups to continue the fiction that government is wasteful and not important in how society works. In all this they are aided by accountants. Both here and in private life, accountants help to cover up the social world as well as reveal it. Here as elsewhere, Americans need to bring the assumptions they use to collect and give meaning to data into the open. Here as elsewhere, Americans should not so much search for assumptions that provide objective knowledge as those that facilitate political creativity and negotiation. At present, powerful groups with the help of private and public accountants, cover up their failures and misdeeds by obscuring their spending, indebtness, and so on, thus making it very difficult for shareholders, consumers, and citizens to monitor and evaluate their behavior.

NURSES, SOCIAL WORKERS, TEACHERS, AND LIBRARIANS

These four semiprofessions[35] have been clustered and highlighted to illustrate four things:

1. They are large.
2. They are distinctly gendered, composed largely of women.
3. Despite their drawbacks, these occupations, relatively speaking, are still desirable jobs and it should be noted that they are held largely by non-Hispanic whites.
4. They work for large organizations as subordinate employees serving socially devalued or less-valued clients.

Though the point will not be elaborated, one should note that males who enter these "feminine" fields face negative stereotyping by outsiders, but are favored on the inside. Tokenism, Williams tells us, works differently in female-dominated occupations and desegregating these occupations requires different remedies than desegregating male-dominated occupations.[36] Williams could have pointed out that some of the advantages males receive could also contribute to the fact that males dominate the authority positions in or over these professions.

Nurses

Nursing has a long history of trying to increase its educational-training requirements in order to upgrade its status. While it has succeeded to some extent, it has run up against the strict ceiling on what nurses can do set by the medical profession (this ceiling may be crumbling—see the section on physicians in Chapter 6). Nursing's resort to education is understandable. Education provides legitimacy (by claiming that it provides its clients with a unique knowledge base through meritocratic processes) and thus allows control over labor flows. Nurses have also resorted to state licensing, another time-honored way to uphold both needed and unnecessary standards (with the latter serving to restrict entry artificially).

Nursing is of interest because its "failure" has come about not so much because its claims about professionalism are false (all such claims are false), but because they have collided with the false claims of doctors. Nursing has also been thwarted by the fact that nursing is labor-intensive and constitutes a major payroll expense. From 1994 on, hard-pressed hospitals have replaced many on their nursing staffs with semitrained aides and have put pressure on nurses to give up various benefits. Here nurses share a burden with teachers, social workers, librarians, middle managers, and the American working class in general as corporate capitalism adjusts to the world market by squeezing its employees while maintaining the income of owners and upper level executives. An important reform in health care is to redefine the role of doctors, physician assistants, and nurse practitioners, all with a view toward making it easier for many aspects of health care to be administered in new and better ways. Of course, an even larger payoff will occur if patients become an integral part of this cooperative effort.[37]

Nursing has had many creative, militant, and courageous leaders throughout its modern history. Many of its leaders have been feminists, even radical feminists. While success can be measured on some fronts, failure has occurred in conventional areas (pay, security, work satisfaction) as well as in the goal of radical feminist nursing, as seen by Roberts and Group, that nurses

> be given the authority to do their jobs, the respect and recognition for what they really do, the freedom to do all they can do, and the economic support that rewards them fairly. The alternative is the present system of enforced and subordinated silence in which physicians overcharge for what nurses can do

instead, take credit for what nurses actually do, and deny patients access to nurses' expertise; a system in which hospital administrators demand more and more competence from nurses and increase their responsibilities, but expect nurses to do their work without full authority or the economic rewards to make it worthwhile."[38]

Roberts and Group provide a rich history of nursing's many and varied struggles in the context of feminism. Unfortunately, they end defining militant feminism in nursing as an aid in helping nurses achieve a better professional status. While some important reforms in health care are desirable and perhaps even possible within corporate capitalism, the authors might have seen things differently if their enemy was not men and physicians, but the highly concentrated, ideologically defined system of corporate capitalism now fully implicated in the world market. To take only one example of the need for social system analysis, the powerful pressures to cut costs in health care in recent years that have squeezed nurses (and hospitals and even doctors) have come from American corporations faced by domestic and foreign competitors who have far lower health-care costs.

Social Workers

An insightful history of social work has been written in terms of how society handled the needs of single, pregnant women between 1890 and 1945.[39] Kunzel reminds us that illegitimacy has meanings that stretch far beyond itself—it not only explicitly involves definitions of morality, sexuality, marriage, family, and nation, but implicitly, it involves considerations of class, race, and gender. The story of social work is part of the rationalization and professionalization of American life that accelerated in the late nineteenth century. By the 1890s, white, middle-class, evangelical Protestant women had established a large network of maternity homes for single mothers (largely from rural, working-class backgrounds). Kunzel tells the story of social work in terms of the struggle by white women in the upper classes to gain control of these homes and establish jurisdiction over illegitimacy in the name of science and expertise (it should be noted that the major problem that generated a need for social work was poverty). But social work's strenuous campaign to establish itself in the name of professionalism was also its undoing. In the 1930s the working class character of (visible) illegitimacy changed as more white middle-class girls appeared in need of help. This led to a changed approach as social work defined middle-class illegitimacy as a personal failing due to emotional deficiencies. Ironically, this placed social work under the authority of doctors, psychiatrists, psychologists, and sociologists (not to mention public officials). In the 1940s, black illegitimacy became visible and while the black sociologist E. Franklin Frazier explained black family problems as a legacy of slavery and oppression (seconded by Gunner Myrdal's *An American Dilemma*, 1944), others (for example, Daniel P. Moynihan, *The Negro Family*, 1965) suggested that it was rooted in black culture. That meant that the United States would have separate ways of viewing illegitimacy (and all other problem behavior): one derived from class ideology (the individual explains all), and two, race (the races are different in biology or culture, or both). It meant that as traditional family structure (headed by a male breadwinner) would become a fantasy ideal performing multiple social functions for America, the inability of many African Americans to meet this ideal would marginalize them still further (this fantasy family is still powerful today as both Republicans and Democrats vie to see who can uphold "family values" while saying little about the runaway corporate, global capitalism that is disrupting and destroying both white and black families).

Kunzel's history has a subtheme that should be noted. Single women in maternity homes forged bonds and asserted themselves as best they could vis à vis their "betters." Here again we see that relations among professional and client are never unilateral. This point should not be overshadowed by Kunzel's major theme which shows how the powerful forces of professionalism, class, gender, and race defined, uplifted, and ultimately subordinated social work.

Social workers handle cases made up of individuals and families who need help. The field is of interest because social work cases are the result of structural problems: A property-oriented society generating unnecessary unemployment, underemployment, economic insecurity, poverty, and assorted personal and family pathologies. The field of social work is a way to depoliticize this fact. A study by Knudsen corroborates the suspicion that social work merely deals with symptoms. The social-service professional model in regard to abused and neglected children, reports Knudsen, emphasizes one-on-one and family counseling, and crisis intervention: Characteristically, it does not tackle the known causes of child abuse.[40]

The field of social work is financed largely by public money and it is easy to see why public caseworkers support the Democratic party. The sharp cutbacks in social services from the Reagan through the Clinton administrations have led large numbers of social workers into private practice (counseling, mental health care) where they earn more than other social workers by catering almost exclusively to middle-class clients.[41]

Teachers and Librarians

Elementary and high school teachers are employees of large public-school systems, some of them very large, and some huge. Since American education is largely local (residential school districts and state government), its quality corresponds to the hierarchy of the American class system (see Chapter 3). Affluent districts routinely spend five times as much on their students as poor districts and this means that elementary and high school teachers (and school librarians) are subject to a steep hierarchy of income and benefits.

Education at this level has never been able to establish the same mystique about knowledge as higher education. Everyone considers themselves qualified to talk about and judge lower-school education; in short, there is no mystique about science, a unique knowledge base, the curriculum, or how to impart knowledge to protect teachers from clients. Teachers are also subject to hostile objections to a secular, humanistic education by various religious and right-wing groups.

The Republican party has launched attacks on the public-school system to curry favor with both secular and religious conservatives and, of course, to curb the political power of the Democratic party. This is part of its attack on any and all professionals or semiprofessionals who are financed by taxes: lawyers, doctors, professors, social workers, police officers, as well as teachers. The Republican party's ideology of laissez-faire (the magical market) and returning power to the people (putting citizens under the thumb of state and local governments, more readily controlled by propertied and elite professional groups than the federal government) is a major reason why the federal government has shallow pockets, cannot reduce sharp inequalities in education and elsewhere, and is unable to provide national direction.

Librarians have also been unable to convince outsiders that they have a unique theoretical knowledge base (this may change as information science expands). They also suffer from being employees of public libraries and schools serving children (and adults) for free, or being employees of colleges and universities serving others. Like other established professions, but not so successfully, librarians have sought to enhance their occupation by linking what they do (storing and making knowledge accessible) to important social functions (education, an informed citizenry) and by requiring more and more education.

ARCHITECTS AND PHARMACISTS

Architecture has a long association with society's power structure. In a brilliant essay, Larson has connected it to priestly power in Mesopotamia and Egypt, royal power in Sumer, to a more secular, popular society in ancient Greece, to state needs and private wealth in Rome, to state patronage of art in the Renaissance, and to a diversified structure of private and public power groups in modern, especially industrial-urban society.[42]

The Renaissance separated the various elements of constructing a building: conception, construction, and commissioning. For the first time, conception, or the artistic rendering of a building, could be stressed independently of construction and sponsor—indeed, artist-architects could confer their special status on the customer-sponsor, a change that also inaugurates the incorporation of architecture into the modern class system. By the nineteenth century, hope was expressed that the architect could combine the aesthetic with the techniques of construction to forge an autonomous professional role. That hope was shattered by the full onset of industrialization and the growth of other professions, most notably engineering. In addition, new building materials destroyed the possibility of preserving a few classic architectural forms. The nineteenth century also diversified taste, and everyone, or rather anyone with money, could choose their own style of building. In one way, this represented a great opportunity for architecture to serve more sectors of society than ever before in history, but in reality, the architect was undermined as an autonomous professional by the autonomy of the rich, near-rich, and middle-class, by the power of corporate and state patrons who commissioned what they wanted, by the proliferation of styles, and by the rivalry of engineers. Larson concludes her history by saying the aesthetic philosophy of *modernism*, or the attempt to link architecture to a vision of a society constructed around the machine, represented a last-ditch ideology to shore up a profession that could not use sponsorship by power groups, as did say medicine, to establish a monopoly.

Two important aspects of the history of architects must be added to Larson's account, the incorporation of the solo practitioner into the architectural firm[43] and the occupation's origins in a masculine world and the difficulty women have had in entering it.[44] The transformation of architecture into a business meant that efficient service to clients became paramount and a *de facto* abandonment of ideals for aesthetically and morally superior private and public spaces.

Pharmacists have also struggled to develop a professional status, but they too have been caught in a number of binds. Their long history of being druggists, that is, a combination of businessperson and pharmacist made it difficult to establish the professional image of being above commerce and concerns about money. Two, pharmacists have now become employees of large drugstore chains or hospitals and have become closely monitored labor costs (even as they employ assistants to help them). Third, their basic product, drugs, is under the control of doctors. And fourth, any contribution they could make to health care is also being made by a variety of health-care aides assisting doctors more directly.[45] Nonetheless, they have struggled with some success to establish the specialty of clinical pharmacy, a claim to professional expertise in evaluating the impact of drugs in direct health-care use.[46]

APPLIED SOCIOLOGISTS

Applied sociology courses gained momentum during the 1980s when academic enrollments in sociology slumped. Today there are two applied sociology organizations. The smaller, the Sociological Practice Association, publishes two annual volumes (one devoted to journal-type articles, the other to articles on the general state of the field). In his review of the 1989 volumes of the SPA, Jaeckel's overall conclusion is that the field's objective of promoting constructive social change is contradicted by its primary thrust: Applied (clinical) sociologists are oriented, not toward dealing with structural variables, but toward helping individuals.[47]

The larger group, The Society for Applied Sociology, founded in 1978, has a broader focus: the application of sociological knowledge in a wide variety of settings to generate knowledge-based change. It also devotes itself to the special educational training needed by applied sociologists. To these ends, it has a newsletter, an annual magazine, and a professional journal, *The Journal of Applied Sociology.*

AIRLINE PILOTS, CAREER CRIMINALS, COMPUTER SPECIALISTS, DETECTIVES, FUNERAL DIRECTORS, AND SOLDIERS

Grouping these occupations is not meant to disparage them or even to indicate great similarity. It has been done to indicate that professionalization is the way that modern capitalism has defined upward mobility and service to society and is, therefore, attempted by a wide variety of occupations. Aside from the fact that more research is needed on these and other aspiring occupations, a few generalizations about them is possible:

1. They are deeply dependent on the requirements and ups and downs of the American economy and the wider society.
2. Many are employees who work in hierarchic, profit-seeking organizations and find it difficult to avoid having their skills standardized.
3. Most have sought to require education as a prerequisite to the occupation, often excessive education. (The most flagrant case is the attempt by detectives to require a college degree despite the fact that studies have shown that detectives—as well as patrol officers—have relatively no effectiveness in fighting crime.)[48]

A word can be said about the occupations listed to indicate their distinct identities.[49] Airline pilots have not been studied. They enjoy high prestige and high income, have an association that negotiates with the airlines as a trade union, and are subject to the needs of large organizations pursuing profit. They require extensive education and enjoy a monopolistic licensing system. As the servants of a complex technology, closely regulated and supervised as to how they perform, airline pilots fall short of the professional image of autonomous appliers of knowledge.

Computer professionals are an emerging profession which has experienced explosive growth in recent decades. They are also diverse and a hierarchy among them has appeared. Academics and software engineers are the theoreticians and creators of the programs that do the myriad types of work through computer hardware. Systems analysts run the programs for banks, airlines, insurance companies, and so on. The latter are certified after passing an examination by the Data Management Association. Computer engineers are those who design the hardware (they have their own association).

Using a catch-all category of *computer worker*, Wright and Jacobs show that, at least for the time being, the large entry of women into this field has not led to the usual gender resegregation but has tended to be integrated by gender both across specialties and in income.[50]

Criminologists have recognized that many criminals are professionals. Edwin Sutherland's *The Professional Thief* [51] cited the many correspondences between the professional and the individual thief who makes a full-time living stealing. The focus on career criminals reveals professionalism in burglary, shoplifting, pickpocketing, forgery, confidence swindling, and the like, as well as organized crime. [52] (Our own focus will be on crime and other forms of deviance among professionals—see Chapter 9.)

Funeral directors and soldiers have been listed to illustrate the difficulties of making sense of the professions. Funeral directors have tried and failed to professionalize: the mix of commerce and formalized funerals (and of course, the type of service performed) have been drawbacks. [53] Soldiers have been listed to show that a demanding and skilled occupation requiring considerable education and a comprehensive code of conduct can still receive poor pay and little prestige except in wartime (or in artificially created periods of crisis such as the Cold War). [54] At present, a career as an officer in any branch of the military is still a very good job, and minorities, including women, have breached the citadel of both elite and lesser military academies though the battle is far from won.

The all-volunteer military and enhanced benefits have tended to move the American military away from being an "institution" (total organization) toward being an occupation. Aside from the importance of this issue to those concerned about military effectiveness, [55] it raises similar concerns about the effectiveness of other professions. Do institutional supports for academicians, law enforcement officers, executives, doctors, clergy, and so on, produce better professionals? Are America's professions following the trend in the military toward becoming mere occupations? To phrase these questions better, perhaps we should ask, Is the relentless competition and instrumental reason of advanced capitalism undermining commitment to its own work ethic?

SUMMARY

Psychotherapists: Our knowledge of mental illness is limited (largely because we have tried to explain it in non-social terms) and a large number of mental-health specialists have had little success in treating its many forms.

Applied psychology: The capitalist belief that psychology is a causal system has provided psychologists with large opportunities to serve corporate and government interests. Since the premise behind psychology is false (individuals cause their own behavior), applied psychology is class biased and ineffective.

Journalists: Journalists are part of a highly concentrated news business, and the news they produce and transmit is biased, fragmented, and dependency creating. The social construction of reality is even more apparent by journalists than by other professionals.

Accountants, nurses, social workers, teachers, librarians, architects, pharmacists, applied sociologists, and a host of other occupations have not been powerful enough to put together the mixture of assets needed to become a profession on the same level with the established professions.

The world of applied professions is dynamic and there is considerable jockeying for advantage among the professions and within them; and there is steady pressure from new claimants.

NOTES

1. *New York Times*, May 17, 1990, p. B12.
2. For a valuable overview of the psychotherapy profession, its various therapies, ongoing research, and the profession's lack of response to research, see Nikki Meredith, "Testing the Talking Cure," *Science* 7 (June 1986): 31–37.
3. D. L. Rosenhan, "On Being Sane in Insane Places," *Science* 179 (January 19, 1973): 250–258; widely reprinted.
4. As reported in Annette Ehrlich and Fred Abraham-Magdamo, "Caution: Mental Health may be Hazardous," *Human Behavior* (1974); reprinted in Glen Gaviglio and David E. Raye, eds., *Society as It Is*, 3rd ed. (New York: Macmillan, 1980), pp. 125–136.
5. Stuart A. Kirk and Herb Kutchins, *The Selling of DSM: The Rhetoric of Science in Psychiatry* (New York: Aldine de Gruyter, 1992).
6. *New York Times*, April 19, 1994, p. C1. For a case study of the long and successful struggle by the psychiatric profession against feminists and medical researchers to get premenstrual syndrome defined as a mental illness and into DSM-1994 (and a clear case of empirical evidence being overshadowed by "political" considerations), see Anne E. Figert, *Women and the Ownership of PMS: The Structuring of a Psychiatric Disorder* (New York: Aldine De Gruyter, 1996).
7. For some pioneering essays that direct psychotherapy away from an individual actor helping another individual actor reach a rational or knowledgeable state and toward viewing both as constructors of identity along a number of dimensions, see Sheila McNamee and Kenneth J. Gergen, eds., *Therapy as Social Construction* (Newbury Park, Calif.: Sage, 1992). For a valuable, if diffused, history of American psychotherapy that undercuts the latter's scientism by relating it to the social and political functions it performs for capitalism, see Philip Cushman, *Constructing the Self, Constructing America: A Cultural History of Psychotherapy* (New York: Addison-Wesley, 1995).
8. Donald S. Napoli, *Architects of Adjustment: The History of the Psychological Profession in the United States* (Port Washington, N.Y.: Kennikat Press, 1981), esp. chap. 2. Also see Michael M. Sokal, "James McKeen Cattell and American Psychology in the 1920s," in Josef Brozek, ed., *Explorations in the History of Psychology in the United States* (Lewisburg, Penn.: Bucknell University Press, 1984), pp. 273–323. Loren Baritz, *The Servants of Power: A History of the Use of Social Science in Industry* (Middletown, Conn.: Wesleyan University Press, 1960) focuses on how industrial psychologists served the interests of corporations.
9. James L. Wood and Amy C. Wong, "GRE Scores and Graduate School Success," *Footnotes*, November 1992, p. 6.
10. *New York Times*, November 29, 1983, p. B7.
11. *New York Times*, March 17, 1988, p. B9.
12. Carl Milofsky, *Testers and Testing: The Sociology of School Psychology* (New Brunswick, N.J.: Rutgers University Press, 1989).
13. Joseph G. Ponterotto, J. Manuel Casas, Lisa A. Suzuki, and Charlene M. Alexander, eds., *Handbook of Multicultural Counseling* (Thousand Oaks, Calif.: Sage, 1995).

14. Mark Fishman, *Manufacturing the News* (Austin, Tex.: University of Texas Press, 1980).

15. Peter Dahlgren, "TV News and the Suppression of Reflexivity," in Elihu Katz and Tamas Szecsko, eds., *Mass Media and Social Change* (Beverly Hills, Calif.: Sage, 1981), pp. 101–113.

16. For a fully developed analysis of journalism as part of the world it is reporting on and thus its inability to avoid distorting the facts to suit American assumptions, see Alan Rachlin, *News as Hegemonic Reality: American Political Culture and the Framing of News Accounts* (New York: Praeger, 1988). To substantiate his argument, Rachlin provides case studies of bias in the way American journalism handled the downing of the Korean airliner in 1983 by a Soviet fighter plane (Canadian accounts were quite different and more objective), and in its coverage of labor unions at home and abroad (strikes at home are unwelcome interruptions, threats to society and its proper functioning, whereas the Polish trade union movement, Solidarity, was a welcome development in Communist Poland).

17. Herbert I. Schiller, *The Mind Managers* (Boston: Beacon Press, 1973), chap. 1.

18. Oliver Boyd-Barrett, "Media Imperialism: Towards an International Framework for the Analysis of Media Systems," in James Curran et al., eds., *Mass Communications and Society* (London: Edward Arnold, 1977), pp. 116–135; William Steif, "On the 'Objective' Press," *The Progressive* 43 (January, 1979): 23–25; Edward W. Said, *Covering Islam* (New York: Pantheon, 1981); Soheir Morsy, "Politicalization through the Mass Information Media: American Images of the Arabs," *Journal of Popular Culture* 17 (Winter 1983): 91–97. The enormously influential *National Geographic* invariably leaves out conflict, exploitation, civil war, and imperialism in its portraits of developing countries—Herbert I. Schiller, "The 'National Geographic': Nonideological Geography," *The Mind Managers* (Boston: Beacon Press, 1973), pp. 86–94.

19. Philip Elliot and Peter Golding, "Mass Communication and Social Change: The Imagery of Development and the Development of Imagery," in Emanuel DeKadt and Gavin Williams, eds., *Sociology and Development* (London: Tavistock, 1974), p. 230.

20. Steven Brint, *In an Age of Experts: The Changing Role of Professionals in Politics and Public Life* (Princeton, N.J.: Princeton University Press, 1994), pp. 123–126.

21. Ben H. Bagdikian, 4th ed., *The Media Monopoly* (Boston: Beacon Press, 1993).

22. Mark Fishman, "Crime Waves as Ideology," *Social Problems* 25 (June 1978): 531–543. For a fuller discussion, see Kevin N. Wright, *The Great American Crime Myth* (Westport, Conn.: Greenwood Press, 1985). The false crime wave is part of the widespread pattern in American professional and business life of identifying and exaggerating the dangers faced by the public, all the more to make them dependent on existing power structures (who are rarely identified as the cause of these dangers).

23. Shanto Iyengar, *Is Anyone Responsible? How Television Frames Political Issues* (Chicago: University of Chicago Press, 1991).

24. S. Robert Lichter, Stanley Rothman, and Linda S. Lichter, *The Media Elite* (Bethesda, Md.: Adler & Adler, 1986).

25. For further discussions of journalism and TV news in the context of entertainment, see the sections on popular culture in Chapter 8.

26. *Wall Street Journal*, August 31, 1994, p. A14.

27. Interview, *New York Times*, December 12, 1994, p. D7.

28. For a picture of bias in the news media stemming from a variety of sources, see Peter Golding, "The Missing Dimensions—New Media and the Management of Social Change," in Elihu Katz and Tamas Szecsko, eds., *Mass Media and Social Change* (Beverly Hills, Calif.: Sage, 1981), pp. 63–81.

29. Peter Dreier, "The Position of the Press in the U.S. Power Structure," *Social Problems* 29 (February 1982): 298–310; Ben H. Bagdikian, *The Media Monopoly*, 4th ed. (Boston: Beacon Press, 1993).

30. Herbert J. Gans, *Deciding What's News: A Study of CBS Evening News, NBC Nightly News, Newsweek, and Time* (New York: Pantheon, 1979).

31. Jyotika Ramaprasad, "How Four Newspapers Covered the 1992 Los Angeles 'Riots,'" in Venise T. Berry and Carmen L. Manning-Miller, eds., *Mediated Messages and African-American Culture* (Thousand Oaks, Calif.: Sage, 1996), pp. 76–95. This essay has the added merit of providing a review of scholars and commissions, both black and white, that have severely criticized news coverage of black behavior from the 1920s on.

32. For informative histories of African-American journalism (and for more examples of biased treatment of blacks), and for data on the absence of blacks from positions of authority in journalism, see Jannette L. Dates, "Print News," and Lee Thornton, "Broadcast News," in Jannette L. Dates and William Barlow, eds., *Split Image: African Americans in the Mass Media*, 2nd ed. (Washington, D.C.: Howard University Press, 1993), chaps. 7, 8.

33. The following relies on the comprehensive summary in Peter Miller's introduction to Anthony G. Hopwood and Peter Miller, eds., *Accounting as Social and Institutional Practice* (New York: Cambridge University Press, 1994).

34. Bruce G. Carruthers and Wendy Nelson Espeland, "Accounting for Rationality: Double-Entry Bookkeeping and the Rhetoric of Economic Rationality," *American Journal of Sociology* 97, no. 1 (July 1991): 31–69.

35. For background on teachers, nurses, and social workers, see Amitai Etzioni, ed., *The Semi-Professions and Their Organization* (New York: Free Press, 1969), and Nina Toren, *Social Work: The Case of a Semi-Profession* (Newbury Park, Calif.: Sage, 1972). For background on librarians, see William Goode, "From Occupation to Profession?" *The Library Quarterly* 31, no. 4 (October, 1961): 306–318; reprinted in H. M. Vollmer and D. L. Mills, eds., *Professionalization* (Englewood Cliffs, N.J.: Prentice-Hall, 1966), pp. 34–43. See also Michael F. Winter, *The Culture and Control of Expertise: Toward a Sociological Understanding of Librarianship* (Westport, Conn.: Greenwood Press, 1988).

36. Christine L. Williams, "The Glass Elevator: Hidden Advantages for Men in the 'Female' Professions," *Social Problems* 39, no. 3 (August 1992): 253–267.

37. For a full analysis that also recognizes that "physician-extender roles were designed by corporate rationalizers," see Arnold Birenbaum, *In the Shadow of Medicine: Remaking the Division of Labor in Health Care* (Dix Hills, N.Y.: General Hall, 1990), chaps. 3, 4.

38. Joan I. Roberts and Thetis M. Group, *Feminism and Nursing: An Historical Perspective on Power, Status, and Political Activism in the Nursing Profession* (Westport, Conn.: Praeger, 1995), p. 335.

39. Regina G. Kunzel, *Fallen Women, Problem Girls: Unmarried Mothers and the Professionalization of Social Work, 1890–1945* (New Haven, Conn: Yale University Press, 1993).

40. Dean D. Knudsen, *Child Protective Services* (Springfield, Ill.: Charles C. Thomas, 1988), p. 31.

41. For an analysis of the profession which criticizes this movement and calls for a return to a community-based focus for dealing with social problems, see Harry Specht and Mark E. Courtney, *Unfaithful Angels: How Social Work Has Abandoned Its Mission* (New York: Free Press, 1995). For an extremely valuable analysis that outlines how expert social work practices at the level of poverty households can and must be connected with national, justice-based initiatives that redistribute resources to neighborhoods and communities, see June Gary Hopps, Elaine Pinderhughes, and Richard Shankar, *The Power to Care: Clinical Practice Effectiveness with Overwhelmed Clients* (New York: Free Press, 1995).

42. Magli Sarfatti Larson, "Emblem and Exception: The Historical Definition of the Architect's Professional Role," in Judith R. Blau, Mark La Gory, and John S. Pipkin, eds., *Professionals and Urban Form* (Albany, N.Y.: State University of New York Press, 1983), chap. 2.

43. Bernard Michael Boyle, "Architectural Practice in America, 1865–1965: Ideal and Reality," in Spiro Kostof, ed., *The Architect: Chapters in the History of the Profession* (New York: Oxford University Press, 1977), chap. 11.

44. Gwendolyn Wright, "On the Fringe of the Profession: Women in Architecture," in Kostof, ibid., chap. 10.

45. For these trends, see Albert I. Wertheimer and Mickey C. Smith, eds., *Pharmacy Practice: Social and Behavioral Aspects* (Baltimore: University Park Press, 1974).

46. For a full analysis, see Arnold Birenbaum, *In the Shadow of Medicine: Remaking the Division of Labor in Health Care* (Dix Hills, N.Y.: General Hall, 1990), chaps. 5–7.

47. The following is based on Martin Jaeckel, "Review Essay: Clinical Sociology," *Teaching Sociology* 19 (January 1991): 96–102.

48. David H. Bayley, *Police for the Future* (New York: Oxford University Press, 1994), pp. 25–28.

49. Actors, artists, fashion designers, television writers, athletic directors, coaches, and athletes are discussed in Chapter 8.

50. Rosemary Wright and Jerry A. Jacobs, "Male Flight From Computer Work: A New Look at Resegregation and Ghettoization," in Jerry A. Jacobs, ed., *Gender Inequality at Work* (Thousand Oaks, Calif.: Sage, 1995), chap. 12.

51. Edwin H. Sutherland, annotated and interpreted by, *The Professional Thief, by a Professional Thief* (Chicago: University of Chicago Press, 1937).

52. For a followup to Sutherland's pioneering work, see James A. Inciardi, *Careers in Crime* (Chicago: Rand McNally, 1975).

53. The classic study of funeral directors and their pretensions to professionalism is Jessica Mitford, *The American Way of Death* (New York: Simon & Schuster, 1963), chap. 15. Also see Vanderlyn R. Pine, *Caretaker of the Dead: The American Funeral Director* (New York: Irvington, 1975).

54. The classic study of the military profession remains Morris Janowitz, *The Professional Soldier* (New York: Free Press, 1960). For an analysis of the military from a wider perspective, see Adam Yarmolinsky, *The Military Establishment: Its Impacts on American Society* (New York: Harper & Row, 1971). No one can claim to know the military and its creativity, its incredible hideboundness, its similarity to civilianship, its acute realism mixed with wide departures from reality, and its career satisfactions and insecurities, who has not read James Fallows, *National Defense* (New York: Random House, 1981).

55. For a comprehensive analysis of the American military and analyses of the military in a wide variety of countries centered on this issue, see Charles C. Moskos and Frank R. Wood, eds., *The Military: More than a Job?* (Elmsford, N.Y.: Pergamon, 1988). Meaty and readable analyses of gender and race relations in the American military may be found in chapters 7 and 8: Patricia M. Shields, "Sex Roles in the Military" and John Sibley Butler, "Race Relations in the Military."

8

Professionalism and the Occupations and Subject Matter of Popular and Elite Culture

◆ ◆ ◆ ◆

◆ ◆ ◆ ◆

The commercialization and professionalization of all reaches of culture have proceeded apace in modern capitalism—individuals and groups have to purchase medical care, legal services, higher education, and the services of the professions in general. Here we analyze commercialization and professionalization in popular and elite culture: entertainment, visual and performing arts, publishing, sports, and auxiliary offshoots. As we see, occupations in this diverse area (actors, artists, choreographers, dancers, directors, fashion designers, musicians, theatrical technicians, and writers) have not been able to professionalize; that is, they have not been able to develop a unique knowledge base, formalize and control access to that base through education, and have thus been unable to increase their collective income and prestige by controlling labor entry or interference by outsiders.[1] The only occupation in this area that has succeeded in formalizing entry through education is fine art teaching.[2] If one includes athletes, athletic coaches, athletic directors, and the communication industries, one also sees a trend toward formal education.

The occupations in the world of elite and popular culture are not oriented toward science and both they and their subject matter are defined by themselves and outsiders as aesthetic, moral, or political, in short, as subjective. Because of this and because of the powerful communication technology that they employ, trends in elite, and especially popular, culture have prompted theories of cultural closure and monopoly. To establish the context for this chapter, we start, therefore, with the concept of hegemonic culture.

THE CONCEPT OF HEGEMONIC CULTURE

The concept of a hegemonic culture is associated with Antonio Gramsci. Gramsci's concept of *hegemony* asks us to stop thinking of dominance only in terms of universal values, political control, and propaganda-ideology. The process of domination, argued Gramsci, is a pervasive and enduring part of our entire experience: at home, in school, in church, at work, at leisure, attending festivals, as well as politics and government. But hegemony, he argued, is always problematic—elites and masses are always in a process of negotiating the terms of domination.

A hegemonic culture has its roots in the basic economy from whence causes flow to embrace the polity, the voluntary sector, and personal and family life. Explaining the hegemony of culture consists both of showing relative unanimity across the top and how the masses are absorbed into elite thought forms. C. Wright Mills and Herbert Marcuse led the way in the 1950s and 1960s in developing the concept of an American hegemonic culture by pointing to economic concentration and the absorption of the masses through ideology, fear, and consumerism. Since Mills and Marcuse, many have contributed to the idea of a monopolistic culture, though the person most associated with the idea is Herbert I. Schiller.

CORPORATE CAPITALISM AND THE COMMERCIALIZATION OF CULTURE

Culture, Inc.

Schiller's analysis of culture rests on the assumption that the prime cause in modern society is the concentrated economy, and its auxiliary, the polity. Here Schiller is continuing the radical conflict tradition in American life that stretches from Veblen through Mills and Marcuse. Schiller's contribution to this tradition is to call attention to the new trends in knowledge generation and transmission made possible by twentieth-century communication technology. Schiller's basis thesis is that the corporate economy, and its helpmate, the polity, has reached out to commercialize knowledge, indeed, all of culture, both at the macro and microlevels of society.

The commercialization of knowledge, information, art, entertainment, and sport is an integral and growing part of the economy itself, the culture industries. These include "publishing, the press, film, radio, television, photography, recording, advertising, sports, and more recently, the many components that make up the information industry (data-base creation, production of software for computers, and various forms of saleable information)." The culture industries include "museums, art galleries, amusement parks (Disneyland, Sea World . . .), shopping malls, and corporate 'public' spaces." In addition, Schiller claims, the entire range of the creative arts such as dance, drama, music, and the visual and plastic arts have been separated from their group and community origins and turned into commodities.[3]

Schiller's focus on the direct buying and selling of symbols directs him away from the disguised manner in which symbols protecting and furthering corporate interests are generated and transmitted by education, research institutes, foundations, charities, and churches. And the role of professionals in commercializing culture is not highlighted. Nonetheless, he provides many new insights into the deeper meaning of some well-known trends. In the corporate world itself, says Schiller, knowledge comes from the top and trickles down the hierarchy on a need-to-know basis, hardly an experience conducive to the development of democratic personalities. Schiller (along with others) has also sounded the alarm at the strong trend toward the privatization of knowledge. In recent decades, a more explicit trend toward the privatization and commercialization of knowledge (as information) has occurred as private information businesses have multiplied and the federal government has shaped its data-gathering operations to accommodate them. The basic pattern that has emerged is that the government pays to amass data, reduces its free distribution, and allows private companies to use its data free of charge as a profitable commodity. Congress and the courts have helped in privatizing symbol creativity by extending the types of knowledge that are patentable[4] and the U.S. Supreme Court has given the sanction of law to corporate power by protecting its right to speech both through advertising and contributing to political campaigns.[5]

The computer has made selling data profitable and today a thriving business has developed providing information on the private lives of individuals. Computer searches of tax, bankruptcy, lawsuit, asset, lien, and other records are valuable to many businesses as they check potential employees or try to identify credit risks and markets. Market research has long used survey methods, but few realize that polling on public issues is also a private business that tends to ask only the questions that paying customers are interested in.[6] This is merely an extension of the power uses of empirical research in natural and social science that we identified earlier (see "Symbolic Activities and the Needs of Power" in Chapter 1).

Schiller is also insightful in pointing to the public mall as an extension of the power of private property (its owners can prevent political and intellectual expression even as they immerse citizens in commerce).[7] Sports, and many cultural activities, including theater, parades, and festivals in parks and streets, along with public television, are now thoroughly encased in advertising and corporate sponsorship. By and large, the nonpartisan sponsorship of sports, art, and public television does more than provide corporate visibility and recognition, does more than make the corporate world appear altruistic—it tends to create the false impression that these reaches of human expression have no social base and no politics.

In a related argument, but focused on intellectuals, Elliott argues that we are witnessing a "shift away from involving people as political citizens of nation states toward involving them as consumption units in a corporate [global] world." The result is to curb two-way interaction, restrict the public sphere, and undermine the power of politically aware intellectuals.[8]

The Globalization of Corporate Expression

Schiller (along with others) has called attention to the outward thrust of America's (and other countries') transnational corporations, not only to establish a free flow of capital and labor (and goods and services), but a free flow of information.[9] With the help of the American government, corporate capitalism mounted an onslaught against all nationalized systems of communication (including the well-regulated, quasi-public monopoly AT&T in the United States) in both developed and developing countries. And it worked hard to curb anyone who defended the need to have communication systems under public supervision, whether at home, in other countries, or at the United Nations. Along with the transfer of communication technology and systems into private hands has come an elaboration of "intellectual property" law and its application to all countries and their interchanges.

The capture by corporate capitalism of communication around the globe means not only that the number of messages running counter to capitalism are reduced (often through misinformation, or the deliberate creation of false realities), but the marketing messages of consumerism now blanket the world. And the messages are not merely transmitted formally by voice, picture, or print, but permeate the atmosphere at international sporting events from the Olympics to autoracing. In addition, the international nature of scientific knowledge creation and exchange, whereby knowledge is assembled in global corporations, privatized, and wedded to profit, often amounts to the appropriation by industrial countries of the culture of developing countries (as we saw in the case of plant science). This process of appropriating the culture of others is far more extensive than is commonly understood.[10]

POPULAR CULTURE: THEMES AND TRENDS

The Concept of Popular Culture

Scholars from a wide variety of fields have expressed interest in popular culture, but have not agreed on its meaning. In the broadest sense, it refers to the culture (symbols, emotions, things) of ordinary people as opposed to the culture of elites. Popular culture, therefore, emerged with the advent of social stratification in the complex horticultural and agrarian societies, and varies depending on type of society. Its most distinctive development occurred with the rise of capitalism, especially after industrialization.

The term *popular culture* also has a narrower meaning: for many specialists in sociology, psychology, literature, and political science, it refers to the symbols, sentiments, and things that are accessible during leisure (recreational) time. These analysts often distinguish between popular and elite culture, with some finding much to praise about popular culture,[11] and some much to condemn.[12] The view this study adopts is that popular culture is composed of beliefs and norms that are pro-status quo (elite art is also largely a way to keep people within certain boundaries, not least when in rare instances it points to the need for political reform[13]).

Popular culture appears to require no training. People respond to it easily, again giving a false appearance of spontaneity. But popular culture is part and parcel of how Americans are socialized, and people respond to it easily *because* of training. Of course, popular culture (unlike elite culture) does not require much *formal* training—but both elite and popular culture require participants who can respond to the sounds and sights projected through assorted technologies. By definition, therefore, all participants in popular culture are social actors who can decode the intricate symbols fired at them.

Sociopolitical and Academic Perspectives

Concern about the political implications of mass communication technology and popular culture surfaced quickly with the onset of yellow journalism in the nineteenth century, the use of the printing press to sway mass audiences. The concern swelled with the advent of radio in the 1920s and 1930s, especially because of its use in Nazi Germany for political propaganda. Though the value-neutral, academic approach has done some important work in this area, starting with empirical research into the relation of radio and its audience in the 1940s, the main creative contributions for understanding the mass media and popular culture have emerged from the sociopolitical perspective.

Probably the most creative scholarly movement focused on popular culture has emerged in Great Britain (wedding British radicalism to ideas from France, Germany, and Italy). British scholars have emphasized class, race, and gender themes in their analyses of popular culture (and so will we, using American examples). British scholars have also argued that themes of popular resistance as well as elite dominance can be found in popular culture.[14] Building on Gramsci, British culture studies have emphasized hegemony (not dominance), or the continued need by the upper classes to negotiate their control of society with the lower classes.

The British, who employ a "relativistic" outlook, derived from Marx, phenomenology, and feminism, properly insist that the powerful and the less powerful are in constant interaction and that domination is not a mechanical one-way street. They also point out that power relations continuously manifest themselves in new forms and that one must not reify concepts such as *the people* or *popular culture*. Nonetheless, this does not mean that popular resistance of any political significance takes place, at least not in the well-developed capitalist societies. It is important (and a form of resistance) that the mass public knows how to discount statements made by governing elites, that anti-authoritarian political jokes thrive under certain circumstances, and that anti-establishment music is well-established in American society, but it is also important not to exaggerate the political significance of such phenomena. While the liberal mainstream wishfully sees multiple positive effects in popular culture, the radical left wishfully sees popular resistance to elite domination.

In studying popular culture, the wishful thinking of both radical critics and the mainstream must be avoided. One should be free, of course, to advocate popular resistance as a way to promote pluralism or an alternative society. Positive functions, such as stability or integration, can be identified and celebrated. But the "ought" world and the "is" world should not be confused. Art, both high and low, is now deeply professionalized and capitalized (though some areas are still open to amateurs and to those with little capital). The various arts require long years of schooling and/or training, expensive equipment and facilities, and like the other professions, each of the arts develops as a specialty with its own journal(s) and association(s). And all seek secure income either directly from a paying public or indirectly through tax-generated subsidies or tax deductions.

THEMES IN POPULAR CULTURE THAT PROMOTE PROFESSIONALISM

Popular culture is an integral part of America's legitimation process. To legitimate is to make something true and moral, and to put it beyond the level of conscious-critical concern. Some think of popular culture as voluntary, spontaneous, diverse, unstructured, everchanging, the opposite of enduring, classical art forms. But these are half-truths. Popular culture is highly structured and contains many enduring themes. Its many technologies (books, magazines, newspapers, painting, sculpture, stage, radio, phonograph, film, television, VCR, computer) should not be confused with diversity of content. Its large variety of individual personalities, behaviors, and situations (romance, adventure, detective stories, espionage, fairy tales, sports, comedy, the supernatural, science fiction, pornography) should not be taken as cultural pluralism or change. Within its diverse subject matter, fads, and trends, popular culture is highly structured around a few simple themes, all of which support the dominance of property and professional groups as a taken-for-granted reality.

Individualism

Popular culture's main theme stresses individualism as both ideal and explanation. For much of American history, the model individual was a young male confronting life and succeeding largely through the force of character. The heroes in the Horatio Alger novel are a prominent example. Though poorly written, the Alger novels contained the mythic elements found in all complex cultures—a young male leaves home to achieve, performs a noble deed, is rewarded by a powerful figure, and rejoins the community by returning home and marrying. Using American materials (making one's fortune in the city in conformity to the Protestant-bourgeois ethic), Alger succeeded because his stories were in line with the American middle class ethos of individual mobility and success.[15]

Americans also respond to the loner, the outsider, and the inner-directed individual. Sometimes the loner is portrayed as a man of action, self-employed, hard working, and productive. A decisive leader, the loner is suspicious of bureaucrats and contemptuous of the well-educated who are always depicted as indecisive.[16] At other times, the loner is depicted as an outsider who deviates from social norms.[17] Sometimes the loner is a vigilante hero (a staple of popular culture for over fifty years) who does good using bad means.[18]

In recent decades the heroic model has changed to resemble society's diversity. Popular-culture heroes now come in all ages, sexes, and skin colors, and from all ethnic groups and economic classes. Heroes are physically diverse as well—tall, short, fat, handicapped, beautiful, not beautiful. Some heroes are charismatic, others are mediators and brokers. Heroes win, lose, and draw. Some are clever and some are befuddled.[19] Although heroes are recognizable social types even when they are marginal or total strangers to society, they are rarely explained in social terms. This is especially evident in times of crisis, for example, during the Great Depression, the individual achiever became a superhero, often superhuman.

Both popular culture and American culture in general also use individualism to explain evil, often by using the physically different as a metaphor for evil.[20] Sometimes the evil individual is a metaphor for self-interest, corrupt government, or greedy corporations. For the most part, however, the clash of good and bad individuals is depicted as an emanation of human nature and tends to take the spotlight off society, its institutions, and its power groups.

American individualism in all its forms is essentially a way to ensure that the well-to-do have a headstart in the scramble for position and a way to blame the lower classes for their failure and deviance. All this is not left to chance, however: the ideology of individualism is given support (as we see in the following sections) by various myths, the ideology of professionalism, and by ideological definitions of love, family, and religion.

Our Threatened Eden and the Need for Professionals

A second theme in popular culture is to depict society as a threatened Eden. Popular culture invariably posits a community whose peace is shattered by an evil of some sort. The evil can be a nature gone berserk (disaster films), incompetent or greedy businesspeople, criminals, the mentally ill, sinister foreigners, and so on. The assumption of a ready made, natural social order appears in various ways. Often the focus is on primary groups, for example, the soap opera's obsessive focus on kinship relations, the situation comedy's focus on a break in the family routine. Sometimes the orderly world of a family, a town, a business, or a ranch is disrupted by an act of lawlessness. Sometimes the notion of an orderly, benign, self-sufficient world is presented in terms of metaphor. For example, the spaceship *Enterprise* in the television series *Star Trek* is a multiple metaphor that can stand for a smoothly running corporation, the United States, or American foreign policy. Or the various individuals who made up the members of the television series *MASH* represent the full spectrum of American statuses and values, form a "family," resolve their minor conflicts, and are thus a way of saying "all's right with the United States."[21] Throughout these stories, the heroes are professionals.

There is evidence that popular culture no longer depicts society as orderly, benign, and rational. The classic detective story that emerged in the nineteenth century presupposed an orderly world in which a small, momentary disruption takes place. The hero detective is more a thinking amateur than a professional. The amateur detective can explain the disruption through observation and logic because the detective (like the rest of the newly emerging scientific, capitalist culture) can assume an otherwise orderly and supportive world. The classic detective story has been pushed aside by crime, espionage, and adventure thrillers in which action takes place in an essentially disorderly and unpredictable world.[22] Hence the increased reference to vigilante action and the need to fight evil with evil. Here one can see a kinship with soap operas and their double-dealing characters and unpredictable experiences. Hence the enormous emphasis on the breakdown of marriages or love relationships and on the untrustworthiness of others: spouses, roommates, nannies, co-workers, officials, friends, or neighbors. Hence the heavy reliance on assorted professionals to extricate people from their predicaments.

The popularity of such stories means that popular culture is in touch with how people feel about the world. Hesitation about the certainties of life have also affected the rare American political film. For much of the history of Hollywood, American films about politics spelled out who was good and who was bad, plots and characters were simplistic and idealistic to a fault, and we knew who to root for (America) from the beginning to the happy ending. European political films are far more complex, do not deal in absolutes, and leave the choice up to the viewer.[23] But a change has occurred in recent decades. The new image of the community and politics is one that is permanently compromised and which can resist the efforts of the heroic redeemer.[24] By and large, the American political film joins popular culture in catering to elite prejudices by painting an almost uniformly negative picture of politicians and government officials. Here it builds on the paranoid style of American politics, and on the laissez-faire, anti-authority tradition found among both left and right liberals. What better climate for the nonpolitical professional to thrive in.

Achievement above Love and Family

A third theme in popular culture that promotes professionalism is the priority given to achievement over love and family. Complex societies require achievers (heroes) who can solve problems lying beyond the home. A common theme depicts an individual (often male, often young) who must transcend an unsatisfactory family in order to achieve. In the classic achievement story, young males must leave home, adult males must forgo romance and sex, or leave wives behind. Individualism and achievement beyond the home come before all else.

The postponement of sex, marriage, and family in favor of masculine heroics has a long history in popular culture from the Western novel and film to Walt Disney. Men are either indifferent to women or under siege by them. Even *Playboy* magazine, as Jewett and Lawrence argue, is part of this pattern. Its focus on sex and nudity has nothing to do with love or commitment. Instead, it creates a uniform world of cool, faceless men and an image of lustful women imploring men to satisfy their needs.[25] Like popular culture in general it makes clear that love and commitment between the sexes must not interfere with masculine achievements, all of which lie beyond home and hearth.

Popular culture's sexless male achiever still exists but today, it is much more common for heroes and heroines to engage in sex, with or without marriage, as part of their normal schedule of activities. The reason is not so much to liberalize human sexuality but because clear cut professional goals are no longer unambiguously and morally achieved. In point of fact, the latent function of illicit sex is to reaffirm traditional morality much as prostitution supports the family and crime supports the moral-legal order.

Popular culture's achievement theme nowadays focuses on professional exploits in the hospital, law enforcement, outer space, the past, the future, or in foreign lands. And problems in personal relations are now routinely presented as somehow inevitable given the imperatives of professional achievement (for example, every doctor in a leading role on the hospital drama *E.R.*, whether male or female, black or white, has severe personal problems). In addition, it is clear that other social problems—achieving full employment, livable cities, a clean environment, a humane health-care system, and so on—are not proper spheres for professional achievement (though problems from each of these areas are routinely presented, conventionally analyzed, and "solved" without raising questions about institutions or power groups).

Love, Family, and Religion as Consolation Prizes

The universalist theme of individual success, combined with the careful control over access to good jobs through excessive educational and credential requirements, enforced by state licensing, mean that most cannot succeed. American society has many control mechanisms that address the problems that this creates: prisons, asylums, tracking in high schools, and community colleges (complete with their cooling-out process). Among the social control processes that legitimate the dominance of property and professional groups is a fourth theme in popular culture, the seemingly contradictory emphasis on love, marriage, family, the little things in life, and religion (for more on the romance novel, love, marriage, and family theme in popular culture, see below, "Popular Culture and Gender").

Television's pervasive "family" format in which a small collection of individuals, related by blood, friendship, or occupation, solve a variety of problems is an obvious way in which attention is deflected from the macrostructure of power. The emphasis on personal and supernatural solutions to alleged personal problems (actually caused by the sociopolitical system) is rampant on television and radio talk shows, "Dear Abby" and similar columns, best-selling self-help and inspirational books, and mass circulation tabloids such as the *National Enquirer*.

Organized religion has voiced criticisms and has supported the reform of society since the earliest days of the Republic. But religion in its various organized, civil, and popular forms has mostly supported the status quo. Indeed, the rationale for establishing American society (the liberal nation-state) was supplied, to a large extent, by Protestantism. Setting up a society based on the free individual was not an appealing prospect to our Pilgrim founders. Individuals are likely to choose self-interest over the social good, likely to quarrel rather than work in harmony. Protestantism reconciled the public good with the free individual by assuming that individuals were in the service of God. It declared the New World the Promised Land, Protestant New Englanders the Chosen People, and society at once a covenant among believers and between believers and God. The affinity between the Protestant worldview and the liberalism of Jefferson and Madison is apparent. In the years after the American Revolution, the Puritan image of society was secularized; or perhaps better said, liberalism was sacralized. The tension between religion and secular society remained, but was transmuted, by and large, into the service of liberalism, providing what one author calls a "Christian industrialism."[26] Eventually, the free individual was reconciled with social order and the welfare of society, not only by Providence but by the providential market.

The intertwining of religion and liberalism eventually became what Robert Bellah has called a *civil religion*, the celebration of Americanism using vague religious terminology.[27] Through its civil religion, the United States seeks to identify itself with both the natural and the supernatural worlds. Through civil religion much about the United States passes beyond conscious thought into the taken-for-granted world.

Civil religion has a number of sources. Christianity supplied the concept of a single God with special plans for the United States. The early secular leaders of the Republic turned this into deism and evoked the concept of a concerned God to buttress the American social order. The Civil War spurred the development of civil religiosity: Memorial Day, Arlington and local cemeteries, and a variety of public monuments imparted sacredness to the Civil War effort. Today, Washington's and Lincoln's birthdays, Veteran's Day, the Fourth of July, and Memorial Day celebrate America and promote solidarity. American exceptionalism rests in large part on Americans' belief that God has specially favored them and their way of life.

Civil religion is a pervasive auxiliary to secular institutions, a celebration and reinforcement of the American way of life, a legitimating process of the first importance. Public bodies and artifacts (for example, legislatures, courtrooms, coins) and public occasions of all sorts from presidential inaugurals to baseball games evoke the sanction of the divine. In effect, American institutions are made divine by clothing them in vague, nondenominational religious terminology.

Organized religion also legitimates American institutions by putting them in a supernatural context. It deflects attention from the present, like liberalism, by projecting a better life into the future. Like liberalism, it explains success and failure in terms of attributes directly in human beings. All in all, American society is identified with God's purposes in a straightforward manner. Less straightforward is "popular" religion. Popular religion is when worship, faith, and miracles occur, and participants are not aware they are in church. Popular religion is when religious themes permeate secular life clothed in secular terms. The social sciences have long had a religious dimension. The concept of Providence was smuggled into economics during the eighteenth century to become the magical market. The concept of a golden age (the Garden of Eden), the idea of heaven, and the idea of the Second Coming were transformed by the French Enlightenment into the liberal (capitalist) concepts of perfectibility and progress.[28] Popular religion is also found in America's many family-centered holidays in which a diffused religiosity celebrates and supports family life. The mass (and elite) media are saturated with religious themes in secular garb. Recent decades have seen more than the usual number of supernatural thrillers, science-fiction morality plays, and disaster films in which inexplicable evil is overcome by individuals displaying faith and courage against great odds.

Whether social problems such as disease, disability, disasters, crime, divorce, or assorted other personal troubles are evoked by secular or religious popular culture, the result is clear: people who cannot do for themselves or cannot wait for magical markets or divine intervention, must look to professionals for salvation. As we see in the next two sections, America's legitimation process leaves little to chance—democratic collective action, especially political action, has been successfully defined as bad and ineffective.

POPULAR CULTURE AND PERVASIVE DEPOLITICIZATION

Though popular culture has been important throughout American history, thanks especially to print technology, the emergence of radio and film from 1900 on is a watershed in its power. Augmented by television at mid-twentieth century, VCRs, and mature computer technology at the end of the century, popular culture may be a growing part of an unchanging power structure. But, whatever its share of power, it upholds professionalism in yet another way (besides emphasizing heroes and individual achievement), by depoliticizing social problems.

The process of depoliticization is anchored in the pervasive themes of America as a threatened Eden and America responding to frontier challenges. These themes blossomed during the 1930s as the old print technology combined with radio and film and eventually television to develop our "national monomyth" (the archetypal plot pattern in American popular culture in which an Edenic community, threatened by nonsocial evil, is redeemed through nonsocial forces, especially superheroism).[29]

The Edenic community is never spelled out, and is never depicted as a tangible goal to be achieved—it just simply is. All questions about its nature were forestalled by another pervasive American myth, the frontier. In a brilliant analysis, Richard Slotkin has outlined the way in which the myth of the frontier emerged in colonial America and was updated to serve American society in the various stages of its development.[30] Though he focuses on popular culture, especially the Western, Slotkin interweaves his account with American socioeconomic trends, social problems, politics, imperialism, and political ideologies.

At first, the frontier myth justified the establishment of white-settler colonies on North America. The myth was deeply colored by the experience of geographic separation from home country, regression to more primitive surroundings, and struggle with a harsh environment and non-white natives. From the beginning the path to progress was through territorial expansion and the displacement through violence of a racially defined group. By projecting problems outward one could distract attention from internal conflict.

The frontier myth became a theory of economic development during the first three-quarters of the nineteenth century. Land and its resources was needed to build the nation's economy and to sustain the ideals of a republic based on a wide diffusion of property. Of course, the resources of the

Midwest and Far West were also needed for the industries of the East and its non-farm population.

After the 1870s, economic troubles (labor unrest and strikes), the failure of Reconstruction, and continued resistance by Native Americans required a new formulation of the frontier myth. Progressives (Teddy Roosevelt and spokespersons for business) used the frontier myth to build an ideology supporting corporate capitalism. The fight against savages and the wilderness was transformed into a Darwinian struggle for existence and a need by hero-adventurers (managerial elites) to overcome the "lower" orders (Native Americans, labor, blacks, immigrants). Progressives also saw a new frontier in overseas expansion. Populists, on the other hand, saw the end of the Western frontier as a crisis for republican ideals based on equal opportunity and widespread property ownership.

Popular culture boomed toward the end of the century and it helped establish the frontier myth in the popular consciousness. The Western novel and film in particular, which elaborated all aspects of the myth, had an enormous popularity from the end of the nineteenth century to the 1970s (see the next section). By and large, the Western film, along with other popular culture, argues Slotkin, helped misdirect Americans away from the real causes of their problems. Instead, Americans were given fictitious enemies (nonwhites, labor, immigrants, foreigners) and told that the nation should mobilize for a new set of frontiers (overseas expansion, the containment of foreign ideologies, a war against poverty and assorted diseases, and the exploration and conquest of space, the atom, and the ocean depths).

In its various forms, popular culture has helped to divert Americans from the real causes of their problems throughout the twentieth century. In this sense, it joined hands with Keynesianism, the New Deal, Great Society programs, and other assorted band-aid treatments of symptoms. National identity was bolstered by the attempt to assert a national literature (the male-oriented classics in undergraduate literature courses—see "Literary Studies" in Chapter 5), and by a developing tradition of ethnocentrism and gunboat diplomacy. A rich fantasy world emerged in which superhuman heroes and unexplained human heroes saved the otherwise sound American community from supernatural and other forms of unexplained evil. Radio comedy distracted Americans and helped them cope with unemployment and poverty.[31] Tough-guy detectives appeared who used bad means to good ends. Best-selling novels depicted Asians as inferior and American films were racist and propagandistic to suit time and circumstance.[32] And the Western film falsified American history for mass audiences much as the high-school history text was falsifying it for America's youth (see the section on history in Chapter 4). Interestingly, the science fiction-utopian tradition has declined drastically in the 20th century, perhaps reflecting complacency, perhaps despair about contemporary industrial society.[33]

Since the Great Depression, popular culture has followed other contours of the larger culture. It now gives a more prominent role to professionals, thereby supporting the new power structure of corporate capitalism. It forestalls real solutions by offering a wide variety of entertainment in which social problems are classless (that is, the upper classes have problems like everybody else), and which are depicted as solvable within the confines of existing institutions.

The ever tighter grip on popular culture by the corporate economy and its ever greater (mostly unintended) use for political purposes are perhaps the best ways to see the similarities between all elements of American culture. Popular culture and the state join to develop a long list of family-centered (ostensibly religious) national holidays. Popular culture forms the stuff of up to one-third of our conversational material. By entering into everyday life, popular culture facilitates secondary interaction and renews primary attachments. As such, it both promotes and constitutes group solidarity and group integration.[34] Film, music, television, best sellers, and sports are big business and its products are manufactured much on the order of shoes, steel, and soap.

Popular culture has become an important dimension of our political life. Movies, radio, and television talk shows, television entertainment, and television news magazines all propound a deeply populist, anti-authority, individualistic (often vigilante) ideology which keeps the American people off balance and unable to use politics and government to promote their interests. The mass media also make possible a new phenomenon—politics and government by cliché. Thanks to television and the computer, political campaigns are now exercises in the manipulation of consensus-oriented formalisms. And mass-media celebrities not only endorse candidates, but run for office and get elected—perhaps nothing illustrates the false reality and limited choices in American life than this confusion among mass electorates between public leaders and celebrities. In 1980, the United States elected a cardboard president to match the cardboard figures in popular culture (actually, it recruited its leader from popular culture). Popular culture, in short, is part of the control structure of society. It helps to dominate people because it operates for the most part beneath the level of consciousness. It helps in social control because it evokes and reinforces the emotions that tie people to the status quo. It supports existing power structures by affirming and updating the popular beliefs that prevent people from holding institutions and elites responsible.

Popular culture is not unitary or homogeneous. Much of it is ad hoc and contradictory because that is the sort of world its creators and audiences live in. Much of its power to control, therefore, lies in its shapelessness. Above all, it contributes to social control by translating social conflicts into personal problems, by providing a variety of fantasy identities, and by depicting fictional others who are experiencing all manner of hardship in nonpolitical settings, thus allowing for a safe discharge of socially induced anxiety, insecurity, and resentment.

Popular culture provides some choice and promotes some awareness, but its main thrust is to conserve a taken-for-granted world. Along with the rest of culture, it actually helps to create that world, including its false realities, for example, that there is more pluralism than there really is, that problem behavior is eternal because its source is an unchanging human nature, that there is no social conflict (among social groups and institutions), and that social institutions and the elites they generate are not the cause of social problems.

Popular culture supports the same abstract, apolitical concept of culture that dominates the mainstream professions and disciplines. Seen sociopolitically, the need to politicize all of culture is long overdue. Culture is created by humans, especially powerful individuals and groups. It defines and defends a particular way of solving existential problems. Culture explains human behavior and makes human society possible. Culture also causes social problems (often the result of solutions imposed by elites). Culture expresses common interests, but also favors elite interests largely by putting the causes of social problems beyond society. Culture also prevents the members of society, including elites, from understanding any of this. Culture is always hegemonic even if it is not totally integrated—indeed its power, embodied in its elites and professions, who are also dominated by it, rests largely on its declared war on depoliticized problems.

Popular culture is part of the corporate economy, big business in its own right. It overlaps and blends with religion and political life. Its penetration of everyday life is all-pervasive and thus invisible. It helps to socialize each generation and reinforces acquired sentiments and beliefs throughout the life cycle. It caters to and blends with the American population by social class, sex, ethnicity, age, and race. It contributes to social control beyond socialization by mediating social tensions and bridging social discontinuities. And it forestalls social explanations of problem behavior and prevents solutions through political action by depoliticizing social problems, largely by handing them over to a professionalized structure of power. Understanding the basic thrust of popular culture increases if the professional theme in both entertainment and sports is highlighted.

POPULAR CULTURE AND THE IDEOLOGY OF PROFESSIONALISM

Will Wright has made a brilliant contribution to our understanding of the professions by analyzing the Western film in sociological terms.[35] Wright employs the concept of *myth*, which he argues, is a structure of principles—good and evil, right and wrong, courage and cowardice, love and hate, and so on. It is also a narrative and a model for social action, a code of advice on how to deal with our everyday world.

Myths have deep roots in a people's psyche, but myths change when society changes. The early western film, says Wright, "corresponded to the individualistic conception of society underlying a market economy" (the stage of capitalist development characterized by small economic units, local markets, a small public sector, and self-directed individualism). The hero (always male) is autonomous, strong, decent, and resourceful. Invariably an outsider, the hero protects, often saves weak society (symbolized by women and old men) against evil (symbolized by another strong, but self-oriented male). Once his mission is accomplished, the hero is eligible for love and sex: He marries and becomes part of a community of equals.

It is clear in the early Western that the actors embody principles. The moral in the narrative clash of principles is also clearly established: The safety of society rests on skillful, courageous, decent individuals with a clear sense of priorities, the well-being of the community above personal interest or gratification. The hero is a private individual (who does not emerge from the community however), there is little emphasis on government as a problem-solver, and the need for collective empowerment is ignored. *Above all, the classic Western resolves the problem of how capitalism can exist if all individuals are pursuing their self-interest.* The reader should note that what makes this myth rather than science is that the hero always remains an unexplained force. A social analyst must ask, If society is weak and most of the human race is declared unfit, where does the heroic individual come from?

After World War II, continues Wright, the *professional* plot emerged as the dominant mythic pattern in the American Western film. The Western changed, says Wright, to reflect a change from a market economy to a "planned, corporate economy," the stage of capitalist development characterized by large economic units, national and international markets managed by large corporations and government, and educated-professionalized elites. Accordingly, the Western hero becomes a professional, often a member of a group of professionals (to correspond to the fact that corporate structures are run by boards, committees, and partnerships). Heroes are now technicians and their relation to society has changed drastically. They now work for money, decide on their own what is needed to solve problems, remain aloof from society during and after the job, and get paid for what they do (often regardless of whether they succeed or fail). Elite values do not harmonize with other values and professionals do not join the community when their job is done. Invariably, the problem faced by the elite group is presented as a technical problem amenable to professional skills. Elites are no longer motivated by personal values, and their actions are no longer connected to social functions and the creation or protection of community values. Though still weak, society is taken for granted, more or less a going concern that supplies elites with enough problems to keep them busy. There is no suggestion of evil coming out of the basic principles of society (private property embedded in individual self-interest) as in the classical Western. *Problems are now part of the eternal human condition.*

The Western declined in popularity during the 1970s and its place was taken by the detective and espionage story. Unlike the classic detective story, the contemporary detective or secret agent is often an outsider or maverick (whether in private or public life) who is forced to break the rules (exemplified by the movies *Dirty Harry*[36] and *Death Wish*[37]). A major break with the past is that social goals are now ambiguous, contradictory, and ironic. And like the later stage of the Western film, the hero is now more professional and is often a "group" (to correspond to the specialization characteristic of advanced capitalism and to the policy-making committee structure of modern bureaucracies). The professional hero is also attached to or supported by complex organizations, a theme that subtly asserts the authority of those who own or control the powerful groups of our society.

The overlap and even confusion between entertainment and journalism is nowhere more evident than in the most popular show in television history, *60 Minutes,* a Western film disguised as journalism. Here reporter heroes uphold heartland values (especially individualism as total explanation) by telling adventure stories about good and bad individuals (morality plays) in a world without institutions, groups, or social power. Since the professional reporter as hero has explained all in terms of rotten or good apples, there is no call for institutional reform or collective action.[38]

The elite professional group also has women in it, different skin colors, and different ages (which makes it appear that society is open to achievement by all; for a fuller discussion of minorities and popular culture, see below). And like the professional in Westerns, heroes, whether individuals or groups, are not always fully successful and often fail at their mission. Since elites, and the organizations they represent, are assumed to be the best in human talent and effort, the status quo is affirmed even when elites fail. The shift to this perspective in popular culture could well reflect and be an apology for the growing inability of elites under corporate capitalism to solve society-wide problems or perform society-wide functions.

SPORT: THE TRIUMPH OF PROFESSIONALISM

Sport and Corporate Capitalism

The world of sport is constituted by norms and values that society wants people to have: giving your all in a win-lose competitive struggle, being a good loser and gracious winner, playing fair, personal discipline and hard work, group discipline and obedience, and not giving up. These values are openly espoused and openly declared to be good for people and society.

Sport has followed the contours of capitalist development. The professionalization of sport started in the nineteenth century along with the general growth of professionalism, developed slowly, and accelerated after 1950. During this period the strong tradition of amateurism declined steadily and today is no more. Amateurism had a two-fold connection to pre-corporate capitalism. Agrarian elites stressed versatility and participation in high culture and sport as leisure activities, and shunned activities based on earning income directly from work. Early capitalist elites, who emulated feudal elites far more than we care to acknowledge, also stressed amateurism in sports and versatility in participation in high culture as a way to gain prestige and hide the way they earned their money. Amateurism was also related to the form that individualism took under early capitalism: democratic and egalitarian, early individualism stressed the all-around, versatile, nonspecialized personality.

The movement to corporate capitalism diversified America's concept of individualism by stressing the value of specialization and expertise. Understandably, sport also changed in keeping with the change from entrepreneurial to corporate capitalism (for example, as Eitzen points out, baseball, based on the versatile individual, was superseded by football, based on the specialized individual embedded in a tightly coordinated group—to be discussed further shortly). Football was originally played without rules. The emergence of rules for football at the turn of the century (on the initiative of Yale University and Teddy Roosevelt) bespeaks the transformation of a Darwinian laissez-faire economy to the managed economy of corporate capitalism. Sport became a big business in its own right after World War II.

Sport is hard work conducted according to all the imperatives of the economic world: special training, discipline, schedule, standardization, technology. And the work (rather than play) starts early with Little League, junior high, and high school. Here one encounters the more mature stage of professionalism among athletes—not only do athletes prepare themselves, actually give themselves over to a career much on the order of the other professions, but since the 1970s they have managed through associational activity to achieve collective mobility. For most of the history of sport professionals were underpaid, exploited, indentured employees, but since free agency their incomes have rocketed. Also important is that the mass media and advertising have made them not only wealthy but famous.

Sport and Depoliticizing Society

Sport uniquely supports the status quo, any status quo, simply by virtue of the fact that it emphasizes abstract character traits. In this way, sport blends easily with different power structures.[39] American sports reflect American capitalism—they are competitive, aggressive, impersonal, methodical, specialized, professionalized, and profitable. Sports are designed to yield a small elite as are the economy, the other professions, the polity, and education. Sports also reflect changes in American society: women and minorities are now more prominent in sport; sport has diversified to accommodate all age groups; and there is no longer one national pastime—baseball must now share the spotlight with football and basketball and to a lesser extent with hockey, tennis, and golf.[40]

Sport depoliticizes by allowing all to participate in the reenactment of American values as if they had no contradictions or bad consequences. It depoliticizes by being nationalistic.[41] It depoliticizes by creating the impression that society, like it, is based on equal opportunity, promotes mobility, and has clear winners and losers emerging from a fair, refereed contest.[42] Sport also depoliticizes by providing variations on basic American values. Individualism, for example, is a highly ambiguous value, the source of much social conflict. Sport mediates such conflict by providing successful examples of individualism in a wide variety of contexts by a wide variety of individuals. America's two major sports, baseball and football, for example, provide different versions of individualism. As Eitzen points out, baseball is a nineteenth-century sport (entrepreneurial capitalism): leisurely, not bound by rigid time schedules, egalitarian, and unspecialized. In baseball, players come in all sizes and shapes, play both offense and defense, and are judged as a composite of abilities (the all-around versatile individual).[43] Football (a distinctively American game) is a game more appropriate for twentieth-century corporate capitalism. Here individuals are incorporated into a highly specialized corporate (team) effort. A military-like discipline spells out what is required under any and all circumstances. Players not only play specifically on offense or on defense, but some only kick, some punt, some play only in special situations. Here is the specialized worker who turns a bolt, handles only kidney diseases, or teaches Chaucer.

Michael Real argues that the Super Bowl (which decides which football team is number one) has become the central mythic spectacle of American capitalism. Here Americans collectively celebrate a game that is openly aggressive, violent, and male-dominated, a game committed to seizing territory through force, guile, and technology (a way to legitimate imperialism?), a game that is profitable big business with ties to the corporate world and the polity, a game that openly associates itself with patriotism and the American way of life.[44] The Super Bowl may have surpassed the World Series to become our central mythic spectacle. Perhaps more important, however, is the way football and baseball monopolize the meaning of individualism within a common American-style capitalism.

Sport and the American Structure of Power

Professional sport as a mass opiate should not obscure the similarities and mutual supports that exist between sport and the rest of the political economy. Elitism in sport has yielded world-class athletes and a flabby, overweight population. The courts gave baseball an exemption from antitrust laws and Congress has given professional sports generous tax subsidies. Local governments have built arenas for sports at public expense. And world-market capitalism (facilitated by the NAFTA and GATT treaties) has produced a worldwide flow of sport talent, especially in basketball, hockey, and even baseball (can international leagues in all sports be far beyond). The movement of teams has blurred the sense of place for fans just as the movement of factories has disrupted workers, their families, and their communities. And the cost of attending a game and the vast differences among those who can afford to go, are not only in step with the widening of America's already steep economic inequality, but represents a further reduction of public space in which America's diverse groups can mingle easily.

Professionalism in sport has yielded high incomes for a few athletes and owners, modest incomes for auxiliary personnel, and dead-ends for the hundreds of thousands of youngsters who fail to make big-time sport teams. Sports organizations, athletes, and television networks combine to sponsor public service announcements extolling United Way, or charity, as a solution for unemployment, poverty, disease, and family problems. Professionalism in sport receives massive support from the voluntary groups who sponsor

Little League teams, and from newspapers and television stations that celebrate professionalism as a natural way of life. The similarities with professionalism in all other sectors of society is apparent, forming a seamless political economy that is as powerful as it is invisible. Perhaps its most insidious disservice is to support the myth that talent in all areas of life is scarce.

POPULAR CULTURE AND RACE: AFRICAN AMERICANS

New Forms of Bias

The early content of the mass media (radio, film, and television) expressed America's racism fully and openly: African Americans were either invisible or depicted as lazy, stupid, incompetent, objects of comic ridicule, and always in menial occupations. From the 1960s to the 1970s, changes occurred and African Americans were portrayed in a more positive light. This change corresponded to a major shift in American (white) attitudes toward African Americans during the post–World War II period and to the realities of the civil rights movement. The changed depiction of African Americans has its own shortcomings, however, and a new, more subtle racist stereotyping has appeared: the more "realistic" all-black shows are characterized by "irresponsible and absent black males, esteem given to bad flashy characters, and a general lack of positive attributes in the Black community." Research since indicates that the media are still in this stage.[45]

Tokenism and the Falsification of Black Life

This is a good place to remind ourselves that experience is not always a good guide to reality. Whatever the appearances, research reveals that white males and females have increased their representation in television character roles in recent years, while black males and females are below their population percentages, with black females far below. African-American life is further falsified by the token representation of blacks among the professionals who appear on television. As far as other racial minorities are concerned, America has none if television is our guide. Native Americans, Hawaiians, Pacific Islanders, Asian Americans, and Hispanic Americans are virtually nonexistent as far as the mass media are concerned. (Print media does have occasional stories about Native Americans and gambling casinos, and Asian-American complaints against affirmative action.)

As for types of roles, black males lost ground in both major and supporting roles and black females lost even more ground. Another major pattern on television is segregation. Whites and nonwhites do not interact much on friendly, respectful terms in mixed-race shows, and the bulk of African-American representation on television is on all-black shows. Incidentally, there is also a strong tendency for whites and blacks to watch like-race shows. In one poll of top ten shows watched by black and by white audiences, there was not one overlapping show!

The Mass Media and African Americans

Researchers report that Americans who watch entertainment programs believe that African Americans are much better off than they are, while those who watch television news programs think they are worse off than they are. Both here and elsewhere, an important reform in improving the depiction of African Americans is to have more black reporters, commentators, and executives in the various media, where they are very underrepresented. A striking example of racial bias by commentators is from sports: in a 1977 study, white commentators gave white players "more play-related praise and more favorable comments on aggressive plays, while blacks were more subject to unfavorable comparisons to other players, and all eleven negative references to nonprofessional past behaviors were to black players.[46] The recent influx of black commentators into the broadcast booth has not been studied to see if improvements have occurred, but one can guess that they have.

Sport and Racial Inequality

African Americans are prominent in many professional sports (basketball, baseball, and football, but not hockey, tennis, golf, auto racing, or horse racing). African Americans succeed in sports that are accessible to them, in other words, in terms of class position and their racially segregated, underserved residential areas. In addition, African-American success in professional sports belies their lack of success in American society. Perhaps the most bitter irony is that the success of a tiny handful of African Americans on the playing field took place at the same time that the American economy was moving away from muscular labor toward cerebral labor (1950s on) leaving black (and white) manual workers in the lurch. The civil rights movement and the integration of sports allowed professional sports teams to expand dramatically in the South and Southwest from the 1960s on, but they also allowed northern and midwestern corporations to move to the cheap labor of the nonunionized South and Southwest. One result was to leave many African Americans stranded in decaying, older industrial urban centers.

On a concrete level, stacking (positional segregation by race and ethnicity to positions that are deemed not to require leadership or cerebral ability) is still prevalent. In addition, African Americans have not been able to move into managerial positions in sports. Professional basketball has a better record than baseball and football in recruiting African Americans into coaching and front office jobs, but progress in all areas stalled in 1991.[47] African Americans are also underrepresented in higher-education managerial positions (athletic director, head coach, offensive and defensive coordinator, assistant coach at NCAA Division 1-A institutions) even though they are highly overrepresented as athletes. In addition, there is a pattern of segregating African Americans in managerial positions corresponding to stacking in player positions, the latter pattern affecting black chances in the former.[48]

POPULAR CULTURE AND GENDER

Mass Media and Women

Trends in the area of gender are similar to those in the area of race and ethnicity. From the 1960s on, the blatant sexism of the media diminished. Women were better represented in achievement roles—they appeared as doctors, lawyers, detectives, and so on. That movement in the depiction of women has continued. The fourth sequel (1995) to the television program *Star Trek* has a woman as its central character, the captain. A 1996 episode of *This Old House* featured female plumbers.

But the overwhelming bulk of media characters and stories still feature males in achievement roles. Women are depicted—and it seems increasingly so since the backlash against feminism that began in the 1980s—as feminine, that is, as nurturing, engaged in household activity, by their appearance, including body shape, and by their relationships to others (mother, wife, daughter).

Underrepresentation on television is too abstract and, in any case, the idea of representing any aspect of American society accurately would not be entertaining and thus not profitable. The media not only reflect the American population's values and beliefs, but they sidestep problems and contradictions. For example, they may not be underrepresenting women in the medical or legal worlds, but they have little to say about the deep segregation of women in these professions into less-rewarded, less-prestigious specialties. When a woman does achieve standing in one of these specialties, she is apt to be referred to as a *female* surgeon.

Women are not prominent among the owners, executives, producers, directors, or writers[49] in the mass media. And as with all professional fields, one must always ask, what does an increase in the number of minorities who are in positions of authority actually mean? It means, of course, that equally qualified individuals are being treated fairly. It means that minorities are likely to receive more favorable attention, be it medical care, justice, jobs, or depiction in the media. But it could also mean that a system that inherently sacrifices many, if not most, will simply be doing it without resorting to racism and sexism.

Soap Operas

The soap opera (from the 1930s on)[50] stressed the importance of romantic interaction, the blossoming of true love, marriage, domesticity, and kinship values. The daytime soap opera presupposes and affirms an ideal family order: true love as the basis of marriage, having children as a woman's fulfillment, parent-child love and devotion, and generational continuity. All problems boil down to the need to maintain a happy, moral family life. Good people associate sex with love, marriage, and children. The world of everyday life is meaningful and small decisions have big implications. Life is filled with many different examples of human nature, all humans behave blindly, life is not always fair, but in the long run (which never comes) good triumphs and evil is punished.

Soaps have increased the number of women with careers, but these are token jobs, a ritual bow to the women's movement. (Actually, women on soap operas who devote too much time to their careers are punished.) Soaps are extremely popular and reflect deeply held values, at least among women. In recent decades, the evening soap opera has developed the family theme (which dominates the daytime soaps) to include the world of big business, including the international economy. Here again, a variegated human nature reigns supreme, but unlike the daytime soaps the evening soaps have a greater tendency for individuals to do good and evil in personal relations as these bear on business relations and vice versa.[51] The (small) movement of women into the business world and the growing importance of the international economy are also reflected in the evening soaps.

The soaps do not have a straight narrative with a strong patriarchal climax and this has led some feminists to see the soap opera as a feminist text that can inspire resistance by viewers. But research has failed to produce such sophistication among soap audiences. As critics have pointed out, the soaps render the individual insignificant and its multiple characters and plots make it difficult for the viewer to identify with any of them. Soap operas have many limited egos in conflict and no one is really able to take charge because each is ignorant about what everyone else is going to do. Thus, far from inciting resistance to male power, the soap opera's format of narration without end; its themes of ideal love, marriage, and family constantly thwarted; its many-sided explanations for evil and failure; and its transgressions that offer vicarious enjoyment for hidebound housewives all reflect the unsatisfactory life of audiences and offer fake justifications and temporary solace for it. Unlike the masculine narrative, which has a strong character coping with his world, the feminine "story" is a never-ending melange of episodic events in which self-oriented individuals struggle without avail in a world that is moral because people get what they deserve. It is not stretching things too far to add that the soaps bear a direct kinship with the social-action tradition of sociology, the rational-choice tradition in economics, and the interest-group politics of political science—which is to say, they legitimate the capitalist world of managed scarcity, except that in the case of the soaps, all instead of most fail.

Romance Novels

The romance novel has a predictable formula and is easy for busy women to read; it is also inexpensive. Aspiring authors are given a tip sheet spelling out the formula: a vulnerable woman meets a powerful man who excites her sexually. They spar, she makes clear that she wants love with sex, they separate. She fears that she has lost him, but in reality, he respects her. Some plot twist threatens their relationship, but they finally declare their love for each other, presumably a love that will last forever.[52]

Like much of the mass media, romance novel publishing is a lucrative monopoly using exploited labor, in this case, female authors.[53] And its female readers are clear about why they read them—for escape. Janice Radway has studied a nonscientific sample of such readers and has offered contrasting interpretations of what the romance novel signifies. On the one hand, readers are escaping from patriarchal marriages into a world where love and commitment, not competitive pursuits for success, reign supreme. On the other, such reading and its content probably do very little to change the patriarchal marriage to which the women must return. Or rather, concludes Radway, we will not be sure until we trace what happens to readers and their spouses over time.[54]

Female Heroes

Popular culture has many females in heroic roles. A female in a heroic role was a heroine in the gothic novel because she triumphed over adversity pursuing a feminine goal, marriage to a man of substance. Today, females are heroic in male roles, for example, as detectives (*Cagney and Lacy, Murder She Wrote*), journalists (*Murphy Brown*), the *Star Trek* captain, doctors (*E.R., Chicago Hope*), or predators (*Fatal Attraction, Disclosure, Thelma and Louise*). Some have even interpreted *Roseanne* as a feminist text because it features a housewife who openly ridicules feminine values.

The great romantic comedies of the 1930s and 1940s signaled the emergence of the capable, intelligent woman, largely among the upper classes. The rise of the middle-class careeer woman has been portrayed on *Mary Tyler Moore* and women can even be superheroes (Wonder Woman, Bionic Woman, Xena: Warrior Princess). The feminist movement, essentially a broadening of opportunities for middle- and upper-class women, is reflected in popular culture in many ways. Women have been given new motives, personalities, and statuses, often conforming to male values and usually according to their social class.[55] Significantly, the rise of the professional plot has included females among the professional group; this is necessary not only to satisfy liberal feminism, but because contemporary male elites are depicted as self-sufficient—no longer do male heroes return to the community when their work is done. Since elites are no longer organically connected to society, it would not do to have males appear to be homosexuals given America's prejudices. Actually, elites engage in sex and romance *during* their adventures, not after as in earlier heroic tales, thus creating the impression that the here and now is where everything worthwhile takes place (a reversal, obviously, of the Protestant-bourgeois, early capitalist theme stressing gratification postponement for the sake of a better future).

The Nancy Drew stories also suggest a new status for women, but have left an ambiguous legacy. Drawing on the Horatio Alger tradition but reflecting the new world of corporate America, the Nancy Drew stories (along with the Hardy Boys series by the same male author) stress success through intellectual-professional creativity rather than character. But Nancy remains feminine and attractive and is thus a superwoman.[56] Here again popular culture, increasingly working through professionalism, mediates a conflict rather than solving it.

Sports and Gender Inequality

Progress in giving girls and women equal opportunities in lower- and higher-education sports has been slow since Title IX of the Education Amendment Act of 1972 guaranteed gender equality for schools receiving federal aid. As late as 1997, women were still suing to get colleges and universities to provide them with equal treatment in sports. Given the economic constraints faced by schools, and resistance by male sports directors and organizations (resulting in slow-motion enforcement by the Department of Education), schools dragged their feet in extending equality to women. Ironically, or should one say, predictably, the large increase in the number of female athletes led to a displacement of women coaches and athletic directors by males.[57]

Women have had only mixed success in establishing professional women's sports. Baseball, football, basketball, and hockey are male monopolies and given the masculine (muscular, violent) style of play are likely to remain so. Women must be aware that participating in masculine-defined sports has serious latent consequences, the chief of which is that it reinforces notions of their inferiority (horseracing is one sport where female participants—jockeys—do as well as male[58]). Women have succeeded in establishing themselves professionally in two (segregated) important sports, golf and tennis. But two things should be noted about these two sports and about women in sports in general. One, professionals (both male and female) have emerged increasingly from private tutoring, largely all-white country clubs, and the athletic programs of higher education—all available only to the upper classes. What this means is that the small opportunity for working-class whites, and male and female racial and ethnic minorities to succeed in golf and tennis has declined. In short, in regard to gender alone, golf and tennis are now dominated by white women from the upper classes.[59] Two, women do not appear much among the various upper-level occupations that manage or report on the many-sided, lucrative world of either male or female professional sports.[60]

CORPORATE CAPITALISM AND THE INTEGRATED PRODUCTION AND DISTRIBUTION OF CULTURE

The production and distribution of culture has been an important part of capitalism, especially since the nineteenth century. For most of this time, including the period of corporate capitalism, the production and distribution of culture was done separately (sometimes mandated by law) and there were separate corporations for various forms of culture: newspapers, trade books, textbooks, radio and television broadcasting, the production and distribution of films and television programs, and so on. Understandably, each area saw the emergence of large-scale organizations and oligarchic competition.

America's concentrated culture industries underwent a significant change during the 1990s induced largely by the computer. Rapid changes in computer technology had raised the prospect of integrating all forms of communication—more concretely, the distinct promise of being able to project any and all symbols through sight, sound, and print through combined wire and wireless media in response to consumer demand. All that remains in the late 1990s is to perfect the computer data systems and the switching-bookkeeping devices still needed and a fully integrated, interactive multimedia system will be reality.

America's media giants in film, publishing, journalism, cable, television, radio, and telephone have not waited for the technology to appear. In the late 1980s and in the 1990s, a frenzy of merging took place that produced a small number of giant multimedia corporations. These giants combine both the production and the distribution of all forms of symbols using all forms of communication under one command structure: broadcast and cable television, wired and wireless telephones, film, radio, music recording, newspapers, newsmagazines, magazines in general, and trade and textbooks.

Since the new computer technology that connects these media can also translate symbols instantaneously into any language, these media giants are expanding with a view to reaching everyone on the planet. As such, they are a force to reckon with in their own right and a powerful support for world-market capitalism and its other global corporations.

Generating and distributing culture as a business also requires educated, often professionally trained personnel. Understandably, special educational programs have sprung up to meet this need.

FORMALIZING OCCUPATIONAL ENTRY INTO POPULAR AND ELITE CULTURE

Routine education through either two- or four-year colleges (or special schools) is the usual route to occupations that produce and distribute popular and elite culture. Football, basketball, golf, and tennis athletes now routinely attend college to learn their craft and they become the source for athletic directors and coaches. The entire range of artistic pursuits also involve formal education at a variety of specialized schools. Aside from college teachers of art and of communication, occupations in this area have not been able to require advanced degrees as a requirement of entry.[61]

There is a need to do research on a number of areas in regard to elite art. To what extent have dance, music, creative writing, fashion designing, the decorative arts, and painting and sculpture come under the processes of formalized education in keeping with the logic of capitalist cultural institutions for production and distribution? Are these areas forces for innovation or have they been stifled by America's piffling public support of the arts? Or said differently, has the arts' reliance on wealthy individuals and private foundations fostered the elite arts and protected them from outside interference only to curb them in conformity to the tastes of the upper classes?

One example can illustrate the promise of research in this area. There are only three graduate programs in the decorative arts in the United States and the latest, the Bard Graduate Center for Studies in the Decorative Arts (New York City), was started by a wealthy woman with her own philosophy of the decorative arts. In line with a major trend in art education, the Bard Center stresses the historical context of art objects (furniture, porcelain, wallpaper, and so on).[62] Is this sociopolitical approach to art safe from political pressure only if done privately? When the taxpayer funds art, either through the National Endowment for the Arts or the Humanities, does it have to undergo the Philistine onslaughts that these programs have endured in recent years? In other words, what is needed to support the arts without undue political interference, as other capitalist countries have managed to do?

The huge growth of popular culture has created a large demand for workers with an education in communication studies. The explosive growth of communication programs has "professionalized" occupations in this area, but only in the sense that specialized education is required, not in the sense that it can control labor entry. Communication programs have twice the faculty of any social science and hold interest for various reasons. The study of communication was once an academic specialty (or topic) that excited sociologists, historians, and political scientists. The power of communication technology to influence behavior and serve power commanded attention. From the printing press to radio and film, academics explored this world, sometimes in nonpolitical and sometimes in political terms. The sociopolitical perspective, never very strong in the United States, has been overshadowed in recent decades by the pronounced nonpolitical and increasingly professionalized perspective of the communication disciplines. This has been accompanied by academic programs in communication to prepare people for the growing needs of the communication industries.

No exact studies of communication education exist and therefore the following is an impression garnered from a perusal of texts and college catalogs. The first impression is that the study of communication is no longer related to the structure of social power, but is largely a technical, nonpolitical introduction to an academic field. This applies even when the topic is the influence of the mass media in politics. The second impression is that the field is a technical introduction to either a set of new occupations or the improvement of existing occupations.

Research will probably also reveal that similar patterns have occurred in a host of related areas. The commercialism that dominates information, journalism, entertainment, and sport has led to formal (professionalized) education in the occupations of these areas and to a pronounced (liberal) professionalism theme in their subject matter. The same processes may be at work in the creative arts (elite culture), and the trends in both popular and elite culture may represent a closure and updating of the hegemonic culture of corporate capitalism (the liberal monopoly).

SUMMARY

The concept of *hegemonic culture* refers to the prevailing influence of elite values and beliefs and to the institutions that maintain them. The power of elite culture must be continuously reinforced against popular resistance. The liberal monopoly in the United States has led to enormous deviance but little resistance to the fundamentals of American-style capitalism.

Elite values and beliefs are expressed formally through the various disciplines, churches, and political parties, but are also found in everyday family life and leisure activities.

The commercialization of culture under capitalism means that health care, justice, education, and other professional services must be purchased and are distributed by social class.

The commercialization of culture is also true of other areas such as information, news, art, sport, and entertainment in general.

Usage varies among liberals and radicals, but the concept of *hegemonic culture* appears to make the most sense when used to refer to the absorption of both elites and masses into a culture that has a comprehensive answer to all problems, including the ability to excuse or hide the failures of the powerful by referring to human nature, nature, or supernature.

Liberals believe that culture is adaptive, while radicals say it is not, but that the masses are resisting. Our own view is that culture is not adaptive and does not permit much leeway beyond American-style liberalism.

To understand how America's hegemonic culture works, a new area of professionalism is explored, the occupations and subject mattter of the culture industries. Thanks in good measure to the phenomenal growth of communication technology, the occupations and subject matter of the culture industries have grown exponentially in two ways:

1. Advertising, public relations, and the transformation of knowledge into private property have transformed huge areas of public space into commercial space, that is, a private world that is not perceived as such.
2. Both elite and popular culture—encompassing the world of music, art, sculpture, dance, and mass entertainment and sport—have also been incorporated into the liberal worldview to achieve hegemonic closure.

Occupations in this area (actors, artists, athletes, athletic directors and coaches, choreographers, dancers, directors, fashion designers, musicians, theatrical technicians, and writers), with the exception of college teachers of art (and communication studies), have not been able to professionalize (that is, control labor entry). However, the subject matter of entertainment and sport is permeated by professional ideology.

The occupations of popular and elite culture require expensive education (tutoring, special schools, two- and four-year colleges) and this means that entry is controlled by social class. Some male African Americans and Hispanic Americans succeed in types of sport that can be prepared for through local neighborhoods, high schools, and colleges—football, basketball, baseball—but, by and large, the remaining sports are dominated by whites from the upper classes. Some forms of music do not require much formal training and are open to all segments of society, but, by and large, the worlds of art and the occupations that control them are the preserves of white males from the upper classes.

The commercialization of popular and elite culture has been accompanied by formalizing entry into its occupations and by a pronounced theme of (liberal) professionalism in its subject matter.

Popular culture has grown and now appears to form a larger part of the population's daily existence. The various themes in popular culture and their support of professionalism are outlined and the pronounced trend toward a professional ideology is discerned.

Advances in computer technology have made possible a full integration of all forms of communication and have led to the emergence of huge multimedia corporations that put the production and distribution of all forms of symbols under one, increasingly global, command structure.

All in all, the culture industries (their owners and subject matter) can be seen as a vast depoliticizing force that takes its place alongside the other professions and elites to render American society difficult to see and difficult to democratize.

NOTES

1. For a valuable collection of essays in this area, see Muriel Goldsman Cantor and Cheryl L. Zollars, eds., *Creators of Culture: Occupations and Professions in the Culture Industries* (Greenwich, Conn.: JAI Press, 1993).
2. Sarah M. Corse and Victoria D. Alexander, "Education and Artists: Changing Patterns in the Training of Painters," Muriel Goldsman Cantor and Cheryl L. Zollars, eds., *Creators of Culture: Occupations and Professions in the Culture Industries*, pp. 101–117.
3. Herbert I. Schiller, *Culture, Inc.: The Corporate Takeover of Public Expression* (New York: Oxford University Press, 1989), pp. 30–31.
4. For a previous discussion of this process in plant science and biotechnology, see "The Natural Sciences" in Chapter 5.
5. Schiller, *Culture, Inc.*, chap. 3.
6. Herbert I. Schiller, *The Mind Managers* (Boston: Beacon, 1973), chap. 5. A full-scaled analysis of polling also shows that results (public opinion) emerge from the way questions are asked, their location in the interview, and the class and racial characteristics of the interviewer; see David W. Moore, *The Superpollsters: How They Measure and Manipulate Public Opinion in America* (New York: Four Walls, Eight Windows, 1992). The title of Moore's book is more radical than the book itself, which concentrates on the evolving science and profession of polling and its relative success in "monitoring the pulse of democracy."

7. A few states, for example, New Jersey, have extended free speech protection to shopping malls.

8. Philip Elliott, "Intellectuals, the 'Information Society,' and the Disappearance of the Public Sphere," in Richard Collins et al., eds., *Media, Culture, and Society: A Critical Reader* (Newbury Park, Calif.: Sage, 1986), pp. 105–115.

9. Schiller, *Culture, Inc.,* chap. 6.

10. For a fascinating collection of essays on the transformation of Third World folk wisdom, knowledge about plants, the plants themselves, art, songs, and artifacts into the private property of Westerners, including examples of and suggestions for a more equitable distribution of benefits, see the special issue "Intellectual Property Rights: The Politics of Ownership," *Cultural Survival* 15, no. 3 (Summer 1991).

11. Herbert J. Gans, *Popular Culture and High Culture* (New York: Basic Books, 1974).

12. In a classic analysis along these lines, Dwight Macdonald argues that popular culture undermines elite culture, implying that popular culture is an instrument of political domination and that elite culture is not. See his "A Theory of Mass Culture," *Diogenes,* no. 3 (Summer 1953): 1–17.

13. Of course, elite art can be radical. Mozart's *Marriage of Figaro* was a profound dismissal of the feudal way of life. Verdi evaded the censors to promote Italian nationalism through his operas. Mark Twain's *Huckleberry Finn* was a many-sided assault on American culture, especially its racism.

14. This double theme is expressed in the introduction and Chapter 1 of Tony Bennett, Colin Mercer, and Janet Woollacott, eds., *Popular Culture and Social Relations* (Milton Keynes, England: Open University Press, 1986), and mentioned frequently in the essays that follow. But the main thrust of the essays is to show how British elites have dominated through popular culture and to offer little evidence of popular resistance. The one good example of popular resistance is provided by Stuart Hall's "Popular Culture and the State" (chap. 2), in which he discusses law, the press, and radio and television, all in relation to the state and economy (and of these the only area that the masses have been able to assert some resistance and make some gains is in law). Needless to say, it is stretching definitions to say that law is part of popular culture.

15. Richard Wohl, "The 'Rags to Riches Story': An Episode of Secular Idealism," in Reinhard Bendix and S.M. Lipset, eds., *Class, Status, and Power* (New York: Free Press, 1953), pp. 388–395.

16. For this image in the literature of the political right (the shrinking old middle class of individual producers), see Jack W. Sattel, "Heroes on the Right," *Journal of Popular Culture* 11 (Summer 1977): 110–125.

17. B. Lee Cooper, "The Image of the Outsider in Contemporary Lyrics," *Journal of Popular Culture* 12 (Summer 1978): 168–178.

18. Gary Hopenstand, "Pulp Vigilante Heroes, the Moral Majority and the Apocalypse," in Ray B. Browne and Marshall W. Fishwick, *The Hero in Transition* (Bowling Green, Ohio: Bowling Green University Popular Press, 1983), pp. 185–195.

19. For the latter, see Elizabeth S. Bell, "The Cultural Roots of Our Current Infatuation with Television's Befuddled Hero," in Ray B. Browne and Marshall W. Fishwick, eds., *The Hero in Transition* (Bowling Green, Ohio: Bowling Green University Popular Press, 1983), pp. 188–195.

20. For the widespread use of the physically different to portray evil in popular (and elite) culture, see Bert Needelman and Norman L. Weiner, "Heroes and Villains in Art," *Society* 14 (November–December 1976): 35–39.

21. Peter J. Claus, "A Structuralist Appreciation of 'Star Trek,'" in W. Arens and Susan P. Montague, eds., *The American Dimension: Cultural Myths and Social Realities* (Port Washington, N.Y.: Alfred, 1976), pp. 15–32, and Robert Jewett and John S. Lawrence, "Star Trek and the Bubble-Gum Fallacy," in *The American*

Monomyth, 2nd ed. (Lanham, Md.: University Press of America, 1988), chap. 1; Roger L. Hofeldt, "Cultural Bias in MASH," *Society* 15 (July–August 1978): 96–99, and Peter Homans, "Psychology and Popular Culture: Psychological Reflections on MASH," *Journal of Popular Culture* 17 (Winter 1983): 3–21.

22. Peter Rickman, "Quixote Rides Again: The Popularity of the Thriller," in Ray B. Browne and Marshall W. Fishwick, eds., *The Hero in Transition* (Bowling Green, Ohio: Bowling Green University Popular Press, 1983), pp. 131–140.

23. Michael A. Genovese, *Politics and the Cinema: An Introduction to the Political Film* (Boston: Ginn, 1987), chap. 3.

24. Harry Keyisian, "Heroes in American Political Film," in Ray B. Browne and Marshall W. Fishwick, eds., *The Hero in Transition* (Bowling Green, Ohio: Bowling Green University Popular Press, 1983), pp. 219–228.

25. Robert Jewett and John Shelton Lawrence, "Playboy's Gospel: Better Wings than Horns," in *The American Monomyth,* chap. 4.

26. For a fascinating picture of the organization of an early industrial town in Pennsylvania and the role of Christianity in helping the propertied classes fight socialism and in providing religious support for the expansion and consolidation of American capitalism, see Anthony F. C. Wallace, *Rockdale* (New York: Knopf, 1978).

27. Robert N. Bellah, "Civil Religion in America," *Daedalus* 96 (Winter 1967): 1–27.

28. Marxism has its own version of these themes, but that requires a separate treatment.

29. Robert Jewett and John Shelton Lawrence, "The Birth of a National Monomyth," *The American Monomyth,* 2nd ed. (Lanham, Md.: University Press of America, 1988), chap. 9

30. Richard Slotkin, *Gunfighter Nation: The Myth of the Frontier in Twentieth-Century America* (New York: Atheneum, 1992).

31. Arthur Frank Wetheim, "Relieving Social Tensions: Radio Comedy and the Great Depression," *Journal of Popular Culture* 10 (Winter 1976): 501–519.

32. Tom Engelhardt, "Ambush at Kamikaze Pass," *Bulletin of Concerned Asian Scholars* 3 (Winter–Spring 1971): 522–531; Daniel B. Ransdell, "Asia Askew: U.S. Best-Sellers on Asia, 1931–1980," *Bulletin of Concerned Asian Scholars* 3 (October–December 1983): 2–25; and Jay Weinstein, "Fu Manchu and the Third World," *Society* 21 (January–February 1984): 77–82. For a classic argument, first published in 1971, that Disney comics are an imperialist influence, see Ariel Dorfman and Armand Mattelart, *How to Read Donald Duck: Imperialist Ideology in the Disney Comic,* tr. and intro. David Kunzle (New York: International General, 1975).

33. Donald McQuarie, "Utopia and Transcendence: An Analysis of Their Decline in Contemporary Science Fiction," *Journal of Popular Culture* 14 (Fall 1980): 242–250. By and large, science fiction, such as *Star Trek, Star Wars,* and *E.T.,* reaffirm the existing social order.

34. Irving Lewis Allen, "Talking about Media Experiences: Everyday Life as Popular Culture," *Journal of Popular Culture* (Winter 1982): 106–115. As Allen reminds us, mass media material can also disrupt and disintegrate social relations.

35. Will Wright, *Six Guns and Society: A Structural Analysis of the Western* (Berkeley, Calif.: University of California Press, 1975).

36. Carl B. Klockars, "The Dirty Harry Problem," *The Annals of the American Academy* 252 (1980): 33–43.

37. Robert Jewett and John Shelton Lawrence, "The Golden Way to Violence in 'Death Wish,'" in *The American Monomyth,* chap. 3.

38. For a rich descriptive analysis that bends over backward not to be too critical, see Richard Campbell, *'60 Minutes' and the News: Mythology for Middle America* (Urbana: University of Illinois Press, 1991).

39. Fascist and communist dictatorships, past and present, have fully recognized the political value of sport.

40. For a good introduction to the sociology of sport, see D. Stanley Eitzen, ed., 4th ed., *Sport in Contemporary Society: An Anthology* (New York: St. Martin's Press, 1993).

41. Individuals and teams from various countries now play on a year-round basis in almost all sports. The Olympic Games are especially nationalistic. The staged wrestling matches that are so popular on television also have a blatant xenophobic flavor.

42. College sports have been scandalized by corruption for decades, but no one seems to care. Sports also have a long history of racism and sexism and the recent success of African Americans in sports has not changed professional sports as much as many believe. For the continued racism of sports, see Richard E. Lapchick with David Stuckey, "Professional Sports: The Racial Report Card," in D. Stanley Eitzen, ed., *Sport in Contemporary Society*, 4th ed. (New York: St. Martin's Press, 1993), pp. 355–371. The many-sided success of women in sports also has many off-setting dimensions—see all four selections in part 11, "Gender and Sport" in the above cited work. Also see the sections on sport and minorities below.

43. The enormous hold that baseball exerted over the American psyche from the latter nineteenth century to the 1950s could well have been a way for Americans to hang on to the fast-disappearing rural, small-town America that made this form of individualism possible.

44. Michael R. Real, "The Super Bowl: Mythic Spectacle," in M. R. Real, *Mass-Mediated Culture* (Englewood Cliffs, N.J.: Prentice-Hall, 1977), chap. 6.

45. Bradley S. Greenberg and Jeffrey E. Brand, "Minorities and the Mass Media: 1970s to 1990s," in Jennings Bryant and Dolf Zillmann, eds., *Media Effects: Advances in Theory and Research* (Hillsdale, N.J.: Lawrence Erlbaum Associates, 1994), p. 303.

46. Bradley S. Greenberg and Jeffrey E. Brand, "Minorities and the Mass Media: 1970s to 1990s," Jennings Bryant and Dolf Zillmann, eds., *Media Effects: Advances in Theory and Research*, p. 289.

47. Richard E. Lapchick with David Stuckney, "Professional Sports: The Racial Report Card," D. Stanley Eitzen, ed., *Sport in Contemporary Society: An Anthology*, 4th ed. (New York: St. Martin's Press, 1993), pp. 355–371.

48. Dean F. Anderson, "Cultural Diversity on Campus: A Look at Intercollegiate Football Coaches," Richard E. Lapchick, ed., *Sport in Society: Equal Opportunity or Business as Usual?* (Thousand Oaks, Calif.: Sage, 1996), pp. 35–41.

49. Women television writers are paid less than men; for a rare empirical study of gender, occupation, and income, see William T. Bielby and Denise D. Bielby, "Cumulative versus Continuous Disadvantage in an Unstructured Labor Market: Gender Differences in the Careers of Television Writers," in Jerry A. Jacobs, ed., *Gender Inequality at Work* (Thousand Oaks, Calif.: Sage, 1995), chap. 8.

50. The following is a composite interpretation of Deborah D. Rogers, "Daze of Our Lives: The Soap Opera as Feminist Text"; Karen Lindsey, "Reading Race, Sexuality, and Class in Soap Operas"; John Fiske, "Gendered Television: Femininity"; and Tania Modleski, "The Search for Tomorrow in Today's Soap Operas," all in Gail Dines and Jean M. Humez, eds., *Gender, Race, and Class: A Text-Reader* (Thousand Oaks, Calif.: Sage, 1995), pp. 325–354.

51. Mary S. Mander, "Dallas: The Mythology of Crime and the Moral Occult," *Journal of Popular Culture* 17 (Fall 1983): 44–50.

52. Marilyn M. Lowery, "The Traditional Romance Formula," in Dines and Humez, *Gender, Race, and Class,* pp. 215–222.

53. Richard Pollack, "What's in a Pseudonym: Romance Slaves of *Harlequin*," in ibid., pp. 223–227.

54. Janice A. Radway, *Reading the Romance* (Chapel Hill: University of North Carolina Press, 1984). The 1991 reprint has a new introduction.

55. By 1980, popular music had begun to drop the traditional sex role standards that prevailed in the 1960s and 1970s; see Kathleen L. Endres, "Sex Role Standards in Popular Music," *Journal of Popular Culture* 18 (Summer 1984): 9–18. In addition, women rock stars like Madonna have assumed the same aggressive, sexual, calculating, money-hungry swagger that has long been characteristic of male rock stars. For other changes in the depiction of women, see Cornelia Butler Flora, "Changes in Women's Status in Women's Magazine Fiction: Differences by Social Class," *Social Problems* 26 (June 1979): 558–569, and Victor Gecas, "Motives and Aggressive Acts in Popular Fiction: Sex and Class Differences," *American Journal of Sociology* 77 (January 1972): 680–696.

56. Susan P. Montague, "How Nancy Gets Her Man: An Investigation of Success Models in American Adolescent Pulp Literature," in W. Arens and S. P. Montague, eds., *The American Dimension: Culture Myths and Social Realities* (Port Washington, N.Y.: Alfred, 1976), pp. 99–116.

57. Lina Jean Carpenter and R. Vivian Costa, "Back to the Future: Reform with a Woman's Voice," in D. Stanley Eitzen, ed., *Sport in Contemporary Society: An Anthology*, 4th ed. (New York: St. Martin's Press, 1993), pp. 388–395.

58. Margaret A. Ray and Paul W. Grimes, "Jockeying for Position: Winnings and Gender Discrimination on the Thoroughbred Trak," *Social Science Quarterly* 74 (March 1993): 46–61.

59. For a more detailed analysis of the class basis of women's golf, see Todd W. Crosset, *Outsiders in the Clubhouse: The World of Women's Professional Golf* (Albany: State University of New York Press, 1995), chap. 13.

60. For a discussion of the explicit tie-in between corporate America and professional sports, the difficulty women's sports have had in the professionalizing, the decline and low numbers of women in sports management, promotion, and reporting, and an alternative to masculine-commercialized sport, see Pamela J. Creedon, Judith A. Cramer, and Elizabeth H. Granitz, "Pandering or Empowering? Economics and Promotion of Women's Sports," in Pamela J. Creedon, ed., *Women, Media, and Sport* (Thousand Oaks, Calif.: Sage, 1994), chap. 7.

61. Professional athletes have achieved enormous collective mobility since the 1970s without advanced degrees, but the main reason is that sports are enormously lucrative and useful to team owners, media companies, and outside commercial interests.

62. For background on Susan Soros, the founder of the Bard Center, by Dinitia Smith, see *New York Times*, March 7, 1996, p. C1.

9

The Professions and Deviance

◆ ◆ ◆ ◆

◆ ◆ ◆ ◆

THE SOCIAL CONSTRUCTION AND MAINTENANCE OF DEVIANCE

Liberal Ideology and Deviance

Modern society spawns considerable deviance, but understanding why actors break norms has been a slow process. Early sociology spent much of its time studying deviance by the lower classes. The far more extensive and socially damaging deviance committed by the upper classes was largely ignored. Though more awareness has emerged in recent decades about the deviance of the powerful, most attention has gone to business crime and political corruption. Though professionals are sometimes included in this analysis, the professions as such have not become a focus of attention in the sociology of white-collar deviance.[1]

The following analysis of professional deviance builds on the basic insight of the sociology of deviance, namely, that it stems from the basic structure of society. Criminal deviance (along with other forms of deviance) is generated by America's universalistic and monopolistic values of individualism and economic success combined with a *de facto* class system that is a powerful barrier to success through lawful means.[2] What this means is that deviance is normal and systemic and to understand it one must focus not on rotten apples (individuals) but on that the barrel (liberal society). Actually, the proper focus for the study of deviance is on the upper classes for the simple reason that their wrongdoing is far more costly and morally damaging to society than that of the lower classes.

The lawlessness of the upper classes may now be more fully recognized, but analysts still find it difficult to penetrate American liberal ideology. Liberal ideology in the United States stresses freedom for all to pursue their self-interests. Freedom can be stated in absolute terms because it allegedly results in many vital benefits: economic growth, knowledge, personal growth and satisfaction, and the reduction of social problems. Freedom also yields a natural economy containing a self-equilibrating process, an economy that requires no political or governmental direction. The ideology of freedom is supported by a host of auxiliary ideas and values: constitutionalism, civil rights, objective law, fiduciary responsibility, voluntarism, and ethics. In the world of the professions, freedom is expressed as a demand for autonomy. Again, common sense would dictate that giving the powerful autonomy is an invitation to deviance, but again American ideology obscures understanding. It is no wonder that Merton's theory of structural anomie, for example, has been interpreted as compatible with American society—textbooks referring to it conclude that what is needed to overcome anomie is to expand and equalize opportunity.[3] The idea that American society is contradictory at the core is not a congenial idea to Americans. The common sense idea that a universalistic, enforced scramble for scarce benefits is bound to lead to systematic deviance cannot compete with America's deeply entrenched liberal ideology.

Professional Ideology and Deviance

The ideology that helped professionals escape public control was well developed during their rise in the nineteenth century.[4] From the mid-nineteenth to the mid-twentieth century, the professions, with the help of social scientists—for example, Emile Durkheim and Talcott Parsons—succeeded in convincing themselves and others that there were professional attributes and processes that solved the problem of social control and power, making it possible for an integrated society to emerge from specialization and interaction among strangers without explicit public control. These attributes and processes were:

1. The long years of training required to acquire the knowledge and skills of each profession gave assurance that all professionals were competent, or at the least, the best possible.
2. Free and fair competition assured that those who had the natural talent or inclination for particular professions would go into them, and that in any case, the intrinsic connection between knowledge and virtue would ensure altruistic service to clients and the community.
3. The professions would also be harnessed to social functions by ethical codes and by professional associations.[5]

Thus, argued professionals, they must be free to pursue service through knowledge. Only their fellow professionals could judge them and clients had to accept their authority on trust.

Monopoly Power and Deviance: The Culture of Liberalism

All in all, the culture of liberalism was a way for property groups (business people and professionals) to achieve a monopoly of power. In good part, it was an understandable reaction to the unfolding complexity of industrial capitalism. Liberal thinkers built on the metaphysics of Western rationalism and proclaimed a natural economy, a natural polity, a natural civil society, and a natural individualism. Out of this metaphysical concoction came specific norms and practices to make it all work (and of course, to ward off other ways of seeing things). Property ownership was stewardship, public officials (elected and appointed) held fiduciary positions and were nonpartisan promoters of the public interest, professionals were disinterested promoters of service, sports were under the cleansing power of rules, referees, and amateurism, and a wide variety of private groups such as colleges and universities, hospitals, charities, foundations, and museums were governed by *trustees*, and alleged to be non-profit. For good measure, the social distance between the holders of power and the masses was augmented by also lodging power relations in the supernatural.

The separation of elites and masses did more than provide huge opportunities and incentives for elite deviance. It did more than make for a series of hidden worlds in which deviance was difficult to detect. By lodging society in human nature, nature, and supernature, liberalism created a depoliticized world in which evil could only be attributed to evil individuals and concrete situations (rotten apples in a sound barrel). By creating a seamless world based on an alleged cosmic bedrock of rationality, the discoverers of evil could only propose minor remedies and refer solutions to power holders and professionals themselves. Nothing illustrates better the deep depoliticization of American society than the fact that even flagrant violations of the Constitution, not to mention law and morality, do not raise questions about liberal institutions. Actually, as Durkheim pointed out long ago, deviance tends to outrage the non-deviant and serves to rekindle society's basic sentiments. In the United States, which more than any other capitalist country steers the attention of its citizens toward rotten apples and away from institutions, the net effect of even the most serious scandals is to stabilize the overall system that produces them.[6]

The Trend toward Formal Mechanisms of Social Control

Most social control comes from routine processes of socialization. American society promotes conformity to its basic cultural values and norms through its family system, churches, schools, mass media, and the lure of consumption and career advancement. Social control also comes from everyday interaction. Americans use ridicule, violence, and moral regimentation to curb deviations from conventional behavior. American intolerance has often been directed against those who think differently; the relation between nonconformist thinkers and assorted private and public censors has been a stormy one throughout American history (the sinner seems to be far more acceptable to Americans than the heretic).[7]

Social control also results from the actions of groups that are organized for that purpose. The United States (and all complex societies) has had to rely increasingly on such groups. Over time, the structures of social control have become more formal, more professionalized, and more official (part of the political-legal order). Traditional forms of social control are still important; families, friendship groups, neighborhoods, religious sects, and so on, still enforce conformity through traditional means (explicit training, ostracism, fear). But formal agencies of social control (both private and public), often basing themselves in law and claiming the authority of science, have grown in size and number. Corporations hire and fire in an effort to develop competent employees, labor unions and churches struggle to control dissidents, and professional associations discipline wayward members. But the two basic thrusts toward formalizing the definition and control of deviance are professionalization and the development of law and government. A wide variety of professions and professionally run agencies deal with mental illness, personal problems, and family pathologies. And government has also grown and professionalized its approach to crime and to deviation from law and regulations in general (for an earlier discussion of the widespread concern with social control in the nineteenth century, see "The Culture of Professionalism" in Chapter 2).

All this is to say that the new forms of social control are part of the growth of corporate capitalism. The complex organizations that deal with deviance emerged in the nineteenth century along with bureaucratic administrative structures in the world of business, government, and the military, and their fate has been intertwined ever since. What all sectors of corporate capitalism have in common is an attempt to rationalize the way in which society does its work.

The two approaches to deviance—social control through socialization (we internalize norms and values) and social control through hierarchic external coercion—can be found in six mixtures say Davis and Anderson. External control can be highly pervasive (as in a total institution such as an asylum or prison) or of low pervasiveness (as in a bureaucracy). One can internalize the norms of a highly demanding transformative group such as Alcoholics Anonymous or a less demanding self-help group like Weight Watchers. Or one can be in a traditional demanding group that relies on both external and internal norms, such as the family, or a less demanding group such as one of the professions.[8] Davis and Anderson argue that the six ways of yielding social control are all responses to the decline of a comprehensive, functional social world. And all six ways are ineffective and politically conservative. Only a healthy society, they conclude, can yield social control.

How to achieve a healthy society has long preoccupied social theorists. In the past century or so, the basic thrust of social policy has been to seek a better, healthier society through professionalization and scientific legislation. How effective has this been and what are its prospects for the future?

Law, Science, and Social Control

The United States relies heavily on legislation to curb undesired behavior and promote approved behavior. Although it is always dangerous to generalize about complex matters, one can safely say that there has been no great success in improving behavior through law. Efforts to protect the environment or to eradicate unemployment through law, for example, have not been successful. The most notorious failure is the fight against crime. American crime rates are high and efforts to curb them through law have had little success. The widespread use of law enforcement technology has not only been a failure but has put into place a vast, secretive system of information gathering that goes largely unmonitored despite its obvious dangers.[9] Law is a blunt instrument that itself often creates deviance. Laws passed to prohibit drink, contraceptives, abortion, prostitution, and marijuana are major examples of how the law creates both conformists and deviants.

Research and experience have yielded considerable knowledge about deviant behavior. Over the generations, a tug-of-war has emerged between those who want to control deviance through science and the application of knowledge and those who want to control it through moral and legal prohibitions. But the contest between these camps is not always what it appears to be. The new scientific approach to deviance appears more liberal and humane, but it can also be interpreted as a defense of the status quo.

From Badness to Sickness: Medicalizing Deviance

In folk society, deviance is explained largely in terms of evil. Religious leaders simply assert that the world is subject to unhealthy forces and that some humans fall prey to demons, witches, or evil spirits. In agrarian society, evil remains a fixed feature of the universe, but religion provides new and more sophisticated ways to deal with deviance, especially through that momentous cultural invention, sin. In the more complex world of feudal-authoritarianism the concept of sin permits society (its power groups) to hold individuals accountable for their behavior in a more direct fashion. From the neolithic or agricultural revolution (about eight thousand years ago) to roughly a hundred years ago, the religious definition of deviance held sway. The rise of industrial society instituted new explanations for deviance. The main thrust of the modern view of deviance is to explain it through science. Here we are not talking of sociology, but medical science. Thus the major thrust of social control in twentieth-century America has been to think of madness, alcoholism, drug addiction, delinquency, hyperactivity, child abuse, homosexuality, and many forms of crime as sicknesses.[10]

As Conrad and Schneider point out, medicalization has its advantages. Deviants thought of as sick are entitled to care and treatment. Instead of being shunned or despised, deviants are placed under the wing of society's most prestigious profession. Treatment is often more flexible and efficient than under the sin model of social control. And deviants become part of society's belief in progress; they are put into rehabilitation programs. But the medicalization of deviance has its drawbacks. Deviants who are sick are no longer considered responsible or free agents. The individual becomes a dependent, no longer a full citizen. The medical model also promotes control by technical experts, which here as in other areas, generates citizen dependency because it is hard for lay people to object to what experts are doing. The medicalization of deviance also keeps the focus of explanation on the individual, which of course depoliticizes deviance. As long as the focus is on allegedly weak or deficient individuals, it is difficult to look for the social causes of deviance and difficult to think of alternative ways of defining social reality or seeking remedies.[11] In short, it takes the heat off society, or rather, off the power groups whose behavior, policies, and values cause deviance.

Creating and Consolidating Corporate Capitalism: Professionals and the Social Construction of Devalued People

Deviance is best understood in terms of six hundred years of capitalism's construction of who is considered valuable (and scarce) and who is considered a burden (surplus and devalued). Capitalism's most important invention in this regard is poverty and unemployment—from England's Vagrancy Act of 1349 through Elizabethan Poor Law to today, capitalism, especially in its American version, has a continuous history of not only creating but castigating the poor. Given over six hundred years of socially created poverty, one can also argue that capitalism needs poverty if it is to be itself.

Society's inability to find places for all has a long history. Medieval society also had to deal with the destitute and it established special places for surplus men and women (it also abandoned millions of babies to their deaths). Under the ironic banner of liberating humanity, capitalism has created a wide variety of definitions and devices not merely to deal with surplus people but to create the ones it needs. It may not be too far fetched to say that capitalism invented the category of *ignorant person* (now known as uneducated) and *illiteracy*, not in keeping with clearly defined social roles, but to legitimate the monopoly over good jobs and the power of the upper classes. The role of professional educators in all this, in earlier years more innocent than today, has been outlined (see Chapter 3).

The nineteenth century also witnessed the emergence of the social constructions called *criminals, mentally ill, mentally retarded,* and *bad girls* and their *illegitimate* babies along with the organizations and buildings required to remove them from society (all complementing the school): prisons, asylums, and homes for wayward women. In all cases, professionalism emerged to legitimate these definitions and practices in the name of science. The history of how American society has dealt with its deviants is one of removing them from the normal community (the social construction called *democracy*), thus avoiding the vexing question of why a constant human nature was producing a rising tide of deviant behavior.

To the above can be added other professionally induced constructions of devalued people that served to create and consolidate capitalism. The concepts of *foreigner* and *foreign country*, the assorted menaces of *immigrants, Native Americans,* and *freed slaves,* all served to generate clear structures of solidarity. Is it stretching things to add *housewife* to the inventions that went into the creation and consolidation of nineteenth-century (1800–1950) capitalism?

It is important in all this to see not only the similarities across the various hierarchies that constitute the United States, but the interlocking nature of these hierarchies. The American economy cannot absorb all those who want and need work and thus economists create the idea of paid work, natural rates of unemployment complete with arbitrary and patently false ways of measuring it. Schools help in all this by creating the concept of the uneducated and thus unemployable, a concept based on academic knowledge in no way connected to economic, political, or personal life.

When the above leads to crime, school dropouts, or emotional problems, more professionals come to the rescue, funded by the taxpayer and supported by state agencies. One illustration will suffice to bring out the interlocking (largely sincere and mindless) power structure at work throughout American society. Mercer has identified how mental retardation is created by educators who employ false definitions of students. Once put into operation, these falsehoods become true and therefore tend to validate the false definitions. Mercer reports that empirical studies in California show that Spanish-speaking and African-American students tend to be assigned to special classes (thus beginning the process of *learning* how to be mental retardates) at significantly higher rates than English-speaking white students, *even white students with similar scores on intelligence tests.*[12] And in a full-scale study of Riverside, California, a city of 85,000, Mercer again documents the class-ethnic-racial basis of mental retardation. Of further value in this study is Mercer's argument that there is a sociocultural (middle-class) bias in the evaluation of what is considered normal intelligence, and that this bias is deeply institutionalized in the individualistic clinical approach of professional diagnosticians and in the interlocking network of organizations that allegedly uncover and treat mental retardation—especially the public schools, public-welfare vocational rehabilitation agencies, law enforcement agencies, medical facilities, the Department of Mental Hygiene, and private organizations concerned with mental retardation.[13]

Carrier has shown that biased professional and political judgments create much of what is called *learning disability*. But Carrier goes much further. In a brilliant synthesis of existing research, he connects class bias about learning disability to similarly biased naturalistic arguments about a wide range of alleged deviations from normality: IQ, educational potential, mental retardation, mental illness, physical disabilities, sexual deviation, being gifted, and crime. And he also shows how professional judgments by psychologists, guidance counselors, medical researchers, teachers, and educators combine with economic and family interests to produce political pressure that results in the legalization of the alleged deviation from the normal. What we have, Carrier argues, is class society (its schools, professions, and the state), not nature, creating inequality and then reproducing itself.[14]

Trent's history of mental retardation documents in detail and puts a human face on the above analyses by Mercer and Carrier.[15] Trent shows that the treatment of the mentally retarded changed depending on whether the United States was at war or peace, prosperous or in recession. Throughout the history of how the mentally retarded were treated, professionals used the language of medicine and science to arbitrarily define a wide variety of the cognitively different and to justify warehousing them (often in conditions far worse than other capitalist societies) and always with a view to getting larger budgets. The debate over whether professional care in custodial institutions is the answer or if the mentally retarded should be returned to the community is a false one, says Trent. Professionalism has failed and the community has clearly shown an unwillingness to provide the resources that are needed to make the mentally retarded as functional as possible.

We now turn from the role of professionals in the social construction and maintenance of deviance and devalued people during the emergence and consolidation of corporate capitalism to deviance by the professions themselves.

TYPES OF PROFESSIONAL DEVIANCE

Failure to Perform: The Deviance of Unnecessary Incompetence

The professions deviate considerably from their norms and values of competence and service. A simple way to see this is to note that doctors whose education is subsidized by the public then refuse to abide by their agreement to serve in communities that lack doctors. Another example, drawn from the academic disciplines, is deviation in the practice of peer review and journal reviewing (considerable fraud in the form of falsified data escapes detection by reviewers; reviewers are biased against young scholars with non-establishment views, and many reviews are shoddily done).

The medical profession has a large number of non-performing doctors and a large number of errors by overworked doctors. Doctors also fail to keep up with effective new remedies, are rendered incompetent by specialization, and employ common American biases in their diagnoses (see the section on physicians in Chapter 6). The legal profession requires excessive education and yet fails to train lawyers to do many of the things that lawyers do. Excessive doses of the wrong kind of education and the failure to train students in the necessities of their respective lines of work is also characteristic of all Ph.D. programs as well as the MBA.

Fallows and Luttwak report enormous departures from both professionalism and common sense by the military.[16] Admission to higher educational institutions (from undergraduate to graduate and professional schools) does not reflect high standards or the academically most qualified. Ninety percent of American institutions of higher education are noncompetitive and the remaining schools admit many alumni, athletes, and minorities who qualify but are not always the most qualified academically.

Unnecessary incompetence is also present in the case of educators who persist, despite mountains of evidence to the contrary, in trying to reform education from the inside using traditional ideals. Unnecessary incompetence is also characteristic of the academic disciplines, especially those that have had ample opportunity to show what they can do, for example, economics and psychology. Deviance here is both by individuals and aggregates and by the professional organizations that have accepted the responsibility for service and performance.

Unnecessary incompetence can be approached in terms of professional stereotyping that continues despite having known harmful effects. David Sudnow was one of the first to expose this practice in his study of public defenders. Sudnow found that public defenders employ stereotypes about their clients from the lower classes, use typical crimes to categorize defendants, and negotiate convictions. In return for more lenient sentencing, the public defender does not criticize the law enforcement system for violating rights, breaking the law, or ignoring the interests of the wider community.[17]

Scheff extended Sudnow's finding that public defenders rely on typical or normal cases to define individual clients and defendants in other problem areas: disease, welfare, probation and parole, divorce, adoption, police handling of juveniles, and mental health.[18] Scheff argues that the more numerous the stereotypes the more likely that they will fit the individuals experiencing problems. The validity of stereotyping declines when the clients are members of marginal classes or racial and ethnic groups (patients with money can negotiate about their diagnosis). When the knowledge base of an occupation is high, then incompetence and careless stereotyping are curbed. Scheff concludes by citing the need for further research into the way control agencies socialize their members into typification practices.

Since these promising beginnings a great deal has been learned about professional stereotyping, though there has been no systematic research. We know that the sighted have used false definitions of blindness, thus denying the blind opportunities to lead far fuller lives.[19] We know that doctors use different images of health for men and women, on the one hand, and overlook distinctive female medical problems by *not* being biased in the direction of their distinctive biological processes and medical histories. One of the most flagrant examples of professional incompetence is in mental health and psychological testing and counseling (see the sections on psychotherapists and applied psychology in Chapter 7). We have also begun to understand that universalism in professional practice and the *absence* of ethnic and racial stereotyping may *retard* professional performance in medicine, psychological therapy, law, and social work.[20]

The expression "unnecessary incompetence" implies that professionals are making mistakes through inadvertence, habit, and deficiencies in their education. Even the large number of biases in the various academic disciplines (with the exception of fraud) can be thought of as accumulation of unintentional mistakes over time. One could interpret incompetence in the professions as a need to reform their educations or improve their practices. But incompetence is so pervasive and persistent that one cannot but suspect that professional incompetence is institutional and systematic, that is, a result of illegitimate power. This can be seen clearly in the way in which American power groups create false realities.

The Systematic Creation of False Realities

The nineteenth century saw the socially created false realities called *criminals, mentally ill, mentally retarded, ignorant people, illiterates,* and so on, all legitimated by professionals and all generating larger and larger budgets for payrolls and buildings. Earlier we reported on false crime waves that appear at budget and election time. We also reported that politically biased information (for example, from government) is routinely reported by journalists as objective fact. Persistent failure in foreign policy does not produce changes in policy.[21] A continuous stream of reports citing basic flaws in the

Department of Defense's procurement practices produces no reforms. Systematic and persistence exaggeration of Soviet strength created a false reality that was transparent to many knowledgeable analysts.[22] The U.S. Corps of Engineers has a long history of unrealistic cost estimates based on obviously unreal interest rates. The Federal Bureau of Investigation collects crime data and reports to Congress in a way that puts the Bureau in the best light and makes it impossible for Congress to monitor its activities.[23] Advertising and public relations specialists, along with political consultants, form a cluster of professionals who systematically create and maintain false realities.

Creating false realities is not an isolated act by rotten apples, nor is it merely typical of the various professions (which it is). It is organized or systemic (just as we see shortly that crime by the upper classes is often organized crime). Each of the above examples benefits other groups besides the creative deviant. Congress and defense contractors were part of the wasteful system of military procurement that benefitted from the exaggeration of Soviet strength. Local and state governments, along with farmers and real estate developers, are quite willing to go along with unrealistic cost estimates by the U.S. Corps of Engineers. Many in Congress and outside were more than willing to give the FBI a free hand. Creating false realities, therefore, is not a random collection of discrete acts easily rooted out or amenable to long range forces like science and education.

To understand the process of creating false realities fully, however, one must see not only that it produces results (crime-fighting budgets rise, products sell), but that the false becomes true (we arm because we believe the USSR is strong causing it to arm, causing us to arm further, and so on). Education affords striking examples of how false realities emerge from a deeply entrenched, self-perpetuating power relation that remains invisible partly because its falsehoods become empirically true. Educators, along with most of the upper classes, believe that education can identify the talented through IQ tests, grades, and diplomas, and that the best educated will make corresponding contributions to the economy and polity. As we saw in Chapter 3, however, behavior in school (by aggregates) has no positive relation to behavior outside school. Why do myths persist? As long ago as 1970, Ivar Berg, summarizing research in this area, found no positive relation between education and various aspects of work behavior, including productivity.[24] In a major work Bowles and Gintis[25] also pointed out that education did not have a positive relation to economic behavior, a fact (anomaly) that since has been substantiated many times over (again, see Chapter 3). Yet the belief that education is a potent problem solver continues undiminished. Why?

Bowles and Gintis attempt an answer by identifying a process whereby false beliefs became part of a class society reproducing itself. Simply put, employers hire those with good academic records falsely believing that they make better workers, *thus making it appear* that education has positive results for the economy. Those who succeed in the economy then send their children to school, where they succeed academically, and the process repeats itself. The fact that this process continues despite being repeatedly exploded by empirical research means that we are dealing with a fundamental part of the American power structure.

Betraying Clients: White-Collar Crimes against Individuals, Groups, and the Public

Deviance by the professions also consists of violations of law, the commission of white-collar crime. White-collar crime is many-sided and can refer to pilferage by employees of retail stores, or to crimes by small businesses (for example, arson to collect insurance). But its most important form, both in money and impact on public morality, is crime by property owners, highly placed executives, public officials, and professionals who steal from businesses (embezzlement), use business to defraud the public (price fixing, adulterated or counterfeited products), steal from clients (securities fraud), defraud the government (doctors and Medicare-Medicaid, the Pentagon and defense contractors), steal from other businesses (industrial espionage, securities fraud, patent fraud, stealing fashion designs, kickbacks, bribery, payoffs in the construction business), or use the state to defraud workers, consumers, taxpayers, and so on (corporate-state crime, lax enforcement of the laws, corrupt legislators, public officials, judges, and so on).

The sociology of white-collar crime is the most important development in criminology in recent decades. Its focus so far has been on business crime and properly so. Research has now begun to disentangle property owners from managers, see the connection between business crime and support by the state, and the difficulties of prosecuting owners and corporate entities. Despite the considerable knowledge that we now have about criminal behavior by the upper classes, our knowledge of crime (and deviance) by the professions has not proceeded apace. An important first step in understanding crime by the professions is to see them as members of the upper classes, some secure, some insecure, some marginal, and some aspiring to reach the highest levels. A second step is to recognize that crime by the upper classes is often highly organized and requires cooperation among various elites. (We refer to organized crime by the upper classes and its professions as *collusion* to distinguish it from the well-known term referring to professionalized criminal groups.)

An interesting background note on crime by elites is that much of it is committed by those who set their own incomes. Executives of large corporations and doctors are two prime examples. This practice bespeaks a larger autonomy that is fertile ground for crime. Doctors engage in a wide variety of questionable practices stemming from their investments in hospitals, nursing homes, laboratories, and medical supply and pharmaceutical companies, and thus stand to benefit from self-referral.[26] Doctors break the law and their service oath by not reporting diseases and disabilities caused by the corporations they work for. Doctors fail to report cases of child and spousal abuse.

The medical profession (a small number of doctors) also defrauds the government, insurance companies, and patients of very large sums of money (more than all the money stolen by the lower classes put together).[27] Lawyers (again not all of them or even most) also violate canons of trust in a variety of ways. Accountants are guilty of giving false audits to benefit themselves and client firms. Accountants, lawyers, and financial planners, who advise clients on investments, sometimes accept fees from those who are selling investment instruments, a fertile field for collusion. Professionals who are entrusted with the finances of others also engage in large-scale embezzlement from individuals (the elderly, widows, heirs and ordinary investors) and from organizations (pension funds, corporations, banks, and so on). Corporate directors tend not to oversee the behavior of management on behalf of stockholders.

Brokers and brokerage firms "churn" their accounts (excessive buying and selling) to earn unwarranted commissions. They also engage in insider trading, the use of information garnered from one side of their professional role used to benefit themselves and others in another side of their role.[28]

Though federal and state employees are subject to conflict of interest laws, the problem of both elected and appointed officials working on behalf of private interests, while ostensibly fiduciary agents, remains a serious problem at all levels of the American polity.

The above focus on deviance by professionals may have created the impression that individual deviance is the main type and cause of norm breaking behavior. Certainly this is the impression garnered from mass media accounts of elite wrongdoing. It is important to remember, therefore, that role conflict is endemic to modern society and that the upper classes of American society have institutionalized enormous autonomy for themselves. The focus, in other words, must be on corporate capitalism as the generator of deviance (by both elites and ordinary individuals). A few examples of how even public agencies in full view deviate from their responsibilities provides an introduction to a macrosociology of deviance by professionals. The Atomic Energy Commission, now called the Nuclear Regulatory Commission, was commissioned to both promote and regulate nuclear energy. Its history is one of promoting nuclear energy and neglecting nuclear safety. The same conflict between safety and promotion contaminates the Federal Aviation Administration. The U.S. Department of the Treasury is the trustee of Social Security funds and is also a large-scale borrower. The Department consistently lends itself social security funds at the lowest interest rates (making the government look better, protecting the taxpayer, but also favoring private investors and neglecting its pension obligations). The above betrayal of trust is widespread throughout American society. The above examples are not individual cases but represent "cooperation" among the powerful to betray the public. This is best discussed in a separate section so that deviance by the powerful can be put in the context of America's deviant form of capitalism.

DEVIANCE IN AMERICA'S DEVIANT FORM OF CAPITALISM

American capitalism is different from all other capitalist societies in having a deeply underdeveloped polity. America's polity is *under*developed not undeveloped—that is, it has been massively shaped to be a strong supporter of property and professional groups and a weak supporter of ordinary citizens, the poor, and minorities.

Collusion Among the Powerful and Near-Powerful

Many white-collar crimes represent criminal alliances among powerful groups; for example, kickbacks, bribery, and payoffs in the construction business often involve the architect, contractor, labor unions, workers, government inspectors, and the owners of the building. White-collar crime connects with street crime as banks launder ill-gotten gains from drug sales and other crimes. White-collar criminals keep abreast of the latest technology; for example, they use the computer to steal money from banks or information from whoever has it. White-collar crime stems from and also consists of the failure to enforce antitrust laws, banking laws, environmental laws, and civil rights laws. It means government officials biasing decisions in favor of companies they will eventually work for. It means criminal networks involving city and state officials, businesses, professions, and police and law enforcement officials.

White-collar crime occurs on a wide scale because the United States relies heavily on voluntary adherence to legal, ethical, and moral norms by powerful groups. Or rather, Americans have been persuaded by these groups, who hide behind fictional notions of pluralism and competition, that this is the way society should be run. When capitalism arose, it developed extensive relations among strangers and these relations have continued to grow. Relations among strangers require new social-control techniques, including laws, ethical codes, and personalized morality. But the most important of these, law, has lagged badly as enterprising economic and professional groups commit new crimes out of developing opportunities much faster than the politically organized public can keep up with. Even when laws appear, they are not enforced because government represents the powerful, not the American people. Much of that representation (our executive, judicial, and legislative branches of government) is itself a result of crime and other deviant behavior.

White-collar crime by elites takes place in all developed capitalist societies, but evidence points to the United States as the leader. Insight into this unique status can be gleaned by noting that the United States provides huge subsidies to the upper classes, including the professions and disciplines, but unlike other capitalist societies, there is little monitoring by government to see to it that elites use subsidies for intended purposes (for the contrast between how the professions arose in the United States and all other societies, see "The Rise of the Professions: National Contexts and Variations" in Chapter 1).

Perhaps the greatest weakness in the American control system, therefore, is the widespread use of fiduciary or trust norms, the almost universal reliance on voluntary compliance to law, ethics, and professional codes. This, of course, is the other side of the laissez-faire coin (or reliance on abstract markets) to achieve social goals, including the control of powerful groups. What makes this a structurally defective system can be seen most clearly by remembering the enormous encouragement of self-interest.

Voluntarism and unmonitored trust relations is like hiring foxes to protect the chicken house. Reliance on abstract markets and the good behavior of the powerful represents an admission that we have given up trying to figure out how to run an industrial society that yields multiple but contradictory values. Rather than tackling the trade-offs that should be made about conflicting values, American power groups have opted for anomie, that is, an abstract commitment to one value (economic growth and success) and a faith in abstract markets.

So far are we from recognizing this structural flaw that we have actually reenergized our commitment to it. The Carter administration began a process of deregulation in the late 1970s that was accelerated by the Reagan administration of the 1980s, which acted legally and illegally (that is, it was itself a deviant, perhaps the most deviant federal government in U.S. history). The net result over the past few decades has been reduced government oversight of one sector of the economy after another. One concrete result was the most colossal scandal in American history, the savings and loan bank debacle in which hundreds of billions of dollars were lost to fraud because of deviance from accepted norms of prudent banking. The scandal is much larger if one includes the huge losses in the commercial banking and insurance business. What all these deviant businesses have in common is the use of other people's money on trust, combined with lax government supervision. It is not enough to refer to this as being somehow connected to finance capitalism or to blame the Reagan administration. The culture of American-style capitalism obscures the danger of allowing powerful groups to go unchecked; it does this by depoliticizing power relations and by relying on hollow control processes (markets, voluntarism, capitalist governments, that is, governments derived, for one thing, from elections that reflect money). A naive reliance on voluntary compliance to law is pervasive throughout the economy (for example, oil industry, safety laws, hospitals, Medicare-Medicaid, airlines and airplane manufacturers, drug companies), and fiduciary relations are fundamental to the professions. Not only do large portions of each of these groups fail to abide by laws, but they often cooperate to provide the multiple skills needed to defraud and otherwise harm the public. For example, the savings and loan scandal required collusion among bank owners, accountants, lawyers, appraisers, architects, real-estate developers, investment brokers, bank examiners, and elected officials.

Scandals also develop because long-term shifts in the economy put economic groups in jeopardy. Understandably, threatened groups fight to stay alive. The bank scandal is a prime example. Restricted by law as to where they could invest, in competition with other places to save (for example, mutual funds and stocks and bonds) and to obtain credit (for example, low-overhead mortgage companies, automobile companies that finance automobile purchases), banks had to promise high interest to lure savers and then had to make risky loans to earn the money needed to pay it. The failure of public policy makers to redefine banking laws also contributed to the banking scandal. Actually, public officials, as far back as the Carter administration, responded to the developing squeeze on banks by loosening regulations while maintaining government insurance over bank deposits. The result was predictable: institutionally induced deviance of enormous proportions.[29]

Relying on nonexistent abstract forces to safeguard society is characteristic of all complex societies. From the emergence of universalistic beliefs and norms in feudal-authoritarian society to the present, elites protect themselves, not society, with empty concepts. Perhaps the easiest deviant-producing policy to see and avoid is the type that emerged when the Reagan administration evoked a nonexistent force, the market, to provide housing. Reducing government grants (which were there to make up for the mismatch between the income of large numbers of Americans and the cost of housing) was supposed to spur housing, but did the opposite. But by reducing government grants precipitously, misguided policy makers promoted huge amounts of corruption as well. Government grants were in place because construction companies, real-estate developers, banks, architects, and realtors needed them. These businesses and professions were threatened when the grants slumped and fierce competition for the dwindling grants occurred. Faced with bankruptcy by an anomic world constructed out of empty concepts by policy makers, businesses and professions predictably resorted to bribery and other forms of corruption to stay afloat.

White-collar crime is huge and difficult to deal with because it is committed by the powerful and respectable. Combating it requires new laws, the enforcement of old laws, and the training of lawyers and law enforcement officials to deal with both old and new forms of white-collar crime. Above all, it requires a better-run economy and society. In any event, the focus on deviance by middle- and upper-level owners, executives, and organizations is the most important development in criminology in recent years and tells us a great deal about the American system of power.

It is not always easy to distinguish between criminal behavior and incompetence. Behind the terrible record of the U.S. Department of Energy's handling of nuclear production for the military, the horrendous hemorrhaging of public funds in the savings and loan debacle, and other shortfalls involving professionals is secrecy and preferential access by power groups to governmental and legislative officials.[30]

Violation of Antitrust, Consumer, and Environmental Laws

Perhaps the most important white-collar crime is violation of anti-trust law, something that requires the help of legislators and government officials. Corporations engage in collusive price-fixing and this finds its counterpart in the restrictive labor practices of the various professions and disciplines (organized as professional associations, these groups fix the price of labor by requiring unnecessary education for entry into the field).

Businesses and professions also violate laws protecting consumers, a violation that is systematic and requires the collaboration of government. There is also widespread violation of environmental laws which also requires help from the government. An interesting and neglected aspect of collusion by the powerful to violate law and the environment is the long history of competition between the U.S. Corps of Engineers and the U.S. Reclamation Service to see which could do the most to upset the way nature wanted water distributed in the western United States (not to mention their mistakes and illegalities elsewhere). In a word, the entire social structure of California and much of the rest of the West and Southwest is based on water distributed by dams or pumped from a giant aquifer (a natural underground reservoir accumulated over tens of thousands of years) underlying seven states. The dams have a limited life expectancy (because of silting) and the aquifer is being exhausted. Much of the long history of building dams and encouraging development is premised on a long-term supply of water that is probably not forthcoming. The government agencies involved have not been controllable by law, largely because their interests coincide with the interests of private business (farmers, ranchers, real estate developers, industry) and publicly elected and appointed public officials.[31]

Collusion in Defense Contracting

A varied group of professionals (military specialists, accountants, lawyers, engineers, researchers, Congressional policy analysts, and intelligence specialists) collaborate in an intricate process of defense contracting. The interrelations among the Department of Defense, Congress, and giant defense contractors has been called an *iron triangle*.[32] Adams's case study of eight of these contractors reveals a world in which the federal government and Congress enjoy a tight, often secretive relation with each other and with military contractors in violation of basic American norms and values (including the violation of legal norms). Defense contracts are noncompetitive, and in addition to their wasteful cost-plus basis, they include many hidden subsidies. There is a revolving door of personnel from the Pentagon to defense contractors and vice-versa. There is a questionable emphasis on high-technology weapon systems and a neglect of conventional weapons and combat readiness. And the general public is excluded from participation in the formulation of defense policy. Not only does this concentration of power not yield the best military readiness, but has been a huge drain on national resources and a contributor to America's declining productivity in the post-1960s.

Of special interest in assessing the power of this network of groups and professionals is that it successfully survived periodic reports severely critical of its practices and demanding reforms. Whether the end of the Cold War can dismantle this power complex remains to be seen.

Collusion in Education

Public programs to support higher education are ways for legislators and elected officials to curry favor with important constituencies (the parents of students, administrators, academic and applied sciences in all areas, and so on). But support is given in abstract terms (education is a good thing) with few questions asked about results. As happens in all problem areas, instead of defining the problem accurately, new "professionals" and new agencies are developed to create the facade of problem solving: for example, financial aid officers (complete with an association and journal) and agencies specializing in student loans.

Federal aid to local government to support education in poor districts appeared in the 1960s but never worked as intended. Clearly earmarked by Congress for poor districts, state legislators and government used the funds to aid all districts, thus keeping relative positions intact.

The widespread fraud and failure to produce is most apparent in the for-profit vocational schools. Many studies going back many years have reported the same dreary message to no avail. Banks make publicly guaranteed and subsidized loans without evaluating the schools that students will attend. Vocational schools are accredited by agencies that receive their income from the schools being accredited. Federal and state governments, despite one critical report after the other, continue to subsidize flagrant fraud and utter ineffectiveness.

HOW PROFESSIONALS HIDE RESPONSIBILITY FOR FAILURE BY THEMSELVES AND OTHERS

It is difficult to evaluate elites because it is they who supply the standards and explanations both for success and failure. Once freed from elite assumptions, however, one can readily see how elites both escape responsibility for failure and take credit for what goes right even when they are not the reason things turn out right. Elites and professions deal with difficult, dangerous, fearful, mysterious problems. They are charged (often self-charged) with explaining and warding off evil, disease, drought, crime, war, adultery, mental illness, corruption, and economic boom, bust, and stagflation. Elites assume responsibility for health, justice, peace (domestic and external), prosperity, and peace of mind. Since the record in all these areas is never satisfactory, how do elites and professions manage to stay on top?

The prospect of not achieving the above values generates acute anxiety and much fear, especially among ordinary people. Achieving important values is far from being a mere matter of skill and knowledge. Those who rely merely on skill and knowledge to solve problems (for example, mail carriers, plumbers, nurses, housewives) are given less power and receive fewer rewards than those whose skill and knowledge *are not up to* the problems they deal with (for example, lawyers, doctors, and economists). Elite occupations always face problems containing a large measure of uncertainty. It is their acceptance of the challenge of uncertainty and their claim that they know the best and only way to deal with it that gives elite occupations great power and high rewards (remember too, that elites also exaggerate these evils, thereby creating the passive, fearful customers they need). In addition, when things go right, elites get the credit, when they go wrong, elites have a built-in way to explain failure.[33]

Preindustrial elites established their jurisdiction over problems with magic and religion. Early elites prayed to god(s) and enacted rituals to seek relief from problems. If things did not work out, preindustrial elites could blame god(s). Modern elites have turned aspects of science into a functional equivalent of magic and religion. Today, elites still rely on magic and faith, but these now go by the name of markets, science, technology, progress, rule of law, incentives, excellence, education, and research. Today, when things go wrong, we are told we need more of one or more of the above.

In the past, a priest could plead ignorance in the face of God's majesty and mysteriousness and still remain a priest. Today's elites can also admit ignorance, but now they keep their jobs by calling for research. The call for research has a number of advantages. It postpones problems, allows elites to define problems in their own way, thus predisposing all toward certain solutions and not others, and makes it possible to build in plausible excuses for failure at the beginning of problem solving rather than have to tack on lame ones at the end. In a basic sense, research is a way for elites of all kinds to escape responsibility. Once they have successfully established themselves as the best (a function served by a higher education camouflaged by the concept of excellence), they can then safely plead ignorance and call for more research. Elites, of course, will do the research, controlling the statement of the problem, and thus the results. They will also control the distribution of research results, thereby often controlling who sees it and who does not. Thus the blame for failure shifts to abstract ignorance and away from ignorant elites.

Holding elites responsible is not easy because they are surrounded by ritual and "sacred" procedures (diagnostic tests, citing the law, giving lectures). Their identity is well established by their clothes; they practice in buildings that awe ordinary people (free-born Americans will speak in whispers and stop chewing gum when they enter the Supreme Court building). Elites practice in prestigious settings with established meanings (laboratory, examining room, courtroom, boardroom, college campus, legislative chamber). And the various elites are seen in terms of well-established interlocked stereotypes. Until recently, for example, American elites were white, male, Protestant, and invariably depicted as clean-cut, well-spoken, successful, and doing serious work.

Professions are in the enviable position of being able to get credit for successes (even when they do not deserve it) and for escaping blame for failure (even when they are at fault). When surgeons perform unnecessary operations, blame is thrown on the individual practitioner rather than the uncontrolled specialization on which the profession is based. Professions also get or are given credit for things that they do not achieve—doctors are given credit for the rising standards of physical well-being over the past hundred years when the main credit should to those who have provided more and better food, cleaner water, better sewage systems, and easy-to-wash clothing. Some professions go unmonitored completely, for example, those in higher education. When dissatisfaction appears, faculties will juggle the curriculum or advising system, but never question the process of education itself.

Elites also escape responsibility (as C. Wright Mills pointed out long ago) by espousing a vague, naturalistic (human nature) explanation of success and failure. As long as society is thought of as the free and full expression of human nature, there is no way for people to get a grip on the levers of power. This also leads to the ultimate way in which elites escape responsibility—they persuade ordinary people that society is natural and just because it represents the forces in human nature. Accordingly, when things go wrong, the place to look is not up but inside.

Elites invariably take a functionalist view of their role in society. All of the above mechanisms for escaping responsibility converge when elites call for nonpolitical, technical solutions to abstract issues in the name of the common good. That this takes place even when it is apparent that a particular institution or group is the cause of the problem shows how successfully they have deceived others as well as themselves.

The world of professions has been in ferment since the nineteenth century. Tensions have existed inside each profession, among professions, and among the professions and outside forces (mostly other elites, but occasionally lay people). The net result, however, has not been to establish a healthy system of pluralistic power; on the contrary, nothing has interrupted the trend toward monopoly and nonresponsibility. The task of holding the professions (and all elites) accountable for the performance of social functions remains the major unfinished business of American society. The many attempts at reform should not mislead us—reform efforts not only have a history of failure, but they create the impression that we are a sound society with problems and make it difficult to ask, Are we a problem society?

THE SOCIAL FUNCTIONS OF PROFESSIONAL FAILURE

Some deviance has positive consequences in a straightforward manner, for example, when scholars and scientists challenge old ways of knowing or doing things. But even undesirable deviance, such as theft, murder, and political extremism, has positive results (see "Monopoly Power and Deviance: The Culture of Liberalism," above). Remember that there is no human nature and therefore no innate way for human beings to know who they are, what they stand for, or what they are against. To refer again to Durkheim, the latent function of deviance is to tell the straight members of society who they are. Deviance provokes disgust and outrage, in effect, rekindling, recharging, and reinforcing social sentiments.

A focus on deviance, therefore, helps us understand how society functions and how it achieves social control even as social-control mechanisms fail. In a classic analysis, Kai Erikson asked an interesting question in this regard: Does society (different power groups with fundamentally different interests) create deviants in order to maintain and revitalize itself? His answer is yes. Society, he argues, seems to need deviants so that it can establish its boundaries and maintain itself over time.[34] Another analyst has found the use of political witch hunts widespread across different kinds of society, including the United States. He concludes that witch hunts, or deviance from political norms to counter imaginary threats to society, helps promote social solidarity.[35]

In broader terms, what is the major purpose of social-control agencies and the professions who run and staff them: courts, police, prisons, juvenile and family courts, regulatory agencies, fair employment agencies, environmental control agencies, mental health facilities? When we condemn or confine the mentally ill, are we performing the latent function of unifying society?[36] Are our social-control professions combating deviance, or are they maintaining the status quo and serving the interests of other power groups? If deviance comes from participation in a contradictory institutional-normative system, then social-control professions and agencies are merely dealing with symptoms.

Social-control agencies and professions are notorious failures. Crime monopolizes our concerns about deviance and there is no denying its prevalence. But law enforcement cannot be said to have had much success against crime.[37] Efforts to cope with deviance in other areas have been no more successful. Self-help and voluntary programs are also ways to help a few while failing the many. Alcoholics Anonymous, Mothers Against Drunk Drivers (MADD), neighborhood movements, Weight Watchers, and various groups to promote self-esteem are basically ways to deflect attention from causes and to put responsibility for change on ordinary individuals.

The significance of pervasive professional failure is profound. That people think and behave in terms of group context is important in interpreting many different kinds of behavior, including professional behavior. Once someone is assumed to be mentally ill, then all facts are interpreted in this direction. Once you are in a social setting, say a mental hospital, a host of habits take over to control perception. But beyond the field of mental health, the same process occurs in the White House, State Department, the corporate board and executive suite, the school and university (from classroom to academic-administrative policymaking bodies), courtrooms (public defenders, lawyers, judges), law firms, pollution-control agencies, voluntary agencies (for example, the American Cancer Society), hospitals, newspapers, news magazines, network news departments, Congress and state legislatures, hospitals, and so on.

All these failures, however, become successes if we look at them in terms of latent functional analysis. What we then see is a conflict society in which the interests of power groups do not harmonize with the interests of society. Social-control professions and agencies are not so much seeking to curb or rehabilitate deviants, or even to protect society from them. What they are doing (unintentionally) is protecting power groups from having to acknowledge that *they* are the deviants and that they are responsible for society's shortfalls.

This is an important insight because it puts our eye, not on the ordinary deviant, but on power groups. It helps us resist the accepted practice of giving the problem of deviant behavior over to experts. What professionalism means is that a problem is being rendered unproblematic, that is, nonpolitical. Powerful pressures to depoliticize have been detrimental throughout American history to dissidents, trade unionists, people with personality problems, lawbreakers (especially from the lower classes), racial and ethnic groups, the handicapped (differently able), gays and lesbians, and women's groups demanding rights. In addition to depoliticizing deviance by stressing personal responsibility for behavior, by medicalizing some of it, and by placing large amounts in the hands of law-enforcement officials, the United States has prevented the lower classes from developing their assorted discontents into a coherent, conscious body of dissent. In this sense, the professions that have struggled to cope with deviant behavior must be linked to the agencies of social control represented by the two major political parties, the school system, the pulpit, and mass media, which, when taken as a whole, have succeeded in blanketing the masses with an ideology of personal responsibility that is not in their interest.[38]

THE PROBLEM OF SOCIAL CONTROL: ASKING THE POWERFUL TO CONTROL THE POWERFUL

The story of the past hundred years can be told in terms of the failed devices adopted by liberalism as safeguards against deviance by elites: blind trusts for public officials; laws against public officials going directly into private employment in areas that they worked in; establishing separate sections in acounting firms and brokerage houses to guard against insider trading; computerized monitoring of stock transactions to identify suspicious volumes of security trading; guardians; trustees; bonding; independent auditors; inspectors; government regulators and examiners; government agencies to certify and license occupations and professions; oversight committees for intelligences agencies; accreditation agencies and oversight commissions for hospitals; mandatory education in brush-up courses; whistleblowers; and ombudsmen. The reason for failure is not difficult to determine. Consider the following examples. Those who use the services of brokerage firms must submit their complaints against brokers to arbitration. The arbitration boards are run by the Stock Exchange, but financed by the brokerage houses. Clients are also not served in a second way. Stock analysts who advise clients to sell (because their research has led them to expect a downturn in a company's fortunes) have been bullied by the same companies and some have been fired by their brokerage houses. One suspects that the credibility of research has been contaminated when 95 percent of brokers' advice to clients is to buy or hold.

Perhaps the first step in curbing professional deviance is to begin collecting reliable data on crime by the upper classes. But the bigger problem remains—how can we expect the powerful to control the powerful? How can they be controlled when they are hidden by the ideology of free enterprise, markets, voluntarism (which includes self-monitoring), pluralism, and moral outrage against rotten apples? The obvious answer to preventing the misuse of power is countervailing power. The enormous concentration of economic power is the prime problem. Ways to decentralize the economy without unduly jeopardizing efficiency must be devised. The connection between private money and political power must be broken. Better ways of balancing power groups must be instituted. Some promising leads as to the concrete forms that balanced power should take concludes our discussion of professional deviance.

CONTROL GROUPS BEYOND THE COURTS, POLICE, AND PRISONS

Society has many control groups outside traditional law enforcement. Professional baseball and football have (fairly effective) groups to monitor the behavior of players and owners. College athletics is also governed by an association (largely ineffective despite the fact that corruption is rampant and longstanding). The various professions have disciplinary processes to oversee the behavior of their members (ineffective), and there are professional groups (for example, hospital or college accrediting bodies) that monitor how professional groups behave (effectiveness not known, but probably low).

Relying on groups to control groups goes far beyond traditional law enforcement even when the control groups are government agencies. The Securities and Exchange Commission (allegedly) protects owners against fraudulent investment practices. The Environmental Protection Agency (allegedly) protects the public against business polluters. The Federal Drug Administration, Federal Trade Commission, and so on (allegedly) work to protect the public against unscrupulous businesses. Which of these types of social control agencies is effective and why?

Ermann and Lundman have developed a topology of organizations in relation to their prime controllers that provides many leads for social-control professionals who want to be more effective.[39] Ermann and Lundman identify four kinds of social organizations that commit deviance and four control organizations (each with a social control function and beneficiary sanctioned by a considerable consensus):

1. Trade unions versus National Labor Relations Board (beneficiaries are participants in a mutual benefit group, in their case, members of a trade union).
2. Business versus Securities and Exchange Commission (beneficiaries are owners).

3. Hospitals versus Joint Commission on Accreditation of Hospitals (beneficiary is the public-in-contact, in this case, in relation to hospitals).
4. Police versus Civilian Review Board (beneficiary is the public-at-large, in this case, in relation to police).

The effectiveness of control agencies, suggest Ermann and Lundman, rests on a number of structural features in the organizations themselves:

1. Control organizations that rely on complaint systems are less effective than those that seek out deviance on their own.

2. Control agencies protecting secondary beneficiaries are likely to temper their efforts so as not to interrupt the flow of primary benefits (for example, the EPA has always put the profits of business before the protection of the environment or the public's health and safety).

3. Control organizations that inspect and do not monitor, that monitor continuously, or that wait for violations are not as likely to succeed as those that rely on a variety of control procedures.

4. Since organizational deviance is deliberate and calculating, penalties must be certain and severe if they are to be effective. Corporations fix prices or pollute knowing that the benefits far outweigh the costs. The CIA, FBI, and police departments continue to engage in illegal acts assuming that benefits will exceed penalties.

5. Effective social control stems from the legitimacy of the control organization. Legitimacy can be defined as the number of groups competing in the same control activity. The SEC is the single control group in the case of investment practices and is powerful and effective in protecting the interests of owners. In contrast, many consumer groups seek to protect the consumer against business and have much less effective control.

6. The greater the disparity in resources between the controller and the controlled, the less effective the controls. (For example many large corporations can outgun and outlast even the federal government in legal contests).

THE CONTROL OF CONTROL: THE AUDIT SOCIETY

The most important thing that can be said about American society is that American culture declares that humans (as opposed to human nature) are not in charge of society and should not be. Instead, American society is alleged to be structured and directed by cosmic forces or natural-supernatural laws (revelation, human nature, truth, economic, political, educational markets, equilibrating processes, constitution, law, knowledge, research, objective indicators, including accounting). Humans enter the picture either as contributors to the above process or as deviants from it.

America's history can be understood as a continuing attempt to assert human controls, actually elite controls, over the pervasive failures of American society while hanging onto the fictions of normative ideology, thus pragmatism, the Populist and Progressive movements, New Deal–Fair Deal–Great Society programs, the Contract with America, and so on. More concretely, America has enacted reforms in keeping with its beliefs, for example, through antitrust laws, deregulation, war on poverty, and student loans, without questioning whether its foundational beliefs, such as competition, individualism, private property, and self-interest are compatible with a stable, predictable, lawful, equitable society.

America (its governing classes) has also tackled its problems by professionalizing, that is, by assuming that knowledge in the hands of non-political experts, educated by and fed new knowledge by other experts, can solve problems. Professionals are considered to be our best doing their best, thereby foreclosing other approaches no matter how dismal the problem-solving results.

The hypocrisy that society should not be directed by humans (an obvious benefit to America's upper classes) is maintained despite the enactment of a whole series of controls and monitoring devices. Law, lawyers, courts, police, the FBI, and prisons holding one million Americans represent human effort to curb crime. The government also monitors the economy to see if stock fraud, pollution, discrimination, and so on are occurring. When corporations and farms find markets causing them problems, the government helps out. When the entire economy falters the government steps in. When housing and education markets do not work the government provides help.

Legislators also require evaluation reports on legislation to see if programs are working. The SEC requires a large amount of information in regard to stock offerings. The Freedom of Information Act gives access to government documents to help citizens understand their world. Requiring open hearings and diverse membership on policymaking bodies are intended to ensure better policy and enhance citizen understanding. Laws to protect whistleblowers are enacted to help uncover mistakes and illegalities. There are inspection systems in both civilian and military bureaucracies. In law enforcement, there is the dreaded Internal Affairs unit to patrol for wayward police officers.

Industry and businesses have inaugurated controls on a massive scale. Bureaucratization is a term that covers a host of controls over work and the quality and quantity of goods and services. Time-clocks, supervisors, paperwork, personnel evaluation, inspectors, specialized unit reports, annual report, and so on. There are special controls needed by special types of goods and services: parachutes and medical supplies require tighter and higher standards than the manufacture of brooms and buckets. Hospitals have to keep a sharp eye out for germs and human error and appoint watchdog committees to do their seeing.

The educational sector is filled with control systems: tests, grades, references, accreditation, and demands for more controls such as national standards and tests for teachers and students. Higher education includes reappointment and promotion reviews, course evaluations, annual submission of resumes, and so on.

The proliferation of controls suggests an innovative, adoptive set of elites acting out the drama of America's basic beliefs and values. But it also suggests fingers in a failing dike since our first line of controls often fail. Here enters our second line of controls, the "control of control," or the "audit society."[40]

Power cites the pervasive use of audits in Great Britain: "financial audits, value for money audits, management audits, quality audits, forensic audits, data audits, intellectual property audits, medical audits, and many others besides." Audits are so pervasive that they seem to constitute a constitutive principle of social organization. The audit emerges in response to a society that can no longer rely on trust[41] and which has generated a wide array of risks. The purpose of the audit is to reaffirm accountability and performance and thus restore trust, comfort, and legitimacy to all institutional sectors. But, argues Power, the audit is not an intellectual process based on accepted procedures and criteria and thus remains invisible. That it be done is far more important than how it is done. It too is taken on trust. In the name of openness and service to the public, as well as to specific groups such as shareholders, the audit is a dense and mysterious thing that shuts off communication and relies not on persuasion but on the presumed independence of the auditors. The all-purpose audit undermines the efficacy of direct control in concrete unique sectors, while affirming the appearance of control. By being above particular contexts, it reaffirms the rationality of the overall system. Though it declares the world an open book, Power concludes that the audit is a substitute for democracy.

Though Power's analysis could be qualified to bring it into line with American practices, for example, the Freedom of Information Act, legal requirements for open hearings, and the capitalist world's most stringent rules on financial disclosure, his analysis does point to a formalistic process that diverts attention from direct analysis and evaluation of how we generate goods and services. The audit is now merely the apex of a pervasive system of arbitrary assumptions and vague principles that modern propertyowners, government officials, and professions use to derive biased abstractions to depict, especially in quantitative language, power relations. The result is to depoliticize that which shouldn't be, thus preventing not only democracy but the knowledge that the governing classes need for even the successful management of failure.

SUMMARY

The rise of capitalism and its maturing stage of industrialization generated social diversity, conflict, and deviance.

With the triumph of liberalism, the problem of controlling deviance took center stage. Between 1790 and 1850 American liberalism established an absolute freedom to use one's property as one saw fit, to think as one wanted, and the right of property groups to act politically to achieve their ends. One response to the resulting diversity and disorder was the utopian doctrine of laissez-faire and other forms of "naturalistic" thinking (especially social Darwinism), all under the assumption that it would take some time for a fully rational society to get established. In the meantime, deviance had to be controlled. Given the liberal world view, this meant professionalism and formal mechanisms of social control.

Deviant individuals do not occur as natural phenomena but are socially created. The creation of a wide assortment of devalued people is associated with the emergence and consolidation of corporate capitalism and the professions that helped create them in the name of science.

Like liberalism in general, professionalism was animated by agrarian-religious norms and values. Like feudal elites, liberal elites demanded freedom from interference promising service to society on a voluntary, fiduciary basis. Like feudal-religious elites, liberals assumed a homogeneous integrated world of values and beliefs. Like feudal-religious elites, they assumed that deviance ultimately came from unremedied defects from the past and uncontrolled desires in human nature.

The professions adopted the same normative-value orientation of the dominant property groups and demanded freedom (autonomy) from interference in their respective fields of competence. The result of organizing society so that all its powerful groups are elevated above ordinary people and absolved of responsibilities for seeing to social functions has resulted in widespread deviance by the upper levels of American society. The mass of ordinary people also exhibited widespread deviance, given a society based on the utopian fantasy that automatic equilibration would negate the negative effects of self-interest..

The growth of deviance led to a shift away from socialization forms of social control (family, religion) to a more formalized system based on law and professionalism (science). Early efforts at formal social control centered on deviance by the lower classes. But in recent decades, attention has shifted to deviance by propertied and professional groups.

Professional groups commit a wide assortment of deviant acts. They also act together combining their skills to commit deviant acts of great complexity and of great cost to society. But deviance by the upper classes is still not fully recognized as structural, that is, a result of fundamental power relations.

The dilemma of American society is that it must rely on the very propertied and professional groups that are causing widespread deviance to curb it.

The most effective control groups are those that have resources, use a variety of methods to monitor compliance, and are clearly responsible for their area. But the only way to curb deviance effectively is to equalize economic and political power.

Modern society is alleged to function naturally but has also instituted large numbers of control devices. These devices do not work or are distrusted, and an audit society—the control of control—has appeared. Audits give the appearance of rational control but are not effective, serving to undermine democratic scrutiny and evaluation of power relations.

NOTES

1. This can be seen in what is perhaps our best collection of readings on white-collar crime, Gilbert Geis, Robert F. Meier, and Lawrence M. Salinger, eds., *White-Collar Crime: Classic and Contemporary Views*, 3rd ed. (New York: Free Press, 1995). The vast bulk of the twenty-four readings is about business crime and only two are about professional white-collar crime—deviance by Medicaid doctors and solo practitioner lawyers.
2. Robert K. Merton, "Social Structure and Anomie," *American Sociological Review* 3 (October 1938): 672–682.
3. R. E. Hilbert and Charles E. Wright, "Representations of Merton's Theory of Anomie," *American Sociologist* 14 (August 1979): 150–156.
4. For an earlier discussion, see the section, "Science and the New System of Power" in Chapter 2.
5. The key idea here, consisting partly of sound sociology and partly of wish-driven ideology, was supplied by Émile Durkheim. Durkheim argued (in *The Division of Labor in Society*, 1893) that fear about the diversity produced by the growing specialization of labor in modern society was unfounded: occupations, he argued, form into cohesive subcommunities and maintain social control without any need of outside management.
6. Andrew Szasz, "The Process and Significance of Political Scandals: A Comparison of Watergate and the 'Sewergate' Episode at the Environmental Protection Agency," *Social Problems* 33 (February 1986): 202–216.
7. The United States has a long history of also promoting conformity through the suppression of books, the intimidation of teachers and professors, and the corruption of journalists. For the large and systematic attempt by J. Edgar Hoover's FBI not merely to suppress but to shape public opinion, see Natalie Robbins, *Alien Ink: The FBI's War on Freedom of Expression* (New York: Morrow, 1992).
8. Nanette J. Davis and Bo Anderson, *Social Control: The Production of Deviance in the Modern State* (New York: Irvington, 1983).
9. For an informative essay, see Richard V. Ericson and Clifford D. Shearing, "The Scientification of Police Work," in Gernot Böhme and Nico Stehr, eds., *The Knowledge Society: The Growing Impact of Scientific Knowledge on Social Relations* (Boston: D. Reidel, 1986), pp. 129–159. The same secretive and discretionary gathering and generation of information on a broader and higher level of power should also be noted.
10. Peter Conrad and Joseph W. Schneider, *Deviance and Medicalization: From Badness to Sickness* (St. Louis: Mosby, 1980).
11. For an interesting discussion of this process in the case of mental illness, see Herbert H. Haines, "Cognitive Claims-Making, Enclosure, and the Depoliticalization of Social Problems," *Sociological Quarterly* 20 (Winter 1979): 119–130.
12. Jane R. Mercer, "Sociological Perspectives on Mild Mental Retardation," in H. Carl Haywood, ed., *Socio-Cultural Aspects of Mental Retardation* (New York: Appleton-Century-Crofts, 1970), pp. 378–391. This publication is an indispensable reference on mental retardation. The concluding summary by H. Carl Haywood is especially valuable.

13. Jane R. Mercer, *Labeling the Mentally Retarded* (Berkeley: University of California Press, 1973).
14. James G. Carrier, *Disability: Social Class and the Construction of Inequality in American Education* (Westport, Conn.: Greenwood Press, 1986).
15. James W. Trent, Jr., *Inventing the Feeble Mind: A History of Mental Retardation in the United States* (Berkeley, Calif.: University of California Press, 1994).
16. James Fallows, *National Defense* (New York: Vintage, 1981) and Edward N. Luttwak, *The Pentagon and the Art of War* (New York: Simon and Schuster, 1984). For a fuller discussion, see "Foreign and Defense Policy" in Chapter 11.
17. David Sudnow, "Normal Crimes: Sociological Features of the Penal Code in a Public Defender's Office," *Social Problems* 12, no. 3 (Winter 1965): 255–276.
18. Thomas J. Scheff, "Typification in the Diagnostic Practices of Rehabilitation Agencies," in Marvin B. Sussman, ed., *Sociology and Rehabilitation* (Washington D.C.: American Sociological Association, 1965).
19. Robert A. Scott, *The Making of Blind Men: A Study of Adult Socialization* (New York: Russell Sage Foundation, 1969).
20. For the need to pay special attention to ethnic and racial cultural differences in these areas of professional work, see Monica McGoldrick, John K. Pearce, and Joseph Giordono, eds., *Ethnicity and Family Therapy* (New York: Guilford, 1982); Stanley Sue and James K. Morishima, *The Mental Health of Asian Americans* (San Francisco: Jossey-Bass, 1982); Jay C. Chunn II, Patricia J. Dunston, and Fariyal Ross-Sheriff, eds., *Mental Health and People of Color: Curriculum Development and Change* (Washington, D.C.: Howard University Press, 1983); Man Keung Ho, *Family Therapy with Ethnic Minorities* (Newbury Park, Calif.: Sage, 1987); and Joseph G. Ponterroto *et al.*, eds., *Handbook of Multicultural Counseling* (Thousand Oaks, Calif.: Sage, 1995).
21. Lloyd S. Etheredge, *Can Governments Learn? American Foreign Policy and Central American Revolutions* (New York: Pergamon, 1985).
22. For a fuller discussion, see "Foreign and Defense Policy" in Chapter 11.
23. James Q. Wilson, *The Investigators: Managing FBI and Narcotics Agents* (New York: Basic Books, 1978), pp. 97–100, 143–147, 172–174.
24. Ivar Berg, assisted by Sherry Gorelick, *Education and Jobs: The Great Training Robbery* (New York: Praeger, 1970).
25. Sammuel Bowles and Herbert Gintis, *Schooling in Capitalist America: Educational Reform and the Contradictions of Economic Life* (New York: Basic Books, 1977).
26. For a full analysis of physicians' conflicts of interest, see Marc A. Rodwin, *Medicine, Money, and Morals: Physicians' Conflicts of Interest* (New York: Oxford University Press, 1993). Rodwin shows that the widespread conflicts of interest in medicine have not yet resulted in legal and ethical norms to resolve and control them. This contrasts with more fully developed fiduciary law and ethics for lawyers, federal employees, and business-financial professionals. Rodwin provides a valuable discussion of the concept *conflict of interest*, but fails to identify corporate capitalism and its complex private and public organizations as the primary cause of it and of deviance. Nonetheless, his suggestions for managing physician conflicts of interest through auditing and review boards are worth considering.
27. For an analysis, which also argues that the very organization of public health subsidies through Medicare and Medicaid invites fraud, see Henry N. Pontell, Paul D. Jesilow, and Gilbert Geis, "Policing Physicians: Practitioner Fraud and Abuse in a Government Medical Program," *Social Problems* 30 (October 1982): 117–125.
28. For the classic analysis of these and other status-role conflicts of the stockbroker, and for attempted safeguards against deviance in this area, see William M. Evan and Ezra G. Levin, "Status-Set and Role-Set Conflicts of the Stockbroker: A Problem in the Sociology of Law," *Social Forces* 45, no. 1 (1966): 73–83.

29. For a valuable reading suitable for undergraduate students that captures the relation between the banking scandal and politics, see Lenny Glynn, "Who Really Made the S. and L. Mess?" *Dissent* 38 (Spring 1991): 195–201. For a detailed analysis that calls attention to the shift to finance capitalism as the generator of new opportunities for white-collar crime, see Kitty Calavita and Henry N. Pontell, "'Other People's Money' Revisited: Collective Embezzlement in the Savings and Loan and Insurance Industries," *Social Problems* 38 (February 1991): 94–112. The term "collective embezzlement" might have served better, however, had it referred to America's extreme version of laissez-faire capitalism and its collusive network of deviant elite groups rather than to "the siphoning off of company funds for personal use by top management."

30. For one account, see Robert Nelson, *A World of Preference: Business Access To Reagan's Regulators* (New York: Democracy Project, 1983).

31. Marc Reisner, *Cadillac Desert: The American West and its Disappearing Water* (New York: Viking, 1986).

32. Gordon Adams, *The Iron Triangle: The Politics of Defense Contracting* (New York: Council on Economic Priorities, 1981).

33. For an interesting development of this perspective, discussed in terms of doctors, lawyers, and clergy, see Linda Burzotta Nilson, "An Application of the Occupational 'Uncertainty Principle' to the Professions," *Social Problems* 26 (June 1979): 570–581.

34. Kai T. Erikson, "Notes on the Sociology of Deviance," *Social Problems* 9 (Spring 1962): 307–314.

35. Albert K. Bergesen, "Political Witch Hunts: The Sacred and Subversive in Cross-National Perspective," *American Sociological Review* 42 (April 1977): 220–233.

36. Thomas Szasz, *The Manufacture of Madness* (New York: Delta, 1979).

37. For two books that argue that our basic beliefs and practices about crime really see to it that there is enough crime to make sure that the causes of crime are not uncovered, see Jeffrey H. Reiman, *The Rich Get Richer and the Poor Get Prison* (New York: Wiley, 1984); and Harold E. Pepinsky and Paul Jesilow, *Myths that Cause Crime* (CabinLock, Md.: Seven Locks Press, 1984). In a third book, Jackson argues that the criminal justice system is not really a system, does not reduce crime, and does not achieve justice. It is really an informal, ad hoc response to false definitions of behavior by a set of unrelated agencies bent on getting rid of people and ensuring their own survival. See Bruce Jackson, *Law and Disorder: Criminal Justice in America* (Urbana: University of Illinois Press, 1984).

38. For a classic analysis, see Michael Mann, "The Social Cohesion of Liberal Democracy," *American Sociological Review* 35 (June 1970): 423–439.

39. M. David Ermann and Richard J. Lundman, "Deviant Acts by Complex Organizations: Deviance and Social Control at the Organizational Level of Analysis," *Sociological Quarterly* 19 (Winter 1978): 55–67.

40. Both terms are from Michael Power, "The Audit Society," in A. G. Hopwood and Peter Miller, *Accounting as Social and Institutional Practice* (New York: Cambridge University Press, 1994), chap. 12.

41. Readers will recall that the United States still relies heavily on voluntary compliance to many basic laws, a misplaced use of trust and a potent generator of deviance by many of our power groups.

10
The Policy Professions

◆ ◆ ◆ ◆

◆ ◆ ◆ ◆

To understand the policy sciences (or any of the professions and disciplines), two things should be recalled about the relation between social
structure and knowledge:

1. The elites of all complex societies generate universalistic explanations
   of themselves and their societies, seeking to legitimate their power
   with abstractions that link it to forces in supernature, nature, and
   human nature.
2. The complex society of the West generated a universalistic way of addressing the world that was distinctive, namely, rationalistic.

Universalistic explanations are those that rely on broad generalizations to explain where everything comes from, why humans are here, how
they got here, why they suffer and die, and so on. Universalistic explanations are transhistorical and trans-social; they transport people out of time
and place into some version of supernature, nature, and human nature. The
result, of course, is to anchor a particular power structure in forces that are
permanent, that is, outside politics, or deliberate human action to solve
problems. The West, it should be noted, from the ancient Greeks to the present shares this characteristic with the non-West even though its way of
generating abstractions relies on human reason.

By and large, the rationalism of the West has focused its energy on finding
universals (or laws or principles) directly in nature and human nature. The idea
that society is a human creation wrought half-blindly by power groups out of
historical necessities and emerging opportunities has as little appeal to power
groups in the West as in the non-West. The idea that society is a human creation
was first broached by Herodotus only to succumb to the more alluring image of
the world developed out of logic by Socrates. The search for generalizations
about humans and their world was embraced by modern society and even
today continues to shun the sociohistorical perspective.

In this chapter on the modern policy professions, we encounter the
power of the transhistorical view over yet another part of the modern cognitive spectrum. As offshoots of the academic disciplines and as groups that
want to establish themselves as professions, it should surprise no one that
the policy sciences, odd as it may seem, are profoundly antipolitical in how
they define and conduct themselves. Despite this, the relation between the
West's general scientific (or rational) tradition and politics (policy) is rich
and not unpromising. To uncover its riches and develop its promise, the
next section traces the relation between view of society and view of politics
(policy). The section after that outlines the general policy orientations available to the American public.

THE RELATION BETWEEN VIEW OF SCIENCE
AND VIEW OF POLITICS (POLICY)

Many have noted that there are associations between type of theory (the
philosophy and method of science and substantive images of society) and

type of politics (how public power should be organized, what values the state should serve, what stance one should take toward the state and society).[1] Though many have commented that idealism is associated with conservatism, few have spelled out the reasons. One reason that deductive or rationalist idealism, and social theories based on it, has been conservative (from Plato on) is that it invariably claims that the ability to think resides in only the few. Furthermore, idealist thinkers characteristically posit an objective, fixed social world that allegedly corresponds to the distribution of abilities in human populations. (Theorists who hold this view tend not to acknowledge that mental abilities stem from education and the other advantages of property). In addition, those who posit the reality of society as established by reason (idealism) also tend to stress order, stability, hierarchy, and unity through consensus.

In contrast to idealist theory and politics, thinkers who stress the validity of knowledge acquired through experience tend to be more democratic, as, for example, Democritos and Protagoras, the *philosophes*, and American pragmatists. It is also true that those who take a nominalist view of society, or who emphasize conflict and exploitation as basic features of society, tend to be progressive, to stress the autonomy and/or equality of individuals, or to assert the sovereignty of the people.

On the whole, therefore, epistemologies are broadly associated with political orientations: Deduction with conservative politics and induction with the politics of individualism and equality. But one must not allow this association to become transhistorical. Like all human behavior, human thought is embedded in history. Deduction can also be progressive and critical as witness Plato, who used teleological deduction to transcend the ascriptive society of his day; Jesuits, who used natural-law arguments against royal absolutism; Hobbes, who used mathematical deduction to erase feudalism, and many others. On the other hand, the empirical or nominalist outlook, especially one that stresses the validity of ordinary experience, while often associated with democratic, progressive politics and with a critical stance toward social institutions, is no guarantee of progressive politics. While empiricism was critical and progressive during the French Enlightenment and during the rise of liberal reformism and socialist social theory, it can now be thought of as part of established liberal societies, performing (among other things) the latent function of helping to manage and stabilize existing systems of privilege and exploitation.

As opposed to most views of the relation between theory and politics, a sociopolitical or historical analysis of this relation assumes that no social system has a self-evident intellectual, moral, or political claim on scientists. All societies are historical power structures disguised in garbs of spurious or problematic legitimacy—custom, magic, religion, birth, progress, achievement, science, the people, representative government, people's democracy, and so on. From this point of view, policy scientists (both natural and social) should ask themselves: What is the structure of power of my own society? How well does my society function when judged by its own values and beliefs? What are the possibilities revealed by history and comparative analysis for alternative institutions and values? As we see, this approach to policy is not found much in the American policy sciences.

The sociopolitical approach to the policy sciences derives from Max Weber's sociology, though of course, there are many other contributors to it both in and out of sociology. Weber's sociology, argued for a value-neutral approach to phenomena infused by a felt value problem, all with a view toward political or other action—it was not the static, naturalistic, value-free positivism of mainstream science but a sociopolitical positivism. Perhaps the crucial insight underlying Weber's sociopolitical approach is that beyond the rudimentary folk systems, human societies are diverse and changing melanges of contradictory values, practices, and beliefs held together by verbal magic, ad hoc compromise, exploitation, oppression, repression, and/or waste, raising the real possibility that no general theory of society is possible. It follows that the scientist is first and foremost an evaluative or moral being who analyzes the world in terms of value problems. Values come not from biology, psychology, reason, patriotism, or empirical analysis, but from experience—and, for the aware policy scientist, from self-conscious, reflected-upon experience. For Weber, the policy scientist must always be aware of the moral-political consequences of his or her actions and keep the following question at the forefront of consciousness: Should I try to reform society (that is, try to make it function better according to its own lights), or should I seek to transform the present power structure into something better?

The sociopolitical approach is relativistic (truth is a temporary consensus negotiated by power groups) and seems to have little appeal for American policy scientists. As with all fields, the policy sciences are animated by the metaphysics of objectivity and final truths. Two general types in the contemporary policy sciences can be distinguished, the liberal and the radical conflict.

THE SPECTRUM OF POLICY ORIENTATIONS

The dominant liberal perspective has three subtypes: the openly conservative liberal, the laissez-faire or rational-choice liberal, and the reform liberal.

The Openly Conservative Liberal

Some policy-oriented social scientists argue openly against government-driven reforms as harmful to other American values. Daniel Bell and Nathan Glazer are examples of conservative liberals who do not want a strong directive government even if it is directed toward enhancing American values. Bell has advocated a decentralized Madisonian democracy,[2] while Glazer, who specializes in race and ethnicity, argues that all minorities will be absorbed eventually and that strong government intervention is not necessary.[3]

George Will represents another variation on liberal conservatism.[4] Will is opposed to a government that directs the economy or interferes with markets, but believes that government has a large role to play in seeing to it that citizens have the values and personality needed to participate effectively in society.

The openly conservative policy scientist tends to limit the role of knowledge in the political life of society. This aspect of conservatism-openly-advocated can be seen most clearly in the inconsistent thought of Charles E. Lindblom.[5] Lindblom's argument is that society is essentially a system of "impairment processes." Both ordinary individuals and elites, as well as groups, are unable to act rationally. Lindblom emphatically includes professionals and social scientists among those impaired. Therefore, no attempt at shaping or guiding society should be attempted—society as it exists, something Lindblom refers to as the *self-guiding society*, is all we have despite its faults. This society is based on markets which Lindblom does not depict as rational systems for allocating resources, but as processes of mutual adjustment. We do not know enough to manage or coordinate society, though we might help it work better if we strengthen free speech, civil rights, and education, and reduced gender and racial inequalities. Any attempt to base society on reason or science, however, whether derived from Plato, Marx, or reform liberals, is wrongheaded. Social science does not have "a single finding or idea that is undeniably indispensable to any social task or effort" (p. 136).

Lindblom goes to considerable lengths to undermine all pretensions to efficacy or knowledge by economists, political scientists, psychologists, and professionals in general. He criticizes corporations as well as governments, and acknowledges that we do not have a pluralistic power structure, in effect, rejecting rationality even as the outcome of markets. Why is all of the above inconsistent? Because Lindblom's thesis, that humans are not rational and that social science cannot supply knowledge for us to use in the management of our collective life, is based on a long grocery list of social science findings. And it is inconsistent because Lindblom says some reforms through politics and government are possible while at the same time denying that reform is possible.

Robert Formaini provides another variation of liberal conservatism. Formaini argues that scientific public policy is a myth because a science based on probability mathematics is a myth.[6] Risk assessment and cost-benefit analysis are both technically faulty and do not provide a basis for a public policy based on the truth of science. Instead, says Formaini, we must rely on the collective wisdom (beliefs and value judgments) of the public as expressed through our political system. Formaini is a conservative liberal because it does not occur to him that our political system systematically steers the public into a limited range of policies (ruling out many plausible choices).

Formaini's argument is similar to other conservative positions because it attacks the ability of science to provide knowledge on which to base policy. But it is one thing to say that science cannot make value judgments (as he does) and quite another to say that statistical analysis cannot provide knowledge. All human behavior—whether scientists doing probability analyses, voters expressing themselves through representative government, or individuals and groups conducting their private affairs—is engaged in probability reasoning (is not majority rule based on the assumption that the more frequent a thing is the more valid it is?). Formaini is right to say that ultimately human policies must be political and value-based. He is wrong to reject probability mathematics as inherently faulty. It is the political uses and misuses of science which must receive critical attention, not science per se.

The Laissez-faire, Rational-Choice Liberal

Another form of conservativism (advocated by thinkers who do not think of themselves this way) derives from liberals who advocate free markets in all sectors of society to produce a society based on the rational choices of individuals and groups. The vast bulk of Republicans and American economists fall in this category.[7] In sociology, exchange, rational-choice theorists also belong here.[8] A Nobel Prize winning economist, James Buchanan, has influenced political scientists to think of politics in rational-choice terms. Another Nobel Prize winner in economics (Gary Becker) has used sociological analysis to influence rational-choice theory in economics.

The reason why rational-choice advocates are conservative is that they believe in competition among individuals and groups, but do little to make real (equal, fair) competition a reality. Advocates of rational choice think they are moving in the direction of maximizing choices, but by not tackling poverty, unemployment, and economic concentration, they are merely defending the existing power structure (the upper classes have the choices). Rational-choice liberals are also inconsistent since they use government for their purposes while denouncing government as inherently ineffective and wasteful.[9]

The Reform Liberal

Most sociologists (for example, Amitai Etzioni and Anthony Giddens) and political scientists are reform liberals; that is, they accept American society as a sound system, but want it to work better. Liberals in this category see more of society in individual behavior than do other liberals. Thus they stress that individuals are socialized to be evaluative, not clinically rational actors. Reformers are aware that some individuals are poorly socialized for participation in our society and need help. Reform liberals also stress the group nature of behavior and this leads them to advocate ways to help the family, make corporations more responsive internally to minorities, enforce antitrust laws, and so on.

Reform liberals openly advocate the use of government to solve problems. They tend to be full Keynesians in regard to the economy, that is, the Federal executive, Congress, and the Federal Reserve Board should use tax, spending, monetary, and interest-rate powers to manage the economy. Reform liberals can be quite critical of American society; nonetheless, they remain liberals to the extent that they advocate nonstructural solutions.[10]

Radical Policy Orientations

The distinguishing mark of radicals is that they connect social problems to basic institutions, especially the American economy. Radicals question whether private decisions about investment are compatible with a sound society. They argue that American capitalism is based essentially on the primacy of property over labor and that our institutions and public policies are designed to protect property and ensure surplus labor (that is, an unsupportable wage structure).[11]

Radical feminists argue that patriarchy or patriarchy plus capitalism is the source of women's troubles and that only a restructuring of society will end women's dominance by men or men-using-capitalism to dominate them.[12]

Radical environmentalists argue that the problem with the environment stems from industrialism per se. Solving environmental problems piecemeal will not work unless the problem of industrialism is also tackled.[13]

THE GROWTH OF THE POLICY SCIENCES

The deliberate enactment of public measures to improve society in keeping with the latest scientific knowledge emerges as an ideal during the eighteenth century in both the French and Scottish Enlightenments. The credit for policy as a more technical approach to updating society and running it more efficiently should probably be shared by Jeremy Bentham and Frederick the Great. Empirical research as the basis of public measures to improve society does not appear until the great, largely government-run projects in nineteenth-century Britain (see "Symbolic Activities and the Needs of Power" in Chapter 1). No significant empirical research either in general or oriented toward the solution of social problems occurred in the U.S. until the creative surge known collectively as the Chicago School emerged in the 1920s. The United States lagged in developing policy research and policy-oriented social scientists because problem solving was long considered a local affair. The Great Depression and World War II changed all this when much of the responsibility for problemsolving shifted to the national level. The policy sciences benefitted from the influential set of readings edited by Daniel Lerner and Harold Lasswell in 1951.[14] But the real impetus to the policy sciences occurred when the Great Society reform programs were enacted in the 1960s, and further impetus occurred during the 1970s and 1980s as American elites experienced an accumulation of unsolved social problems.

It is important to note that the policy sciences and the great reform movements of the past three-quarters of a century are largely elite-driven. The policy sciences and reform movements not only do not originate in the lower classes, but the values and interests they serve go far beyond the problems of the poor, minorities, workers, or inner cities. Both manifest and latent analysis tell us that the policy sciences, wittingly or unwittingly, support the interests of the powerful even as they propose reforms on behalf of the downtrodden (see "Symbolic Activity and the Needs of Power" in Chapter 1). Today the policy sciences consist primarily of specialized professionals emerging from economics, political science, and sociology; their story can be told in terms of any of them, but perhaps best in terms of applied sociology.

Sociology as an Applied Science

The classic tradition in sociology (as C. Wright Mills reminded us in *The Sociological Imagination*) was composed of activist intellectuals, sociologists who did not hesitate to see practical benefits in their work for humanity-at-large. The great sociologists had many different orientations, but at least one thing in common, a deep interest in using science to benefit and direct society. Condorcet, Saint Simon, Fourier, Comte, Karl Marx, Herbert Spencer, Max Weber, William Graham Sumner, and Lester Ward represent a wide range of sociological creativity across a number of countries, but all agreed that scientific knowledge should be incorporated into the life of society. In this century, American sociology pioneered the understanding of urban problems during the 1920s, played a significant role in changing American racist beliefs and practices, and was in the thick of the War on Poverty and the Civil Rights movement of the 1960s. Today, sociologists are busy trying to develop practical solutions in many problem areas, for example, crime and punishment, mental illness, family pathology, and school integration.

Sociology, therefore, is both a pure and an applied science. Under its pure hat, it searches for generalizations about human behavior that are free of the distortions of time and place. Under its applied hat, it searches for knowledge that will help solve problems. Morris Janowitz has characterized these two traditions as "enlightenment" sociology (the stress on pure research and the belief that science can and should exert its influence, but only on the general intellectual climate of the times, especially through teaching), and "engineering" sociology (the direct application of science to problem solving).[15]

Eager to establish itself on the same basis as natural science, sociology (from roughly the 1920s to the 1950s) emphasized ahistorical, quantitative (pure) research and tended not to think of itself as an applied science. Today, all this has changed. For various reasons, sociology now openly avows that it is both a scientific and a humanistic discipline, interested in both pure (not immediately relevant) research and applied research (what is the best way to help children succeed in school, what will be the effects of an urban renewal project, what is the best way to introduce technological innovations, and so on). A call for more emphasis on social policy research has been heard lately in the addresses of Presidents of the American Sociological Association. The programs of sociology conventions at both national and regional levels have also reflected a renewed interest in applied sociology. Perhaps most important, the period from the 1960s on has seen a veritable explosion of applied sociology courses, programs, and degrees at both the undergraduate and graduate levels.[16] The American Sociological Association's *Careers in Sociology* (1991) states that a "fundamental change" has occurred in sociology: the once rigid distinction between pure and applied research has blurred and the two are now seen as complementary (p. 8).

The heightened interest in sociology in knowledge applications has a number of sources: falling enrollments, declining research funds, and a growing sense that social problems are growing in extent and depth. Recent decades have seen a growth in Marxism in the social sciences and some liberal radicalism, but, by and large, the new interest in policy appears to be by mainstream sociologists eager to shore up their discipline in a period of declining enrollments and research funds.

Comparative Public Policy

The field of comparative public policy has burgeoned in recent years as social scientists have sought answers to both academic and policy issues by looking beyond their own societies. Political science has long had a comparative politics specialty which includes a policy dimension.[17] More recently, it has tackled public-policy issues on a comparative basis more directly.[18] Sociologists have also begun to show interest in comparative public policy.[19] Unfortunately, neither of these two otherwise admirable studies in comparative policy has anything on the impact of the international political economy on domestic policy. Interestingly, mainstream economics has shown little interest in comparative public policy though it is by far the most influential policy adviser to government and politicians.

The most serious resistance to a genuine policy science lies in mainstream political science. Our reason for picking on political science should be clear. The main avenue for the better management of society is political action, but the American political system has serious deficiencies. The two parties, drawn largely from the upper classes and competing for the allegiance of voters on vague, limited platforms, effectively control the public agenda. The power of money gives the business and professional world effective control of the political parties and a deeply gerrymandered Congress. Despite the hurley-burley of American politics, therefore, it is best understood as having been thoroughly depoliticized. Mainstream political science contributes to this process of depoliticizing politics by defining itself as an empirical, value-neutral science.

Gabriel Almond, one of the most creative scholars in the field of comparative politics, epitomizes all that is good and bad about mainstream political (and social) science. The comparative politics text he helped assemble no doubt leads the field and has had a positive influence on generations of political science students. Nonetheless, the text does not include the United States as one of the countries studied (references to the United States are used to develop the analytical tools with which to analyze the rest of the world, in effect, assuming that the United States and its political scientists are the benchmark for analyzing and understanding polities around the world), is still Eurocentric, excessively focused on details about political institutions (if priority must be given to variables, economic and historical factors must come ahead of all others), and has almost nothing to say about the enormous impact of the international political economy on domestic social and political structures.[20]

The Flourishing Policy Sciences

The policy sciences are flourishing in two senses: one, there are numerous policy-studies organizations, a large number of journals with the word *policy* in the title, a large number of undergraduate and graduate public-policy programs, scores of policy-research centers both in and outside universities, and a declared interest in policy by book publishers, scholarly associations, and interest groups. Of great importance is the expressed interest in policy research and policy evaluation by local, state, and federal governments.

The policy sciences are also flourishing in the sense that applied offshoots have appeared in all disciplines, part and parcel of the explosive specialization that has enveloped all of them. There are numerous applied journals in economics, sociology, psychology, and so on through the natural sciences. There is little doubt that the hunger for usable knowledge is there. Whether it is being satisfied is another matter.

THE PROFESSIONALIZATION OF REFORM

Reform, or the attempt to solve problems by a change in law and a new distribution of resources, has become a routine part of liberal society. This is true of the United States as well as other developed societies and as true of Republicans as it is of Democrats. The process of reform has also been professionalized, which is to say, reform has been defined in such a way as to guarantee failure. Liberal reform, American style, is inherently nonstructural, that is, it does not tackle the basic causes of problems. American reform liberalism is an ad hoc search for rotten apples and the depoliticization of the barrel.

All this is to say that Americans at all levels assume that they live in a natural, just, sound, pluralistic, adaptive society, and that social problems come from social change (a progressive movement away from ignorance and obsolete ways) and from willful wickedness on the part of individuals and special interests. So deep and pervasive is the consensus on society's validity that even most deviants believe that society is on the up and up, for example, the bulk of ordinary and white-collar criminals, the mentally ill, adherents of pie-in-the-sky religion, drug and alcohol abusers, wife-beaters, spouse killers, the passive unemployed, and the millions who undergo cosmetic surgery or sign up for therapy programs that promise to straighten out whatever is wrong with *them*.

The professionalization of reform appeared early in the nineteenth century, accelerated during the late nineteenth century, and really came into prominence from the 1930s on. Everywhere and at all times, it is a "middle-class" movement. During its earlier stage, reform movements were in keeping with the nature of entrepreneurial capitalism (small town, rural, small business, solo professional). Here one finds the urban morality and beautification movement,[21] the Temperance movement,[22] and the sociologists who framed social pathologies in terms of human nature, Protestant morality, and abstracted artificial situations.[23] Later, and more in keeping with corporate capitalism, one finds the growth of graduate schools (devoted to professional research and application), the beginnings of policy-research institutes, and the rise of the great foundations and philanthropies. The essence of corporate or elite liberalism consists of cloaking reform and the policy process in the garbs of science, neutrality, and professionalism. Today, elite liberalism has both a right and a left wing.[24]

The ideology of political reform dissolves the American people into individuals and emphasizes the need to facilitate their choices. The Republican and Democratic parties have different versions of this ideology. The Republican party emphasizes choice by parents (through vouchers) of where to send their children to school or where to rent apartments. They also emphasize choice on the part of business people (supported by government subsidies or relaxation of regulatory laws) to go into various businesses, communities, or countries. Liberal democrats emphasize choice and the empowerment of ordinary citizens by emphasizing civil rights laws (including the right to choose abortion), income support for the poor, and more public services, including tax-supported lawyers for the poor. Neither party, however, says anything about popular choice over capital investment, full employment, or the huge welfare state for the well-to-do and rich.

Both parties may stress the empowering of ordinary people, but this is more than counterbalanced by an emphasis on leadership and professional direction. It is clear, moreover, that the professionalization of reform has its sources in the dynamics of corporate capitalism, that is to say, it is now geared to the needs of large corporations and nationally oriented upper-middle class individuals.[25] Essentially, the arguments about reform take place between a regionally diverse set of local property and professional groups and a set of elites who are nationally-internationally oriented. Indeed, much of what is called reform is really the extension of professionalization and the struggle among types of professionals.

The reform of education during the first half of the twentieth century, for example, was part of the effort to shift control of schools away from local communities to the state and federal levels.[26] The same is true of the general emergence of the federal interventionist-welfare state. By and large, the professionalization of problemsolving at the policy level is part of the overall emergence of a national state to service a national-international economy.[27]

This is the background needed to understand civil service reform (the Pendleton Act of 1883), the establishment of the national regulatory agencies from the late nineteenth century on, the emergence of the Keynesian state from the 1930s on, and the use of professional advisory bodies such as the Council of Economic Advisers, National Security Adviser and Council, the National Science Foundation, the National Science Academy, the National Health Institutes, and the National Endowments for the Humanities and Arts. The rise to prominence of elite liberal arts colleges during the same period provided ideological cover for the rise of professionalized academic disciplines and the applied professions.[28] Here too lies the meaning behind the interest by many professions and disciplines in improved statistical services—they need information about how the various actors of society are behaving in order to tackle their problems for them.

Finally, the professionalization of reform created a host of political-interest groups. In a real sense, the deeper meaning of the rise of the federal state is that it helped to legitimate, indeed, helped to create, the very business, farm, and professional groups that it ostensible existed to regulate and harness to the public interest. The federal state (no less than local and state governments), not only is in the service of property and professional groups, but it helps create and sustain the groups themselves.

THE PROFESSIONALIZATION OF PLANNING

Planning is an important characteristic of all societies in the contemporary world. By planning is meant the attempt to allocate and schedule resources to produce desired effects. As in other countries, planning takes place even in American society, but with one conspicuous exception. Alone of all the developed and almost all the developing societies, the United States has no commitment to or process for national planning. American planning is done by private groups and when it is public it is hidden by euphemisms and defined as nonstructural and nonpolitical.

The planning idea is strong in the United States and it too has been professionalized. A number of professionalized approaches can be distinguished. In his informative history of the idea of planning in the United States, Wilson distinguishes among five approaches to planning: rational, incremental, mixed-scanning, general systems, and learning-adaptive.[29]

Planning also goes by other names: management science, information science, planning-programming-budgeting-system (PPBS), strategic planning, risk assessment, cost-benefit analysis, and, of course, central planning under state socialism. Professionals may argue about the virtues of these approaches, but beneath secondary differences, one theme stands out: *Planning is the attempt by elites to develop an efficient use of resources to achieve vague goals without input from ordinary people.* Elites may develop specialized types of planning, say for the federal government (PPBS), or planning software applicable to hospitals or universities. They may focus on the needs of a corporation, of a city, or a transportation system. But all these plans have one thing in common—the overall structure of power (the subordinate position of ordinary people) is taken for granted.

Openly conservative liberals like Lindblom oppose planning, arguing that human beings are not rational enough to plan, that organizations are rife with habits and emotions, and that we should accept muddling through as our best strategy for rational action (incrementalism). But Lindblom's distinction is false—the so-called rational planning tradition is merely a variation of muddling through. Or rather it is a disguised form of laissez-faire; basically, the liberal planning tradition rests on the uncoordinated, self-seeking behavior of a wide variety of social units, all in the faith that the combined effect will add up to the most rational society. Rarely do the professionals who discuss planning ever argue that the values and beliefs of all the relevant parties must be incorporated into the planning process. Rarely, in other words, do they ask that the political system be reformed to see what priorities the population has for capital investment. So far the planning process in both capitalist and socialist countries has been technocratic, something imposed on the bulk of the population by those who claim to know best.

POLICY PROFESSIONALS: THE COMPROMISING TIE TO THE ACADEMIC WORLD

The Policy Sciences as Warmed-over Academic Disciplines

One would expect that if the academic disciplines are value-free and nonpolitical, the policy sciences would be the opposite. This is not the case: The main thrust of the policy field, as is true of knowledge elites in general, is to depoliticize problems.

The public-policy (or social-policy) professions emerged in the nineteenth century in a hostile environment of radical laissez-faire. Explicit social planning is opposed by America's most powerful groups. Accordingly, the various specialties that emerged under the general heading of public-policy professional kept a low profile and employed euphemisms to camouflage their activities (for example, urban planning was located in schools of architecture). Throughout their development, these specialties maintained deep ties with the academic professions. Public administration and foreign policy–defense analysis are connected to political science. Housing, energy, transportation, foreign trade, economic development, and so on are attempts at applied economics. Urban planning, law enforcement, penology, and social welfare (income maintenance, family, and the like) are outgrowths of sociology. Public health is an outcome of medicine and sociology. Environmentalists have their footing in chemistry and biology, combined occasionally with a social science.

There are many hybrids. Military specialists have backgrounds in sociology, history, and political science. Statisticians have backgrounds in mathematics, economics, and sociology. Educators study psychology, administration, and sociology. Social workers have backgrounds in sociology and administration. And there are subspecialities everywhere, for example, specialists in various kinds of crime or types of family pathology.

Policy analysts agree that there is little consensus about what policy science means. There is no agreement about basic terms or about requirements to ensure competence, and the wide variety of activities and journals that call themselves *policy* are extremely diverse.[30] Both as an overall field and as subspecialities, public policy shares much with other professions. Like the other professions, it too has identified an artificial area and staked a claim to it based on expertise. The result here, as in the other professions, is widespread ineffectiveness and failure.[31]

The Mania for More Research

The once clear distinction between pure and applied research has blurred in recent decades as hardpressed policy makers have called for usable knowledge to help them solve American society's mounting social problems. Higher education has been quick to respond and now contains a large number of policy and applied programs. So far, however, no great success can be reported. These programs and the research conducted in their name are largely disguised versions of our academic programs. Harvard's Kennedy School of Government and the Lyndon B. Johnson School of Public Policy at the University of Texas, for example, focus on technical knowledge framed in value-free, apolitical terms. The failure to develop viable public-policy programs is perhaps the central failure of higher education, but none of the half-dozen higher education reports that appeared in the late 1980s even mentioned this problem. The reason is understandable. Our educators have an ahistorical (or academic) conception of knowledge which takes the usefulness of elite-generated knowledge for granted. To submit it to the test of usefulness would require a profound alteration in the mental habits acquired over thousands of years.

Most research, therefore, is still framed in terms that policymakers cannot use. Policy research is largely a profitmaking business and clients must be pleased rather than problems solved. The case of Lewin-VHI, a Virginia-based research institute is probably typical. During 1994, at the height of the discussion of health-care reform, a large number of Lewin-VHI research reports emerged containing diametrically opposed conclusions, indeed the conclusions corresponded to the political positions of the interest groups that were paying for the research. What is of great significance is that all reports were objective and in keeping with scientific standards. The explanation of why all this occurred is that the sponsors of the research specified what assumptions to use and what questions to ask.[32] Recent doubts about studies about the comparative cost-effectiveness of drugs conducted by drug companies themselves have highlighted the absence of standards in this field.[33] In addition, much of the research supporting the safety of drugs, airplanes, the workplace, oil production, and so on is done for the government by the interested parties themselves.

When research appears that runs counter to the interests of powerful groups, it is simply denied or ignored (for example, research on smoking, pornography, strategic bombing, and supply-side tax cuts). Research appears to be largely a way to dodge problems and protect the status quo that causes problems. Research, for example, into the cause of cancer and its cure, was spurred by President Nixon, rich individuals, and the American Cancer Society during the 1970s, effectively undermining efforts to prevent cancer by curbing our chemical companies, putting scrubbers in smokestacks, and reducing our intake of high-fat food and exposure to the sun. A call for more research is the way that the Reagan administration of the 1980s forestalled action on acid rain for more than eight years. Research into a magical defense system ("star wars") was obviously a way to block serious arms control negotiations. A call by former Education Secretary Bennett (via a handpicked panel) for more research in higher education effectively blocked the needed coordination and planning of American education that his department should have engaged in.

Liberalism began to develop the mania for value-neutral, nonpolitical research (and education) in the nineteenth century. Science not only worked with self-evident values, but it could no longer pronounce on values. In one variant or another, this position is found in William Graham Sumner, Vilfredo Pareto, W. I. Thomas, and mainstream American sociology, including theorists as dissimilar as George Lundberg and Robert K. Merton. In short, the emergence of empirical sociology helped to consolidate capitalist society by helping to define and identify its problems with an eye toward reforms, by improving its administrative structures, and by developing support structures for a private-property, profit-oriented exchange economy (a supportive state, better education, voluntary groups, and so on). At mid-twentieth century, liberalism in social science and sociology was characterized by narrow empirical studies and by abstract theories that, by and large, rendered the essentials of liberal democracy unproblematic. Science, argued social scientists, could take place without regard to values or politics, indeed its knowledge is applicable to any kind of society. By and large, this is the position taken by policy analysts.[34]

Richard P. Nathan exemplifies the apolitical policy researcher who has put his liberal reform orientation in abeyance.[35] Writing extremely well and utilizing his extensive government experience, Nathan provides a valuable historical picture of the rise to prominence in the federal government of Keynesianism, the PPBS orientation to government operations, and demonstration and evaluation research (the latter is an offshoot of PPBS and focuses on the question, Is the program working or paying off?). One thrust of Nathan's analysis is to stress careful monitoring of pilot programs. So far, he tells us, reforms have met almost universal failure. But he warns against broad theory or research into social conditions and trends. To help learn from experience, he provides valuable case studies of demonstration and evaluation research. But what Nathan is advocating in the final analysis is that we make nonpolitical, technical analyses of existent policies and that we ignore the power structure which is the cause of both problems and ineffective policies.

POLICY PROFESSIONALS: THE COMPROMISING TIE TO INTEREST GROUPS

Applied professionals work for a large number of groups, which while varied, have one thing in common: All claim to be nonpartisan seekers of the truth on which to base policy. The "nonpolitical" councils, committees, institutes, corporations, advisory boards, and foundations (such as the Carnegie Foundation, Council on Foreign Relations, Rand Corporation, Committee for Economic Development, Twentieth Century Fund, American Enterprise Institute, Heritage Foundation, and Brookings Institution) that many policy professionals work for, however, are far from being nonpartisan.[36] These groups are characterized by a narrow class composition, direct ties to specific business and professional interests, and great influence over domestic and foreign policies.[37] In recent years, we have learned more about these allegedly neutral groups. A study of the Carnegie Corporation, for example, has shown how it steered policy making away from economic and political issues and reforms, favoring an approach that stressed science, education, and elite culture. And within science and education, it favored certain approaches and fields of knowledge, thus helping to define the knowledge-producing elites (not just knowledge areas but also racial, gender, and class attributes of the knowledge elites). The high-minded reforms promoted by the Carnegie Corporation should not blind us to the fact that corporate liberalism is merely one of alternative approaches to policy problems.[38]

Applied professionals also work for the "nonpolitical" undergraduate and graduate programs in public policy, social work, business, public administration, natural-science research, engineering, computer science, and environmental studies. They work for government, for example, applied professionals work for legislative committees (as staffers) and for government directly as engineers, geologists, chemists, space scientists, lawyers, economists, and statisticians. Applied professionals also work for corporations and for for-profit research businesses such as the Rand Corporation, Battelle, and the hundreds of economic consulting firms.[39] Clearly, by appearing prominently across the apexes of the American power structure, applied professionals help to create the illusion of national problemsolving, thus contributing to the undeserved legitimacy of corporate capitalism.

SUMMARY

The knowledge elites of complex societies put causation outside of society and history. This is true even in the West despite its rationalist orientation. The policy sciences share the same transhistorical orientation of the other professions and disciplines.

The view one holds of science (deduction versus induction) is associated with the view one holds of politics (policy). Deductive theorists tend to be conservative, inductive theorists tend to be progressive and democratic. Nonetheless, since all thinking is embedded in history, it reflects history's unique configurations and ironies: deductive theorists (for example, Plato and Hobbes) can be revolutionary, while inductive theorists (for example, most of those who have pioneered empirical research) can be upholders of the status quo.

The policy sciences have flourished in recent decades as American society has experienced a growing variety of severe social problems. The policy sciences have not become political in the sense that they engage in macrosocial analysis with a view toward redesigning basic institutions—instead, they have professionalized.

The professionalization of policy making means that the policy sciences have transformed social problems into nonpolitical, technical, means-ends problems. It also means that they have hewed close to the academic sciences, and that they have become the servers of those who pay them, the power groups who are causing the problems in the first place (profit-and-nonprofit research institutes, corporations, universities, and foundations).

Two overall reform perspectives in the United States can be distinguished, one, a right-liberal approach which emphasizes a neutral government in regard to the economy, but which can intervene to promote law and order and better morals on the part of the general citizenry, and two a left-liberal position which argues that government can and should help ordinary citizens or beleaguered economic groups to participate more effectively in an otherwise unproblematic capitalism. Both perspectives not only take the United States at face value, but help to legitimate a seriously malfunctioning corporate capitalism.

NOTES

1. For example, Don Martindale, *The Nature and Types of Sociological Theory* (Boston: Houghton Mifflin, 1960), pp. 76–77, 122; Werner Stark, *The Sociology of Knowledge* (London: Routledge and Kegan Paul, 1958), p. 44ff., and *The Fundamental Forms of Social Thought* (New York: Fordham University Press, 1963), p. 8f; and Herman Strasser, *The Normative Structure of Thought* (Boston: Routledge and Kegan Paul, 1976), chap. 1. Needless to say, many of the theorists of the sociology of knowledge (for example, Karl Marx, Max Scheler, Karl Mannheim, and radical feminists such as Dorothy E. Smith) have concerned themselves with the political implications of theoretical orientations.
2. Daniel Bell, "The Revolution of Rising Entitlements," *Fortune* 91, no. 4 (April 1975): 98ff.
3. Nathan Glazer, *Ethnic Dilemmas 1964–1982* (Cambridge: Harvard University Press, 1983).
4. George F. Will, *Statecraft as Soulcraft: What Government Does* (New York: Simon and Schuster, 1983).
5. Charles E. Lindblom, *Inquiry and Change: The Troubled Attempt to Understand and Shape Society* (New Haven, Conn.: Yale University Press, 1990).
6. Robert Formaini, *The Myth of Scientific Public Policy* (New Brunswick, N.J.: Transaction Books, 1990).
7. For the public policy formalisms of American economists, contradicted by even mainstream economic analysis and research, see the section on economics, in Chapter 4.

8. Exchange theory in sociology has changed in recent decades as theorists (Peter Blau, for example), have come to realize that all social relations are mixtures of reason, knowledge, and a variety of values (emotions). A recent attempt to derive a sociological theory from rational choice theory is James Coleman, *Foundations of Social Theory* (Cambridge, Mass.: Harvard University Press, 1990).

9. For a fuller discussion, see the section "Cost-Benefit and Risk-Benefit Analysis: Systematic Bias in Favor of the Status Quo" in Chapter 11.

10. Most social-problems texts in sociology, for example, have a reform liberal orientation.

11. For example, Herbert Marcuse, Michael Harrington, and Immanual Wallerstein.

12. For example, Dorothy E. Smith, Nancy C. M. Hartsock, and Kathy E. Ferguson.

13. For example, William R. Catton, Andre Gorz, and Murray Bookchin.

14. Daniel Lerner and Harold Lasswell, eds., *The Policy Sciences* (Stanford, Calif.: Stanford University Press, 1951).

15. For this distinction and a brief history of sociology's attempt to develop an applied sociology, see Morris Janowitz,"Professionalization of Sociology," *American Journal of Sociology* 78 (July 1972): 105–135.

16. For a valuable summary of some important landmarks in social-policy social science, see Louis G. Tornatsky, Trudy Solomon, et al., "Contributions of Social Science to Innovation and Productivity," *American Psychologist* 37 (July 1982): 737–746.

17. Gabriel A. Almond and G. Bingham Powell, Jr., eds., *Comparative Politics Today: A World View*, 6th ed. (New York: Harper Collins, 1996).

18. Arnold J. Heidenheimer, Hugh Heclo, and Carolyn Teich Adams, *Comparative Public Policy: The Politics of Social Choice in America, Europe and Japan*, 3rd ed. (New York: St. Martin's Press, 1990).

19. Sociologists have contributed important essays in an excellent multidisciplinary effort edited by Meinolf Dierkes, Hans N. Weiler, and Ariane Berthoin Antal, *Comparative Policy Research: Learning from Experience* (New York: St. Martin's Press, 1987). Sociologists have also done important comparative work in the areas of family, education, and health-care policy.

20. For a macrosociology analyzing the adaptive capacity of representative societies (with a main focus on the United States) that stresses the impact of intersocietal relations on domestic structures and vice versa, see Daniel W. Rossides, *Comparative Societies: Social Types and their Interrelations* (Englewood Cliffs. N.J.: Prentice-Hall, 1990).

21. Paul Boyer, *Urban Masses and Moral Order in America, 1820–1920* (Cambridge, Mass.: Harvard University Press, 1978).

22. Joseph R. Gusfield, *Symbolic Crusade: Status Politics and the American Temperance Movement*, 2nd ed. (Urbana: University of Illinois Press, 1986).

23. C. Wright Mills, "The Professional Ideology of Social Pathologists," *American Journal of Sociology* 49 (September 1943): 165–180.

24. For more on private research groups and foundations, see "Policy Professionals: The Compromising Tie to Interest Groups" later in this chapter, "Cost-Benefit and Risk-Benefit Analysis: Systematic Bias in Favor of the Status Quo" in Chapter 11, and "Capitalism versus Democracy: The Conservative Attempt to Revitalize America" in Chapter 12.

25. For the transition from the proprietary-competitive market stage to the corporate-administered stage of American capitalism (or corporate liberalism), see Martin J. Sklar, *The Corporate Reconstruction of American Capitalism, 1890–1916: The Market, the Law, and Politics* (New York: Cambridge University Press, 1988).

26. David B. Tyack, *The One Best System: A History of American Urban Education* (Cambridge, Mass.: Harvard University Press, 1974).

27. For Alvin Gouldner's classic criticism of Howard S. Becker's essay, "Whose Side Are We On?" *Social Problems* 14 (Winter 1967): 239–247, for glibly rejecting the value-neutral approach without realizing that he was siding with national elites, see "The Sociologist as Partisan: Sociology and the Welfare State," *The American Sociologist* 3 (May 1968): 103–116.

28. For the relation between corporate capitalism and higher education, see Clyde W. Barrow, *Universities and the Capitalist State: Corporate Liberalism and the Reconstruction of American Higher Education, 1894–1928* (Madison: University of Wisconsin Press, 1990).

29. For the characteristic of each in tabular form, see David E. Wilson, *The National Planning Idea in U.S. Public Policy: Five Alternative Approaches* (Boulder, Colo.: Westview Press, 1980), pp. 118–119.

30. Milan J. Dluhy, "Introduction: The Changing Face of Social Policy," in John E. Tropman, Milan J. Dluhy, and Roger M. Lund, eds., *New Strategic Perspectives on Social Policy* (New York: Pergamon Press, 1981).

31. A content analysis of six prominent policy journals between 1975 and 1984 revealed that policy analysis fails to live up to its stated ideals of being systematic, relevant, and multidisciplinary. Further, policy research displayed no movement toward such ideals, no integration of the field, and no noticeable differences between it and academic research; see David M. Hedge and Jin W. Mok, "The Nature of Policy Studies: A Content Analysis of Policy Journal Articles," *Policy Studies Journal* 16 (Autumn 1987): 49–62.

32. Hilary Stout, "One Company's Data Fuel Diverse Views in Health-Care Debate," *Wall Street Journal*, June 28, 1994, p. A1.

33. George Anders, "Doubts Are Cast on Cost Studies by Drug Makers," *Wall Street Journal*, June 28, 1994, p. B1.

34. This position is taken explicitly by Edith Stokey and Richard Zeckhauser, *A Primer for Policy Analysis* (New York: Norton, 1978), p. 4, and by default by David L. Weimer and Aidan R. Vining, *Policy Analysis: Concepts and Practice*, 2nd ed. (Englewood Cliffs, N.J.: Prentice Hall, 1991). The same nonpolitical approach is found in two leading political science texts on the practice of public policy: Thomas R. Dye, *Understanding Public Policy*, 8th ed. (Englewood Cliffs, N.J.: Prentice Hall, 1995), and Clarke E. Cochran, Lawrence C. Mayer, T. R. Carr, and N. Joseph Cayer, *American Public Policy: An Introduction*, 4th ed. (New York: St. Martin's Press, 1992).

35. Richard P. Nathan, *Social Science in Government: Uses and Misuses* (New York: Basic Books, 1988).

36. For a pioneering set of essays on the political nature (corporate liberalism) of foundations, see Robert F. Arnove, ed., *Philanthropy and Cultural Imperialism: The Foundations at Home and Abroad* (Bloomington: Indiana University Press, 1980). For a focus on the foreign policy impact (corporate liberalism) of three powerful foundations, see Edward H. Berman, *The Influence of the Carnegie, Ford, and Rockefeller Foundations on American Foreign Policy: The Ideology of Philanthropy* (Albany: State University of New York Press, 1983).

37. William Domhoff has studied the latter phenomenon closely as part of his argument that the United States is ruled by a small upper class; see his *The Higher Circles: The Governing Class in America* (New York: Vintage, 1971), esp. chaps. 5 and 6. See also Thomas R. Dye, "Oligarchic Tendencies in National Policy-Making: The Role of the Private Policy-Planning Organizations," *Journal of Politics* 40 (1978): 309–331. More recently, Domhoff has written "Where Do Government Experts Come From? The Council of Economic Advisers and the

Policy-Planning Network," and Dye has written "Organizing Power For Policy Planning: The View from the Brookings Institution," both in Domhoff and Dye, eds., *Power Elites and Organizations* (Beverly Hills, Calif.: Sage, 1987). Two studies have clearly established that the right-liberal and moderate-conservative think tanks are funded by a national corporate elite: J. Craig Jenkins and Teri Shumate, "Cowboy Capitalists and the Rise of the 'New Right': An Analysis of Contributors to Conservative Policy Formation Organizations," *Social Problems* 33 (December 1985): 130–145, and David Stoesz, "Packaging the Conservative Revolution," *Social Epistemology* 2, no. 2 (1988): 145–153.

38. For a full analysis of the Carnegie Corporation, see Ellen Condliffe Lagemann, *The Politics of Knowledge: The Carnegie Corporation, Philanthropy and Public Policy* (Middletown, Conn.: Wesleyan University Press, 1989).

39. For a discussion of methodological differences among policy professionals depending on their background and the organization they work for, see the section "Cost-Benefit and Risk-Benefit Analysis: Systematic Bias in favor of the Status Quo" in Chapter 11. For a discussion of the ideology of conservative think tanks and their role in the attempt to revitalize American society during the 1970s and 1980s, see the section "Capitalism versus Democracy: The Conservative Attempt to Revitalize American Society" in Chapter 12.

11

The Professions and Social Adaptation

◆ ◆ ◆ ◆

◆ ◆ ◆ ◆

THE PROBLEMSOLVING RECORD

In modern society, problems that cannot be solved in the course of ordinary life become defined as social problems by economic interest groups, social movements, governments, and voluntary groups, including professional associations. The definition of problems and their solution tend to come from established groups, often the same groups that are causing the problems in the first place. As we look into the problemsolving record, our focus will oscillate from this power structure to the policy professionals who work in and largely for it. Our first step is to question the alleged rationality of capitalism.

Capitalism and Rationality

In a radical critique, Kolko (using mostly judgments issued by nonradical, establishment figures and groups) has argued that public policy in the United States is not characterized by rationality and has been a wholesale failure.[1] The independent regulatory commissions were thoroughly ineffective before World War II and have been largely ineffective since. Despite continuous references to science and policies-based-on-fact, the United States failed to cope with both the international and its domestic economy during the 1920s and 1930s. Since World War II, it has had almost no success in predicting or coping with downturns in the economy or with specific economic problems. Economic forecasting by the Council of Economic Advisers has been wide of the mark almost every time. The need to mesh the macroeconomic (Keynesian) management of the economy with legislation relating to unemployment, poverty, housing, urban development, education, and infrastructure spending has been carefully avoided.[2] As far as social research is concerned, measures of unemployment, female participation in the labor force, capital investment, oil use-production-and-imports, bank failure, rate of profit, manufacturing capacity utilization, and money supply have also been faulty in the extreme.

The Index of Social Health

The American problemsolving system has had notable failures over the past few decades. Its inability to direct the economy into sustained productivity, full employment, use values, and price stability is far and away its biggest failure. Economic failure is also the cause of failure elsewhere. Declining investment in infrastructure and public services, including health and education is part of the decline of cities and living standards, and these feed back, both directly and as social overhead, to retard and reduce productivity. Unemployment and job insecurity breed crime and waste and these too reflect back to burden the economy.

The problemsolving failure of the past few decades is well-nigh absolute in the area of blue- and white-collar crime. The United States has been unable to curb family dissolution or the serious problem of violence within the home. There appears to be no overall progress in protecting the environment (some important successes not withstanding). The Index of Social Health, compiled by Marc Miringoff and the Fordham Institute for Innovation in Social Policy, provides data about problems in sixteen areas: infant mortality, child abuse, children in poverty, teen suicide, drug abuse, high school dropouts, average weekly earnings, unemployment, health-insurance coverage, the elderly in poverty, health insurance for the elderly, highway deaths due to alcoholism, homicides, food-stamp coverage, housing, and the gap between rich and poor. The Institute reports that between 1970 and 1994 (the last year for full data on all indicators), there has been a consistent downward drift in the social health of the nation as measured by these indicators.[3]

Foreign and Defense Policy

The failure in domestic policies and intelligence has been matched by a failure in foreign policy, defense policy, and intelligence. Federal intelligence agencies (such as the CIA) and private research groups that work (at twice the cost of public agencies) for the federal government (such as RAND, Institute for Defense Analysis) have records that are far from successful. Private consultants are picked on a political basis and do not contribute useful policy recommendations.[4] The CIA has failed to predict almost every major event adversely affecting the United States since 1945. The overall intelligence-policy failure had its most conspicuous failure in Vietnam. American policymakers would not hear of any evidence that suggested either that the revolutionary forces has vast popular support (which they did because of the grossly inequitable economy), or that they had large military capabilities. In consequence, biased data were compiled to justify American involvement in support of South Vietnam.

American foreign and defense policies are confused, counterproductive, and formalistic. These are also characteristics of the undergraduate and professional programs in these areas which do little to produce effective foreign-policy professionals. International relations in political science, free-trade theory in economics, and modernization theory in sociology are not realistic guides to the world of international politics. By common agreement, the United States is seriously deficient in its knowledge of the developing world (and other countries), in its education for international affairs, and lacks scholars in one field after the other (including Soviet studies during the Cold War).[5] The distortion of knowledge by power groups is perhaps most ominous when it affects matters of war and peace. The federal government had a long history of systematically exaggerating Soviet strength.[6] And it has a fetishistic bias toward high-technology weaponry and away from conventional military forces and readiness.[7] The American military, composed of wasteful, uncoordinated services, won World War II using a production model of war (outproduce and outgun the enemy), but floundered when it used the same approach in a different kind of war in Vietnam.[8]

Foreign and defense policies are subject to contradictory demands flowing from our domestic power structure. They are also distorted by infighting among and within civilian and military bureaucracies. Not surprisingly, American foreign policy, based on faulty, often deliberately distorted intelligence, is characterized by chronic bungling, and our foreign policy establishment is continuously surprised by events—all of which suggests that mistakes here, as in other professional areas, are institutionally induced, not mere human error.

As Kolko argues, America's domestic and foreign policy biases and errors go beyond being normal mistakes—there appears to be a systematic bias in public-policy intelligence and practice that corresponds to structural imperatives (the American power structure).[9] Our public-policy deficiencies extend to other areas as well—crime data and law enforcement, energy, transportation, housing, and environmental protection. A third of a century after the rise of the environmental movement, the United States lags badly in its ability to identify and assess the risks to the environment and human health of industrial-business practices in one area after the other. The Reagan administration of the 1980s inaugurated a curtailment of our already deficient data-gathering and a transfer of public information-gathering to private-profit businesses. The process of coordinating information-gathering and research among the various elites began to accelerate.[10] The Republican Congress of 1994–96 continued the onslaught against data-gathering by the federal government.

THE AMERICAN DREAM: REALITY OR NIGHTMARE?

The modern world is essentially the outcome of economic growth. Economic growth from 1200 to 1800 produced a middle class that undermined feudal society and eventually shaped Western society and the globe in its own image. Economic growth yielded a diversified group and power structure that generated representative government and constitutionalism (first in England, the United States, France, and then in many other countries). And from 1850 to roughly the 1960s, it yielded a rising standard of living. But since the 1960s, the United States (and many of the mature industrial societies) has experienced slow economic growth and stagnant, even declining, living standards. Today, a large and growing social overhead (for example, crime, pollution, military expenditures, wasted resources in curative medical care and ineffective education) prevents economic growth from being translated into higher living standards.

The economic slowdown since the 1970s may be reversible. But few seem to realize that the slowdown is more than a phase of the so-called business cycle. The slowdown comes from lagging productivity which is caused by many factors. The rising productivity from the mid-nineteenth to the mid-twentieth century may have been historically unique. Much of it was due to cheap human and material resources (much of it generated by government policies) that could be combined easily to yield mass manufacturing through complex organizations (the corporation). That era has passed; economies are now far more complex and require expensive capital and raw materials. The giant bureaucracies that dominate our economy are difficult to manage both internally and in regard to the outside world. A large number of new values (for example, equality for minorities, protection of the environment) must be added to old values (for example, efficiency, profit). Labor skills for many reaches of the economy have gone up even as much of labor is degraded by being pitted against labor in the developing world. The accumulating shortfalls of the past lead to increases in the social overhead, further retarding economic growth. And so on.

Chronically slow economic growth has also created a negative political environment. Slow economic growth means a zero-sum society as all struggle, using the expectations of the last century, to get a bigger share of a shrinking pie. Slow economic growth means a rising social overhead to cope with crime, to beef up military security, to pay for rising needs in health care and education, and to subsidize the economy in a thousand and one ways. In turn, the heavy social overhead retards productivity and shrinks the portion of the pie available to support and increase living standards. The economic slowdown is really a self-reinforcing process and much more difficult to reverse than most of America's elites and professionals are aware.

Understanding what is happening to the American Dream requires new ways of looking at familiar facts. In George Washington's day over 90 percent of working Americans worked on farms. By 1900 the percentage had dropped to 70 and today less than 3 percent of the labor force works on farms. But what does this change mean? The term *farmer* still evokes an image of a healthy, happy farm family pulling together doing honest work associated with farming. It also falsifies the present. Today's farm economy is dominated by large corporations (agribusiness), the government pays farmers not to grow food, and the government buys what farmers can't sell at prices far above the world price. That same economy also poses a danger to the environment because of its heavy reliance on machinery, pesticides, and fertilizers. Professionals have been an integral part of the emergence of our highly concentrated farm economy: agricultural research in plants and chemicals, farmer education, engineers to develop machinery and built infrastructure such as dams and irrigation systems. The pattern in agriculture has its counterpart elsewhere. The American economy is dominated by large corporations aided by oligarchically structured professions, all of which receive large and varied amounts of government subsidies and strong normative (legal and moral) support.

Changes in the American labor force have also been depicted as a rise in skill levels. Many argue that we are in a postindustrial age where most people work with their heads, not their hands or backs. The reality is otherwise—the main bulk of new jobs in the United States have been and will continue to be unskilled and semiskilled; the labor force will continue to have shortages of trained people even as there are surplus workers. There are as many sweat shops today as there were a hundred years ago. The image of a bright new world of high technology hides a dark, unchanging reality: the United States' economy has always rested on cheap labor and the future promises to be the same. The sources of cheap labor were vastly augmented with the enormous expansion of the world-market economy. Today, significant portions of the American labor force can be considered to be in the developing world. In addition, significant (legal) immigration has brought over one million skilled and professional foreign workers per year into the United States since World War II. In the next twenty-five years over 45 million foreigners will be legally admitted into the United States to ensure the continuance of what is certainly one of the most important and overlooked features in American history—plentiful supplies of socially generated cheap labor.

The declining fortunes of American labor extended far beyond blue-collar workers. One-third of college graduates report that they are in jobs that do not require a college education (and the number is now undoubtedly higher). Casualties among managerial ranks have been high and there is considerable hidden unemployment and underemployment among professionals (for example, an estimated 43 percent of all higher-education faculty are part-time or temporary workers with lower pay and no benefits[11]). In addition, employment firms have experienced an enormous growth in placing professionals in part-time, temporary jobs.[12] And there is an ominous trend (made possible by the computer) toward exact monitoring of all workers, including many professional practitioners, to prescribe exactly how they will work and to determine how tasks can be further specialized.[13]

The computer's negative features deserve far more attention than they have received: the elimination of skills (for example, tune-up mechanics, bank tellers, musicians), degrading of skills (for example, medicine, law, social work, airline pilots, chess players), tight monitoring of work (for example, airline reservation clerks, clerical workers), the substitution of temporary and part-time workers for full-time, full-benefit workers, and unemployment as the computer allows work to be done in cheap-labor areas of the United States and abroad. In the past, the negative aspects of new technology have always been offset by the creation of new, good jobs—for the first time in the history of technology, the computer appears not to be offsetting labor negatives with new, good jobs (in the United States).

Despite claims by computer manufacturers, the computer has not led to increases in productivity.[14] In some ways, the computer is similar to labor-saving devices in the home—when the latter devices were introduced they did not reduce labor (and thus "costs" to yield more productivity in relation to a set amount of work), but rather made housekeepers more productive in the sense of being able to do more and better work. Houses were kept cleaner, clothes were washed more often and made softer or more starched, more time was spent on fancier recipes, and so on. The computer has done much the same: fancier work complete with graphs and elegant type and reliance on written (more detailed) messages that are more time-consuming than oral communication.

The computer also increases the volume of communication fragmenting the employee's work day. To a researcher's surprise, it was found that the major variable leading to more productive computer work teams was to provide support staff to answer the phone and prevent work interruptions. The computer's amazing ability to handle data creates a presumptive need to use it (to justify its cost) and there are demands for more information to answer ever more refined applications, even if not essential to the enterprise in question. In addition, administrators overestimate the accuracy and value of computer models (based on quantitative questions and answers), leading to an "illusion of control" and "cognitive conceit." All in all, administrators are not better at administering, become overworked, and not knowing any of this, continually press to upgrade the abilities of their computers. In addition, while lower-paid workers are laid off, a large increase takes place in better-educated, computer-skilled, higher-paid workers. The promotion of the computer by the various technocratic movements continues to be strong (see the section below on successes and failure), though some welcome attempts to assess its worth to society have at last begun. Not to have done so sooner represents an adaptive failure of major proportions.

Ominously, the basic thrust of the American economy is toward a labor force in which the relative number of secure, well-paying jobs is declining and the number of temporary, part-time, low-skilled jobs expanding. Corporate capitalism has already undermined the power of organized labor. Labor unions now cover only 16 percent of the labor force, down from a high of 32 percent in the 1960s. The strike is no longer an effective labor weapon given the large numbers of unemployed and a probusiness government and judiciary. Labor unions have been forced to give back many of their gains. The basic thrust of the Reagan–Bush administration of 1980–92 was especially detrimental to labor. By lowering social-service programs, aid to cities, public housing, and aid to education, the Reagan–Bush administration forced many into the labor market. Since the concentrated economy has drastically reduced the number and power of small business and the self-employed, the historic middle class (augmented by a well-paid blue-collar, middle-income group) that formed the reality behind the American Dream may be on the way out.

IS THE AMERICAN MIDDLE CLASS DISAPPEARING?

The American middle class has long since disappeared if middle class is defined as a moderate-sized property owner or autonomous professional. Today, property is more highly concentrated than ever before and Americans, including professionals, are largely employees of large bureaucratic corporations, hospitals, foundations, voluntary groups, churches, and government.

The disappearance of the middle class was hidden from view by economic growth, especially from the late nineteenth to the mid-twentieth century. Economic growth created a new middle class of salaried professionals and high-income skilled workers. The new economy of abundance also homogenized a great deal of consumption, creating both a real and fictitious mass of middle-class consumers. And labor segmentation, the creation of meaningless gradations among occupations, also misled Americans into thinking that things were getting better.[15]

The broad middle class that appeared in the first half of the twentieth century appears to be shrinking. In assessing trends in household income, it is important to distinguish between middle income and middle class. A middle income can be acquired in a household in which husband and wife both work in blue-collar or working-class jobs. Both the nature of the work and the family background may well make this a working-class family despite its middle-level income. Middle class means a certain level of income, but also from a source that promotes a certain personality. It means awareness about and a desire to live in a certain way: owning a home with enough space for family members to have private lives, and enough appliances, including a second car, to service it. It means vacations as well as savings for the future. It means expectations for future advancement at work. And it means proper socialization of the young for future middle-class (or upper-middle-class) status, especially through a four-year college education.

From the 1970s to the 1990s a distinct bipolar shape appeared in America's income distribution. In the 1970s and '80s there were laments for the skilled workers in smokestack industries. What few realized is that during the same period millions of middle-level managers and professionals were laid off by hard-pressed corporations (many were "hard-pressed" by their own subsidiaries in cheap-labor countries).[16] And all experts predict that layoffs and a wider use of part-time, temporary (benefitless) labor will continue into the indefinite future, effectively curbing opportunities for the formation of middle-class households. By the 1980s, it was clear that high-technology industries and upper-level occupations were also being exported to developing countries.

Trends in the ownership of productive property, household income, and occupation indicate an erosion in the size and power of the historic American middle class. And by the 1980s another change had taken place in the middle class—diversification. The middle class is now made up of singles, married childless, double earners with children, divorced and remarried individuals, and older couples and singles.

The decline of the middle class and its fragmentation into very different types has serious implications for American society. The broad, politically moderate middle class was the mainstay of American representative government. As we have seen, American political life has changed for the worse and this may well be due to the change in the American middle class, which, economically hardpressed, has turned inward, no longer able to keep an eye on the upper class or care what happens to the lower classes.

WERE THE 1960s A WATERSHED?

Has the United States lost its enchanted world of manifest destiny and inevitable progress, its sense of being in tune with the cosmos? Fifty years of on-average prosperity seem to have created rather than solved problems. Not only have the consequences of prosperity contradicted basic American beliefs, but little has been done to prepare Americans for coping with what may be a no-growth future. Instead of a creative set of elites able to deal with problems one by one, the United States has an interlocked set of power groups that seem unable to tackle the deep tangle of intertwined social problems.

The elaborate welfare state erected during the past century is no doubt a source of stability for American society and has helped to correct some injustices and prevent some hardship and suffering. But the welfare state has also locked all power levels of American society into a structure of dependency and immobilization. The attempt by the Reagan administration in the 1980s to unclog American society by reducing the role of government and returning it to its past condition (an alleged era of individualism and free market competition) failed largely because of resistance by the wealthy and well-to-do who are the main beneficiaries of the welfare state and the main supporters of the Reagan administration.

The basic group dynamic in American society is competition among the various levels and types of propertied groups to maintain or increase relative advantage. The higher morality guiding rivalry among the haves is economic growth, not as measured by meaningful work, healthy consumption, or husbandry of resources (use economy) but in the abstract (exchange economy). Ever large portions of our gross domestic product are going into unproductive, unsatisfying social overhead: unneeded military preparations, fighting crime, repairing the physical and human costs of pollution, unsafe workplaces, unhealthy lifestyles, and tax and welfare subsidies for unproductive people at all class levels.

The 1960s may be a watershed by another criterion—it may mark new heights of formalism and reliance on myth. Our assorted indices and theories do not provide meaningful categories for judging economic and social outcomes. Expectations soar beyond what society can deliver, and widespread deviance is the order of the day. Absolutist, single-interest groups multiply as demands are unmet. Meanwhile property and professional elites orient themselves to vague, often empty abstractions: excellence, research, annual report, budgets, career advancement, making the top 500 corporations, total assets, dividends, test scores, GDP, interest rates, and so on. Far from being tied to social functions, elites have given themselves the right to look after their own interests and provide solutions to their own problems, under the master myth that self and public interest are the same.

DECLINING LEGITIMACY

The Survey Research Center and the Center for Political Studies (of the Institute for Social Research at the University of Michigan) studied the attitude of trust in government for over two decades. Trust in government showed significant declines beginning in the early 1960s, and plunged during the 1970s. In tracing this development, Arthur N. Miller concluded that "analysis conclusively demonstrates that the current, widespread political distrust of government is rooted in attitudes that are more generic than evaluations of the incumbents."[17] In short, American distrust of leaders is so profound that it seems to be undermining their faith in institutions. Widespread apathy toward elections can certainly be interpreted in this way. Trends in confidence toward institutional leadership rise slightly from time to time as presidents are elected or if the economy improves. But the long-term trend from the 1960s to 1982 clearly indicates a decline in confidence by the American people in leadership. As such, this poses a distinct threat to the legitimacy of American institutions.[18]

Polls since the 1980s have continued to show declining levels of public confidence in American institutions and groups. Polls indicate a growing loss of confidence through 1990 in political leaders, parties, and officials.[19] And by 1994, small business was the only sector of American society that was able to muster a (bare) majority of Americans who expressed "a great deal" or "quite a lot" of confidence in it.[20]

The cleavage between elite and people extends to policy matters. The American people clearly want a strong federal government to solve the problems of war and peace, the economy, and quality of life. Nine out of ten Americans believe that the federal government is responsible for seeing to it that no one goes hungry and that every person achieves a minimum standard of living. Americans clearly express a preference for wage and price controls to fight inflation, and they support a woman's right to an abortion and favor a curb on handguns. Seventy-five percent of the American people express a clear preference for jobs as the best way to curb crime, a preference that runs counter to elite beliefs.[21] Moreover, the American people express clear support for national health insurance. Their attitudes toward nuclear arms and foreign policy were also at variance with those of American elites during the Cold War, with most preferring a nuclear freeze and a less belligerent foreign policy.

The elites of the United States, with some minor exceptions, tend to ignore the public's wishes. There is a tendency among elites, including public officials, to regard the ordinary citizen as uninformed and self-contradictory. American elites, including sociologists, have a longstanding tendency of blaming and ignoring the masses, largely by regarding them as uneducated, selfish, and undisciplined.

The decline in legitimacy can be expressed in different terms. American behavior exhibits a strong trend toward self-centered individualism. Over the past few decades, Americans have participated less across almost the entire spectrum of political and voluntary life. Robert Putnam has compiled the evidence for this decline, calling attention to its implications: a decline in voluntary and political participation (or what he calls "civic engagement") means a reduction in the generation of social capital, "the networks, norms, and trust that enable participants to act together more effectively to pursue shared objectives."[22] In our terms, this means that as faith in the legitimacy of institutions declines, people withdraw from sociopolitical life and thus fail to generate the faith in institutions that is needed to participate in the first place. As social capital declines, Americans participate less, and so on. Conflict sociologists in an earlier generation had referred to the above process as mass society atomizing its members and making them feel powerless and paranoid. Their warning that such a population is extremely vulnerable to political manipulation has had considerable confirmation in recent years.

The decline in legitimacy appears real. By and large, it stems from the deep cleavage between the interests and values of American elites and those of the American people. In another sense, it reflects a decline in the adaptive ability of American elites. Again, the master problem seems to be a social system whose basic institutions separate elites from direct experience with the problems of ordinary people. Elites are separated from ordinary people because institutions allow them to solve their own problems under the false faith that by doing so they are also serving the public.

PROFESSIONS AND PROBLEMSOLVING

Previous chapters on education and the academic disciplines (Chapters 3–5), the applied professions (Chapters 6, 7), and the policy professions (Chapter 10) contain deep criticisms of America's knowledge elites. In the remaining sections of this chapter we look at the record of various kinds of professionals who have accepted responsibility for the solution of social problems. The next section evaluates the professionals who spearhead innovations and reform movements.

Professions and Social Movements: Resource-Mobilization Theory

Resource-mobilization theorists have led the attack against views that explain social movements in terms of abstract individuals experiencing abstract conflicts. Complex society, especially industrial society, argue these theorists, generates discontent as a matter of course. The real question is, Why do concrete movements arise from a constant condition? The things to look for, argue resource-mobilization theorists such as McCarthy-Zald, Oberschall, and Gamson, are resources and how well they can be mobilized, especially by elites.[23]

McCarthy and Zald, who pioneered this perspective, argue that while there has (probably) been an increase in social movement activity, the increase has not come from greater mass involvement in social problems. What has happened, they argue, rather persuasively, is that a significant flow of resources has emerged from wealthy individuals, foundations, churches, and governments (and from labor unions and voluntary organizations of all sorts) and that this has produced groups (social movements) that exist independently of those who have grievances. The flow of money and donated labor has made it possible to professionalize problemsolving. Often, the professionally led group will create its membership after the fact. The case studies that follow amply demonstrate that substantive change reflects social power, not abstract ideas, and that professionals succeed only when their aims are consistent with the structure of power.

Successes and Failure: Environmental and Nuclear Issues, Space Flight, and Computerization

Bringing the environment into public consciousness seems to be a success that can be attributed to professionals (academics, largely in the natural sciences). The same seems to be true of nuclear issues, which were also brought to the attention of the American public by professionals (natural scientists, physicians, and lawyers). The space-flight movement, led by professionals, was able to exploit the felt military needs of Germany during the 1920s and 1930s, and the Cold War rivalry between the United States and the Soviet Union after World War II, to successfully generate public support.[24] These successes look different, however, when assessed from a different perspective. Bringing environmental or nuclear issues to the attention of the public is not the same thing as solving these problems. The space-flight movement succeeded because its interests coincided with the interests of government (especially the military) and was part of intersocietal hostility after World War I.

The technocratic nature of professionally led reform movements can be seen in computerization. Analysts have identified five computer movements forming a general social movement in favor of computerization.[25] These movements appear in five areas: urban information systems, artificial intelligence, office automation, computing for instructional purposes, and home computing for personal purposes. Though not organized as one movement, all five share basic ideological beliefs and values. Those advocating computerization are middle- and upper-middle-class professionals. The ideology of computerization is politically conservative (a part of the overall process of depoliticization). Emphasis is placed on knowledge, reduced costs, enhanced efficiency and thus productivity, the elimination of drudgery, and the promotion of individualism, flexibility, and cooperation. There is also an emphasis on the need to keep up to date since computer technology is continuously improving and extending its scope.

As Cling and Iacono state, computer ideology includes all things not said and all things assumed. Computer advocates do not mention the costs of computerization or the threat to other values. They do not focus on employment loss, threats to privacy, ways to bilk consumers, or the quality of work. They rarely stress computer breakdown or poor servicing. They define many of the above problems as people problems, the inability of people to keep abreast of technology. And the stress on the future of computer technology allows computer advocates to gloss over the conflicts of the day while holding out hope of an ideal social order in the future. In short, computerization is both explicitly and implicitly part of postindustrial ideology, part of technocratic liberalism.

Cling and Iacono state that no effective opposition exists to the general computer movement. Special interest groups, for example, civil rights organizations, consumer groups, and labor unions, oppose or question specific aspects of computerization. Computerization proceeds because powerful interests want it, especially professional groups who identify with the computer industry in general: accountants, doctors, teachers, and urban planners. The net result has been to "reinforce the patterns of an elite-dominated, stratified society."

The computer will no doubt help in achieving technical mastery of many things. Will it result in the technocratic ego? To be able to program everything and anything must be psychologically exhilarating. Will programmers be able to keep track of what they are programming? Already the incredibly fast and flexible programs of yesterday are locked in place, like obsolete steel mills and machine tools, too useful to throw away, too obsolete to be profitable or competitive. These computer programs are understood by no one because no one is responsible for all of a program of even moderate complexity; new is grafted to old without anyone really being in charge.

Seen in this way, is the computer a metaphor for modern society? Are we directionless and filled with cross-purposes like an old computer filled with long-forgotten programs? Is modern society a haphazard result of a series of technical advances that have led to oversized, overloaded, ultimately unworkable societies? A simple society creates simple personalities that are easy to keep track of. Complex (computer) society bombards its members from all directions sending some this way and some that. Does it produce the "saturated self"? Rather than purge itself of the past and the no longer useful, modern society allows all norms and values to hang on. Does the real danger in the computer lie in the possibility that it is deceiving us into thinking that we have control over our destiny?

The Cooption of Professionals: The Cases of Energy Researchers and BART Engineers

Professional cooption is widespread. While doctors and lawyers provide high-quality services for high-level individuals and powerful groups, medical and legal services cannot be improved as long as these services are deemed to be private enterprise on a one-to-one basis. Educational services cannot be improved as long as the academic profession is splintered into artificial disciplines. Mental health cannot be improved as long as individual practitioners deal with patients one by one. Public policy professionals cannot succeed as long as they tackle the symptoms of a problem using cost-benefit analysis.

The failure of professionals is often the story of those who set policy and own the skills and knowledge of professionals. The CIA is not as unknowing as it appears—its knowledge was used selectively by elected administrations. The HUD, EPA, and banking scandals clearly show that professional staff were overruled by political officials who were pursuing private-power interests. Many doctors, lawyers, and educators understand the need to provide structural solutions, but are confronted by the owners and controllers of health-care, legal, and educational systems.

In an interesting analysis, Feldman found that policy researchers at the Department of Energy worked hard and diligently despite knowing that their research would be ignored. Feldman tends to interpret this in terms of classical laissez-faire theory. Despite the fact that self-oriented individuals are not always able to achieve goals predictably, argues Feldman, the [magical] market will yield desirable results. In Feldman's interpretation, the fact that policy research by professional researchers is not used nonetheless yields order and mutual education among contending research interests.[26] A much simpler interpretation is that while American elites do not base their rule on professionally produced knowledge, they have a need to pretend that it is (associating state power with science has a long history back to the absolute monarchies of Europe). Their rule then receives the legitimacy of science and their misrule can be blamed on abstract ignorance. The nonuse or misuse of research provides a handy excuse for failure across the apex of American economic, voluntary, and professional elites.

The case of Bay Area Rapid Transit (BART) is another example of how politically powerful economic groups hide behind a technocratic approach to social problems.[27] The Bay Area Rapid Transit system, proposed to help solve the problem of air pollution and traffic congestion in the San Francisco region, is a multibillion-dollar failure. Why? A fragmented political system made it impossible to frame the problems of Bay Area pollution and transportation in terms that could reasonably be met. Government in the United States is not expected to do most things directly or to raise its own capital. America's fragmented political jurisdictions make it difficult to mobilize or harmonize divergent interests. The basic (largely latent) purpose of BART was to revive and enhance the economy and thus the property values of downtown San Francisco. The four surrounding counties, having little direct interest in the problems of San Francisco, voted against the bond issue to finance BART and were opposed to paying higher taxes to support BART's operations. A rigged referendum, however, made it appear that the project had adequate public support. Instead of the normal two-thirds support required in *each* jurisdiction, only 60 percent was required and that for an *average of all four* jurisdictions (which of course gave heavily populated San Francisco the edge). The referendum passed by 61 percent.

BART's Board of Directors and its general manager had no firm foundation in law, no firm source of funds, and no one to whom they were responsible. From the beginning, BART stressed space-age technology, glamour (automated, clean, aesthetic), and inexpensive service. Technical problems multiplied and serious questions of safety arose. Cost overruns also multiplied and the project ran far behind schedule.

BART's professional employees were not integrated into the project, but had been hired to monitor the private contractors who were actually building BART. BART's engineers tried to protect the public's interest, but because they did not understand the overall project, their whistleblowing tended to stress technical questions. Capital cost overruns were 50 percent over original estimates and operating costs were almost five times original estimates. Revenues were much lower than expected because passenger patronage turned out to be half of original estimates. The fare is much higher than that on buses and considerably higher than the cost of using a private automobile. Very few passengers have been lured away from cars, so air pollution has not been curbed. And like most mass transit systems around the country, the main users are not the poorer classes, but the better-off and well-to-do. Rapid transit is not an alternative form of transportation as many think and a tax subsidy to the poor to make up for airline and highway subsidies for the well-to-do. It is part of a vast system of largely invisible public subsidies for the upper classes. And because BART is heavily financed by regressive property and sales taxes, the poor are paying 40 times more than the well-to-do for a system they do not and cannot use.

How many other BARTs are there? Given its fragmented and weak political institutions, the United States continually sets up irresponsible boards, authorities, and commissions to conduct a huge array of "public" services in the realms of transportation, energy, water, agricultural marketing, sports, occupational licensing and certification, education, the arts, health, and legal services. Instead of focusing on the causes of problems, America's problemsolving elites are committed to a professional or technocratic approach, that is, they believe they can solve problems without changing fundamental power relations. What they are doing, of course, is protecting the status quo and thus their own interests.

The Cooption of Professional Artists

Art is always an expression of a society's basic values, beliefs, and power structure. It also expresses new ways of seeing and feeling in response to new social currents.[28] Art is a complex world of sculpture, literature, painting, theater, film, music, and exhibiting, and takes both elite and popular forms. Though generalizations about art are hazardous, a number of trends are discernible. Art in all its forms has been deeply commercialized. Understandably, the production of art is now industrialized. Artists are often employees of corporate structures: record companies, film studios, greeting card companies, fashion magazines and fashion houses, symphony orchestras, and universities. The funding of art is openly political and strong pressures exist to curtail art that deviates from accepted norms. Art is also critical, but much of its criticism is about secondary issues and it cannot be said that artists are a force for even reform, let alone social-system change (for a fuller discussion of art as popular culture, see Chapter 8).

Professionals and the Failure of Reform Through Judicial Action

Handler has analyzed attempts to use the judicial system to solve problems in order to answer a larger question: Do social movements reflect a pluralist democracy? Do they enlarge or maximize pluralism, thereby helping to turn it into a viable ideal? Addressing these questions, Handler focused on thirty-eight cases of social-reform efforts over a twenty-five-year period in four areas: civil rights, environmental protection, consumer protection, and welfare rights. These efforts all used litigation as an instrument of social change, and the efforts were directed largely at government. Here were weak challenging groups relying on the legal system to change its norms and procedures and force government to enforce existing laws or reinterpret them. The use of litigation, and thus the use of lawyers and public-interest law firms, became so widespread after the 1950s that Handler regards it as a social movement. In a fascinating analysis, he assesses benefits and losses and the general strengths and weaknesses of a variety of social groups in each of the four areas. He concludes, by and large, that no significant change of power relations occurred and that the United States is still more "corporatist" than pluralist.[29]

Rosenberg has focused directly on the U.S. Supreme Court (and other courts) to assess which view of the court, the Dynamic or the Constrained, is more in line with the facts. Though he focuses on lawyers leading or opposing "significant reform" only implicitly, his analysis rounds out our understanding of the power and effectiveness of both the legal profession and its embodiment as a judicial institution. Using primarily *Brown* (racial desegregation in education), *Roe* (legalization of abortion), and women's civil rights (but also other issues), Rosenberg argues convincingly that litigation produces significant change only if it has political and social support (even when legal victories are obtained). By and large, those who want change should use their resources to mobilize political movements and not squander them on the fly-paper of litigation.[30]

The most recent attempt to assess the effectiveness of lawyers and the law, while providing valuable insights into legal symbolic processes, is a throwback to the era before resource-mobilization theory.[31] Delgado and Stephancic condemn the bias and unimaginative thinking that has characterized judges and lawyers when dealing with race, ethnicity, and gender cases. They cite typical ways in which bad thinking is justified and the status quo is upheld. Professionalized research and classification systems and the need to cite precedents also bias thinking toward the status quo. But while Delgado and Stephancic link error and bias to the larger world of law and legal practice (using occasional references to the social construction of reality perspective), they do not embed the legal system in a larger sociohistorical frame. They are insightful in places when they show how objective empiricism can block novel, morally better subjective definitions. But by and large, they neglect the historical basis of error and bias, institutional imperatives, and sociopolitical power. Quite explicitly, their argument is that our inability to rid ourselves of the self-evident evils of racism and sexism is a failure of the legal imagination.

Professionals as Activist Reformers

Organized movements to achieve goals being thwarted by normal institutional functioning have arisen from within the ranks of professionals. Hoffman has documented two such movements based on nineteen case histories of activist organizations over an eighteen-year period (1960–78), eight in city planning and eleven in medicine, largely set in Boston and New York.[32]

Though not statistically representative, Hoffman believes that these organizations represent typical activist strategies and dynamics across the country.

Activists in city planning and in medicine faced similar problems and adopted similar strategies. They both sought to improve planning and medical services for low-income and minority communities. Planners involved themselves, for example, in helping communities resist proposals to run highways through their neighborhoods, while doctors set up storefront health clinics. Their efforts, however, were not successful. The communities involved had different priorities: planning and medical services were not of primary importance to these communities (except when their homes were threatened). Indeed they looked on the new proposals as a way to increase their power and as sources of jobs.

The reform effort was sobering for professionals who realized that their professional status was not part of a consensus about fundamental values and that much of what they assumed may have been class-based and self-serving. Activist professionals came to realize that a professional orientation, based on individuals and on technically defined situations and problems, did not lead to positive results. Many began to think far more structurally and to search for the causes of problems. And many began to realize that in trying to empower their clients, they were undermining their professional claim to a unique knowledge base. Indeed, their clients not only wanted a transfer of knowledge to themselves, but community leaders turned out to be "conservative", often wanting themselves to become the providers of services.

In summary, reform efforts based on the assumption by professionals that they faced a rational but underserved community in a rational social order did not lead to improved services. Realizing that they were merely being used to pacify the poor and minorities, professionals turned to community empowerment only to find that the community was conservative and that professional claims to autonomy based on knowledge was threatened. Relying on professionals to spearhead significant reform, concludes Hoffman, may be a poor substitute for an alternative image of a good society.

In many ways, all reforms and all social movements, whether in civil rights, education, or the environment, are professional movements. The movements studied by Hoffman were relations between activist professionals and low-income, minority communities. Other reform movements are professionally led groups against professionally led groups, both of which can assume only limited interest by the general public. As the next section illustrates, the key to reform success is always to think politically, not technically, and to mobilize a coalition strong enough to get results.

Professionals versus Professionals: Public Policy as Negotiated Reality among the Powerful

One of the most obvious things about professionals is that their work involves mystery and unpredictability. In exploring the unknown, claims are made and controversy occurs. Sometimes these controversies remain within the confines of a scientific specialty. Often, however, disputes about scientific matters erupt into the public arena and we have the phenomenon of scientists publicly disagreeing with each other.

Most of the public controversies involving such matters as car safety, smoking, nuclear power, nuclear arms, clear air, the greenhouse effect, and so on have been "settled," not by science, but by political power. A case study that illustrates the social nature of perspectives on science and the ultimate negotiated nature of what is decided (reality) is the controversy over estrogen replacement therapy (ERT).[33] Starting with the claim that menopause is an estrogen deficiency, Americans divided over ERT because its use was associated with cancer. Nonetheless, estrogen was widely prescribed for women despite the warning that it was linked to cancer. The question of estrogen becomes much more interesting when American divisions are compared to British divisions on the identical matter.

American researchers, using statistical correlations, emphasized the risk of using estrogen, while British medical research, relying on direct cause and effect relations, emphasized the benefits of using it. American doctors (in the pay-for-service American system) strongly supported the use of estrogen (which requires considerable medical monitoring). British doctors (on salary in the socialized British health-care system) were reluctant to prescribe estrogen. By 1979, only 2 to 5 percent of British women over 40 received ERT compared to an estimated 20 percent in the United States.

American feminists opposed ERT and its claim that it would keep women "feminine forever," because they had a strong political agenda, one of whose aims was to free women from the alleged confines of biology (and, of course, to protect them from cancer). British feminists, with a strong socialist political tradition to rely on, condemned the reluctance of doctors to prescribe estrogen as yet another example of elites withholding resources from the weak. Finally, American regulators succeeded in getting an insert in every ERT patient package warning of the cancer risk, whereas British regulators issued a statement saying that estrogen did not cause cancer.

RESISTANCE TO KNOWLEDGE

Resistance to knowledge, both inside a profession and among the various elites, is well known. Religious elites do not all accept the fact of human evolution. Legislators and government have largely ignored the connection between a deficient, out-of-control economy and crime. A wide variety of elites believe that the public wants tax cuts and reduced government spending despite repeated surveys indicating that what the public wants is good—not necessarily less—government.

Resistance to knowledge by professionals is of special interest to this study.[34] Military professionals in the United States Air Force still believe in strategic bombing despite the fact that four of its own studies have found no strategic value in bombing. Economists continue to believe (a belief shared by business in general) that tax cuts lead to increased savings and capital investment despite overwhelming evidence to the contrary. Economists continue to believe that markets actually exist (as opposed to markets as an ideal) when it is clear that they do not in every sector of the economy (food, housing, health care, education, and so on) and that corporations often raise prices when demand slumps, giving the lie to the alleged principle of supply and demand. The government (through the public school system), along with psychologists and professionals throughout higher education, continues to rely heavily on IQ and similar testing despite the fact that testing has been thoroughly discredited. The same knowledge elites (supported by other elites) have also resisted the knowledge, gleaned from dozens of studies, that the only way to improve education is by improving the class conditions from which students come.

All knowledge elites have resisted findings questioning the value of laissez-faire, or unplanned, research. They have resisted knowledge that unnecessary education is required for all professions. They have resisted knowledge that exposure to knowledge does not result in knowledgeable behavior. Here we are talking not only of the many findings that taking a particular academic course does not change behavior—for example, doctors, who have taken courses in nutrition are not more likely to use that knowledge in their practices than those who have not taken such courses—but of the overall finding that *education as such* has little impact on students and cannot be related to their behavior beyond school.

The patterns in resistance to knowledge are clear enough. A first pattern is resistance through habit and ignorance, which occurs because knowledge elites have demanded autonomy from others and freedom among themselves (the leave-us-alone-and-all-will-be-well syndrome of laissez-faire capitalism). An example of this can be taken from medicine: it was established in the mid-1980s that ulcers are caused by a virus and can be cured with antibiotics; nonetheless, most doctors continue the time-honored treatment that addresses only symptoms.

A second pattern is that knowledge elites resist knowledge because knowledge upsets powerful clients who benefit from being able to pursue nonscientific policies in the name of science.

A third pattern of resistance to knowledge emerges when knowledge threatens the foundations of the profession itself or requires significant changes in it. What would happen to economists if their logic had to match behavioral reality, or if their basic definitions, on which that logic is based (for example, of capital, labor, unemployment, savings, productivity, efficiency), are seen for what they are, arbitrary, time-bound, and at best, useful fictions. What would happen to all knowledge elites if they had to acknowledge that all scientific work is value based, that is, political? For one thing, they would find it difficult to maintain the separation that now exists among themselves and, of course, between themselves and laypeople.

A case study can illustrate how professionals resist and reject knowledge about their behavior that threatens their obsolete practices. Mechanic reports that research findings in biomedical research and technology are accepted easily since they do not interfere with the interests of professionals and actually complement and extend them. Research in the area of health-care and services tends to be neglected, however, and when done, ignored. The reason for this is that research into health-care practices upsets habits and threatens a professional monopoly.

As an example, Mechanic reports on a study at Yale–New Haven (Yale University's teaching hospital). Children scheduled for tonsillectomies were randomly divided into experimental and control groups. The control group received the normal care. Mothers of the children in the experimental group were admitted to the hospital and given a realistic picture of what to expect. The mothers in this group experienced less stress and their children had much better medical readings, made better adaptations to the hospital, and experienced a more rapid and better recovery after leaving the hospital. These findings are of added significance because tonsillectomies are widely performed and psychological problems are known to have important adverse effects on health. Neither Yale–New Haven nor other hospitals acted on the findings.[35]

KNOWLEDGE AND POLICY AS EXPRESSIONS OF POWER

The search for knowledge is not a technical operation removed from a culture's values and beliefs and a society's structure of power. Sociology (and social science) has developed a fairly good picture of the American power structure. Power, first of all, is highly concentrated and bears little relation to both professional and popular myths. The main structure of power lies in the American economy. There is overwhelming evidence that power flows from the economy and that political, religious, educational, and family institutions have relatively little control over it. There is also strong evidence that the American power structure is connected to those of other societies and could not exist without such connections.[36]

The policy scientist must be aware of the power groups that run our society and shape our image of it. Despite their well-motivated desire to confront reality, power groups consistently create false and contradictory images of reality, and perpetuate outmoded images of it. American elites clearly have interests contrary to mass interests (as well as contrary interests among themselves). One reason for all this is the concept of reality itself. Policy scientists must stop assuming that they are engaged in uncovering the one reality beneath or beyond the secondary world of ignorance, vestiges from the past, and human fallibility. Policy scientists must build on the basic insight of creative social science and humanities—society is a created reality (for a fuller discussion, see Chapter 1).

Once seen in this way, social reality ceases to be unitary and fixed. Society is then seen for what it is, a hodgepodge of elements accumulated over thousands of years. Much, even most of it, comes, not from a nonexistent abstraction, the people, but from powerful groups. What has been called democracy over the past few centuries is really an enlargement and diversification of power groups, who are now forced to negotiate the nature of reality. Ordinary people have always had some say in these negotiations, but developments over recent decades have brought more and more of them into the political process. The policy scientist (and knowledge elites) must always keep the negotiated nature of social reality in mind: The family, the corporation, the school and voluntary group, the state, the individual, society, and the world system of societies are all historical creations. They must always ask: Is what I am studying working in terms of clearly stated values? What are the real choices available to the various parties and are they communicating effectively in their negotiations?

Understanding the Policy Process

Professional myths and biases abound when it comes to understanding the policy process itself. Economists minimize the role of policy (value-laden, information-short, political decisions) in the behavior of economic, political, and social actors even as they work mightily to curtail it. Political scientists exaggerate the role of the political system in public policy even as they discover that the sources of power over policy lie outside the political system. A recent summary by Burstein of what sociology and political science understand by the overall policy process illustrates how difficult it is for the technocratic disciplines to incorporate power into their analyses.[37]

Employing the "garbage-can model of organizations" (the world is open and malleable, organizations are unstructured, all could have turned out differently), Burstein reviews what is known about "three aspects of the political process (in the United States): agenda setting, the development of policy proposals, and the struggle for adoption of particular proposals." Burstein argues that sociology (along with political science) has concluded that policy domains (or areas) are autonomous and specific unto themselves (health, energy, agriculture, and so on). One cannot relate them to general social development, class, or unified elites. His report concludes that the policy domains are socially and politically constructed and that while we know something about the enactment of policies, we have a long way to go before understanding the overall process.

Burstein's review of the field would have been far different had he adopted a different set of assumptions to see it with. For one thing, the world of policy-making and state-society relations look much different if the time frame used is five hundred instead of fifty years. Thus seen, the approach of capitalist society toward the poor, for example, exhibits enormous similarity over the centuries, say from at least the Elizabethan Poor Law of the sixteenth century to the U.S. Family Support Act of 1988 (and subsequent squeezes on the poor). Seen over time, from a macrosociological focus, America's policies about education, health care, housing, race, fair employment, family, children, women, the environment, defense procurement, energy, agriculture, and so on have never run counter to the interests of the upper classes. Burstein also fails to mention that reform movements succeed or fail only if they have money (or are willing to use violence).

There is also no discussion of the fact that many laws are adapted as tokens of vitality and concern and then not enforced. And, there is no discussion of the enormous corruption that fouls the American political process.

The garbage can theory of the policy process assumes a society without power (naive liberalism, technocratic liberalism). An analysis focused on the power structure of capitalist society would note that the noisy world of policy controversy and apparent resolution has solved no problems. Our politics merely recycles issues creating the impression that actors are concerned and behaving rationally. The ultimate assessment of the American policy process is that we have only one policy: not to have policies anywhere since we want to achieve a market society—a society marked by rational actors in accord with a rational social universe. In such a society there is neither power nor public policy since equal, rational actors are all pursuing rational policies. The difficulty (impossibility?) of achieving this ideal, and how far current practices are from it, can be seen in the following section.

Power, Theory, and Facts: The Political Nature of Official Data

Power groups construct reality in part by creating symbolic representations of the economy, family, ethnic groups, the polity, causation, other countries, themselves, and those without power. How they think determines what facts are seen and how facts are interpreted. Power groups specializing in symbols, be they shamans, priests, or contemporary social scientists, invariably downplay the role of assumptions in science, and thus the created nature of reality, stressing instead the objective reality of facts quite apart from the human beings discovering them.

The reliance on assumptions to tell us what facts to collect is nowhere more apparent than in the Bureau of the Census and other data-gathering bodies of the federal government. Even the head-count census required every ten years is political because it must make decisions on what heads to count. The same applies to the unemployment rate, and so on, through the entire system of social indicators. Americans have now grown so accustomed to debating the nature and health of their economy and society in terms of official data supplied by the federal government that few realize that such data are inherently political (causing them to see things in only one way since the data have been mislabelled as objective), or that the data are often defective (also see below, "Reconstructing Our Social Indicators").[38]

In addition, current trends point to a deliberate curb on "official data" and the rise of private firms who specialize in information to be sold for profit. Clearly, this trend reinforces the existing structure of economic and social power. It not only makes knowledge available only to those with money, but the collection of data, carefully geared only to the concrete questions that interest our business and professional elites, may not be that useful to them in their role as a governing class. Needless to say, the commercialization of knowledge is not likely to promote an informed, democratic citizenry.

Power as Money

Money gives power. In its most direct expression, it enables you to buy knowledge. People with money can buy the knowledge of a doctor or a lawyer, whereas the poor cannot. Those with money can also obtain knowledge by sponsoring research. Governments have money and therefore can do research into population characteristics, weapon systems, nuclear energy, the secrets of its citizens or of foreigners, pest control, and so on. By definition, all power groups have the resources to obtain knowledge, either through purchase or research.

Power as Secrecy

One of the reasons existing knowledge is arbitrary is because much of what goes on in the world remains secret (that is, the search for knowledge is conducted secretly and once found, is often kept secret). The ability to keep things secret is a good index to social power. Governments conduct many activities in secret largely because government is involved with the conflicts and secrets of private groups and must somehow manage the problems that these groups (and legislatures) cannot settle.[39]

Corporations are also very secretive, not only about their technical processes, quality controls,[40] and creative designs, but about basic financial matters, including debt, assets, costs, profits, and ownership (these matters are often falsified to hide the true nature of the firm's economic status). Enforcing housing standards and fighting arson are not easy because for one thing it is difficult to identify the owners of slum properties. The United States has great difficulty in prosecuting antitrust cases because often it cannot obtain the facts it needs. Corporate secrecy also prevents the U.S. government from obtaining data on oil production and refinement, and on oil and gas reserves. Of great significance is the fact that secrecy has also helped to prevent a uniform way of computing profit. Also significant is the fact that knowledge about the rich is very difficult to obtain (especially their wealth) and that most of what we call social-science knowledge is about the middle, working, and lower classes.

Other groups besides the very powerful hide their behavior. Alcoholics, drug users, wife beaters, burglars, embezzlers, tax evaders, gamblers, prostitutes, and so on hide their behavior making knowledge about these activities difficult to obtain. Some deviants are better able to hide their actions than others. By and large, deviance by the powerful is much harder to uncover than deviance by the weak. Sociology as a discipline has yet to confront this problem though individual researchers have tackled it. A promising development is the new focus on deviance by private and public organizations. Vaughan, for example, provides a fascinating case study, combining knowledge about deviance and organizational theory, of the enormously complex problem of uncovering carefully hidden Medicare fraud from within a large pharmacy corporation, a process that required great secrecy by five government agencies to prevent evidence from being erased.[41] (See also "Control Groups beyond the Courts, Police, and Prisons" in Chapter 9).

Shaping and Transmitting Biased Knowledge

Bias is as prevalent in policy research as in other forms of research. Even a small bias can lead to a large and expensive mistake. A classic example is an energy report by the National Academy of Sciences. The academy serves the federal government and Congress in an advisory capacity. Its committee reports carry great weight because of the academy's reputation for careful analysis and review. A 1980 report by this prestigious organization raises disturbing questions about American policy-making as well as about the academy. In a mammoth report on energy (which took 350 experts four years and four million dollars to complete), the academy's committee on Nuclear and Alternative Energy Systems gave a pessimistic appraisal of the outlook for solar energy and an optimistic one about coal and nuclear energy. Its general perspective was based on a comparison of relative costs. For some incredible reason, cost estimates for solar energy were based on the assumption that the cost of solar technology would not change over the next thirty years. This flies in the face of all experience with technology and rendered the report worthless.[42]

Other examples of bias can be cited, many of them deliberate and politically motivated. An estimate on the cost of a new dam can be wrong because of a biased assumption about interest rates (the U.S. Corps of Engineers has a long history of using unreal interest rates to hide the true cost of public projects). In estimating the cost of nuclear energy, results will differ depending on whether the costs of all plants are averaged, or the common practice of averaging only the costs of those built before the high inflation of the late 1970s. Perhaps the most damaging mistake in American policymaking, which persisted uncorrected despite our myth that error inevitably succumbs to science, is the CIA's error in computing Soviet military spending. This error coincided with the political interests of elected administrations and thus continued over many years, despite criticism, and resulted in a large overspending on military defense by the United States (an overspending that damaged the American economy and curtailed the adaptive ability of tax-starved public bodies).

Power and Multiple Realities

Power groups erect barriers to knowledge in yet another sense. Complex industrial society is marked by considerable rivalry among power groups. In their struggle, power groups create different symbolic worlds (or versions of reality) to support and further their interests. Religious groups have a different reality from secular groups, and among religious groups there is a differing reality for Protestants, Roman Catholics, Jews, Muslims, and Navahos. The worldviews of corporations, trade unions, professions, and lower classes all differ in important ways. The reality of a male is different from that of a female, a husband from wife, and parents from their children. These diverse realities are no mere systems of ideas; they are embedded deep in the emotional structure of the human psyche and maintained by daily interaction routines.

Social scientists also have a reality different from outsiders such as government, the world of business, and the broad public. Hansen has outlined cleavages that separate political elites and academics researching the policy process (for example, political elites lack historical perspective, do not work with clear beginnings and endings, are skeptical about policy evaluation, believe that what they are doing is objective not political, and are disbelieving when told that the policies they are pursuing have failed elsewhere).[43] There is even a separate reality for each of the social sciences[44] and multiple realities within each.

Davidson provides a case study of a federal agency funding research proposals from university staffs in which tension existed between professional groups, the evaluators of the proposals, and the staff leaders who decided on the overall mix of accepted grants. The evaluators focused their work on the merit of each proposal and identified with the university staff, even offering suggestions on how to improve the proposals. The leaders of the agency were policy oriented and more attuned to the political ramifications of the agency's work (the allocation of scarce funds had to satisfy members of Congress). Though all were professionals, tension existed because of the organizational setting.[45]

Those who aspire to know more about the world must not assume as they read or practice social science, therefore, that they are escaping the forces of power and entering the world of objectivity (assuming objectivity is possible). Objectivity is a worthy, but difficult-to-reach goal. Being realistic about how easy it is to be biased is an important way to stay on the road to objectivity. Members of complex industrial society live in a world of *multiple* (symbolic) *realities*. For this reason, one of the most important of all urban-industrial behavior skills is *empathy*, the ability to put oneself in another's place. Skill at putting oneself in the place of others is also useful to the social scientist and such figures as Vico (mental reconstruction), Max Weber (*verstehen*, or understanding), and Cooley (dramatic perception) have called for its use in analyzing human behavior.

There is no doubt that the history of the various sciences and professions has been a struggle to achieve the ideal of objectivity. Many have now come to understand that science is a form of *social* behavior and that objectivity is whatever people agree on. The ideal of objectivity was easier to achieve when society was simpler and consensus was deeper and wider (or was thought to be). The ideal of objectivity also had a practical purpose—it provided professionals with a way to cope with the conflicting interests that surrounded them. Recall, for example, that the ideal of objective journalism (as opposed to interpretative journalism) arose because newspaper owners, to avoid offending readers and advertisers, encouraged a bland, consensus-oriented type of reporting.

To some extent, the same thing happened in sociology from the nineteenth century until recently. Sociologists, along with power groups in general, exaggerated the consensus about which it was possible to be objective. Ironically, the ideal of objectivity hid many of the conflicts and shortcomings of society. Today, it is much better understood that science rests on assumptions. Those who agree on assumptions will agree on facts; thus research is valid only in terms of the assumptions on which it is based. Today sociologists understand that a single perspective, or way of seeing, is also a way of not seeing (Kenneth Burke). They know that creative science is the interplay of contrasting perspectives and that science is inescapably implicated in value judgments.

The need to understand all this has only begun to be felt in the field of policy analysis and evaluation as currently practiced. What follows shows how the name of science hides the power uses to which cost-benefit analysis, the most prevalent form of thinking about public problems, has been put.

Cost-Benefit and Risk-Benefit Analysis: Systematic Bias in Favor of the Status Quo

A special way of thinking about problems and conducting research, which has deep roots in basic American values and beliefs, poses a danger to policy analysis. This perspective is alternatively known as cost-benefit analysis, risk-benefit analysis or risk assessment, exchange theory, rational-choice analysis, or most simply, as market analysis. Essentially, this cluster of procedures for arriving at decisions about how to handle problems relies on the old nineteenth-century rational individual decked out in glittering scientific garbs. By and large, it is mainstream economics and social science focused on a policy problem. Genuine policy analysis, on the other hand, is always implicated in value conflicts. For example, to judge economic benefits by money alone in a short-time frame may conflict with long-term economic benefits. To stress economic benefits may further economic concentration and create political imbalances. To stress justice for minorities may cause political divisiveness. To favor women may create a sense of injustice among males. To favor birth control may save on welfare costs, but cost the support of Roman Catholic voters or clergy. And so on.

Cost-benefit analysis (along with professional specialists) came into its own during the 1960s largely to forestall proposals and even legislation to protect the environment and the health and safety of Americans. Basically, business interests (helped by the White House under both Democratic and Republican presidents) argued that no measures should be taken that cost more than their tangible benefits to society. Since the costs of safer workplaces and a cleaner environment could be calculated and the value of human health and life and the survival of the planet could not be calculated without employing value judgments, the results were predictable: Do not impose costly burdens on business.

Cost-benefit analysis is favored by engineers, economists, and natural scientists and is found in corporations, research institutes, and the federal executive (Office of Management and Budget and the EPA). As an approach, it conforms to the cultural belief that a value-neutral science can provide answers even if they are expressed in the language of probability. Environmentalists and value-oriented social scientists reject this approach. For one thing, it puts a price tag on nature and human beings. Second, the price tag conforms to the existing class system: The lower on the class ladder you are, the less your life (or neighborhood) is worth. Cost-benefit analyses that put a monetary value on all things favor the existing distribution of wealth and power. Cost-benefit analysts, say environmentalists, know the price of everything and the value of nothing.

In 1992, a new wrinkle was given to cost-benefit analysis by the Office of Management and Budget (OMB), the president's office for monitoring federal regulations. In a memo blocking a major proposal to reduce worker exposure to contaminants, the office argued that the regulations would adversely affect workers' employment and wages, and therefore health.[46] The analysis was obviously meant to help business, but the argument was a two-way sword. The direct connection (admitted by a business-oriented administration) between employment-wages and the health of workers leaves the economy open to charges that it must be restructured to eliminate unemployment and low-wage labor. It is interesting to note that the OMB's argument was quickly abandoned.

Those who favor cost-benefit analysis also stress the ignorance of the public and its need to be educated. What their general position amounts to is that experts can be rational, but that the broad public cannot. This is a contradictory position because the same people also argue that the individual (the broad public made up of individuals) knows best how to consume, find work, invest, raise a family, and so on, and should be let alone. What is really being said, it seems, is that the broad public should not organize or support collective measures for the public good since it cannot act rationally through politics and government.[47]

Reconstructing Our Basic Indicators

The Gross Domestic Product is probably our most outmoded and harmful economic indicator. Critics have charged that it records all economic transactions without discriminating among activities that promote human well-being; enhance productivity in socially useful areas; represent waste, pollution, and other harmful costs; or deplete natural resources. And it utterly ignores unpaid household work and community service. The GDP vividly illustrates the formalism inherent in the liberal tradition of objective, value-neutral analysis, not only in economics but in all of science. Employing a disguised value judgment in favor of efficiency, economics undermines efficiency by tallying all monetary transactions regardless of their uses to the American people (felt standard of living). By relying on exchange economics instead of use economics, the GDP puts making shoes, growing food, and stitching clothing on the same plane as money spent on prisons, car accidents, preventable diseases and disabilities, divorce, and so on. In effect, the GDP endorses any and all forms of material and human capital with no questions asked. As such, the GDP is an irrational way to keep national accounts and it contaminates all areas of public policy.[48]

Reconstructing our basic economic-government-social indicators to enhance the effectiveness of public policy has already been done with a proposed new poverty index. The current poverty level is based on criteria established in the early 1960s: families (adult couple, adult couple with two children) and unrelated individuals (singles, elderly) were assumed to be poor if their cash income before taxes did not cover a minimum diet multiplied by three to cover other expenses.

A new way to measure poverty has been proposed to take into account the diversity of poor households; noncash benefits such as food stamps, health care, subsidized housing, school lunches, and energy; tax credits; regional differences in the cost of living (especially housing), child care, and other work expenses; health-care costs; and child-support payments. The new poverty index does not change the overall number of poor from the old index but it has one great advantage: it allows legislatures, governments, and others to assess the impact of various public policies on the poor.[49]

The major advantage of the new index will not appeal to those who do not want evidence that government programs work. The antipoverty program of the 1960s was abolished precisely because it worked. The Republican party sabotaged President Clinton's legislative program in 1993–94 and after their victory in 1994, it proposed eliminating one successful program after another. One of its motives was political strategy—successful government programs create supporters for the Democratic party. Another is that it justifies government intervention as a way to solve social problems, something that its business and professional supporters fear will ultimately lead to explicit economic and social planning (and thus a loss of their present freedom from public accountability). A third motive is that successful government programs run counter to the groups that are causing the problems, the main supporters of the Republican party.

All this is a reminder that improving our ability to solve social problems requires far more than a professional technical fix. The central problem is still our concentrated structure of power, or said differently, the need to get past those who are causing the problems in the first place.

Policy Science and Ethics

Professional norms and values are sometimes held in check by or come into conflict with other values and norms. The medical profession could often advance knowledge if it felt free to experiment on human beings. Law enforcement officials would have an easier job of it if they could violate the privacy of individuals, not to mention other rights.[50] Sociologists also face ethical conflicts. Research on homosexual behavior contains a classic case. Before the Gay Rights movement, most homosexuals kept their identities secret to avoid embarrassment, the law, and economic penalties. Laud Humphreys's study of impersonal sex by males in public restrooms ("tearooms") made it necessary to gain their confidence. Humphreys posed as a lookout to warn those engaged in "tearoom trade" of approaching outsiders. This made it possible to take down the license plate numbers of his subjects and eventually he interviewed a number of them at home posing as a researcher on another matter. His purpose in all this was to understand a largely hidden type of impersonal sex. One interesting finding was that a majority of males who engaged in sex with other males in public restrooms were married and many were not homosexuals. Though Humphreys was extremely careful to keep his subjects' identities secret, his research had sticky ethical implications.[51]

Ethical problems in social science take many forms. Social scientists who do research into mass communication or consumer habits may be helping power groups to convey false messages or sell faulty products. Social scientists may be unaware of the purposes of their research or insensitive to its ethical implications. A classic case concerns the participation of social scientists in furthering a foreign policy objective of the federal government: Project Camelot. In the early 1960s, the United States Army enlisted social scientists to study the causes of revolution and insurgency in developing countries with a view toward countering them. Project Camelot collapsed when its purposes were revealed. The social scientists involved merely wanted to pursue their research and seemed unaware of the ethical implications of participating in research to establish the best way to intervene militarily in other countries for political purposes.[52]

In recent years, professional associations have become more aware of problem behavior in their ranks (a sure sign that something was amiss was the growth of malpractice suits). One response by professional groups was to develop ethical codes. Ethical norms can have a significant impact on behavior and should not be dismissed out of hand. But ethical codes are also ways to prevent a critical, realistic evaluation of a profession and its members. The emergence of a formal ethical code for a profession is associated historically with a rise in its prestige, income, and its ability to restrict entry into its ranks. In addition, ethical codes are notoriously weak in their provisions for enforcement and professional groups rarely take action against deviant members.

Ethical codes also emerge or are revised when a profession experiences widespread loss of confidence. The legal profession, for example, embarked on a major revision of its professional code as a result of the Watergate and other scandals involving lawyers. Recently, sociology adopted a new code of ethics prompted largely by cases in which the rights of research subjects had been violated. Research often involves keeping subjects in the dark about the nature of the research project and informed consent by subjects is now a prominent theme in sociology's new awareness about research ethics.

But even here researchers must not lower their guard and forget the everpresent forces of power. The new ethics of informed consent protects the weak, but it also means that researchers must negotiate with the powerful before they can study them. What if the powerful refuse to be studied, or worse, give their consent, but only on their terms?[53]

SUMMARY

America's problemsolving record is poor for as far back as we have records. The fairly reliable empirical record of the past half-century tells the same story.

America's poor problemsolving record may have become qualitatively worse since the 1960s. Records show a steady decline on almost all indicators of social health. The American Dream and its visible expression as a broad, politically stabilizing and progressive middle class have both begun to fade.

A variety of efforts by professionals to solve problems reveals pervasive failure. The reason for failure goes beyond the tradition of empirical, value-neutral, objective science that all professions are based on. That tradition is itself a product of the sucesses that property groups, including the professions, have had in deflecting attention away from social structure as the cause and thus the remedy for social problems.

Contemporary society and knowledge elites exhibit considerable resistance to knowledge.

A wide variety of studies analyzing the role of professionals in problemsolving has found widespread failure and impotence when professional aims run counter to the structure of power.

The creation of knowledge is shown to be a social process determined by power. All professionals must recognize that science is fundamentally based on assumptions and that conclusions result from these assumptions. A democratic society must recognize that assumptions are derived from one's location in a system of power and that only a pluralistic power structure will yield balanced assumptions. In the final analysis, if we want the knowledge that we need to create a better society, we need to change power relations, not improve our knowledge-making process.

NOTES

1. Gabriel Kolko, *Main Currents in Modern American History* (New York: Pantheon, 1976). His argument is also found in "Intelligence and the Myth of Capitalist Rationality in the United States," *Science and Society* 44 (Summer 1980).
2. For a detailed history of this avoidance in regard to welfare spending, see Margaret Weir, Ann S. Orloff, and Theda Skopol, eds., *The Politics of Social Policy in the United States* (Princeton, N.J.: Princeton University Press, 1989).

3. Marc L. Miringoff, *The Index of Social Health, 1996* (Tarrytown, N.Y.: Fordham Institute for Innovation in Social Policy, annual). However valuable, this annual is not a full coverage of social problems. For example, it does not focus on productivity, crime by the upper classes, or the spoilation of the environment.

4. Daniel Guttman and Barry Willner, *The Shadow Government: The Government's Multi-Billion-Dollar Giveaway of Its Decision-Making Powers to Private Management Consultants, "Experts," and Think Tanks* (New York: Pantheon, 1976).

5. For our failure to research the developing world, see Kenneth Prewitt, "Social Science and the Third World," *Society* 21 (May–June 1984): 84–89. For our deficiencies in education for international competence, see the Commission on International Education, *What We Don't Know Can Hurt Us* (Washington, D.C.: American Council on Education, 1984), and Cassandra Pyle, "Our Shortfall in International Competence," *AGB Reports* (March–April, 1984).

6. For a critical analysis, see Robert H. Johnson, "Periods of Perils: The Window of Vulnerability and Other Myths," *Foreign Affairs* 61 (Spring 1983): 950–970. For a detailed analysis of Soviet world power (judged by the number of countries in the Soviet camp, their share of world population, and GNP), which concluded that it was quite small and that it had declined since its high point in 1958, despite the claims by conservatives and many liberals, see Center for Defense Information, "Soviet Geopolitical Momentum: Myth or Menace?" *Defense Monitor* 15, no. 5 (1986).

7. For a penetrating analysis, see James Fallows, *National Defense* (New York: Vintage, 1981).

8. For an analysis from a right-liberal perspective, see Edward N. Luttwak, *The Pentagon and the Art of War* (New York: Simon and Schuster, 1984).

9. It could well be that career professionals in the State Department and in other intelligence services have performed well, but that the elected "owners" of these bureaucracies have disregarded their reports and have pursued poor policies on their own. Testimony to this effect was given in 1991 during the Senate hearings on the nomination of a new CIA director.

10. David Dickson, *The New Politics of Science* (New York: Pantheon, 1984).

11. *Chronicle of Higher Education*, June 14, 1996, p. A13.

12. *New York Times*, May 23, 1996, p.1.

13. Barbara Garson, *The Electronic Sweatshop: How Computers are Transforming the Office of the Future into the Factory of the Past* (New York: Simon and Schuster, 1988).

14. Douglas H. Harris, ed., *Organizational Linkages: Understanding the Productivity Paradox* (Washington, D.C.: National Academy Press, 1994).

15. David M. Gordon, Richard Edwards, and Michael Reich, *Segmented Work, Divided Workers: The Historical Transformation of Labor in the United States* (New York: Cambridge University Press, 1982).

16. One revealing outcome of unemployment among professionals is that (at least in one case) they are not politicized by it. For the apathy among the large numbers of engineers and computer specialists laid off by companies on Massachusetts's famous Route 128 in the severe economic slowdown of the 1970s, see Paula Goldman Leventman, *Professionals Out of Work* (New York: Free Press, 1981), chap. 9.

17. Arthur H. Miller, "The Institutional Focus of Political Distrust" (paper delivered at the annual meeting of the American Political Science Association, 1979), p. 46.

18. For a comprehensive review of the many polls tapping public confidence, and an analysis of the relation between declining confidence and the legitimacy of American society, see Seymour Martin Lipset and William Schneider, *The Confidence Gap: Business, Labor, and Government in the Public Mind* (New York: Free Press, 1983).

19. Michael Oreskes, "Alienation from Government Grows, Poll Shows," *New York Times*, September 19, 1990, p. A26. The same lack of interest and distrust of government appears regularly in polls of college students.

20. U.S. Bureau of the Census, *Statistical Abstract of the United States: 1995* (Washington, D.C.: U.S. Government Printing Office 1995), Table 457.

21. As reported by Elliott Currie, "Fighting Crime," *Working Papers* 9 (July–August 1982): 22.

22. Robert D. Putnam, "Tuning In, Tuning Out: The Strange Disappearance of Social Capital in America," *PS: Political Science and Politics* 28, no. 24 (December 1995): 664–683. For an abbreviated version, see *American Prospect*, no 24 (Winter 1996), or the Internet, http://epn.org/prospect/24/24putn.html.

23. John D. McCarthy and Mayer N. Zald, *The Trend of Social Movements in America: Professionalization and Resource Mobilization* (Morristown, N.J.: General Learning Press, 1973); Anthony Oberschall, *Social Conflict and Social Movements* (Englewood Cliffs, N.J.: Prentice-Hall, 1973); and William A. Gamson, *The Strategy of Social Protest* (Homewood, Ill.: Dorsey Press, 1975). For a wide variety of essays within the general framework of resource-mobilization theory, including a reprint of the McCarthy and Zald essay, see Mayer N. Zald and John D. McCarthy, eds., *Social Movements in an Organizational Society* (New Brunswick, N.J.: Transaction, 1987).

24. William Sims Bainbridge, *The Space-Flight Revolution* (New York: Wiley, 1976).

25. Rob Cling and Surname Iacono, "The Mobilization of Support for Computerization: The Role of Computerization Movements," *Social Problems* 35 (June 1988): 225–243.

26. Martha S. Feldman, *Order Without Design: Information Production and Policy Making* (Stanford, Calif.: Stanford University Press, 1989).

27. The following is based on Melvin M. Weber, "The BART Experience: What Have We Learned?" *Public Interest*, no. 45 (Fall, 1976): 79–108, and Robert M. Anderson, Robert Perrucci, Dan E. Schendel, and Leon E. Trachtman, *Divided Loyalties: Whistle-blowing at BART* (West Lafayette, Ind.: Purdue University Research Foundation, 1980).

28. The sociology of art owes much to Pitirim Sorokin, *Social and Cultural Dynamics*, 4 vols. (New York: American Book Co., 1937–41); rev. and abr., 1 vol. (Boston: Porter Sargent, 1957). For a full-scale Marxist analysis of the sociology of art, see Arnold Hauser, *The Social History of Art* (London: Routledge & Kegan Paul, 1951), 2 vols.

29. Joel F. Handler, *Social Movements and the Legal System: A Theory of Law Reform and Social Change* (New York: Academic Press, 1978).

30. Gerald N. Rosenberg, *The Hollow Hope: Can Courts Bring About Social Change?* (Chicago: University of Chicago Press, 1991).

31. Richard Delgado and Jean Stephancic, *Failed Revolutions: Social Reform and the Limits of Legal Imagination* (Boulder, Colo.: Westview Press, 1994).

32. Lily N. Hoffman, *The Politics of Knowledge: Activist Movements in Planning and Medicine* (Albany: State University of New York Press, 1989).

33. For a valuable discussion and the following ERT case study, see James C. Petersen and Gerald E. Markle, "Controversies in Science and Technology," in Daryl E. Chubin and Ellen W. Chu, eds., *Science Off the Pedestal* (Belmont, Calif.: Wadsworth, 1989), chap. 1.

34. For a related discussion, see "Failure to Perform: The Deviance of Unnecessary Incompetence" in Chapter 9.

35. David Mechanic, "Sociological Critics versus Institutional Elites in the Politics of Research Application: Examples from Medical Care," in N. J. Demerath et al., *Social Policy and Sociology* (New York: Academic Press, 1975), pp. 99–108.

36. Michael Useem, *The Inner Circle: Large Corporations and the Rise of Business Political Activity in the U.S. and U.K.* (New York: Oxford University Press, 1984), and Kees Van der Pijl, *The Making of an Atlantic Ruling Class* (London: Verso, 1984).

37. Paul Burstein, "Policy Domains: Organization, Culture, and Policy Outcomes," *Annual Review of Sociology* 17 (1991): 327–350.

38. For a fascinating set of essays on the history of public data-gathering and current trends and problems, see William Alonso and Paul Starr, eds., *The Politics of Numbers* (New York: Russell Sage, 1987).

39. Secrecy in the federal executive has been reduced somewhat thanks to the Freedom of Information Act of 1966, amended in 1974. The federal legislature and judiciary and state and local governments still conduct their affairs with considerable secrecy, most of it with little functional justification.

40. Companies often get court orders to keep records on product safety (which are available to plaintiffs suing them for defective products) secret from both the government agency responsible for safety and the general public.

41. Diane Vaughan, *Controlling Unlawful Organizational Behavior: Social Structure and Corporate Misconduct* (Chicago: University of Chicago Press, 1983).

42. *New York Times*, March 1, 1980, p. 20.

43. Susan B. Hansen, "Elite Informants and Theoretical Guidance in Policy," in Edward Bryan Portis and Michael B. Levy, *Handbook of Political Theory and Policy Science* (New York: Greenwood, 1988), chap. 13.

44. For a classic analysis of how sociologists and political scientists arrive at different conclusions about the nature of community power because of their methods, see John Walton, "Discipline, Method, and Community Power: A Note on the Sociology of Knowledge," *American Sociological Review* 31 (October 1966): 684–689.

45. Robert E. Davidson, "Professional Conflicts Within Organizations," *Sociology and Social Research* 69 (January 1985): 210–220.

46. *New York Times*, March 16, 1992, p. A13.

47. For a criticism of risk assessment professionals in an overall study showing how the sociology of risk should be conducted, see Charles Perrow, *Normal Accidents: Living with High-Risk Technologies* (New York: Basic Books, 1984), chap. 9. For an argument stressing the importance of theory in fact collection (and thus the need for conceptual pluralism) and criticizing rational-choice theory, see Lawrence A. Scoff and Helena M. Ingram, "The Influence of Theory on What We See," and for a critique of cost-benefit analysis showing that its adoption by the White House favored business over the health and safety of Americans, see Susan J. Tolchin, "The Political Uses of Evaluation Research: Cost-Benefit Analysis and the Cotton Dust Standard," both in Dennis J. Palumbo, ed., *The Politics of Program Evaluation* (Newbury Park, Calif.: Sage, 1987), pp. 235–248, 249–269. For an analysis of the age, sex, race, education, and organizational affiliation of risk professionals in relation to theoretical outlook, see Thomas Dietz and Robert W. Rycroft, *The Risk Professionals* (New York: Russell Sage, 1987).

48. Clifford Cobb, Ted Halstead, and Jonathan Rowe, "If the GDP is Up, Why Is America Down?" *Atlantic Monthly*, 276, no. 4 (October 1995): 59–78.

49. Constance F. Citro and Robert T. Michael, eds., *Measuring Poverty: A New Approach* (Washington, D.C.: National Academy Press, 1995).

50. Needless to say, there is a considerable amount of secret and/or illegal medical/drug experimentation on human beings and a considerable amount of illegal invasion of privacy by both public and private power groups.

51. Laud Humphreys, *Tearoom Trade: Impersonal Sex in Public Places* (Chicago: Aldine, 1970). Humphreys discusses the ethics of his research in a 1975 edition of his work.

52. For a background on Project Camelot, see Irving Louis Horowitz and James Everett Katz, *Social Science and Public Policy in the United States* (New York: Praeger, 1975), chap. 6.
53. For this insight, see Robert S. Broadhead and Ray C. Rist, "Why Social Science Discovered Morality," *Social Policy* 9 (May–June, 1978): 36–40.

12
Harnessing the Professions and Disciplines to Social Functions

◆ ◆ ◆ ◆

◆ ◆ ◆ ◆

THE IDEAL OF AN ADAPTIVE SOCIETY

An adaptive or functional society is a problemsolving entity, not a problem-free utopia. The members of a functional society can feed themselves, reproduce and socialize new and old members, settle disputes, and adjust to new conditions. Adaptive power groups are those that can develop the motives, ideas, and skills needed for replenishing, sustaining, and adapting a given way of life to both old and new circumstances. A functional society has legitimacy which means that people take it on faith that power groups deserve their power. Hierarchy, laws, taxes, unequal wealth and income, discipline, high standards, and competition are not suspect because ordinary citizens see direct and beneficial consequences flowing from them. Setbacks and failures are not resented because they appear to occur in a *just* society. A functional society has statuses and norms which, by and large, produce intended and desired results. The adaptive society is an ideal, but it is not beyond reach—to repeat, it is problemsolving rather than utopian.

What is it that yields an adaptive society? Mainstream American social theorists and social scientists assume that the development of science, technology, professionalism, and liberal institutions, especially the market economy, political markets (elections, lobbying), and educational markets, guarantee a progressive (adaptive) society. The record of the past three decades casts serious doubts on all aspects of this axial assumption.

THE SEPARATION OF ELITES AND PROFESSIONS FROM SOCIAL FUNCTIONS

Americans are wrong to be puzzled about why their problems are not being solved. The answer is fairly simple. The United States has gone further than any other capitalist society in divorcing its productive property and its professions from performing social functions. Because of our broad and false consensus about the nature of property and professional practice, few can really see what has happened. The major reason for recessions, periods of inflation, family problems, crime, unemployment and underemployment, urban decay, productivity decline, and an ineffectual foreign policy is the highly concentrated and self-oriented economic-professional world.

The major power relation (institutional and group structure) that makes up American society is the autonomy of property (including human capital) from accountability. Americans have been led to believe that market forces and open competition determine the hierarchy of wealth and income. This is not true of wealth and not true of the incomes of professionals. The American upper classes, by and large, have the power to determine their own incomes and to enhance and protect their wealth. In turn, the high incomes they give themselves (leading to the largest gap, by far, between their incomes and ordinary people in the capitalist world) allows them to live apart and keeps them ignorant of how ordinary people live. Perhaps more important is the fact that their separation from ordinary people means that they do not experience the full negative consequences of the decisions they make about the running of America, especially their decisions about the generation and uses of material and human capital.

We Americans are problem-oriented, but our approach to problems protects the status quo and creates as many problems as it solves. We tend to individualize the cause of problems; instead of evaluating the medical profession, for example, we initiate malpractice suits. The mythology of doctor-patient relation hides the service-for-fee profit system undergirding medicine. When the cost of American medicine outstripped the number of customers who could afford it, we never got a chance to discuss the best way to deliver health care. We foolishly allowed health care to be defined by collective bargaining, which means that the unemployed and many of the employed have to do without health-care insurance. We blundered through piece-meal reform into financing medicine indirectly through taxes, Medicare, Medicaid, and private insurance, including Blue Cross-Blue Shield, thus ensuring plenty of money for private-profit health care with few questions asked about it and even less evaluation and accountability. Incidentally, does our productivity index capture the fact that doctors (a minority of them) are performing over one million unnecessary operations every year, or the fact that doctors (again a minority) are stealing more from the public than all the muggers, burglars, and stickup-persons in the country put together?

In all areas of behavior we have an elaborate system that blames victims and individual evildoers, but rarely the real cause, the organized groups that dominate particular areas. When we focus on problemsolvers, our characteristic focus is on heroes (profiles in courage, Nobel Laureates, whistleblowers) and empty abstractions (excellence, the gold standard, balance the budget, non-partisanship, voluntarism). The closest we get to real causes is when we complain about unrepresentative and thus unresponsive policy-making bodies: Congress, labor unions, the Supreme Court, the United Way, colleges, professional boards, foundations, and of course, corporations. *But few see the absence of broad public participation in decisionmaking as a system-wide pattern and few can relate apathy and alienation to the oligarchic nature of our economic, social, and political life.*

The failure of our various elites has led to a significant and steady decline of popular trust in political leaders and the professions, a decline that threatens the legitimacy of institutions.[1] The failure is evident in the political stalemate that prevents the United States from generating majority coalitions with a mandate to govern. Our failure to develop a well-structured economy has generated an insecure, alienated, and depoliticized citizenry that is easy prey for demogogues. That same citizenry, with the help of lawyers, vents its experience with professional failure in malpractice and liability lawsuits.

The failure of our knowledge elites is also apparent. Economists have failed to develop practical theories to help citizens and the government deal with the economy. Political scientists have yet to learn that political institutions do not have much independent impact on society (the same is true of education, public and private). Textbooks seem not to promote learning, while biased and incomplete high school history texts (which characterizes all of them) have probably done much harm. Government cannot generate useful data on crime, energy, unemployment, inflation, and productivity.[2] Economists and sociologists have done poorly in forecasting social and economic developments, the CIA misses revolutions under its nose. It may be no exaggeration to say that because of our knowledge elites we don't know where we've been, where we are, or where we're going.

Failure is far more pervasive than we are aware because elites have ready excuses for their inadequacies—who can tell if they are really saving souls, removing a dangerous uterus, formulating a good system of taxes, developing a sound energy or foreign policy, and so on. When you think of it, we do not value our elites because of what they know or can do. People who know how to do something predictably, like making a shoe, cutting hair, teaching elementary school, or delivering a letter are looked down on. We value elites because they claim they know how to deal with our collective ignorance and fears. Elites have a great stake in keeping the world unpredictable and dangerous. They have a lot to lose if peace breaks out, if health care or education become routinely available, if personal identities are easily formed, if meaningful jobs are plentiful, and so on. Is this why research results are so little used? A leading sociologist estimates that no more than 5 percent of the data reported in sociology journals treats variables that policymakers would ever dream of changing. Seen from this perspective, scientific research is a way of indefinitely postponing the application of science to our problems.

Elite failure is also difficult to identify because elites define problems and give us what they claim is the only path to follow. In effect, the professionalization of problemsolving closes the door on alternatives and leaves us with no outside standards by which to judge elites. The crash program on cancer research, from the early 1970s on, for example, has been a relative failure (large amounts of money have been wasted and stolen, basic research has been distorted) and yet the full magnitude of failure could not be assessed because as a people we did not decide between genuine alternatives and therefore could not imagine what would have happened had the unneeded cancer research money been put into known ways of *preventing* cancer. Incidentally, the crash program of cancer research is instructive on another account—it illustrates how elites cooperate to solve their problems while failing to solve the public's. Rich people supported a tax-supported cancer-research program because private wealth was not up to the job (and no amount of money could buy the rich a cancer cure). The American Cancer Society, Sloan-Kettering and other medical centers, and government agencies all had many motives for medicalizing cancer, not least because it diverted attention from the interests (their own included) threatened by cancer prevention: dairy farming, tobacco growers and manufacturers, food processors, polluting corporations, and nuclear arms plants. And the whole idea appealed strongly to then—president Richard Nixon—what better use of billions of tax dollars than to spend them on an apple-pie-and-mom program that would help his reelection.

Our magical market is our most conspicuously incompetent problem-solver. Magic is extremely useful to elites because they get the credit if something goes right while evil spirits (communism, OPEC, terrorists, Cuba) get the blame if something goes wrong. Our economic and political elites—from corporation executives, MBAs, lawyers, accountants, foundation executives, reform groups, and strategic planners to the Federal Reserve Board, the Congress, and the president—do not really do much to attack the economic problems of the country (which are also the main source of almost all other problems) because to do so puts them in conflict with their own interests. Again and again the American people respond to polls stating that they are in favor of government action, including wage and price controls, to cure economic ills. In contrast, the Republican party and large segments of the Democratic party call for voluntary efforts, the magical market, moral effort, or local government to solve our problems.

Problemsolving in the United States is a vital and effective tradition among powerful groups as long as they are acting on their own problems. But in solving their problems they create problems for others. The movement of capital out of Cleveland or New York to cheap labor, low-cost areas such as Orlando or Seoul is an imaginative solution for those faced with rising labor costs and taxes, and a problem for stranded workers and cities. The movement of elites (and the broad middle class) into the suburbs solves their problems of getting decent housing and education, but erodes the tax base of cities, undermines communities, and reduces the forces of law and order. Computers are installed to make corporations more efficient, but do not. Instead, they enhance bureaucratic power, creating electronic sweatshops, economic concentration, and overseas investments not sanctioned by public discussion or legislation.

The upper classes solve their various health, education, travel, housing, and other problems under the general principle that if each is successful the whole will be too. This obsolete market mentality is alive and well in America and no doubt solves some problems, creates others, and aggravates still others, leaving the country dynamically the same at best. When the hustle and bustle is over, little has been done to change the fundamental process by which one group's victory is another's loss. Economic growth and a well-managed system of victimization (liberalism, racism, sexism) has hidden this process for much of American history. The decline in real wages and stagnant living standards of the past two decades, and the increase in social problems has brought a vigorous response from the Republican party. Completely ignoring the fact that only 40 percent of the electorate voted in their 1994 Congressional sweep, the fact that they received only 21 percent of that, and polls indicating that voters had never heard of their Contract with America, the Republican party inaugurated a legislative program that would cripple the federal government and put the entire burden of problem solving in private hands and our ineffective, corrupt, and totally plutocratic state and local governments. Far from noticing that the American economy (and polity) has been increasingly disconnected from the American people, that market failure is rampant, that America's state governments are under the thumb of private interests, and that our professions are largely ways to hide economic and political failure, the Republican party considers it the height of adaptive creativity to intensify our reliance on the same principles and forces that are causing all our problems.

CAPITALISM VERSUS DEMOCRACY: THE CONSERVATIVE ATTEMPT TO REVITALIZE AMERICA

The elites of complex societies in the past formulated ideologies to justify the existing order. By and large, they steered everyone, including themselves, away from the mundane causes of evil. Modern capitalist society is no different. Its professions and disciplines are part of a network of elite-mass power relations. Some disciplines and professions are more fully part of the elite and others are auxiliaries, but all are parts of an adaptive system whose ideological codes are at wide variance with its problemsolving record.

The recent slowdown in problemsolving is obscured because the outlook of American elites was deeply influenced by the spectacular economic growth from the early nineteenth to the mid-twentieth century and by the fact that economic growth increased living standards. What may have been a purely historical—that is, unique—occurrence was framed in metaphysical terms by American elites, including the various social science disciplines. Confronted with the fact of economic slowdown and living standard stagnation, and faced with popular restiveness and some radical demands during the 1960s, American elites mobilized to both quell demands from below and to revitalize American society. American business mobilized politically to curb demands for welfare spending, to undermine the power of labor, to reduce taxes, and to augment American military power to match American economic interests around the globe. The conservative backlash to popular demands and to economic troubles in the 1970s included a flourishing network of policy institutes. The most important of these groups self-consciously adopted a conflict approach, seeing the major conflict between a dynamic, rational capitalism and a meddling, wrongheaded, wasteful democracy as the major barrier to America's revitalization.[3]

The conservative backlash was split, ranging from the once liberal Brookings Institution to right-wing institutes promoting free-market, less-government policies and on to conservatives interested in using government to enforce law, order, and morality. Business interests that looked on government and reform as ways to stabilize and harmonize both the economy and society (corporate liberalism) went into abeyance.

The conservative backlash found (created?) a ready agent in the Reagan–Bush administration (1980–92). But after getting a great deal of what they wanted, conservatives succeeded only in producing huge debt, underinvestment in private and public facilities, and yawning trade and domestic deficits. Not only were their basic ideas (less government in the economy is good, more government in morality is good) proven wrong, but they undermined the public's faith in government even further by causing the worst corruption in American history.[4] What America needs, and what the public consistently asks for is *good*, not less, government, one that directly tackles and solves problems. Conservative Republicans (and this includes many Democrats) are not interested in good government because that would raise serious questions about the nature of American-style capitalism and its relation to our present political system.

The conservative attempt during the 1980s to revitalize the American economy through across-the-board tax cuts and other aids to the upper classes failed. The parallel attempt to revitalize the American people through moral exhortation and the discipline of self-reliance and competition also failed. The formalisms, across-the-board tax cuts, and fewer public services (for the public) are favored by conservatives because they allow the concrete use of government for their own purposes while making it possible for them to deny that government and politics are useful. Across-the-board tax cuts undercut the use of targeted tax cuts—the latter can be evaluated more readily than abstract cuts and would provide experience and knowledge in directing the economy. Across-the-board tax cuts also make it possible to obscure the fact that such cuts invariably favor the upper classes while making it appear that all income-wealth classes are being treated the same. Fewer public services for the public, while stressing American principles of self-reliance and personal responsibility, hide the fact that most public services (the ones that continue) favor the upper classes.

Supply-side Keynesianism and explicit reliance on markets to solve problems from 1980 to 1992 can be considered a full-length experiment with fairly conclusive results: The abstract reliance on markets by right liberalism does not work. Indeed, the consequences were negative: the rich got richer and everybody got poorer, crime of all kinds, especially by the upper classes soared, and the American people became anxiety-ridden and fearful. The most significant result of the 1980s was not the breakdown of Soviet-style socialism, but the bankruptcy of American-style liberalism.

By early 1992, as the recession that began in 1989 continued, it was clear that both right and left liberals (Republicans and Democrats) were still thinking in terms of stimulating an unproblematic economy. Few voices were saying the obvious: The long-term slump in American productivity was the real problem and could not be solved with ad hoc stimulation (for example, lower interest rates or tax cuts). Decades of mismanaged and unsolved problems were contributing to the growing social overhead and were having a cumulative negative effect. One clue to all this was that consumer confidence was far lower than objective conditions warranted. The main reason was that large portions of the population was unemployed, had experienced unemployment, were insecure in their jobs, and/or did not have enough money to meet their bills easily. In addition, it was clear that the Republican party advocated doing nothing and that the Democratic party was advocating band-aids for a running sore. The grand laissez-faire experiment of 1980 to 1992 made it abundantly clear that individual competition is destructive, and that rampant self-interest undermines the institutions that can make moderate self-interest socially useful. It also became clear that relying on trust instead of building it, and relying on voluntary solutions instead of political solutions openly arrived at breeds free riders, crime, and cynicism.

The failure of the conservative experiment of the 1980s means abandoning the fiction that a rational economy exists somewhere by nature, a rational economy devoid of contradictions and compromises, that is, devoid of value judgments and politics. Business interests and the Reagan–Bush administration established an approximate version of this "rational" or laissez-faire economy during the 1980s. They disciplined labor with unemployment (resulting in low plant capacity utilization); they kept interest rates high, making the dollar strong and imports cheap; and they reduced taxes on business, all of which led to a higher rate of profit *share* (profits divided by total output). But they failed to increase that which is of most interest to capitalists, the profit *rate* (profits divided by capital investment). The use of unemployment (and other anti-labor actions) devastated the American labor force, but it also led to low plant utilization and thus a low profit *rate*. High interest rates kept the dollar high (as foreigners rushed in to lend us money); this succeeded in keeping imports cheap, further lowering business costs. But high interest rates inhibited capital investment as did idle plant capacity. The result was a continuing slump in productivity. And there was no reversal of the stagnation and even decline in living standards that had begun in the early 1970s. Ironically, even the "winners" did not win because they failed to improve the profit rate.[5]

Laissez-faire economics had failed many times before the 1980s, but failure had been masked, or excused, by the upward trend in living standards. By establishing an approximate version of a "rational" or market economy (and society), the Reagan-Bush administration from 1980 to 1992 became a vast social experiment. Because it failed to raise living standards (leading to massive debt and an anxiety-ridden populace), failed to increase productivity, and failed even to raise the profit rate (income on capital stock), even right-liberals should be persuaded that a rational market economy and society is fiction. The right kind of economy can only be one that results from trade-offs in basic values made by a democratically organized people.

Both conservatives and radicals are right—there is a deep conflict between capitalism and democracy. Insurgent professionals in many areas have sensed this and have mounted political protests of various kinds. But most professionals have avoided their political responsibilities by adopting a value-neutral stance about their work and swallowing dubious propositions about the value of abstract knowledge and technology. This occurs even when professionals operate in the field of public-policy analysis. Herbert Stein, an influential mainstream economist and adviser to presidents, epitomizes this stance. Stein argues that economics is a search for the timeless and placeless and that the advice that it can give to public policymakers consists of a few elementary concepts and prepositions that can be found in any introductory economics course.[6] He then goes on to say many sensible things about the role of an economics adviser, especially the need to know how government works, how policy advice will impact on the fortunes of elected officials, how to communicate effectively with lay audiences, and, above all, the need for empathy, objectivity, and judgment in developing the options paper, the choices available to decision makers, including arguments that the adviser does not agree with. Stein does not realize that what he is saying is that economics as such has very little to say about the economy and that the real action lies not in being an economist, but a political economist—better still, a sociopolitical actor conscious of the value choices being made. The real action lies in interpreting the significance for the economy of new or unique historical factors. By maintaining a false distinction between economist and adviser, Stein was misdirecting the president, Congress, and the public. During the Bush administration, economic advisers Dorman and Boskin should have stated publicly that public-policy options had shrunk because previous policies derived from empty economic principles had led to declining productivity, debt, deficits, and an angry electorate. Instead they relied on more empty economic principles to advise the president that he ought to do nothing about a relatively severe recession (1989–92).

ENHANCING ADAPTIVE CAPACITY

The Problematic Society

The emergence of capitalism led to a new way of defining human beings, society, and nature: as abstract, unfixed, interchangeable forces and processes. The emergence of "possessive individualism" (humans own themselves and have the right to mix their labor with nature or to sell their labor) in the thought of Hobbes and Locke[7] completed the capitalist symbolic world. A dynamic, ever more complex private economy needs to escape from the static and diffused demands of morality and custom. It needs a nature that can be transformed and recombined in whatever way science and technology make possible. It needs, above all, a labor force composed, not of slaves, serfs, or families, but of interchangeable, easily bought, moved, or discarded individuals. Thus the general thrust of the impersonal, abstract economy leads directly to the abstract natural and social sciences, and ultimately to a deadening formalism, the image of a self-equilibrating society fueled by the uncoordinated input of specialized researchers and practitioners dealing with artificially defined phenomena and problems.

The problem with science and the professions is not a matter of epistemology or education. Their problem is caused by the problematic nature of modern capitalism (and in a wider sense, modern industrialism, since the socialist societies have done no better in managing their affairs). The problematic nature of modern society simply means that nothing about human behavior or institutions is a given, and therefore, there can be no such thing as data. It means that liberals, Marxists, minority theorists, and postmodernists have acknowledged in varying degree that society is a constructed reality. It means that the complexity and dynamism of society can be captured only by an interpretive science not wed to any set of assumptions. It means that all issues and problems must be politicized, put in a sociohistorical context, and solved on the basis of political decisions (beliefs plus values).

There is a new realism afoot in social science. Even mainstream social scientists are beginning to recognize that social science has not had much success in nourishing or guiding public policy.[8] In a refreshingly candid analysis, Eva Etzioni-Halevy has argued that modern knowledge elites (for example, economists) have had no success in translating their knowledge into prophecy (useful predictions or forecasts with which to make public policy).[9] The United States appears to have a hegemonic culture, which like all cultures is profoundly antipolitical. Breaking the hold of this culture requires an image of a problem society, not a society with problems. Far from being problemsolvers, the professions are busy solving elite problems, including their own and their solutions become the problems of the masses (for example, they solve the problem of inflation by slowing down the economy thus causing unemployment and bankruptcy, they maintain high, irrelevant academic standards to control labor flows into the professions causing widespread student failure and dropping out).

In analyzing society as the problem, it is important to distinguish between better policies with which to address problems, and policies designed to improve adaptive capabilities (our main focus has been and remains on the latter). The main barriers to better adaptation and problemsolving are the elites themselves, the institutions they create, and the metaphysical ideologies they concoct to justify their respective interests and the social system that promotes them.

Changing America's Power Relations

The most important way to make the upper classes creative is to reduce their power. The central reason why America does not work as it is supposed to is that wealth is highly concentrated and decisions about how to use material and human resources are made by a small number of unaccountable individuals and groups. The most important way to get society organized for better problemsolving is for an organized public to have far more to say about the basic investment process. No other reform can do much good unless investment decisions are democraticized.

The professions emerged in the nineteenth century in the heyday of small-scale economic units oriented toward local markets. Not surprisingly, the professions thought of themselves as entrepreneurs (self-employed, solo practitioners). As late as 1960, half of our Managers and Administrators (the Census Bureau's inadequate category for professionals) were self-employed. By the late 1970s, that figure had dropped to below 20 percent. The ranks of lower and upper white-collar employee ranks have continued to grow (due to the shift to a service economy and to the internationalization of the American economy), but the most important new thing about professionals is that they have become employees. Far more attention must be paid to the conditions of work and the restraints imposed on professionals by the hierarchies they work for. And professionals must become aware of the role they play in the structure of power, not only in individual hierarchies, but in the overall network that connects the apexes of all hierarchies.[10]

Instead of an unthinking acceptance of the goals set by those who own or control the organizations they work for, professionals must become more policy-conscious. Should professionals continue merely to provide technically framed knowledge about their areas of expertise to hospital boards, publishers, governing boards, the Secretary of State, CIA director, and so on through the rest of government, the voluntary sector, and the basic corporate economy? Does it make any sense to allow our most educated people to be coopted by the fiction that the most important things about society (private property, capital investment, representative government, law, education, and science) are nonpolitical?

Improving Our Policymaking Institutions and Groups

Directed change or planning requires knowledge about how society works, thus our earlier call for a reconstruction of our economic and social indicators. But knowledge is acquired and used by social groups. People must do the planning, but people see the world from their location in groups. Above all, directed change and better policymaking means structuring groups so that they can function better. The major change needed is to put less faith in nonexistent market mechanisms. Basic decisions about the economy must be made by a public organized for that purpose. The second major change is to improve our political institutions, especially by freeing them from the power of private money and eliminating the practice of gerrymandering (or creating noncompetitive, homogeneous electoral districts). The third is to transform education to emphasize applied knowledge from kindergarten on with a view toward improving our professions, occupations, and above all, the competence of ordinary citizens. And all reform must be guided by the overriding principle that policy groups are effective only if they have heterogeneous memberships and are operating in a genuinely pluralistic system of power.

Avoiding "groupthink" is crucial for better policymaking.[11] We need to do more than educate professionals (and citizens) to look at (create) facts using different assumptions (especially important in the development of economic, government, and social indicators). To rely on that alone is to rely on the rational-choice, individual responsibility approach. We need to reform institutions to guarantee that a healthy *pluralism of assumptions* is present in all policy groups.[12] We need to rotate the membership of policy groups to make it possible for citizens to aquire policy experience, to provide policy makers with a wide variety of experience, and to make sure that groups are invigorated by new members.

Paul Sabatier has suggested that policy-oriented mutual learning will occur if advocacy coalitions are required to participate in a professionally run forum. Such fora will force professionals to examine fundamentals, weed out weak data, and eliminate improbable causal assertions. Recognizing that the professional personality has a deep core of fundamental norms and values, Sabatier acknowledges that most learning will occur outside this core in the areas of primary and secondary beliefs about policy issues. Mutual learning by professionals, he argues, is especially likely about issues involving natural as opposed to social systems, and if good quantitative indicators are available.[13]

Perhaps above all, policymaking must be comparative. In turn, comparative policy analysis must be grounded in a macro analysis of significant sociopolitical units (nation states). It must be aware of historical differences in development among the several capitalist (and socialist) systems. It must be aware that similar outcomes can emerge from different policies. It must delve into the purposes of policies and not rely merely on abstract quantitative data since most of it is supplied by governments that lack motivation to report failure. It must take due note of the importance of external factors on a nation's life (the international economy and polity). Implied in all of the above is that it must be focused on social power.[14]

Understanding the Service Economy

The rise of the service economy has not been acknowledged in political life, has not been adequately depicted in social science, and has not been properly related to inflation, productivity, unemployment, and other social problems. The failure to understand it is also part of why professionalism is not understood. The white-collar service economy has been referred to as a split between property (allegedly greedy and self-oriented) and management (allegedly educated, enlightened, and public minded). Not true. Others have struck a similar theme by citing the growth of highly educated managers and professionals presiding over a knowledge-based economy and society as evidence of a postindustrial society (also not true). Others misrepresent the service economy (using misleading census categories) by seeing it as the elimination of physical and mental drudgery and the dawn of a new era of challenging, professionalized work—the information society (also not true).[15]

What is a service economy? What is it in the context of the basic structure of the American economy? The most important feature of the American economy is high concentration (oligarchic competition) in basic sectors. Our service economy still means a bureaucratized society made up largely of lower-level employees across the private and public sectors. It is an economy with a large number of women in the pink ghetto of waitressing, hairdressing, retailing, entertainment, hostessing, billing, and typing. It is an economy that has upwards of 500,000 prostitutes (part of the huge underground economy not captured in official statistics). It is an economy that employs large numbers in advertising, work that requires considerable skill because the products to be sold are largely identical and often either useless or harmful. It is an economy in which corporations spend huge sums to polish their images and hide their mistakes, thus public relations experts thrive. The service economy includes the large number that produce assorted entertainment through sports. What is the overhead on our national life of supporting professional sports with their entourages, sports palaces, and endless criss-crossing of the country burning up jet fuel? Should some of the resources devoted to professional sports, which includes varsity college sports, be devoted to providing sports for our flabby masses?

The service economy refers to the large number of educational personnel from kindergarten to elite universities who do not produce better citizens or workers (see Chapter 3). The large numbers of students supported in higher education, plus the buildings, fuel bills, and faculty and staff salaries, are a huge drain on the national economy (and a large subsidy to the upper classes). The United States has far more college graduates in supervisory, middle-level support positions throughout the economy, government, and military than other capitalist societies with no increase in production, merely a large increase in overhead cost. What college students learn in college can only be imagined; for example, a sizeable majority of white college graduates of both sexes has consistently voted in recent presidential elections for the candidate who says the least.

The service economy includes accountants whose standards are arbitrary and who endorse annual statements by businesses that do not give accurate pictures of assets and debt. The belief that double-entry bookkeeping ushered in capitalist rationality is a myth: accounting is largely a legitimating device for the capitalist economy, something to bolster confidence (whether deserved or not), not a basis for making economic decisions.[16] Incidentally, arbitrary and deceptive accounting practices throughout the American economy link up with misleading government/social science indicators, and misleading government budget practices to prevent the American people, including its leaders from knowing where they've been, where they are, and where they're going.

The service economy includes wasteful practices in our medical establishment—for example, the American open-staff hospital. Unlike European closed-staff hospitals, which rely on salaried doctors, American doctors do not actually work for hospitals. American doctors use hospital technology and services as private-profit entrepreneurs to exact profit through their medical skills under a series of no-questions-asked, largely publicly financed insurance schemes. This leads to large amounts of hospital committee work to cover up or patch up gaps in service. It leads to the huge staffs needed to process the unnecessary paperwork generated by our cottage-industry medical establishment, much of it in error because few can really understand it or keep track of it (one audit found that 100 percent of hospital bills contained errors though the overall average is a 90 percent error rate).

The service economy includes social workers, police officers, district attorneys, probation officers, prison guards, public defenders, and clerks dispensing unemployment checks, all of whom repair the ravages of an economy out of public control. The service economy includes lawyers, over-worked at elite levels, handling the mountain of litigation that comes from poorly written laws, competition-stifling mergers, and from fighting for or against government regulation. Underworked lower-level lawyers hang on tenaciously to title work, simple wills, and accident cases, most of which could be handled by high-school graduates or by citizens themselves.

The service economy means luxury hotels, gourmet food for poodles, demolition derbies, restaurants that could not exist without expense ac-counts, bookies, blackjack dealers, and reshaped noses and buttocks. Ser-vices include firms that specialize in union busting and the $35,000 a year it costs to imprison a youth offender and the $45,000 it costs for adult offend-ers. Services include the six and seven figure incomes of arbitragers and the incomes of unneeded professors.

The shift to a service economy has made it difficult to measure many economic outputs; it is easier to measure toasters and radios than straight teeth and entertainment pleasures. It is also difficult to measure the value of white-collar inputs such as sales, promotion, marketing, and conferences. Nevertheless, we do know that the productivity growth of the American ser-vice economy has lagged behind Europe and Japan. The reason is simple: We have employed more labor because our wage costs have declined as labor supply has swelled.[17] And long before we understand it, the spectacular growth of the service economy will begin to reverse itself in favor of manu-facturing. And we will not be ready for that change because our understand-ing of manufacturing is as poor as our understanding of the service sector.

Perhaps the easiest way to understand the service sector is to remem-ber to include teachers and professors, the academic disciplines, and theo-retical and applied professionals, all with highly deficient records in solving social problems. Included among our ineffective service occupations are policy professionals who provide technical analyses of problems abstracted from the sociohistorical context that is causing them.

POLITICIZING THE PROFESSIONS AND DISCIPLINES

Power, or One Actor's Solution Can Be Another's Problem

The concept of social power is central to understanding and solving social problems. Let us imagine that society is the result of millions of social actors (individuals and groups) seeking solutions to problems. Sometimes the actions that people take will be good for everybody. At other times, ac-tions taken to solve problems will cause satisfaction for some and grief for others. Your neighbor's dog keeps coming into your garden; you solve the problem by putting up a fence, which your neighbor objects to. A young woman has an unwanted pregnancy; she solves her problem by having an abortion, but this is seen as a problem by right-to-life groups. A labor force larger than the number of available jobs constitutes a problem for those who are unemployed, but the same condition is a *solution* for property owners who must hire labor. Arson is a problem for tenants, but a solution for hard-pressed landlords. Insight into how various power groups benefit from social problems and how social groups experience and perceive problems differently according to class, economic interest, gender, age, race, and ethnicity is fundamental to orienting both citizens and professionals toward the real nature of social problems.

The economic recession of 1980–82 is a case in point. At one time, people believed that recessions and depressions were caused by natural economic laws. Today, we may not understand economic downturns completely, but we do know that they are caused by power groups, not impersonal economic laws. The reasons for the deep recession of 1980–82 are fairly simple to uncover. Presidents Carter and Reagan, Congress, and most of the influential leaders of the private world agreed that the economy had to be slowed down in order to fight serious inflation. The method they used was fairly primitive: The federal government (through the Federal Reserve Board) raised interest rates to make it difficult for consumers to buy and business people to invest. The result was predictable—unemployment for millions of Americans and bankruptcies for tens of thousands of small business people and farmers. One set of power groups enacted a solution (they lowered demand and thus eased price pressures on supplies) that caused problems for other social groups. Here is power in its most dramatic and revealing form. Presidents Carter and Reagan, the Federal Reserve Board, Congress, and the leaders of the corporate world did not ask the American people if they wanted to fight inflation with bankruptcy and unemployment. The American people might have suggested other ways to curb inflation—for example, by raising taxes, cutting defense spending, or eliminating tax-subsidized meals and entertainment for business executives. But powerful groups imposed their solution, claiming it was in the best interest of the country. And it worked: the inflation rate of 13 percent dropped to 4 percent by 1984. But their solution, while benefiting many besides themselves, was at the expense of those who lost their jobs, farms, and businesses.

Power groups do not relish having their behavior or policies examined. They work hard to create the impression that their solutions are good for all. By examining power relations, knowledge elites are often at odds with the holders of power. By scrutinizing the habits and myths established by power groups to justify their actions, knowledge elites can explain why things do not work, or why some prosper while others suffer. By understanding power, they generate in us what C. Wright Mills called the *sociological imagination*: the ability to link our personal problems to the solutions imposed on us by others. By understanding power, a people identifies the social forces that control opportunities, shape experiences, and restrict choices.

Contemporary social science is a powerful dispeller of false beliefs. Its insights reveal a social world far removed from conventional beliefs. Even a short list of what it knows makes it clear that many conventional beliefs need to be discarded or revised:

1. Economies are not governed by laws such as those found in nature.
2. The welfare state does not distribute wealth downward, but more resembles socialism for the well-to-do and capitalism for the lower classes.
3. Formal education seems to have very little independent influence on students' beliefs and values, or on their behavior after leaving school.
4. Women do not behave as they do because of their anatomy or hormones.
5. Older people do not lose interest in sex nor does aging diminish their brain capacity.
6. The death penalty does not deter potential murderers.

Obsolete myths persist even in the face of evidence that contradicts them. Why? Because dispelling myths is far more than a matter of education (see item 3 above). To understand the persistence of myths, one need only ask a simple question: Who benefits from false beliefs? To no one's surprise, the answer leads us straight to the structure of social power. False beliefs and ineffective practices are not easy to dispel or dislodge for the simple reason that power groups benefit from them. Put into practice, these beliefs are often solutions imposed by the strong on the weak.

Optimizing Life by Rejecting the Science of Optimization

As the science of optimization, economics does something that is characteristic of all knowledge elites: It takes something it is good at, assumes that all should strive to be as good as it is, and gradually takes it for granted that it knows what is best for ordinary people. Like all knowledge elites, it does little research to find out how people actually perceive and act in their own worlds. *Most research tells us how social scientists perceive problems.*[18]

Once the fiction that there are social groups or categories of individuals that know how to define and solve problems is abandoned, real insights into how people experience and react to problems emerge:

1. People who are expected to act in concert, either in private or in public, have different problems and see the world very differently.
2. People in different social locations see the *same* thing differently, often very differently.
3. America's master assumption, that self-interest is rational—that is, solves problems—is not borne out. The assumption that the pursuit of self-interest (microdecisions) leads to the common interest (macrodecisions) is also not borne out.
4. Individuals at all levels of society and regardless of education tend to take the overall society and its power structure for granted. When they are confronted with problems, they do not relate them to power or to the way society is organized. Instead, they explain and rationalize their problems in terms of an obsolete law, a parasitical bureaucrat, outmoded ideas, evil people, foreign devils, subversives, and so on.

5. Individuals rarely see that one person's problem is often another's solution.

Interconnected Problems and Interconnected Solutions: The Professions as Macrosociologists

Let's start from this last insight and trace a pattern of causation. Mr. Big Business moves a factory overseas or to the South to make it more competitive, causing unemployment for Mr. and Mrs. Blue Collar and bankruptcy for Mr. Small Business. A woman solves her problem of an unhappy marriage by getting a divorce—this means that an extra housing unit is needed, which contributes to the housing shortage, but it is a solution to a hard-pressed landlord, perhaps our bankrupt Mr. Small Business. In the meantime, an absolutistic-minded right-to-life group has managed to get the legislature to ban the use of public funds for abortions. Mrs. Blue Collar is forced to get an unsafe, illegal abortion because her husband is out of work; she develops a serious complication and has to spend three months in a hospital on Medicaid. In the meantime, Ms. Upwardly Mobile, without missing a day of work, buys an abortion for $300 using a hospital paid for largely with tax money, and she continues her support for a political party that is against public spending and against abortion whether paid for with or without tax money.

The above examples and web of causation can be expanded. As the American people experience this world, and as awareness of social problems grows, there is a call for more education, a return to grass-roots democracy, and higher standards for professionals. Except for elites (who tend to take American society for granted), the average American suffers from a nagging and upsetting sense that the world is somehow out of control. All nod their heads in agreement as they read the results of a Gallup poll—the American people are deeply disenchanted with and distrustful of their leaders, and only two occupations still enjoy majority support, doctors and garbage collectors. But having been socialized into American-style liberalism, they conclude erroneously that the root of the problem lies not with institutions or power groups, but with leaders who are dumb, dishonest, and deceptive.

Social causation is a tangled, multisided chain of causes and consequences. The key to almost all problems, though, is a better-managed economy, one that provides a coherent transition from school to work, greater respect for manual work and less respect for professionals, a better monitoring and control over rootless capital, and a clear set of priorities about where national resources should be invested. A better-managed economy would cut back idleness, absenteeism, rape, family violence, and the other behaviors that swell the social overhead and, of course, represent enormous psychic and physical suffering.

A better-managed economy can come only from a more effective polity (and, in turn, that requires a better economy). But many things can help solve problems. Local environmental laws can have a national impact because business people do not want to deal with dozens of different local and state regulations (one hopes that a better national environmental policy will result, but so far pressures have led to lower national standards superseding higher state standards).

Of course efforts to curb smoking, reduce the number of overweight Americans, develop outreach medical programs for low-income Americans (especially pregnant women), and develop safe workplaces and transportation systems would not only reduce overhead costs, but would reduce the number of handicapped.[19] A foreign policy that stressed economic and political rather than military solutions would also release funds for domestic purposes. Those who want to curb the violent and overly competitive nature of American sports could well help us develop a better foreign policy, economy, politics, and family life. Toning down violence in all entertainment would be one step in curbing our use of violence and competition as solutions to problems.

Most problems are the results of solutions. A democratic polity will be better able to trace the chain of causation and avoid the shifting of burdens downward as is the case with contemporary America. A democratic polity will focus, not on educating the masses in the abstract, or releasing elites in the abstract to achieve abstract goals; it will work to make all adaptive, especially owners, managers, legislators, public officials, and professionals. But elites cannot be creative and adaptive if they are insecure. At present, beneficial changes threaten the economic and personal lives of those who pioneered last year's changes. The Owl of Minerva will never fly by day if reform pushes vested interests into a corner. To take an example: Lowering the cost of living and saving planetary resources could be furthered if we rented caskets for funeral rites and got buried in $50 pine boxes. But that reform will flounder unless we provide casketmakers with options for useful livelihoods. Elites must be given a way out so that they can lend a creative hand in fashioning their own updating.

Economic and Social Planning

The American polity, argue reformers, must play a bigger role in explicitly guiding American society. Our present policy of pretending that we do not have policies is not working. Calling all this free enterprise and democracy obscures the issue: The lack of policies to run the country is itself a policy and deserves to be evaluated as such. The American economy must be directed, if not actually planned, so that recessions, unemployment, and bankruptcy can be prevented. Explicit government direction can help modernize and adjust the economy to new conditions—at present threatened businesses dig in and use government to protect obsolete ways. Explicit government direction can help the professions evaluate their performance according to their own achievement criteria—at present threatened professionals dig in and use government to protect the incompetent and preserve obsolete practices. Once the planning process is started in regard to corporations and professionals, labor unions, farmers, and other groups will be obliged to follow suit. The main objective of planning is to make it possible for groups to adjust to new conditions. *An all-important condition for developing adaptive personalities and an adaptive society is to create a public in which all have faith that losses and gains will be shared equitably.*

Planning, it must be repeated, does not mean adhering to an alleged rational scheme concocted by those in power, by those with more education, or by those who claim to have a better science. Planning is a political process in which the many discuss and decide how to design groups and institutions, and arrange resources, to achieve a given structure of values.

Strengthening Social-Policy Research

Social-policy research has emerged in recent years as an encouraging development both in education and American public life. Despite impressive beginnings, much remains to be done. Relations between social researchers and government data-collection agencies must be improved. A wide range of data must be recast to make them relevant to policy formation. Relations between fact collectors and policymakers must be improved. And evaluation must be carefully built into our public policies and programs to make sure that they have their desired effects.

The use of advisory committees and consulting firms to formulate reports and make policy recommendations to our legislatures and political leaders must be reexamined. Critics charge that such bodies disguise the exercise of power, allowing partisan powerholders to appear disinterested and objective while blocking or mismanaging needed reforms. There is also a need to reexamine our policy of burying or postponing issues by asking for more research, as well as using Congressional commissions, independent regulatory agencies, and presidential panels and commissions to make believe that we are basing public policy on objective knowledge.

Public policy educational programs must also come abreast of the new realism about the professions. At both the undergraduate and graduate levels, education for the professions must deal with the real world faced by problemsolvers. They must recognize that running public affairs is not a matter solely for technical knowledge, not a matter to be approached only in a value-neutral way. Ultimately, problems make sense only if they are put in a sociopolitical context and solved through a mixture of cognitive and value judgments. So far the record is not encouraging. America's public-policy education lacks an historical-comparative dimension and a sense of the realities of power (groups pursuing contradictory, unreal, and anti-social goals). Both our public-policy education and research tend to stress narrow technical studies, for example, of housing, health care, land-use, taxation, air and water pollution, transportation, education, and recreation. Such studies are based on the fallacy that science can provide answers and that subjective human decision can be transcended. The largely technocratic nature of our approach to social problems denies the reality of power and fails to promote the ideal of informed decisionmaking by humans living in a moral universe.[20]

The ultimate insight is that science and professionalism are political activities and that politics reflects social structure, especially the corporate economy. If we want better thinking, we must redesign the groups that our thinkers belong to: the federal executive, Congress, corporations, churches, schools, hospitals, academic departments, professional associations, and so on. If we want a better society we must not be content merely to study it or reform it—we must also be prepared to redesign it to yield the behavioral and symbolic results we want.

SUMMARY

An adaptive society is a comprehensive group and institutional structure designed to yield stated outcomes such as material necessities, new members, conflict resolution, and new knowledge and services.

The United States is a utopian society in that it relies on magical processes (allegedly rational markets in the economy, polity, education, and voluntary sector) and ineffective property and professional elites to solve its problems.

The utopian nature of American society is also discussed in terms of its confusion between pluralism as an ideal and the actual world of social power. Rather than exhibiting pluralism, the United States is essentially a diffused oligarchy characterized by poor lines of communication and unproductive quarrelling.

The 1980s witnessed an attempt to revitalize the United States by falling back on its basic laissez-faire principles after a long series of failures by reform liberalism. The failure of right liberalism during the Reagan–Bush administrations of 1980–92 after the failure of left liberalism raises profound questions about the vitality of American society.

The propertied and professional groups that make up America's governing class have the same stake in denying that society is a socially constructed system as did the feudal elites of the past—it enables them to put all the important things about human life in nature and human nature. The first step in breaking this hegemonic symbolic world is to change power relations in the direction of genuine pluralism. The second step is to harness property and professional elites to social functions, a harnessing that can only be done by a democratically organized public.

NOTES

1. See the section "Declining Legitimacy" in Chapter 11.
2. There are important qualifications to this global indictment. The General Accounting Office (GAO), which is an assembly of a wide variety of professionals, has a reputation for scientific rigor, honesty, and a flair for knowing what kinds of questions to ask (although it works for Congress, both political parties and a wide variety of groups, while protesting its findings, concede that its standards are beyond reproach). The EPA is one of the many examples of federal agencies

that do not supply useful data on which to base policy (essentially it does no basic research and its regulations lack credibility). The history of the EPA also provides insight into the dependence of professionals on the wider business elite—its budget was cut consistently by the Reagan administration and in 1993 was 3 percent lower than in 1981.

3. For a sophisticated, critical analysis of the attempt to revitalize American society by the Brookings Institution, the Trilateral Commission, the American Enterprise Institute, the Heritage Foundation, and the Institute for Contemporary Studies, see Joseph G. Peschek, *Policy-Planning Organizations: Elite Agendas and America's Rightward Turn* (Philadelphia: Temple University Press, 1987).

4. Haynes Bonner Johnson, *Sleepwalking through History: America in the Reagan Years* (New York: Norton, 1991).

5. For a technical macroeconomic analysis on which the above is based, in language that makes it accessible to noneconomics majors, see Samuel Bowles, David M. Gordon, and Thomas E. Weisskopf, *After the Waste Land: A Democratic Economics for the Year 2000* (Armonk, N.Y.: M.E. Sharpe, 1991), chap. 10.

6. Herbert Stein, "What Economic Advisers Do," *American Enterprise* 2, no. 2 (March–April 1991): 6–12.

7. C. B. MacPherson, *The Political Theory of Possessive Individualism: Hobbes to Locke* (New York: Oxford University Press, 1962).

8. Perhaps the most sophisticated evaluation of and still the most useful collection of suggestions for linking the academic and policy worlds is N. J. Demerath, Otto Larsen, and Karl F. Schuessler, eds., *Social Policy and Sociology* (New York: Academic Press, 1975).

9. Eva Etzioni-Halevy, *The Knowledge Elite and the Failure of Prophecy* (Boston: George Allen and Unwin, 1985).

10. Self-employment by "professionals" has grown in recent years but most of it is due to unemployment and consists of scraping along.

11. For the classic analysis of the poor policies that emerge from homogeneous groups, see Irving L. Janis, *Victims of Groupthink: A Psychological Study of Foreign-Policy Decisions and Fiascos* (Boston: Houghton Mifflin, 1972).

12. For the broader range of questions that arose in an advisory group to the National Institutes of Health when it included public interest and consumer groups as compared to its regular panel of professionals and business representatives, see *Chronicle of Higher Education,* March 8, 1996, p. A47. Interestingly, the NIH did not change its practice of relying on narrowly constituted panels.

13. Paul S. Sabatier, "An Advocacy Coalition Framework of Policy Change and the Role of Policy-Oriented Learning Therein," *Policy Sciences* 21, nos. 2–3 (1988): 129–168.

14. For an extremely valuable set of case studies of public policy (framed in terms of the concept *welfare state*) in a wide variety of capitalist societies, along some of the above lines, see Richard Rose and Rei Shiratori, eds., *The Welfare State East and West* (New York: Oxford University Press, 1986); Francis G. Castles, ed., *The Comparative History of Public Policy* (New York: Oxford University Press, 1989); and Ramesh Mishra, *The Welfare State in Capitalist Society: Policies of Retrenchment and Maintenance in Europe, North America, and Australia* (Toronto: University of Toronto Press, 1990).

15. For a fuller discussion, see "The Fiction of a Knowledge Society" in Chapter 1.

16. For a discussion, see "Accountants" in Chapter 7.

17. Lester C. Thurow, "American Mirage: A Post-Industrial Economy?" *Current History* 88 (January 1989): 13ff.

18. In a survey of thirty-four sociology textbooks on social problems, Robert H. Lauer reports that sociologists define social problems in ways that deviate profoundly from how the American people define them (as expressed in Gallup

polls); see his article "Defining Social Problems: Public and Professional Perspectives," *Social Problems* 24 (October 1976): 122–130.

19. U.S. Commission on Civil Rights, *Accommodating the Spectrum of Individual Abilities* (Washington, D.C.: U.S. Civil Rights Commission, 1983), chap. 1, reports that between 9 and 15 percent of the American population is handicapped.

20. For an indictment of Harvard's Kennedy School of Government (which can also stand for most public-policy programs in the United States) along these lines, see Jonathan Alter, "Harvard versus Democracy," *Washington Monthly* 15 (March 1983): 32–39.

Name Index

Subject Index

Academic perspective (*see* Functionalism)
Academic profession, 65
Accountants, 37, 75*n*, 168–170
  accountancy as ritual, 169, 240
  and audit society, 238–240
  and capitalism, 168*f*
  and deviance, 227, 229, 231
  as interpretive science, 168
  and iron triangle, 231
  as legitimating fiction, 31
  and liberal ideology, 238*f*
  social power, 70*f*, 269, 240 (*see also* Mathematics, Social indicators)
Actors, 183
Administration
  all-purpose administrator, 39, 146
  comparative study of, 145
  and computer, 271
  and engineering, 39
  as ideology, 94, 145–146
  minorities, 146–148
  public administration, 39, 257
  science of, 70, 94, 143–148
  social power, 144 (*see also* Public administration)
Administrators and executives, 39, 49, 143–148 (*see also* Administration, Public administration)
Advertising, 184, 225, 310*f*
African Americans
  administrators and executives, 146–148
  African American feminism, 28*n*, 52
  deviance, 221, 222
  engineering, 110
  as fictitious menace, 194, 221
  illegitimacy and social work, 172–173
  journalism, 167
  in law, 139
  literary studies, 119, 121, 125*n*
  mass media, 201–203

mathematics, 110
medicine, health, health care, 131–132
in natural science, 109–110
political science, 95–96
popular culture, 201–203
psychology, 110, 117
sociology, 86
sports, 202*f*
theorists, 28*n*, 51, 52, 60
Agricultural science, 109, 111 (*see also* Plant science)
Airline pilots, 176
American studies, 44 (*see also* Literary studies)
Anomie, 55*n*, 100*n*, 216, 229, 230
Anthropology
  anti-racism, anti-biopsychological, 39
  culture concept as ideology, 39, 88
  as ideology of British imperialism, 23, 87*f*
  as interpretive science, 88*f*
  male-oriented bias, 27*n*, 50, 89
  and postmodernism, 118
  as radical, 87
Applied professions, 127 (*see also* by individual profession)
Arbitragers, 312
Architects, 37, 174–175, 228, 229, 230, 257
Art, 39, 55*n*, 183, 184, 279
Artists, 183, 279
Asian Americans, 109–110, 139, 147, 194, 201
Athletes, 183, 198–202, 206, 207
Athletic coach, 183, 202, 206, 207
Athletic director, 183, 202, 206, 207

Biology, 105, 106, 109, 123*n*, 124*n*
Brokers, 227, 229, 236

Capital
  capital formation, 308
  concentration of, 308